THE LABOR BOARD CREW

THE WORKING CLASS IN AMERICAN HISTORY

Editorial Advisors
James R. Barrett, Julie Greene, William P. Jones,
Alice Kessler-Harris, and Nelson Lichtenstein

A list of books in the series appears
at the end of this book.

THE LABOR BOARD CREW

Remaking Worker–Employer Relations from Pearl Harbor to the Reagan Era

RONALD W. SCHATZ

UNIVERSITY OF ILLINOIS PRESS
Urbana, Chicago, and Springfield

Library of Congress Cataloging-in-Publication Data
Names: Schatz, Ronald W., 1949– author.
Title: The labor board crew : remaking worker-employer
  relations from Pearl Harbor to the Reagan era /
  Ronald W. Schatz.
Description: Urbana : University of Illinois Press, [2021]
  | Series: The working class in American history |
  Includes bibliographical references and index.
Identifiers: LCCN 2020026838 (print) | LCCN 2020026839
  (ebook) | ISBN 9780252043628 (cloth ; alk. paper) |
  ISBN 9780252085598 (paperback ; alk. paper) | ISBN
  9780252052507 (ebook)
Subjects: LCSH: United States. National Labor
  Relations Board. | Industrial relations—United
  States—History—20th century. | Labor laws and
  legislation—United States—History—20th century.
  | Labor—United States—History—20th century.
Classification: LCC HD8072.5 .S327 2021 (print) | LCC
  HD8072.5 (ebook) | DDC 331.0973/09045—dc23
LC record available at https://lccn.loc.gov/2020026838
LC ebook record available at https://lccn.loc.gov/
  2020026839

For Cynthia, Lily, and Sam
l'amore conquista tutto

Once, when we were walking together in the Yard, I mentioned a news item about a manned flight to Mars. Dunlop smiled and exulted: "More worlds to negotiate!"

—Robert Rosenblatt, *Coming Apart: A Memoir of the Harvard Wars of 1969*

CONTENTS

PREFACE

I WAS TRAINED IN LABOR HISTORY and began my career writing about workers, unions, and management at General Electric and Westinghouse; about Philip Murray, the Steelworkers union, and the major steel companies; and about Roman Catholic thinking and action about workers, capitalism, and socialism. While exploring these topics, I kept encountering a small group of professors and attorneys who acted as go-betweens for unions and companies. I didn't know exactly who they were, or their motivations and objectives, but they seemed to appear all the time, and so I decided to look further.

I began by investigating the School of Industrial and Labor Relations at Cornell University, which opened in September 1945 with a handful of faculty, 118 students, mostly young armed forces veterans, and great enthusiasm. It offered classes on union-management negotiations, labor economics, labor law, personnel management, and labor history and offered summer internships. Governor Thomas Dewey delivered the inaugural convocation address. "This is not a labor school where dogma will be taught, from which trained zealots will go forth. This is not a management school where students will learn only to think of workingmen and women as items on a balance sheet," the governor declared. "It is a school which denies the alien theory that there are classes in our society and that they must wage war against each other. . . . The State of New York will here provide the equipment to abate the fevers which rise from claims and counter-claims which are now the language of industrial relations." CBS Radio broadcast the speech across the country.[1]

I read transcripts of the hearings of the state legislative committee that had proposed the school, pored through administrator and faculty files, and then began interviewing the founding professors. The first question that I always pose in interviews is "Tell me about your parents and your upbringing." The replies frequently reveal valuable material unavailable in other ways. One example is Jean Trepp McKelvey, a professor of industrial relations at Cornell who not only taught students on campus but gave classes to trade unionists in factory towns and became a renowned mediator. McKelvey was born to a German-Jewish family in 1909 in St. Louis and grew up in Orange, New Jersey. One of her maternal uncles owned a garment factory in Rochester, New York. Another owned Bergdorf Goodman, the luxury clothing store in Manhattan. Jean attended a progressive high school in Orange during the school year. During the summer, she stayed with her maternal grandparents in Rochester. McKelvey was a studious girl who loved to stay home reading. But she was obliged to spend long afternoons at her grandparents' country club, where her relatives sat by the swimming pool, sipping mint juleps and belittling the Russian Jews who worked in their factories.

The experience impelled Jean to decide to study workers and unions when she entered Wellesley College in 1924. Her father was an electric engineer who became friends with Gerard Swope, the future president of General Electric, when they were students at Massachusetts Institute of Technology (MIT). Swope introduced his friend's daughter to Otto Beyer, the engineer who organized the acclaimed union-management cooperative system at the Baltimore and Ohio Railroad. Beyer put her in touch with Matthew Woll, the vice president of the American Federation of Labor. Drawing on those connections, McKelvey wrote a prize-winning senior thesis on why Woll, Sidney Hillman of the Amalgamated Clothing Workers, and the socialist leaders of the American Federation of Full-Fashioned Hosiery Workers broke with American unions' traditional resistance to pay by piecework and accepted Frederick W. Taylor's system of scientific management in the 1920s. It became the basis of her doctoral dissertation in economics at Harvard and later a book. McKelvey ultimately devoted her life to resolving industrial conflicts.

Early experiences also inspired Vernon ("Pete") Jensen, who joined Cornell's Industrial Relations faculty in September 1946. Jensen was a Mormon, born and raised in Salt Lake City, where his parents ran a hardware store and a lumberyard. Jensen went on mission for two-and-a-half years after graduating from high school. He traveled through Georgia and the Carolinas seeking converts. In Waycross, Georgia, he met Mormons who had gotten jobs on the railroads by breaking the picket line during the bitter 1922 nationwide railway shopmen's strike. Jensen also met former railroad workers forced into sharecropping because they remained loyal to their unions. While hitchhiking in spring 1929, he met Communists who were helping to lead the dramatic strike that swept across cotton mill towns from Tennessee and Virginia through the Carolinas to Georgia.

Several months later, Pete returned to Salt Lake City to enter Brigham Young University. He was planning to study history and teach in a seminary. He saved pocket money for Christmas gifts for his family, but the bank where he had deposited his funds collapsed in mid-December. Jensen went home without presents for his family and was unable to return to college. So he taught school, got married, and, when his wife was transferred, accompanied her to San Francisco. In 1933 Jensen enrolled at the University of California at Berkeley in a seminar taught by Paul Taylor, America's leading authority on farm labor. "I joined a special seminar. There were eight of us. And when we started, who was in there but Clark Kerr and John Dunlop!" Kerr and Dunlop were prominent members of the group whose nature I was trying to delineate. Jensen went on to earn a doctorate in labor economics at UC-Berkeley; teach at the University of Colorado and Cornell; write seven books on labor on the docks, in lumber, and in metal mining; and serve as a labor-management mediator and arbitrator during and after the Second World War.

Many other universities also created industrial relations programs in the 1940s. Industrial relations was that era's equivalent of the black studies and women's studies programs of the late 1960s and 1970s and environmental studies, feminist, queer and sexuality studies, and ethnic studies programs today: interdisciplinary programs that challenged traditional academic opinions and attracted students eager to change the world. I went on to explore the archives of the industrial relations programs at Yale University, UC-Berkeley, the University of Illinois, the University of Pennsylvania, and Harvard University.

I also met George Strauss, a UC-Berkeley professor who was an Army Air Force sergeant discharged at Long Beach, California, in early 1946. Hitchhiking home to Philadelphia, he spent one night in a rooming house in Peoria, Illinois, where workers at the auto parts companies, the steel mills, and the railroads were all on strike. "It seemed the whole world was on strike," he remembered. So Strauss decided to enter graduate school in industrial relations at MIT. "At the end of the war, people came back and went into industrial relations because that seemed to be the best way to solve a bunch of social problems: unemployment, inequality, strikes, oppressive working conditions, underconsumption. . . . They could all be solved through unions. . . . It answered social and economic and political and certainly emotional needs."

Even more valuable were two long afternoons with Clark Kerr, a Swarthmore College graduate who had founded the industrial relations program at UC-Berkeley and went on to become chancellor at Berkeley and president of the University of California. Kerr and Pete Jensen were graduate students in the seminar on agriculture labor with Professor Paul Taylor in 1933. When the cotton pickers went on strike that fall, Taylor asked Kerr to go to the San Joaquin Valley and interview the strikers and farm owners. Taylor's wife, photographer Dorothea Lange, accompanied graduate student Kerr on the trip. She gave three photographs of farmworkers to Kerr. They were on the wall behind his desk at the Institute of Industrial Relations where we met.

The 1933 California cotton pickers' strike was one of the most dramatic strikes in American labor history and was an inspiration for John Steinbeck's 1936 novel *In Dubious Battle*. Kerr got to know Mexican migrants who had gone on strike, black farm laborers, and also the white "Okies" and "Arkies" who mostly refused to strike. He also met smaller cotton farmers who were in debt to the banks, and the growers, as the larger landowners were called. He also met merchants, local sheriffs, and federal mediators. Sympathizing with the Latino strikers and the small farmers, the trip was a life-changing experience for Kerr.

Most of the pieces now were on the table for my study, but how did they fit together? The missing piece surfaced when I interviewed John Dunlop—renowned professor of labor economics at Harvard University who was appointed dean of the School of Arts and Sciences after the 1969 student strike, director of the Cost of Living Council in the Nixon administration, and secretary of labor in the Ford administration. Dunlop also chaired many labor-management-government boards, was the principal arbitrator in the U.S. construction industry for decades, and, after George Taylor of the University of Pennsylvania died in 1971, the most influential figure in the industrial relations field. Dunlop was seventy-seven years old at the time of the interview yet still feisty.

"*What* are you studying," he demanded almost before I could say a word. I replied that I was studying "industrial relations professionals," the term that prominent figures in the field used to identify themselves in the latter 1940s.

"*What's* an 'industrial relations professional'?" he shot back. "Isn't a shop steward an 'industrial relations professional'? Isn't a foreman an 'industrial relations professional'?"

"*Who* are you studying," he demanded.

"Well, I am studying you and Clark Kerr, Ben Aaron, Pete Jensen, Jean McKelvey, Sylvester Garrett, Robben Fleming, . . ." I started to reply.

"We all worked for the War Labor Board," Dunlap broke in. This was the office set up by Franklin Roosevelt to oversee relations between workers, unions, and companies during the Second World War.

The book's project crystallized at that moment. It ceased to be a study of the industrial relations field and instead became a biography, a collective biography, embracing their entire lives, not only the world war and U.S. labor-management relations, but their work in other realms of American society and other parts of the world throughout their lives. I would write about their personal backgrounds and education, how they learned to resolve union-management conflicts while working at the War Labor Board, and how they drew on that experience to try to resolve conflicts in other realms throughout the United States and the world.

The National War Labor Board recruited 250 young professors, attorneys, and economists, and a handful of Roman Catholic priests—all white and all but six male. They had so much leverage at the negotiating tables despite their tender age that Philip Murray, the president of the Steelworkers and the CIO, called them "the Labor Board boys."[2] A dozen of the staffers were particularly influential. They tried—often successfully—to resolve conflicts between unions and management for decades in almost every sort of industry in the United States, not only manufacturing, construction, meatpacking, the railroads, the airlines, and the docks, but later in the public schools, fire and police departments, major league baseball and other professional sports, agriculture, and symphony orchestras.

During the 1950s and 1960s, they investigated industrialization throughout the world, research that led them to believe that capitalist and communist systems would ultimately converge, just as unions and management seemed to be cooperating in the United States at the time. They were appointed as provosts, chancellors, top deans, and presidents of the most prestigious universities at the height of the student revolt of the 1960s, where they developed systems of conflict resolutions that were subsequently adopted by colleges and universities across the country. They tried to control prices and wages during the stagflation puzzle of the 1970s—in that instance, far less successfully.

Only one of their hundreds of graduate students was as brilliant, fervid, and tough-skinned as the War Labor Board veterans. That was George P. Shultz. Shultz became a professor of industrial relations, close to his mentors, secretary of labor, secretary of the treasury, and budget director in the Nixon administration and secretary of state in the Reagan administration. He drew on his experience in labor-management relations to help end racial segregation in Southern public schools, introduce affirmative-action programs in American industries, and conduct the negotiation that ended the Cold War. He has remained active in public affairs, flying from his home in California in 2018 at the age of ninety-seven to warn the U.S. Senate Armed Services Committee about the danger of new, smaller nuclear weapons.

This book tells the story of this extraordinary group—their lifelong efforts to bring stability and peace to the United States and the world, their backgrounds, their thinking, their objectives, their achievements, and their failings.

ABBREVIATIONS

AFL   American Federation of Labor
AFT   American Federation of Teachers
BAM   Black Action Movement
CIO   Congress of Industrial Organization
ENA   Experimental Negotiating Agreement
FLOC   Farm Labor Organizing Committee
FSM   Free Speech Movement
HSTA   High School Teachers Association
IRRA   Industrial Relations Research Association
MLBPA   Major League Baseball Players Association
NDMB   National Defense Mediation Board
NEA   National Education Association
NLRB   National Labor Relations Board
NWLB   National War Labor Board
OSHA   Occupational Safety and Health Administration
ROTC   Reserve Officer Training Corps
RWLB   Regional War Labor Board
SDS   Students for a Democratic Society
TAA   Teaching Assistants Association
UAW   United Auto Workers
UE   United Electrical, Radio & Machine Workers of America
USWA   United Steelworkers of America

1

In the Wake of Pearl Harbor

> A generation is composed of all the men and
> women who identify with a formative event
> or a common hardship that determines their
> outlook for the rest of their lives.
>
> —Jacques Julliard

EARLY SUNDAY MORNING. December 7, 1941, George Taylor and his wife Edith met his former student, Allan Dash, at Philadelphia's 30th Street Station. They picked up their tickets and the morning paper and boarded the Red Arrow train to Detroit. A forty-one-year-old professor at the University of Pennsylvania's Wharton School of Business, Taylor was among the top young union-management mediators in the country. He had taken a leave from the university in September 1940 to help the General Motors Company and the United Auto Workers union resolve their grievance disputes. A dyed-in-the-wool Philadelphian, Taylor had been reluctant to take that job. He didn't want to leave the Wharton School and dreaded the frequent trips the assignment would entail. But war was raging across Europe, Africa, and Asia; the War, Navy, and Army Departments needed materiel from General Motors; and labor relations at the company were rocky. So he agreed to work for GM and the UAW for twelve months.

By December 1941, Taylor had already spent fifteen months away from home. The management and union finally agreed to hire his protégé, G. Allan Dash Jr., as his successor. Dash had ten years of experience mediating disputes in the Philadelphia textile industry. They worked out an arrangement under which the two men would crisscross the upper Midwest for three months. George would introduce his understudy to the local union and company representatives, Allan would become familiar with the grievances in each locale, and then Taylor could return home.

December 7 was a fine late-autumn day in Pennsylvania, with clear sky and crisp air. The first few hours on the train would have been delightful except for the news in the *Philadelphia Inquirer*. More than one hundred thousand Japanese sailors and soldiers were assembling on ships and on the frontier of Indochina, preparing to attack. Two Japanese destroyers were steaming to the Gulf of Siam, the Philippine government ordered evacuation of civilians from Manila, Australia was preparing for war, and President Franklin D. Roosevelt had sent a personal message to Emperor Hirohito in a "'final' effort to avert war with Japan."[1]

After lunch in the dining car, George, Edith, and Allan returned to their seats, chatting as the train reached the foothills of the Allegheny Mountains. At that moment, 1:20 p.m. Eastern Standard Time, 190 Japanese bombers and fighters appeared unexpectedly over Oahu, dived down, and began assaulting the U.S. fleet anchored at Pearl Harbor. A second wave of 170 planes followed. The bombardment continued for seventy-five minutes. By the time it ended, 2,335 U.S. sailors and soldiers were dead, as were 68 civilians, and 1,178 Americans were wounded. Three U.S. battleships—the *Arizona*, the *California*, and the *Utah*—were sinking to the bottom of the sea; the *Oklahoma* was capsized; and four other battleships—the *Pennsylvania*, *West Virginia*, *Tennessee*, and *Nevada*—were impaired. Eleven smaller Navy vessels were underwater or disabled, and 150 U.S. airplanes were destroyed.

Japan's strike at Pearl Harbor was as frightening to the American people as Al Qaeda's attack on the World Trade Centers and the Pentagon sixty years later and the loss of lives even greater. Yet it was only the beginning. Ten hours later, 191 Japanese bombers and fighters strafed Clark Field in the Philippines, destroying nearly half of the U.S. Army Air Force fleet of B-17 "Flying Fortress" bombers and two of the four squadrons of P-40 fighters. In less than twelve hours the Imperial Navy Air Force eliminated the sole impediment to Japan's conquest of the South Pacific. General Douglas MacArthur termed the strike at Clark Field "one of the blackest days in U.S. military history."[2]

Taylor and Dash met the president of GM, Charles Wilson, and the vice president of the UAW, Walter Reuther, for lunch the next day, December 8. They were dining at the top of the Fisher Building, the Art Deco skyscraper designed by Albert Kahn to celebrate General Motors, Detroit, and the U.S. auto industry. As their waiter was bringing drinks, the maître d' announced that President Roosevelt was about to address the Congress and the nation. Chatter stopped, all turned to the radio. "Just when I was on the threshold of the biggest arbitration job I have ever held, and we were talking about my succeeding George Taylor, the 'Star-Spangled Banner' came on the radio and everybody in the restaurant stood up and cheered," Dash remembered. "Then Franklin Roosevelt made his famous 'day-which-will-be-live-in-infamy' speech."[3] After years of fighting, America's corporate executives and union officers would have to cooperate to win the war.

The following day, Taylor and Dash began meeting with GM plant managers and local UAW officials. They started in Detroit, Flint, and other factory towns in southern Michigan and northern Indiana. They were in a Chicago hotel shortly before Christmas, discussing workers' grievances with a local union business agent and GM plant manager, when the porter interrupted. There was a phone call for Professor Taylor. George left to take the call. "He returned sort of white-faced," Dash recalled. "When we asked him if he was ill, he replied, 'No, but the call was from the president of the United States, and he asked me to come to Washington tonight.'"[4]

Roosevelt was setting up a new agency, the National War Labor Board (NWLB), to oversee U.S. union-management relations for the duration of the war. He asked Taylor to be vice chairman. Everyone at the table congratulated George, who left, called Edith, packed, and hurried to Washington.

* * *

No Americans today except the most elderly can appreciate the fear that the American people felt in the winter of 1941–42, and fewer still realize how close the Axis powers came to victory. Today most Americans assume that the United States and its allies were bound to triumph. That assumption is not correct, as Japan's extraordinary feats after their attacks at Pearl Harbor and Clark Field suggest. One day later, Japanese troops invaded Thailand and Malaysia, bombarded U.S. air bases and ports at Guam and Wake Islands, and destroyed Britain's air bases at Hong Kong. On December 10, Japanese troops landed on Luzon in the Philippines. On December 11 Japan attacked the Dutch East Indies (subsequently renamed Indonesia), the principal source of natural rubber for the United States and Japan. On December 13 and December 22, Japanese forces captured Guam and Wake Island. On Christmas day they took Hong Kong. Meanwhile, Japanese naval destroyers shelled the Hawaiian Islands. A week later, January 2, 1942, Japanese troops captured Manila, the most heavily guarded port in Asia. The American and Filipino troops retreated to the Bataan peninsula and Corregidor, a two-mile-square rocky island situated at the entrance of Manila Bay. There they were assaulted by Japanese forces from both air and land. Short of food and weapons, the Americans and Filipinos on Bataan surrendered on April 9. The Japanese army marched the 70,000 captured troops to internment camps, beating stragglers with bayonets. More than 7,000 Americans and Filipinos perished on the trek. The regiments on Corregidor held out until May 6, by which time the island's cliffs had collapsed, the woods were obliterated, and shore roads had fallen into the water.

Japan had already occupied Korea, Manchuria, much of southern China, Formosa (later renamed Taiwan), and Vietnam. While attacking Bataan and Corregidor, the emperor's forces also conquered Indonesia, Singapore, and Burma and landed forces in New Guinea. Their next objectives were Australia and Midway Island. In preparation, Japanese ships shelled oil refineries off the coast of California and Oregon and bombed U.S. bases in Alaska and captured Atka and Kiska, the most westerly of the Aleutian Islands. Although not likely since their troops were spread thin, a full-scale Japanese attack on Alaska was not utterly out of the question.

Germany and Italy were no less aggressive. In March 1936 Germany reoccupied the Rhineland, the industrial heartland it had had to concede to the Allies after the First World War. Ninety-nine percent of the German people voted in favor of the Führer in a popular election shortly afterward. In November 1936 Berlin and Tokyo signed the Anti-Comintern Pact, pledging to defend each other against the Soviet Union. The next year, Rome joined the compact. German troops occupied and annexed Austria in March 1938. In his meeting with Adolf Hitler at his summer palace in Berchtesgaden in September 1938, British prime minister Chamberlain promised that Britain would not intervene if Germany annexed the Sudetenland, the mainly German-speaking provinces of Czechoslovakia. The acquisition did not satisfy the Führer. In March 1939 Germany placed the Czech provinces of Bohemia and Moravia under its "protection," annexed Memel in Lithuania, and renounced its nonaggression pact with Poland and its naval agreement with Britain. Italy invaded Albania on April 7, 1939. Italy and Germany signed a military pact on May 22. The Soviet Union and Germany signed a nonaggression treaty on August 23, 1939. A week later, the Soviets and Germans jointly invaded Poland, conquering that proud land despite fierce armed resistance. After a quiet winter, the Wehrmacht turned west, invading and conquering Belgium, the Netherlands, Denmark, Norway, and the bulk of France. Germany had already occupied Romania while fascist Italy conquered Ethiopia and Tunisia and invaded Greece. Meanwhile, the collaborator Marshall Phillippe Pétain ruled in southern France, General Francisco Franco ruled in Spain, and other allies of Germany ruled in Hungary, Croatia, and Portugal. Although Sweden and Switzerland were officially neutral, both governments made compromises with Germany. By June 1941, all of Euro-Asia was governed by fascists, Communists, or compliant neutrals.

On June 22, 1941, Hitler broke his treaty with Josef Stalin and attacked the Soviet Union, the largest invasion in world history. The Red Army was not prepared, and many Ukrainians and others ruled by the Soviets welcomed the German troops. By late 1941, the Germans occupied eastern Poland, Latvia, Lithuania, Estonia, and large swaths of the western Soviet Union. They reached the outskirts of Moscow and had Leningrad under siege. Although the Soviet forces regained some territory in the winter of 1941–42, the Wehrmacht resumed its offensive in June 1942 and by September had crossed the Don River, attacked Stalingrad (now Volgograd), and invaded the southern Caucasus. In the meantime, the Italian and

German tank units under General Johannes Rommel defeated the British Eighth Army in Libya and were pressing toward Alexandria, Egypt.

Even American labor historians have for the most part ignored or discounted the Allies' dire straits. Instead, they have chosen to focus on the controls that federal agencies imposed on unions and workers during the war and American unions' discriminatory treatment of women and African American workers, as if these were the sole consequential issues confronting American labor and the United States during the war.[5] Union leaders of that era knew better, as did the vast majority of the unions' members and other American workers, regardless of race or gender. Although the Red Army had not collapsed, the Soviets had lost much of their industry and the bulk of their arable land. Until the Red Army triumphed in the momentous battle at Stalingrad in February 1943, Roosevelt understandably feared that Stalin might sue for peace, as Vladimir Lenin had done a quarter-century earlier. Although the Royal Air Force's pilots prevented a German invasion of Britain in fall 1940 and Britain possessed the largest navy in the world, the British chancellery was penniless, Britain's army was relatively small, and its food supply meager.[6]

The weeks following Pearl Harbor were "dark days," as *New York Times* foreign correspondent Hanson Baldwin wrote on December 17, 1941.[7] With the Soviets badly wounded and Britain frail, victory in Europe depended on the United States—not only the U.S. armed forces but, equally, America's industrial might. Yet two decades of disarmament and indifference had left the United States with an army that ranked eighteenth among the world's nations in size and an air force of 1,700 aircraft, mostly obsolete. Although the Congress had been increasing defense spending since 1937 at Roosevelt's urging, military production comprised merely 2 percent of the U.S. gross national product in 1940. "When war broke out the United States was still a predominantly civilian economy, with a small apparatus of state, low taxes, and a military establishment that had only reached the foothill of re-equipment," the noted English historian Richard Overy observed. It "faced states which had been arming heavily for eight or nine years and now had more than half of their national product devoted to the waging of war."[8]

The Allies could not defeat Germany, Italy, and Japan unless the United States built, trained, and transported huge armed forces across the Arctic, the Atlantic, and the Pacific. The United States had to raise and ship hundreds of thousands of tons of grain and other food and manufactured unprecedented quantities of airplanes, ships, tanks, jeeps, guns, bombs, bazookas, and other war materiel for its armed forces, the Soviet Union, Britain, China, and other allies.

The United States ultimately achieved those objectives and more. By late 1942, Americans were producing twice as many aircraft and tanks as the Axis powers (although the German Panzers and *Königstigers* were more heavily armored and more powerful than U.S. Pershing tanks). For every major vessel built in Japan, the Americans built sixteen comparable ships. The same was true of weaponry.[9]

Yet success in industry was by no means certain. Employers had to stop making highly profitable consumer goods. Millions of Americans had to leave the countryside and small towns for jobs in Chicago, Buffalo, Seattle, Los Angeles, Norfolk, Mobile, and other factory towns and ports. Housing had to be built for the new workers, women had to be encouraged to take new kinds of jobs, men had to be forced to accept women as coworkers, and white resistance to blacks in industry, which peaked in 1943 and 1944 in union bastions like Oakland, Detroit, and Philadelphia, had to be checked.

Industrial relations were the toughest challenge of all on the home front. The term encompassed a complex of subjects, including keeping strikes to a minimum to increase production, curtailing wage increases to curb inflation, and convincing union and corporation leaders and their staff to cooperate with each other despite the decades of rancor. American businesses opposed labor organization much harder than businesses in any other nation. Employer opposition included spying on unions, firing pro-union workers, obtaining court injunctions to stop strikes, manipulating the press and politicians, recruiting thugs, saboteurs, and strikebreakers, and boycotting businesses who signed contracts with unions. Although the National Labor Relation Act passed by the Congress in 1935 in principle guaranteed workers the right to unionize, Remington Rand, Republic Steel, and Weirton Steel openly defied the law. Meanwhile, American Federation of Labor (AFL) leaders denounced rival Congress of Industrial Organizations (CIO) leaders in congressional hearings, and anti-Communists fought Communists inside CIO unions.

Nearly nine million American workers belonged to the unions in 1939, more than twice as many as in 1936. As war intensified overseas in 1940 and 1941 and the War and Naval Departments issued contracts for military hardware, labor markets tightened. Nearly 2.4 million American workers went on strike in 1941, almost three times as many as in 1936, demanding wage increases and union contracts.[10] To forestall strikes, Roosevelt established the National Defense Mediation Board (NDMB) in March 1941—a twelve-person committee with high-ranking corporate executives, national union officials, and lawyers and professors experienced in labor-management mediation, plus alternate members. Although the board helped avert several dozen walkouts, several large unions rejected their proposed compromises. The most dramatic conflict occurred in early June 1941, when the Communist-led local of the International Association of Machinists struck North American Aviation Corporation near Los Angeles. The strike did not end until Roosevelt sent in Army troops. The NDMB collapsed in early November when the president of the CIO and the secretary-general of the United Mine Workers

(UMW) quit the board to protest the majority's vote denying the UMW demand that every coal miner in pits owned by steel companies be a member of their union. Without those members, the NDMB lacked legitimacy.

Many members of Congress and large sectors of the public were livid about strikes, unions, and union leaders in 1941—above all, about John L. Lewis, the grandiloquent president of the UMW. According to one Gallup poll, 72 percent of the public favored a ban on strikes at defense plants in 1941. "If there is an insurrectionist spirit in America, for God's sake let us find it out now and meet it before it is too late," one congressman exclaimed. "We are already living under a labor government rapidly headed for a labor dictatorship, which, if not checked, will soon run into a labor despotism," another cried out. Other members of Congress chimed in, condemning "coddling of extremists," "racketeers in labor's ranks," and unions "sabotaging the war effort." A bill was introduced into the Congress that would have subjected leaders of strikes at defense plants to punishments ranging from twenty-five years in prison to execution. "If it is necessary to preserve this country, they would not hesitate for one split second to enact legislation to send them to the electric chair," remarked the Democratic chairman of the House Judiciary Committee. "John L. Lewis damn your black coal soul," exclaimed the Army newspaper *Stars and Stripes*.[11]

* * *

If Japan had not attacked Pearl Harbor, the Congress would have passed draconian antiunion legislation and Roosevelt, who had already sent U.S. Army troops to halt the North American Aviation strike, would have signed the measure or would not have issued a veto, thus allowing it to become law. The Japanese attacks allowed the administration to adopt a more sophisticated strategy.

Seventy-two hours after Pearl Harbor was bombed, Roosevelt asked attorney William Davis, chairman of the defunct NDMB, to convene a meeting of prominent union and liberal corporate leaders in Washington. He wanted a new arrangement to prevent strikes, lockouts, and other disruptions. He appointed Davis as moderator and appointed the chairman of the Senate Committee on Education and Labor as associate moderator.

The White House invited twelve prominent corporate executive and twelve union officials to the meeting. The twenty-four representatives met at 10 a.m. on Wednesday, December 17, in the imposing conference room of the Federal Reserve Board's governors. The president arrived late for the opening session. The mood when he arrived was "dead seriousness," one journalist reported. Speaking gruffly without notes, the president told the men that they had to agree on a plan to overcome their disputes "just as fast as you can." There was no time for bickering, he insisted. "The country is expecting something out of you in a hurry. . . . It would be a thrilling thing if we can get something out in the way of a unanimous agreement by tomorrow night, Thursday, or at the latest Friday night. I want speed. Speed now is of the essence, just as much as in turning out things in plants, as it is among the fighting forces. . . . We have to do perfectly unheard of things." Leaning over the lectern, the president spoke about a mythical Army Air Force pilot he named Lieutenant Kelly. "The government did not tell him he had to dive on a battleship and lose his life," he informed the gray-haired union and corporate officials. "That was his 'must': his own personal 'must.' There was nothing in his orders that told him he had to dive his plane into a Japanese battleship. That was young Kelly's personal 'must.' And each one of you, and I too, we have our personal 'musts,'" declared the president, whose battle with polio underscored his message. "The country is looking at you," he told the audience. "I am looking at you. The Congress is looking at you. All I can say is God speed your efforts."[12]

Despite Roosevelt's plea, the industrialists and union leaders refused to compromise. Two issues divided the conferees: the labor leaders' insistence on 100 percent union membership in companies where they had contracts—a policy that no corporation would accept—and guaranteed wage increases for workers. The conference did not end until Christmas Eve, when the president told the press that they had reached consensus. But his announcement was not true. The two sides had agreed to nothing more than to forswear strikes and lockouts during the war and to support a new agency to help settle disputes. There was no compromise on union membership policy or on wage increases. Nonetheless, on January 12, 1942, Franklin Roosevelt issued Executive Order No. 9017, establishing a new office called the National War Labor Board.

"The national interest demands that there shall be no interruption of any work which contributes to the effective prosecution of the war," the executive order began. According to the president, the labor leaders and industrialists at the December conference had "agreed that for the duration of the war there shall be no strikes or lockouts, and that all labor disputes shall be settled by peaceful means, and that a National War Labor Board shall be established for the peaceful adjustment of such disputes." The new board consisted of four leading corporate executives, four top labor leaders, and four members of the public who were experienced arbitrators, designated as "representatives" of America's employers, employees, and the public, plus four alternate employer representatives and four alternate labor representatives who would serve when a regular member of their side could not be present.[13] Unlike the ineffective NDMB, decisions issued by the NWLB had the force of law "by virtue of the authority vested in me by the Constitution," according to the president, a dubious assertion that was never challenged in the courts. "After it takes jurisdiction, the Board shall finally determine the dispute, and . . . may use mediation, voluntary arbitration, or arbitration under rules established by the Board."[14]

Roosevelt appointed attorney William Hammatt Davis and economist George Taylor as the NWLB's chairman and associate chairman. The other public members were Frank Graham, the president of the University of North Carolina distinguished by his relatively liberal views on racial questions, and Wayne Morse, dean of the University of Oregon's law school, with experience arbitrating cases for unions and northwestern shipping and lumber companies. Graham and Morse both served in the U.S. Senate after the war. Graham was defeated in 1950 by race baiting in the Democratic Party primary campaign; he subsequently served as the United Nations mediator in a dispute between India and Pakistan over Kashmir. Morse remained in the Senate until 1969. A maverick who moved from the Republican Party to independent status and finally the Democratic Party, Morse was one of the only two senators who voted against the 1964 Tonkin Gulf resolution that gave President Lyndon Johnson unrestricted authority to conduct the war in Vietnam.[15]

To represent America's "employees," the president selected Matthew Woll, a vice president of the AFL, the president of the Photo-Engravers union, and an old friend of Samuel Gompers; Tom Kennedy, the UMW officer who had resigned from the government's previous mediation board; the president of the United Automobile Workers, R. J. Thomas; and the secretary-treasurer of the AFL, George Meany. Meany quickly emerged as the leader of the labor cohort.

As "employer representatives," the president appointed four relatively liberal industrialists: the chairman of the board of Standard Oil of New Jersey, Walter Teagle; the president of Standard Knitting Mills of Knoxville, Tennessee, E. J. McMillan; the president of Congoleum Nairn of New York (later renamed Monsanto), Albert Hawkes; and the chairman of the board of the American-Hawaiian Steamship Company, Roger Lapham. A San Francisco Republican, Lapham became the principal spokesman for the corporate executives.

Although the NWLB's employee, employer, and public representatives had not been elected to office by their constituents or approved by the Senate, the president gave them the power to settle all union-management disputes and issue edicts to employers and unions on hours of work, working conditions, union membership policies, grievances, and virtually every other aspect of union-management relations. In October 1942 Roosevelt gave the board the power to impose controls on the wages of *all* employees in *every* American industry except in agriculture, whether they belonged to unions or not.

President Woodrow Wilson had set up a similar board a quarter-century earlier, in March 1918. The two boards had the same name, the same number of members, also consisted of union, corporate, and public representatives, and faced similar challenges. Nevertheless, the two National War Labor Boards differed significantly. The board appointed by Roosevelt consisted of equal numbers of union, corporate, and "public" representatives. Wilson, by contrast, had appointed five top union leaders and five business leaders and asked the labor and employer groups to separately select a public citizen who would serve jointly as cochairmen. The business leaders on the 1918 board chose former president William Howard Taft; the trade unionists picked Frank Walsh, an intrepid Kansas City labor lawyer who had chaired the U.S. Commission on Industrial Relations of 1912–15. The first war labor board had a small staff; it functioned for merely eight months, and, despite their stature, Taft and Walsh lacked experience in mediation.

The second war labor board had much more time than its precursor—four years. They had a much larger staff and were able to learn from their predecessors' experience. Many of the business and union representatives on the second war labor board had served on one or more of the tripartite industrial-relations boards that Franklin Roosevelt appointed during his first two terms in office. AFL vice president Matthew Woll served on both war labor boards. And relations between unions and corporations in the United States had changed considerably since 1918. By 1941 no American union leader imagined overthrowing the capitalist system, not even Ben Gold, the president of the Fur & Leather Workers, or Bill Sentner, the president of District 8 of the United Electrical, Radio & Machine Workers of America (UE), both of whom openly acknowledged their Communist Party affiliation. In this regard, they were far removed from revolutionaries of the 1910s like William Z. Foster and Bill Haywood. Although Gold, Sentner, the UE's director of organization James Matles, and the International Longshoremen & Warehouse Union's president Harry Bridges defended the Communist Party's positions on nearly all national and international issues, they were for all practical purposes reformers, fighting to empower their members within the capitalist system. Moreover, the United States and the Soviet Union became allies after Germany and Japan attacked their homelands in 1941, and the Communist Party of the United States, which took cues from Moscow, insisted that union leaders whom they influenced cooperate with the NWLB, employers, and the Roosevelt administration. Finally, the War Department and other administration offices made recognition of unions a condition for receiving federal contracts. Consequently, although employer and labor representatives continued to fight over grievance cases, sometimes sharply, the second NWLB did more than its forerunner to stimulate union-management cooperation.

* * *

William H. Davis was sixty-one years old when appointed as NWLB chairman. A patent attorney by profession, Davis earned his law degree from Columbia University, the most prestigious law school in the country at that time. During the First World War he worked in the Department of War's planning division, which trained many future New Deal administrators. After the armistice, he developed a clientele that included the DuPont Corporation and fought cases up to the Supreme Court. Davis devoted much of his time to public issues during the 1930s, however, particularly union-management relations. Although he originally called this work "recreation," as time passed, industrial relations became his principal interest. Davis served as deputy director of the National Recovery Agency from 1933 to 1935 and director of the New York State Board of Arbitration from 1937 to 1941. At the behest of Roosevelt, he traveled to Sweden and England in 1938, along with General Electric (GE) president Gerard Swope and University of Wisconsin law school dean Lloyd Garrison, to investigate industrial relations there. In 1941, he served as chairman of the NDMB, the NWLB's predecessor.

Born in 1880 in Bangor, Maine, son of an engineer who owned an iron mine in Kentucky, Davis retained a distinctive Maine accent. "Will," as he was usually called, had uncombed white hair, a dry sense of humor, and a natural manner that enabled him to work with trade unionists more easily than the usual corporate lawyer. In a 1942 *Fortune* magazine article, journalist John Chamberlain described Davis as "shambling, salty, rumpled, charming, and red-faced." His greatest strength as a mediator was his patience or, more precisely, his ability to use time as a weapon. "Davis lets both sides to a labor-management quarrel run through what he calls the 'emptying process,'" Chamberlain wrote. "He can sit until five in the morning—and sometimes later. His own contribution is limited to breaking in for purposes of getting a point clarified. But all the time he is busy making notes. . . . When the 'emptying process' is over, Davis draws up two lists, one of agreed-upon items, one of the opposite. The rest is a matter of supervised horse trading." Despite his degrees and previous positions, Davis scorned attorneys and economists, who in his opinion did not understand the real world. "He used to say, 'Don't talk to me like a lawyer,'" remembered Ben Aaron, a Harvard Law School alumnus, former NWLB staffer, and law professor at the University of California–Los Angeles. "And he had the presence and the standing to cut through a lot of this legal stuff when these lawyers would come plastering before the Board. He just wouldn't put up with it."[16]

A generation older than George Taylor, Wayne Morse, and Frank Graham, likable, persuasive, and well connected in Washington, Davis served as the NWLB's public spokesperson at congressional hearings, mediated disputes among the board's members, negotiated on behalf of the board with other federal agencies and the White House, always keeping the board from tilting too far one way or the other when the waters got rough.

While Davis did essential work, the NWLB's vice chairman George W. Taylor had greater impact inside the board, on its staff, and on American industrial relations more generally. Like Davis, Taylor used time as a tool in mediation, listening intently through the trade unionists' and managers' long, often-contentious meetings. Unlike Davis, however, Taylor disdained "horse-trading." His upbringing as a Quaker and his years of mediation with the garment manufacturers in Philadelphia convinced Taylor that he could lead even truculent union men and employers to consensus by posing the right questions at the right time.[17] (See figure 1.)

* * *

Davis and Taylor planned from the beginning to recruit and train promising young economists and lawyers in mediation and arbitration and send the bulk of the staffers to what Davis called "the field." The twelve-member board would remain in Washington, where they would establish broad principles and decide the most controversial disputes, while the staff would resolve almost all the cases in the cities where the war material was produced and shipped.

"All right, gentlemen," Davis began at the opening of the board's first meeting, 11:00 a.m. Friday, January 16, 1942. "We meet here with some familiar faces and some new faces," he noted, referring to the fact that half the board's members had belonged to the NDMB. "I think we meet under a very different set-up from the now defunct Mediation Board," Davis continued. The previous committee was authorized only "to make every reasonable effort to adjust and settle" conflicts, but Roosevelt's Executive Order #9017 gave the NWLB the authority to "finally determine" disputes. While the earlier board could only *ask* a union and company to submit their dispute to arbitration, the new board could issue orders that had the force of law. "We have been given the job and we can't complain that we haven't been given the power," Davis told the board. "We can't complain that we haven't behind us or under us an agreement, and we can't complain that we haven't been given the widest possible discretion. I think that under these circumstances . . . this Board has the job of not just stopping strikes—that has been agreed to—but of creating a morale in management and labor that fits the national situation and gets the maximum production." That was essential to turn the tide of war. "I hope we will be able to discharge that obligation."

Davis began talking about the unresolved disputes that they had inherited from the NDMB when George Meany broke in. Davis and Meany may have planned the interruption. They had been working together for almost a decade, first in Albany and New York City, where Davis had directed the New York State Board of Arbitration while Meany presided over the New York State Federation of Labor, and then in Washington on the NDMB. And, unlike previous AFL leaders, Meany had few if any reservations about linking the labor federation to the federal government. Although Meany was twenty-five years younger than Davis, the two men mixed easily. Indeed, Davis's tone when speaking to Meany at the NWLB's opening session was more than friendly: almost affectionate. "Mr.

FIGURE 1. William H. Davis and George W. Taylor at the first meeting of the National War Labor Board, January 16, 1942. AP photo.

Chairman, don't you think that before we proceed to anything at all we should go over the entire matter of organization and procedure?" His senior AFL colleague Matthew Woll concurred. Davis turned to Roger Lapham, the business delegation's principal spokesman, who said that they had no objections.[18]

Over the next hour-and-a-half the twelve men forged a plan to resolve strikes, lockouts, and workers' grievances that the board followed throughout the war. They rejected the National Defense Mediation Board's approach of handling grievance cases ad hoc. That method was outdated, Meany declared. "We sat for hours and hours and we found that we had to add to the membership of the board. We kept adding and adding all the time. We had forty-one people, I think, at one time on this Board. In fact, we had to have people go on Panels [sic] even before they were officially appointed."[19]

A week before the creation of the War Labor Board was publicly announced, Secretary of Labor Frances Perkins had proposed a solution to this problem. Perkins told reporters that she was giving the president a list of twelve prominent Americans who could serve as mediators. Her list included former Republican presidential candidate Wendell Willkie; former postmaster general Jim Farley; Anna Rosenberg, a veteran New York social reformer; the editor of the Des Moines, Iowa, *Register and Tribune*; and a justice of Utah's Supreme Court. Secretary Perkins's Labor Department had been in charge of mediation and conciliation in Washington until 1941. Like any bureaucrat, she balked at intrusion on her turf. But Perkins had moved too quickly. She had failed to contact Willkie ahead of time and when the Indiana Republican heard from reporters that he was going to receive an appointment in labor relations, he called the president to protest. He "wanted to be in the trenches," in other words, international relations. Secretary Perkins had to back off, to Davis's delight. "I said to her, 'You tell Mr. Willkie that if he comes on this board he will be in the trenches!'" he joked. "But if he doesn't want to, it will be all right with me.' And I said, 'Would you please say to Mr. Early [President Roosevelt's press secretary] . . . that until the war labor board has acted, I shall say nothing more and there will be nothing said by anybody about any further appointments.'"[20] By taunting Perkins, the first woman appointed to a presidential cabinet, Davis consolidated his all-male board.

Davis regarded the National War Labor Board as the industrial counterpart to the U.S. Supreme Court. Just as the Supreme Court presided over the national judiciary system, determined for themselves which cases to consider, and made decisions that set precedents for circuit, district, and appellate courts, so the NWLB would provide guidelines for arbitrators and mediators to follow in their meetings with unions and corporations. He did not want civil courts intervening into union-management cases. Despite their sharp differences in other regards, the corporate executives, labor leaders, and arbitrators on the NWLB all opposed judicial intervention into industrial relations. Davis and the other board members thought of themselves as architects of a new system parallel to the civil and criminal courts, an American equivalent to Australia's industrial arbitration courts.

"Suppose you had an arbitration board made up of Mr. [Supreme Court Chief] Justice [Charles Evans] Hughes, Judge [Learned] Hand, and Mr. [Thomas] Thacher [former U.S. solicitor general]," Davis declared. "If you went to that group, they would want to know first, 'Well, what is it that we are going to decide? What is the issue?' They would have to have a document before them. It would have to be something that was possible to arbitrate, in my opinion, some kind of a rule about it to be applied. . . . Where rules had been established, understood by custom or by the Board, then they would refer the thing to arbitration."

Davis urged the board members to avoid breaking into working groups. Instead, they could appoint deputy tripartite panels that would hear disputes and issue decisions in accordance with the principles announced by the NWLB in its rulings. In other cases, Davis suggested, the board could decide to appoint a single person who would listen to the parties and make recommendations to the members. "See if I have this right?" Meany asked, as if he and Davis had not already hatched out the plan in private.

> This Board will function as a 12-man board with a rule for a six-man quorum that provides at least two employer and two employee representatives be present and that the meetings of the Board will be along the lines as laid out this morning, that this great big body of mediators will not attend meetings of the Board or act as officers, but that if a case is given to, say, a tripartite panel of mediations public, employer, and employee, that when the time comes for presentation of the case to the Board[,] then the mediators will appear before the Board in the role of witnesses.

"Is that the idea?" Meany asked. Yes, Davis replied. "My conception of what we will have to do is to have [tripartite] mediation panels who will take a case and try to mediate it and if they can't mediate, then they can make recommendations to the Board."

"I think that we are going to have a flood of cases," Davis warned his fellow board members. "We have to settle about 99 percent of them by mediation or we would be swamped." He did not want old-timers like Jim Farley, Wendell Willke, and Anna Rosenberg to mediate cases for the board. He wanted young men—he always conceived of the arbitrators and mediators as male—who were trained by, and loyal to, the War Labor Board, not older men and women with prior experience and ties. Davis made another analogy to the Supreme Court: "I think we ought to get young fellows just out of law school for a year or two who are not so expensive as that, and yet picked out as being energetic and competent young men. It is the sort of job that you pick out law school students who made high grades, and make them Secretaries to [the] Justices of the Supreme Court."[21]

Here was a plan for controlling labor-management conflicts so that the United States could win the war: a crew of young economists and attorneys to investigate, mediate, and arbitrate cases for the NWLB—an American industrial supreme court. "I think we ought to keep our hands as clean as we can up here," declared E. J. McMillan, the Tennessee textile industrialist, smiling broadly. The AFL's secretary-general George Meany was delighted. "There will be a number of cases that the Panels will come back and say to us, 'Well, this thing is settled through mediation.' Well, if it is settled through mediation, God bless them."

* * *

Davis handed the job of recruiting, educating, and supervising young professionals to George Taylor, who was twenty-one years his junior and, as a professor at the Wharton School, well informed about recent graduates. When the board began, its staff consisted of Lewis Gill and William Simkin, both Wharton School alumni who had worked with Taylor in Philadelphia garment mediation and assisted the NDMB, and Ralph Seward, an arbitrator who had served as a public member of the NDMB. Soon afterward Taylor recruited the director of the New Jersey State Board of Mediation, David Cole, a forty-three-year-old Paterson, New Jersey, attorney. For the position of general counselor of the board, he and Davis recruited the dean of the University of Wisconsin law school, Lloyd Garrison, grandson of the passionate abolitionist William Lloyd Garrison, a graduate of Harvard College and Harvard Law School and a member of the Harvard Board of Overseers. During the 1930s, Garrison had served on mediation panels in the steel, printing, and railroad industries. He chaired the National Labor Relation Board in 1934 and, at the request the New York State legislature, traveled to Sweden and Britain with Davis and GE's president Gerard Swope to learn new ways to resolve industrial conflicts.[22]

George Taylor then began to recruit the board's staff. Although some of the recruits were attorneys, most were professors of economics. They were young, mainly in their mid- to late twenties, and, with merely one exception, Ruth Dewing, all male. The majority knew little or knew nothing about industrial relations beyond what they picked up in the newspapers, radio, or strikes in their hometowns. Taylor and Davis wanted bright young people who would learn quickly and be devoted to the board. Thinking about the question fifty years later, one of the recruits, Sylvester Garrett, put himself in Taylor's shoes: "Are you going to get older people—more experienced, but less resilient? Or are we going to get younger people who go out there and make mistakes, but who can take a pasting and survive?"

The board's young staffers came to respect, even revere, George Taylor, whom they always called "Professor Taylor." They called him a "genius" and "mediator supreme." The NWLB's vice chairman returned the affection. Married to his high-school sweetheart Edith Ayling but childless, Taylor treated the NWLB's new hires as if they were his sons. Some board staffers called themselves "Taylor-made men." "Thank God for George Taylor!" exclaimed Ben Aaron, referring to career advice that he received from Taylor when the war ended.[23]

The NWLB staff was not like their counterparts in the State Department and the Justice Department, who came from well-heeled white Anglo-Protestant families and were educated at exclusive prep schools and Yale, Harvard, and Princeton. Nor did they resemble the Labor Department's economists, who were mainly immigrants or children of immigrants and mainly graduates of City College of New York. Rather, the NWLB's staff came from what John R. Commons called "the third class," which was neither proletarian nor capitalist. "Two-thirds of the voting population are speculators," Commons wrote back in 1906. "We call them the public. They may be forced to take sides, but they want fair play."[24]

The Labor Board boys' parents were farmers and milliners (for example, Clark Kerr's father and mother), salesmen (Eli Rock, George Hildebrand, and Milton Derber's fathers), painting contractors (Saul Wallen's father), owners of hardware shops (Vernon Jensen's father), an ice-skating rink and dance-hall operator (Robben Fleming's father), Protestant missionaries (John Dunlop's mother and father), or pastors (William McPherson's father). The majority were raised in middle-class families inspired by the social gospel, the social-reform ethic embraced at the beginning of the twentieth century by liberal Episcopalian, Presbyterian, Congregational, and Methodist denominations. Others were from the Society of Friends, or, in some cases, Reform Judaism or Latter-Day Saints, each of which, in different ways, were committed to social reform, missionary work, and conflict resolution. They grew up in the Great Depression, when destitution was widespread among working-class families and strikes frequently turned violent—and, like virtually all Americans of that era, they feared another war.

Although they avoided theory, the Labor Board boys were for all intents and purposes institutional economists, in the tradition of John R. Commons—a strain in economic thought influential between the 1920s and the 1940s. They viewed the U.S. economy as a constellation of institutions—primarily labor unions, businesses, and business associations—whose leaders could speak with authority for their constituents and could forge compromises among themselves or, when needed, with the assistance of intermediaries, namely their group. The Labor Board boys did not align themselves with political parties. Nonetheless, they were basically New Deal–style liberals, although not unqualifiedly so. Several members of the group, including Jean McKelvey and Clark Kerr, joined the Socialist Party's youth groups or at least sympathized with socialism when they were young. On the other hand, John Dunlop, David Cole, and others worked with Governor Nelson Rockefeller in the 1960s and later with Presidents Richard Nixon and Gerald Ford—not because they were Republican economists, but because they were selected by Republican chief executives as labor-management intermediaries. Working with unions and businesses that negotiated pensions and other benefits for workers, they did not advocate government-funded medical care during or after the war. Nor did they support the Communist Party. Yet to call them anti-Communist would not be accurate, since they had no problems with mediating disputes for the International Longshoremen and Warehouse Workers Union, the UE, or other unions whose leaders were close to the Communist Party. In fact, by the 1960s they had become convinced that the world's Communist and capitalist systems would converge.[25]

John Dunlop ultimately became a top member of the board's staff and, as time passed, the top labor-management arbitrator in America. Dunlop was born in 1914 in Placerville, California, an old gold-mining town, where his parents operated a pear ranch. He was the oldest of seven children. When he was four years old, his mother and father decided to become missionaries for the Presbyterian Church. The family moved to Cebu Island in the south-central Philippines, where John and his brothers and sisters grew up. ("My brother and I were the only Americans in our school.") The family did not return to the United States until 1931, and then only temporarily.[26] John entered Marin County Junior College while his parents returned to Cebu. "My parents were devout, and I thought for some time of going into the ministry, as a matter of fact." His perspective soon changed. The nation was suffering badly and, like Vernon Jensen, Dunlop regarded economics as the most compelling issue. "I shifted technically into economics when I went to Berkeley in the fall of '33. And all the excitement about the recession and depression and New Deal . . . impelled me to take the economics major."

He married Dorothy Emily Webb in 1937, spent a year studying with John Maynard Keynes at Cambridge University, and received his doctorate in economics from the University of California in 1939. While in England, Dunlop spent a couple of months in Yorkshire, home of England's textile and steel industries, to become acquainted with the working class, "But basically that was all rather intellectual," he recalled. His thesis was a numerical analysis of wages and prices, not about workers or unions. He returned to the United States to teach at Harvard University, first as a teaching fellow, then as an assistant professor of economics. He and Emily shared a small apartment with another teaching fellow, Ken (John Kenneth) Galbraith, and his wife Kitty.

Dunlop made a splash while in England with a September 1938 article in the Royal Economic Society's *Economic Journal*, which refuted a theory of the relationship between real rates and money wage rates in the short run that Keynes had advanced in his recently published *The General Theory of Employment, Interest and Money*. Contrary to Lord Keynes, it stated that "statistically, real wage rates generally rise with an increase in wage rates, rise during a first period after the peak, and then fall under the pressure of severe wage reduction. Correcting for changes in the terms of trade or for trend does not materially alter the results," Dunlop argued. Keynes replied in March 1939 issue of the same journal conceding the point but added that "further statistical enquiry is necessary before we have a firm foundation of facts on which to reconstruct our theory of the short period."[27]

Dunlop was twenty-four years old when his exchange with Keynes was published. He almost certainly would have remained focused on economic theory if he had not been asked to join the NWLB in 1942. "The thing that really caused me to be a practitioner was the War Labor Board," recalled Dunlop, whose friends at the time called "Johnny." "I held a number of different posts as special assistant to George Taylor and Will Davis." Although Dunlop was only twenty-eight, Taylor and Davis appointed him to chair the Wage Adjustment Board, the auxiliary of the NWLB responsible for preventing inflation in construction, a critical issue for the war. He was also appointed vice chairman of Regional War Labor Board I headquartered in Boston. "I watched the people and developed the capacity and willingness to undertake the costs of managing and settling something."[28]

The Jewish members of the board's staff were not motivated by their religious faith—at least not consciously. Their outlook was secular. But, like many middle-class American Jews of their generation, they sympathized with workers yet feared social conflict. This was true, for example, of Benjamin Aaron—or Ben, as he was called, the first professional hired by the board aside from those carried over from the National Defense Mediation Board. Born in Chicago in 1915 to parents who immigrated from Germany, Aaron was the youngest of five children. His mother died when he was five, and his father died soon afterward. Ben was raised by his paternal aunt and her husband, an attorney. They moved to San Francisco, where he finished school.

Aaron graduated from the University of Michigan in 1936 and Harvard Law School in 1940. "Three years in law school convinced me that I didn't want to practice law in a conventional way," he recalled. "I grew up during the period of the organization of the automobile industry, the sit-down strikes, the Battle of the Overpass at Ford," he continued. "My sentiments were strongly in favor of organized labor. . . . I, in all my naïveté, wrote to Dick Frankenstein [the vice president of the UAW], who I had never met and offered my services on their legal staff. Of course I never even got a reply."

He went to Washington, DC, looking for a job. "It's a terrible thing to say that a war could be a blessing, but in my case [it was]," he confessed. "I had been unemployed and looking for a job for quite a considerable period of time." Ralph Seward, who had been an alternate public representative on the NDMB and transferred to the NWLB, assured Aaron that a job would open up for him in the industrial relations field. As soon as the NWLB was established, he went to Seward, who passed him on to Taylor. "And then began a period in my life with George, who was my principal mentor on the board."

Aaron was well educated, tall, lean, handsome, quick, and articulate and looked even younger than his age. When he walked into the room of union and company representatives in Detroit to convene a meeting, "all these middle-aged or elderly people on both sides . . . look at me, first in complete and utter disbelief, and then with complete and utter disgust."[29] Despite Ben Aaron's appearance and inexperience, he proved so able that Taylor appointed him as his assistant, chairman of the board's Tool-and-Die Commission, chairman of the board's National Airframe Panel, and, finally, executive director of the NWLB.

Only one woman was recruited for the NWLB's staff in Washington. That was Ruth Dewing. Born in 1915, daughter of a Harvard professor and a psychologist, she had attended progressive schools in Cambridge and earned a BA at Bennington College in Vermont. "Everybody's talking about the workers' point of view, but they had never even *known* a worker, much less been in a plant," she remembered. So Dewing went to work for six weeks in a wool mill in 1936. She lived in a boardinghouse with French-Canadian workers so she could "find out what a worker's point of view really was." After living among those women and working in the mill, she realized that there was no common workers' viewpoint. The French-Canadian, Portuguese, and English workers in the mill had distinctive perspectives. This led to her studying for a master's degree at Columbia University, and through her father's friend, a job as impartial chairman at suit and laundry factories in Brooklyn, and then a job on the NWLB staff. "They had to scrape the bottom of the barrel to hire women," she joked in a 2008 interview. At the board she got to know George Taylor and was especially close to Ben Aaron and his wife Eleanor. "We all felt passionately that there are ways of settling labor disputes that are substitutes for strikes." One had to "perceive what the other person is really saying and feeling, not projecting yourself on to them. And then figuring out how all these pieces could possibly fit together. We all had that in common." Dewing didn't remain on the board's staff, however. Instead, she resigned when she married James Ewing, another member of the staff, who had enlisted into the navy. After the war ended, they became newspaper publishers in Bangor, Maine, and Keene, New Hampshire. Consequently, Ruth Dewing's experience at the board proved to be a brief, memorable interlude in her life.[30]

When the board created regional boards in 1943, they hired several other women. The most influential of them was Jean Trepp McKelvey, who became a prominent figure in the industrial relations field. (See figure 2.) As explained in the Preface, Jean Trepp was raised in Rochester, New York, and decided to study labor after watching her grandparents and their friends disparage the Russian Jewish immigrants who worked in their factories. She wrote her senior thesis on why socialist-led unions accepted scientific management in the 1920s. The senior thesis won first prize in a contest sponsored by the Hart, Schaffner and Marx clothing company for the best essay in economics written by an undergraduate. Rejected by Harvard Law School because of her gender, she earned her doctorate in economics at Harvard.

McKelvey was able to get a job teaching economics at Sarah Lawrence College in Bronxville, New York, in 1933 despite the depression, perhaps through family connections. At that time Sarah Lawrence was a two-year women's college, educating young women from well-to-do families. "All these wealthy kids," she recalled. "You know, Weirs and Fords. . . . All of them becoming Communists, by the way, in repudiation of their families." She added that she "was never tempted." She did, however, join the Socialist Party and ran for local office in Bronxville on

FIGURE 2. Jean Trepp as a junior at Wellesley College, 1928. Kheel Center, Cornell University.

its ticket in the mid-1930s. In 1933 she married Blake McKelvey, a historian and son of a Protestant minister whom she met at Harvard. Despite her abilities and accomplishments, Jean McKelvey was not asked to join the NWLB staff in 1942. So she went to work in an electrical parts factory at night to contribute to the war effort while teaching during the day. But when the board created regional divisions a year later, she was appointed as a public representative on Regional War Labor Board II, which covered upstate New York and northern New Jersey.[31]

Ruth Dewing Ewing and Jean Trepp McKelvey, however, were exceptional. The vast majority of the board's mediators, arbitrators, and other professional staff were male. And none better exemplified the Labor Board boys' weltanschauung than Clark Kerr.

Kerr was born in 1911 and raised in Stony Creek, a village near Reading, in southeastern Pennsylvania. His father raised fruits and vegetables on a three-acre hillside plot, with several horses, sheep, cows, pigs, ducks, geese, and guinea hens. "So I was raised as a farm boy. In fact, I had my own team of horses when I was fourteen, and the members of that team, Maude and Kate, really became my best friends. I spent more time working with them than I spent with any human beings," he recalled, a remark that suggests his cloistered character. His father also occasionally taught extension classes for Penn State's agricultural school, but he never earned much money. Although Clark's mother died while she was young, she was the most influential figure in his life. She had been a milliner before she married. Women would bring her photographs and drawings of hats and dresses cut out of magazines; his mother would make facsimiles. Forced to leave school after the sixth grade, she made up her mind that her children would receive the education she had been denied. Much to her fiancé's resentment, she refused to wed until she had saved enough money for that aim. "And her three daughters went to Oberlin, and I went to Swarthmore, out of her hard work," Kerr proudly declared. (See figure 3.)

As a child, Kerr attended two different Protestant churches. Watching the ministers trying to take congregants from each other's churches by claiming that "the way to heaven is through the Reformed Church or the Lutheran Church" disabused him of both denominations. Once he arrived at Swarthmore College, where most of the students were birthright Quakers, he began going to the Friends' meetinghouse and to the American Friends Service Committee, the social-service organization sponsored by the Quakers. Swarthmore was associated with the liberal, Hicksite branch of the Quaker faith, with a Tolstoyan conception of Christianity, with Christ as moral teacher. The meetinghouse he attended was philosophically, rather than textually, oriented. "We believed that your life should be a religious life, not just on Sunday but in your daily life, the way you lived." Entranced, Kerr became a "Convinced Friend," in other words, a convert.

As a member of the Friends Service Committee, he spent the three summers of his college education on peace caravans. Although the early 1930s were the peak of isolationism in America, Kerr and his friends would go to Rotary Club and Kiwanis Club in Philadelphia and ride in buses up to Rhode Island and eastern Massachusetts trying to persuade anyone who would listen that the United States should join the World Court and the League of Nations. While classes were in session, he and other Friends went to the African American section of

FIGURE 3. Clark Kerr as a junior at Swarthmore College, 1932. Courtesy Friends Historical Library of Swarthmore College (1932 *Halcyon* yearbook).

North Philadelphia on Monday mornings to prepare breakfasts for hungry people. They brought day-old bread, milk just ready to turn, and stale apple butter collected by the Quakers. He would set up tables and spread the apple butter on the people's bread. "To see the poverty and desperation of the people in North Philadelphia had a really big impact on my life." He met a black minister, who invited him to speak to his congregation about peace. In their gospel spirituals, Kerr entered "a completely different world" from the tranquil Friends meetinghouse at Swarthmore. Yet "I saw there at these black churches the same sense of goodness in the people as I saw in the Quaker meeting."[32]

Since Kerr had to care for the animals in the barn after classes, he was never able to play sports in high school. It was different at Swarthmore, where he played intercollegiate soccer, basketball, and track and became captain of the college debate board. One Sunday evening in February 1932, he had the honor of debating against the Socialist Party's presidential candidate Norman Thomas. The subject that evening was capitalism. Speaking first, Kerr asked how the socialist policies advocated by Thomas could solve the business cycle. He dismissed Thomas's proposals for the creation of unemployment bureaus, unemployment insurance, public works, and the regulation of the introduction of new technologies as "mere palliative[s]" already adopted in several states and other capitalist nations. Long-term planning of production "will not serve as a cure [either]," Kerr claimed, because the business cycle is subject to uncontrollable factors such as foreign markets, hurricanes, floods, and vicissitudes of credit and investments. "Dictatorial methods are the only solution for the control of production and consumption, and dictatorial methods are not what the socialists want," the college senior insisted. Thomas responded that no system could be a magic answer to all social ills, but that socialism could be more effective than capitalism. The proposed remedies for unemployment mentioned by Kerr had not been "earnestly applied" in America, Thomas added, and if they were, the system would no longer be capitalist. The socialists wanted to plan production and consumption without profit. The time had come to take sides in the battle between capitalism and socialism, Thomas concluded. Impartiality is no longer possible. "Better to take the wrong side rather than no side at all."[33] Recalling the debate sixty years later, Kerr said that although his friends thought that he had won, he was persuaded by Thomas's vision of socialism, at least temporarily.[34]

Kerr graduated in May 1932. He went on one last peace caravan before register-ing for Columbia University law school in September. This one was to California, where he discovered unemployed workers exchanging their skills for spoiled oranges, carrots, and other vegetables with impoverished farmers in Los Angeles County. They "were really trying to do something about the depression, however primitive or feeble."[35] Impressed, Kerr quit law school for economics. He enrolled in the economics program at Stanford University and wrote a five-hundred-page master's thesis on self-help cooperatives of the unemployed in California. He also started a chapter of the League for Industrial Democracy, the junior section of the Socialist Party and progenitor of the 1960s' Students for a Democratic Society.

For his doctorate, Clark shuttled up the Bay to the University of California at Berkeley to work with Professors Paul Taylor and Ira Cross, labor economists who had studied with John R. Commons, in October 1933. He enrolled in Taylor's seminar on agriculture and economics. Several weeks earlier, cotton pickers in the San Joaquin Valley had gone on strike. Vigilantes broke into the union hall, where they killed women and children there. President Roosevelt and Governor James Rolph appointed a three-member fact-finding commission consisting of Ira Cross, president of the College of Pacific Tully Knowles, and archbishop of San Francisco Edward Hanna. Cross asked Taylor to hurry to San Joaquin to investigate. Taylor asked his new student, Clark Kerr, to go in his place. Taylor told Kerr to go to Pixley, the strike's headquarters, and "record what people said in their own words and to send . . . my notes as soon as possible." Paul Taylor's wife, photographer Dorothea Lange, accompanied Kerr. Lange took several of her most famous photographs of farm laborers during that trip.

The 1933 San Joaquin Valley cotton pickers' strike was as intense, violent, and complex as any in America's tempestuous labor history. By the early 1930s grow-ers in that valley were engaged in large-scale, industrial-type agriculture, the first time such production was undertaken in the United States, perhaps the world. The majority of laborers were Mexican and Filipino immigrants, but migrants from Arkansas, Texas, and Oklahoma, both black and white, also worked in those fields.

The first three-and-a-half years after the October 1929 stock-market crash were an era of depression in the United States, both economically and psychologically. The mood began to change in summer 1933 after Congress passed the National Industrial Recovery Act, the Agricultural Adjustment Act, and the Federal Emergency Relief Act. Meanwhile the Marxist-led General Union of Workers and Peasants was conducting a massive farmworkers' strike in Mexico. As farmworkers struck in Mexico, the Communist-led Cannery and Agricultural Workers Industrial Union acquired followers in the San Joaquin Valley. The workers were divided between Latinos following the Communists and "Oakies" and the "Arkies" following Pentecostal preachers. The growers were better organized and refused to make any concessions to the union, for they were being squeezed by the bankers who held the mortgages on their land and machinery. "Every dime I have in the world is in that crop!" one grower told Kerr.

The cotton workers' strike fractured Pixley. Although some local merchants extended credit to the migrant strikers, the Ku Klux Klan shot strikers and union organizers. The Mexican government sent a representative to investigate; the U.S. federal government dispatched mediators; and the governor's fact-finding commission held hearings. Nonetheless, the growers remained resolute.

It was in this setting that twenty-two-year-old Clark Kerr undertook his research project. Having developed skills by meeting so many kinds of people in North Philadelphia, on the peace caravans, and among jobless workers in southern California, he succeeded in winning the confidence of Latinos, Okies, Arkies, African Americans, union organizers, evangelical ministers close to the pickers, owners of large and small farms, and the local sheriffs. He met with merchants, the consul from Monterey, newspaper reporters, and the various state, federal, and clerical mediators. Kerr subsequently gave lengthy excerpts of his interviews to the U.S. Senate Committee chaired by Senator Robert La Follette Jr. exposing the use of espionage and munitions against unions.

As a left-leaning pacifist, Kerr's heart went out to the strikers. But having grown up on a family farm ("It was kind of half-subsistence and half-commercial as we sold some but consumed a lot too"), he also empathized with the smaller cotton farmers. He acquired a more complex perspective on employers and laborers than other socialist students. "You find very quickly that there isn't any such thing as 'capital' and 'labor,'" Kerr remarked years later. "I mean there are a lot of different people, a lot of different factions. And even among the growers who were adamant, there were some more sympathetic than others. And the little farmers, by and large, were more sympathetic to the workers. I was sympathetic to the little farmers coming off a family farm myself. They would work out in the fields with the people, you know. They would know them, while the big farmers, of course, didn't. They worked through foremen."

That was only the beginning of Kerr's discoveries. He went to the camps and shanties where the strikers lived. The suffering experienced by the cotton pickers' families deeply affected Kerr, who lost his mother when he was young. He was especially moved by one boy, the son of Mexican migrants. "I always wanted to adopt a little boy. I wasn't married then and it wasn't really proper, but he was the son of a cotton picker and just in terrible poverty. I just would have liked to have taken him to my home and start a family of my own. They'd drink the [infested] water—and this kid was sick with diarrhea—and they drank their water out of the ditches, irrigation ditches, and they had too little food. It can get cold and foggy in the San Joaquin Valley."

Kerr's sympathies were not confined to this youngster, however. "My sympathies were with the small farmers and with the cotton pickers. Also I developed some sympathy for the sheriffs, some of whom were just terrible, terrible people, but some were people who really believed in the law and its proper enforcement. But then how do they do that [enforce the law] when the workers don't vote and the growers do? And what rules do you have? Can you just shake your fist at people? Can you throw things at them? . . . I developed some sympathy for the difficulty of the law enforcement officer. . . . Their position is difficult."[36]

This story provides the key to understanding the Labor Board boys' outlook. When he was president of the University of California, Clark Kerr became famous—and quite correctly so—for being cerebral and publicly cold, yet tears welled in his eyes as he told the story of the sickly migrant child sixty years after the event. There were good people in each of the parties in that harrowing battle, he concluded in 1933, not only among the strikers and smaller growers but among some honest sheriffs too. Something had to be done to find a way out of the impasse in Pixley, in the San Joaquin Valley, throughout California's farm industry, and, by extension, at the thousands of other farms, factories, docks, meatpacking plants, and railroads in America. Someone had to build a new, less violent system for workers, farmers, and employers. "A few growers are using the opportunity to work toward better housing, better employment methods, and so on. But will the farmers generally and the government see and grasp their opportunity to use power intelligently and deal with causes?" Kerr exclaimed in 1935.[37] Who had the drive? Who had the vision? When Japan attacked the United States, Kerr and the other NWLB staff got their chance.

2

George Taylor and the War Labor Board, 1942–45

I was scared to death. . . . We sent these kids out.

—Will Davis

To American production, without which this war would have been lost.

—Josef Stalin's toast to Franklin Roosevelt at the 1943 Teheran Conference

IN EARLY 1942, prospects did not look good for the United States, the Allies, or the National War Labor Board (NWLB). William ("Billy") Leiserson felt sure that the new board would fail. Because Leiserson was the chairman of the National Labor Relations Board, the government's other top industrial-relations agency, and coauthor of the Social Security Act, the speech that he delivered on war labor policy at the City College of New York's Great Hall on Wednesday evening, February 18, 1942, attracted considerable attention and the audience was packed.

The news that day had been ghastly. Early in the morning, 242 Japanese aircraft directed by Marshal Admiral Yamamoto, who had commanded the attack on Pearl Harbor, bombed the Australian port of Darwin, one of the few Pacific naval bases still in the Allies' hands, and the nearby Royal Australia Air Force base at Parap. The raids killed at least 243 people, 300 to 400 more were wounded, 20 military airplanes were destroyed, 8 ships were sunk, and most of the military and civilian facilities at Darwin were laid waste. The same morning, Japanese bombers escorted by fighter planes attacked Surabaya, the largest naval and air bases in the Dutch East Indies. It was Japan's third raid on the harbor in two weeks.

The lieutenant governor predicted that Japan would invade India or Russia next if the Dutch colony fell. During the same day, Japanese forces crossed the Bilin River, Britain's last defense line before Burma's capital, Rangoon. Six Japanese divisions began moving onto Luzon, the largest Philippine island, and Japanese troops landed on Timor. Later in the day, German submarines struck Allied oil tankers and refineries off the coasts of Virginia, Aruba, and Venezuela. Morale in the Third Reich was high, the British Ministry of Economic Warfare reported, and Germany's weapons production had reached a new peak.[1]

Could the United States, Britain, and the Soviet Union recover from these assaults? No one could be certain, but since Britain and the Soviets depended on American industry for arms and food for survival, much hinged on the War Labor Board. Could the new board and its young staff stabilize union-management relations in America?

William Leiserson doubted it. The administration's decision to allow the War Labor Board to evaluate each case on its merits made no sense, he told his City College audience. Its precursor, the National Defense Mediation Board, had collapsed eight weeks earlier when the president and secretary-treasurer of the Congress of Industrial Organizations (CIO) resigned in protest of a ruling against the United Mine Workers. Why would the War Labor Board do any better? Labor and corporate leaders weren't able to compromise at the conference summoned by Roosevelt after Japan attacked Pearl Harbor, the president's claim to the contrary. Most U.S. companies were still insisting on "open shop" practices in their operations, a policy that no trade unionist would accept. The labor leaders' demand of 100 percent union membership at firms where they had contracts was equally unacceptable to corporate management, even as the tightening labor markets strengthened the unions' hand. When Charles Hook, the president of the National Association of Manufacturers, defended the open-shop principle at Roosevelt's December 1941 conference, John L. Lewis rose to his feet and growled, "I have heard this open-shop talk before. The open shop is a harlot with a wig and artificial limbs, and her bones rattle. But how much production will she give us, Mr. Hook?"[2]

How could the administration forge a union-management compact under these circumstances? "Engaged in a desperate war and fighting . . . on the defensive, this country now confronts a state of labor relations which can only be described as chaotic," the *Wall Street Journal* opined two days after Leiserson's speech.[3] Roosevelt salvaged the December 1941 conference by terming the corporate and union leaders' promises to cooperate with the War Labor Board and not call strikes or lock out employees a triumph, but Bill Leiserson knew better. There was "no essential difference" between the deceased National Defense Mediation Board and the new War Labor Board, he declared. "One was a mediation board that arbitrated; the other is an arbitration board that mediates." The president hasn't given the new War Labor Board wage guidelines or a union-shop policy on which to base its decisions, and so "decisions . . . will appear and, in fact, are likely to be arbitrary and capricious," he remarked. Production for the military will be delayed "unless broad principles" on union membership and wages "are determined in advance," he warned. "It seems rather strange to leave the determination of such crucial national issues to an arbitration board designed to make awards in particular cases." Leiserson urged the president to reconvene the December 1941 conference. If the second meeting fails, the Congress should intervene, he argued, for the National War Labor Board was impotent.[4]

Rather than accepting Leiserson's counsel, the president let the National War Labor Board members decide workers' wage rates, union-membership rules, and virtually every other aspect of labor-capital relations. This approach was typical of Franklin Roosevelt, who would vacillate and form additional committees rather than alienate powerful interest groups.[5] Yet in this case the president's hesitancy proved wise. Within six months, the War Labor Board not only settled the open-shop controversy, which had poisoned union-management relations in America since 1903, but established wage-rate guidelines that survived for the duration of the war. And, despite innumerable conflicts, some of which were quite sharp, the board's young economists and labor lawyers managed to prevent or stop thousands of strikes, resolve grievances, and forge working arrangements with management and union officials that survived throughout the war and for years afterward. These were remarkable accomplishments, inconceivable in early 1942.

* * *

During the 1980s, Nelson Lichtenstein, Staughton Lynd, Katherine V. Stone, Martin Glaberman, and other labor historians, critical legal scholars, and radical authors denounced the National War Labor Board, its Little Steel wage and union-security decisions, and the work of John Dunlop and other prominent members of the staff after the war for imposing an unjust, bureaucratic system that shackled U.S. workers when their leverage was at its peak. They blamed the board and the arbitrator it trained for the decline of unions in America in the latter twentieth century.[6] Their arguments were accepted by almost all labor historians at that time, continue to be advanced and accepted by historians today, and have rarely been critiqued.[7]

On closer look, this interpretation is not persuasive. Although the board imposed a 15 percent limit on wage increases (measured from a base of January 1, 1941, before consumer prices began to rise considerably), the caps were on increases in wage *rates*, not on workers' total *earnings*, which rose very substantially during the war because of extended workweeks, overtime pay (even though rates of overtime pay were reduced), and the new jobs that opened up during the war for

African Americans, Mexican Americans, Puerto Ricans, white women, sharecroppers, farm laborers, the unemployed, disabled persons, the elderly, and teenagers. Moreover, the board's directive gave its staff wiggle room in the form of freedom to rectify wage "inequities" and "maladjustments" and adjust "substandard standards of living."

The board's policies, combined with the ongoing expansion of the economy after the war ended, help explain how wage structure narrowed markedly during the 1940s.[8] In every belligerent nation, except the United States, Canada, and Australia, conditions for the common people deteriorated during the war and remained low afterward. In the United States, by contrast, they improved considerably, a point that the critics of the War Labor Board of the 1970s and 1980s failed to acknowledge.

Similarly, although the board's maintenance-of-membership rulings forced union officials to expel members who led wildcat strikes, the principal alternatives for workers and unions were far worse, in the face of the fierce opposition to strikes and strike leaders in the Congress and much of the public at that time. Many members of Congress became enraged when John L. Lewis called fifty-three thousand miners at coal companies owned by the steel companies out on strike in November 1941. After calming down momentarily after Pearl Harbor was attacked, public hostility to unions and strikers welled again, as the conservatives' victories in the November 1942 congressional elections suggests. By 1943 the preponderance of the public—and indeed a majority of union members—favored laws banning strikes, supported laws against featherbedding, and thought the government had the right to tell workers where to work. When John L Lewis led a strike of four hundred thousand coal miners in June 1943, Congress passed the Smith-Connally Act, which outlawed strikes in any company making war-related products; empowered the president to seize the company if the workers nonetheless walked out; provided fines, imprisonment, or both for any person who encouraged a strike, slowdown, or lockout; and prohibited contributions by unions or employers to politicians. Roosevelt vetoed the law, requesting the power to draft strikers instead. Congress overrode the veto.

The maintenance-of-membership clauses certainly increased the power of the national unions' officers, as Lichtenstein and others argued. That was the board's intent. But would the unions or their members have been better off without the board or those agreements? The analysis advanced three decades ago was so flawed that Lichtenstein disavowed his original analysis when his 1983 widely read study, *Labor's War at Home: The CIO in World War II*, was reprinted in 2003. "In the early years of the twenty-first century, the potential payoff from the corporatist bargain of World War II looks much better than it once did," he wrote in the new preface. "If the industrial relations systems put in place in the 1940s was so hostile to working-class interests," he added, "then why have almost all employers resisted it?"[9]

The War Labor Board had great impact on workers, unions, and corporations but not in the way that the critics of the 1970s and 1980s imagined. First and foremost, by effectively handling hundreds of thousands of grievances, strike threats, and stoppages, the board contributed to the production of goods for the United States, the Soviet Union, and Britain that were needed to defeat Nazi Germany, fascist Italy, and Imperial Japan while averting the labor draft proposed by the president and members of Congress. Second, the board recruited and trained a corps of capable arbitrators who became the principal intermediaries in the unionized segment of the U.S. economy after the war. Third, the board required all corporations and unions to add binding-arbitration clauses to their contracts. Before the war, binding arbitration had been largely confined to the garment industry and railroads. Although scorned by left-wing intellectuals, arbitration generally proved more beneficial to workers and unions over time than to stockholders and corporations, which is why the latter ultimately turned against the system. Finally, the system of conflict resolution constructed in 1942–45 served as a model when public-sector workers, service workers, and professional athletes organized a generation later.

* * *

George W. Taylor deserves more credit than any other person for the creation of the war and postwar industrial-relations system. Although the NWLB's chairman, William H. Davis, represented the board at congressional hearings, press conferences, and meetings with other federal agencies, Taylor not only wrote the board's most important decisions but recruited and trained the top staff. In the process, Taylor imparted his distinctive method of conflict resolution to young arbitrators. In March 1945, he replaced Davis as the board's chairman and organized and directed President Truman's November 1945 National Labor-Management Conference—a month-long parley that concluded by endorsing guidelines for union-management relations for the postwar era.

To understand how Taylor could have such an impact, one needs to go back to Kensington, the northeast section of Philadelphia where he was born. Crowded with sixty thousand textile workers and their families (many of whom were immigrants or children of immigrants from northern English textile towns and Ireland) and home to a thousand wool, cotton, silk, yarn, and carpet mills and other employers, Kensington had a history of worker violence reaching back to a weeklong battle between Protestants and Catholics in 1844. In June 1903, the Manufacturers' Association rejected the unions' demand for shorter hours, and workers in six hundred Kensington textile mills stopped work en masse. When the strike fervor flagged, the legendary agitator Mary G. Harris "Mother" Jones organized a march of one hundred children carrying banners calling for "Justice," "We want more schools and less hospitals," "We want time to play," and "Prosperity is here. Where is ours?" from the district to Theodore Roosevelt's home in Oyster Bay, Long Island. When Philadelphia's streetcar workers struck in 1910, Kensingtonians pushed trolley cars driven by scabs off the tracks and beat the blacklegs. The transit workers won that strike. Other successful strikes followed in Philadelphia. But the 1920s also saw a long series of lockouts and unsuccessful strikes as employers cut wages, moved mills out of the district, increased hours, hired women at rates lower than men's, and imposed yellow-dog contracts.[10]

Born in 1901, George Taylor watched strikers, strikebreakers, company guards, and police confronting each other in the streets from his childhood onward—brutal battles that included strikers stripping female strikebreakers of their clothes and police and company agents beating and shooting strikers and sympathizers.[11] Although Taylor grew up in proletarian Kensington, he wasn't *of* it, for his mother and father were Quakers and better off than most of their fellow residents. Fifteen thousand Quakers lived in Philadelphia at the beginning of the twentieth century, mainly in Germantown and Mount Airy, quiet, tree-lined, well-to-do sections of the city. Hardly any lived in Kensington.[12] Taylor's father and mother were exceptions. A native-born American of English ancestry, Harry Taylor was a supervisor in the Orinoka Mills, a silk upholstery mill. He did well enough that his wife Anna, a Danish immigrant, remained at home, keeping house. They lived in the Fishtown section of Kensington. One of George's uncles owned a textile mill. Harry and Anna Taylor assumed that their son would become a manager in one of Philadelphia's textile and garment factories after graduating from Frankford High School. The principal of the school, however, thought the studious, sensitive boy was better suited for college. At his urging, George applied for and won a Mayor's Scholarship, allowing him to enroll at the University of Pennsylvania's Wharton School of Business.

Taylor earned his bachelor's degree in 1923, a master's in business administration in 1926, and a PhD in economics in 1929 at the University of Pennsylvania. After receiving his BA, he taught economics and business administration at Schuylkill (later Albright) College in Reading and coached its football team. After he completed his doctorate on the full-fashioned hosiery industry, Taylor was appointed as a researcher at the Wharton School. He continued to study unions and employment trends in the silk hosiery industry.[13] After several years he was appointed as an associate professor in the Industrial Relations Department at Wharton.

Silk hosiery manufacturing was a booming industry in the early twentieth century. Based primarily in Philadelphia, it enjoyed high profits, paid comparatively

high wages, and was almost completely unionized. As time passed, however, hosiery employers began to move their operations out of the city to nonunion sections of eastern Pennsylvania and New Jersey, as well as southern New England,
the Midwest, and North Carolina. Employers who remained in the city tried to
undermine the hosiery workers' union, provoking many strikes. In 1931, after a
hard-fought six-month-long strike, the Full Fashioned Hosiery Manufacturers
of America and the American Federation of Full Fashioned Hosiery Workers
signed a new contract that named George Taylor as their impartial chairman.
The contract give the thirty-year-old professor "the duty and power to decide
and adjust all matter in dispute" between the two parties. Taylor succeeded Paul
Abelson, the Yiddish linguist and arbitrator who coauthored the famous "Pro-
tocols of Peace" for the New York garment industry with Louis Brandeis in 1911.
In 1935 Taylor was also hired as arbitration chairman for the Philadelphia local
of the Amalgamated Clothing Workers of America and the city's men's clothing
manufacturing association.[14]

A perceptive son of a mill supervisor, reared in Kensington, and familiar with
the Society of Friends' method of developing consensus by listening to each member's views, Taylor could sympathize with both laborers and employers, much
like Clark Kerr in the cotton pickers' strike in California. The Quaker manufacturers of Philadelphia adamantly opposed unions and strikes. But they rarely if
ever resorted to violence to break strikes. The Quaker manufacturers developed
shrewder ways to make unions unappealing to workers.[15]

Unlike his colleagues at Wharton, George Taylor sympathized with trade
unions, believed that trade unionists and employers could cooperate, and developed a distinctive way to foster "a meeting of the minds," an expression he often
used. Taylor intentionally intermingled "mediation" and "arbitration" principles,
which his peers considered incompatible. "In my judgment there have been too
many befuddled attempts by arbitrators to reason mediation out of grievance arbitration," he wrote in 1949. "Grievance arbitration cannot be viewed exclusively
as a 'mediation process' or a 'judicial process.' There is no 'either-or' choice . . .
because elements of both are inclusive."[16] The War Labor Board staff termed his
method "med/arb."[17]

Taylor would speak as little as possible at grievance arbitration hearings, mainly
posing questions that could lead participants to reconsider their views. His approach often succeeded. Fully one-third of the arbitration grievance cases sent
to Taylor by the Full-Fashioned Hosiery Workers of America and the Hosiery
Manufacturers Association between 1931 and 1940 were formally labeled "Settled
without Disagreement." In other words, the parties' representatives compromised
after meeting with Taylor. Yet he did issue rulings in two-thirds of the grievance
cases he chaired in the hosiery industry. In some of those instances, the union

and company representatives actually had reached a compromise after meeting with Taylor, but nonetheless asked him to issue a ruling as if it were his own decision. Doing so would protect the union representatives and employer from being criticized by union members or other firms for making concessions.

Unlike the other arbitrators of his era, Taylor did not sit above the contending parties like a judge in a courtroom, as was common then. Instead, he would sit at the same table with the trade union and company like a senior member at a Friends' meetinghouse. Those hearings included the employees who filed the grievance, the leader of the shop committee, the local union leader, the superintendent in the department, at least one and often several representatives of the particular company, and representatives of the national union and the manufacturer or manufacturers' association. He would begin each case by reading the letter that he had received from the union who had filed the grievance. A union representative would present their argument next. A representative of the company would then reply.

After the opening presentations, the parties were free to question or counter the others' claims. If the employer or trade unionist hesitated, Taylor would pose a question to prompt discussion. Stenographers were not included in the hearings that Taylor ran, and only occasionally did he himself even take notes. Instead, he would listen to the trade unionists and employers, trying to figure out their motivations and real objectives, which often were not the same as their stated demands. Grievance hearings were sometimes highly contentious, with the representative for one side or the other—more often than not, the trade unionist—shouting and condemning the other party's arguments or actions. The speaker might truly be angry but frequently feign rage for tactical reasons. Taylor did not object to such outbursts, nor did he ban obscenities. He would intervene, however, when arguments became disorderly and would not allow attacks on the character of others in the room.

Taylor tried to develop informal relations with the spokesmen for all parties he met. For that reason, he never held hearings at the Wharton School, lest the trade unionists or small employer feel ill at ease on the Ivy League campus. Instead, he rented an office downtown and held most of the hearings there. Since officers of the Full-Fashioned Silk Hosiery Workers of America belonged to the Socialist Party, Taylor occasionally convened hearings at the Young Women's Christian Association, a favored haunt for the Philadelphia Socialists.[18] And, if a case involved mechanical issues, Taylor—or Dash or Bill Simkin, Penn graduates who succeeded him as impartial chairman at the national hosiery and the Philadelphia men's clothing industries—would meet the parties at the factory where the dispute had occurred so that they could inspect the machinery in question while each side tried to explain why their interpretation of the contract made the most sense.

When a grievance session occurred out of town, Taylor, Simkin, or Dash drove there with the union representative and the employer. "We would go on hosiery cases . . . in somebody's car, and we would stay in the same motel," Dash remembered. "We would have drinks and dinner together and maybe a 'bull session.' It was a very close relationship."[19] The 1930s were tough times, and the roads rough. Traveling together saved everyone money. They took turns at the wheel and talked about the weather, sports, the economy, politics, women, whatever subject came to mind. If the factory was far away, they traveled together by train. Naturally some of these men became friendly, socializing with each other after returning home and visiting each other's homes with their wives at Christmas.

Taylor and Dash continued working in that way when hired to resolve disputes between the Philadelphia local of the Amalgamated Clothing Workers of America and the suit manufacturers. Good working relationships formed in both industries. Good relationships did not prevent the trade unionists and the employers from interpreting contract terms differently or arguing, sometimes vehemently. Nonetheless, disputes could be settled more easily among negotiators who traveled and drank together than between strangers.

Unlike his predecessors, George Taylor did not issue one-sentence edicts. Like the Philadelphia Society of Friends, which produced a series of editions of the *Rules of Discipline* to guide their discussion, his rulings were more nearly treatises.[20] In these "awards," as the rulings were termed, Taylor carefully addressed each question raised by the parties in the hearings and addressed underlying concerns that he perceived as well. He also was sensitive about his choice of words. An employer was vulnerable to criticism from members of the manufacturers' association, from his board of directors, business partners, stockholders, their banks, or, if the firm was family-owned as was common in the garment industry, from the executive's mother, father, grandparent, brother, sister, uncle, aunt, or grown children. Union negotiators were even more exposed. Rivals in their local and other locals in town or the region or the national union might undermine them. It did not matter whether the union was conservative, socialist, or Communist: any trade unionist might waylay a rival.

For that reason, Taylor developed a unique way of protecting the negotiators and facilitating agreement. Rather than issuing a ruling after a hearing closed, as most arbitrators did, he would write a preliminary opinion, show the draft to the union and manufacturers' association's officers, revise his draft, and, if he still was not certain that he had it right, share the revised draft with the parties' representatives. He expressed sensitivity not only to the negotiators' interests but also their circumstances and feelings. Silk hosiery was a highly seasonal industry—slow part of each year, extremely busy at other times. At the height of the season, Taylor would meet negotiators often, even weekly, and would personally hand his written decisions to the parties' representatives. He always spoke to the losing party's negotiator first. Doing so was essential, in his opinion. "You might not talk after the hearing to the winner, but you must talk to the loser," Bill Simkin recalled. "Now, this is born out of the basic notion that it's kind of cold and cruel to pick up a piece of paper, read that and that's your first notion of what's going to happen in that case. . . . You *must* talk to the loser," Simkin continued. "George used to operate—and I've tried to [as well]—on the principle of as few surprises as possible. It might be a casual remark, or if it's a tough case, you'd sit down face to face, go over the whole business with the top representatives of one side and explain the reason for ruling against them . . . which would help sell the notion."[21]

Union-management arbitration weren't like commercial arbitration, civil courts, and criminal courts. The prosecutor and the defendant in criminal cases and the litigants in civil cases would depart after the ruling and seldom or never meet again. Employers in commercial arbitration cases might interact again but not frequently. Trade unionists and employers, by contrast, were likely to meet each other within the week after an award was issued, even the next day. They had to "live and work together in an amicable way, if the business is to operate efficiently," Taylor remarked in 1938. Consequently, he tried to nurture stable relationships among union and employers' representatives. That was his principal objective. He never aimed at perfect justice if such a ruling would seriously damage bonds between the parties. Rather, he tried to "narrow the range of difference" and "the extent of possible loss" from his arbitration awards, he explained. He wanted settlements that both sides' representatives could accept and sell to their constituencies—the union's members on the one side and the stockholders or family members, on the other side. "In all cases, the importance of the 'consent to lose' requires that arbitration be accepted voluntarily by the parties," Taylor explained.[22]

Taylor tried to promote "industrial goodwill," a phrase coined by John R. Commons. "My own notebooks of cases arbitrated include any number of instances where accumulated grievances have made brick throwers out of employees who have much the same ideals and aspirations as 'you and I and the man in the elevator,'" he remarked in 1938.[23] For that reason, he not only chose his words carefully but processed grievances quickly. Highly diligent, he wrote approximately a thousand arbitration rulings in the hosiery industry during the 1930s and heard about four hundred more cases that were settled without decision, while also arbitrating cases in the men's clothing industry, serving on federal agencies, and teaching full time at Wharton.

Taylor aimed to foster "a meeting of the minds" among employer and trade unionists. This was his highest aspiration. Therefore, he barred attorneys from his grievance hearings. Although normally quite amiable, Taylor absolutely refused to compromise on that point, for lawyers intentionally sharpened differences among the parties and did their utmost to discredit their client's opponent. Taylor passed on his method to his protégés at the Wharton School and the War Labor Board. "If you want the strict rules of evidence followed here[,] please get yourself a judge, or get yourself an arbitrator trained in law. But you don't want me because I know very little about the rules of evidence," Allan Dash would say to union and company negotiators. "I just want all the facts because I think the decisions should be based on the facts, and not upon the skills of the advocates."[24] NWLB-trained arbitrators also tried hard to keep the trade unions and employers from acting like lawyers. "The procedure of examination, cross-examination, redirect, re-cross [sic], etc., those terms were never used," recalled Dash, adding that "I seldom dress[ed] in dark clothes . . . to discourage the parties from treating me like a judge and adopting adversary techniques."[25]

A photo of Taylor that appeared in *Business Week* when he was appointed umpire for General Motors and the United Auto Workers in 1941 shows a five-foot-seven-inch-tall man with a round, youthful face, wire-rimmed glasses, black hair greased straight back (as was fashionable then), and a small mouth about to break into a smile. Other photos show Taylor with twinkling eyes, a natural grin, and, on more than one occasion, laughing.[26] Experienced, alert, quick, assured yet self-effacing, George Taylor had the "rare gift for inspiring management and union leaders to have confidence in their ability to make an effective contribution to the relationship," his protégé Lewis Gill remarked.[27] "Dr. Taylor would push you so gently that you didn't know you were being pushed," one railroad union officer recalled.[28]

* * *

From the beginning, the most contentious issue confronting Taylor and the board's other public members was the union leaders' demand for a "union shop"—or "closed shop," as corporate executives and conservative politicians termed the unions' position. The union leaders were demanding that every employee in the firms that they bargained with be a union member. It was different in France and Germany, where several unions often negotiated with a single employer. No union leader would be at ease with such an arrangement in the United States. As late as 1942 the large majority of American employers continued to insist on maintaining an "open shop," which in principle was defined as the freedom of employees to join, or not join, a union, as they prefer, but in practice meant the freedom of employers to fire any worker who tried to unionize. The issue had been the sorest question since at least 1903, when the National Association of Manufacturers began its drive to weaken unions and was revived with the so-called "American Plan" in the early 1920s.

The issue came to a head in the steel industry. More Americans worked in steel mills than in any other industry except agriculture and construction. U.S. Steel was the largest corporation in the United States, generating roughly 40 percent of the industry's output. The United Steelworkers of America was the nation's largest union; its president, Philip Murray, was elected president of the CIO in 1941. The steel corporations successfully defeated union organizing and strikes in 1892, 1901, 1919, and 1934. U.S. Steel and Jones & Laughlin signed contracts with the Steel Workers Organizing Committee, the predecessor of the United Steelworkers of America, in March 1937. These contracts consisted of little more than written agreements recognizing the union's right to exist and oral commitments to higher wages and shorter hours. Support for the union at those companies was so fragile in the late 1930s that the locals had to set up picket lines outside the mills to get the workers' dues.[29] The situation was worse at the other large steel companies—Bethlehem Steel, Republic Steel, Inland Steel, and Youngstown Sheet and Tube—dubbed "Little Steel." Those companies employed 175,000 blue-collar workers in 1940. When the union called strikes at the Little Steel companies in spring 1937, the firms obtained court injunctions against picketers. Police killed at least sixteen strikers and supporters marching on picket lines outside Republic Steel mills in South Chicago and Massillon, Ohio, in May 1937, most of them shot in the back by police; twenty or twenty-one, according to another estimate. In addition, more than twenty strikers were wounded. None of the Little Steel companies signed contracts with the union until 1941.[30]

When the United States went to war, the Steelworkers, like all CIO and American Federation of Labor (AFL) unions, pledged not to call any strikes. To do otherwise was inconceivable in the aftermath of Pearl Harbor. Not only were the labor officials fervent patriots; they would be thrashed if they blocked production. Yet the no-strike pledge put union officials in a bind, for, if they could not threaten a strike, why would a hostile management make concessions? And, since the workers would receive the benefits negotiated by the union whether they were members or not, why would they pay dues? The steel companies were hiring thousands of new employees, many of them from the countryside and unfamiliar with, or hostile to, unions. Would the new employees join the Steelworkers union? If they did join when hired, would they continue to pay dues? If not, the union might wither, for, unlike Germany or Sweden, for instance, the United States had a decentralized form of industrial relations, with thousands of agreements negotiated at the local level. Monitoring those agreements required large staffs. Consequently, the Steelworkers union demanded that U.S. Steel and the Little Steel companies sign "union shop" contracts—that is, provisions requiring all blue-collar workers be union members at mills where the union was legally certified as the bargaining agent, with dues subtracted automatically from their pay. The union leadership also demanded wage increases of $1 per day for steelworkers. "We have given all we can give here. We have given up the right to strike!" the Steelworkers president Philip Murray exclaimed at the December 1941 War Labor-Management Conference.[31]

The NWLB's chairman, Will Davis, proposed a compromise that he called "maintenance-of-membership." Under that arrangement, newly hired workers would have a choice of whether to join the union. If workers did join, they would be obliged to remain dues-paying members until the contract expired, at which point all employees would have that choice again. The arrangement would guarantee a steady stream of dues for the union while satisfying the management's demand of freedom of choice for employees. The corporate heads rejected the idea out of hand. "It furnishes no means of protecting employees from being coerced into signing up and once they have signed up[,] they cannot withdraw," asserted the president of Inland Steel. "This company is opposed to it or any other form of closed shop, no matter what it is called nor how it is camouflaged," declared Republic Steel's management. The maintenance-of-membership proposal was "a new smoke screen . . . and entirely unacceptable," the president of Bethlehem Steel exclaimed. He added, "The real question before this country today is national security, not union security."[32] When negotiations between the Steelworkers' representatives and Bethlehem Steel, Inland Steel, and Republic Steel broke down in early February 1942, the Labor Department sent the case to the NWLB to resolve. "In both labor and employer circles the War Labor Board's action is looked forward to as perhaps the biggest test," the *New York Times* reported.[33]

The steel companies were way off the mark, George Taylor argued. "Total war requires the harnessing of every resource of the nation," he declared in an address to the convention of the Pennsylvania Federation of Labor in Scranton in May 1942. "Collective bargaining and organized labor are among the great resources possessed by America." Those principles have been "democratically endorsed by the people of this country," he exclaimed, implicitly referring to the November 1940 presidential election, when precincts packed with union members and their relatives provided the margin for Roosevelt's unprecedented third term. In late 1941 and early 1942, many members of Congress, not only Republicans but Democrats as well, were calling for severe restrictions on unions, something that many labor historians have forgotten. These congressmen were deluded, Taylor argued. They think that "the right of labor to organize into effective unions . . . is a luxury which can be tolerated only in peacetime[,] . . . that the organization of labor is an actual deterrent to the prosecution of the war."[34]

Unions are essential to winning the war, Taylor asserted. "Our country should be backing the unions, not censuring them! . . . Have those critics forgotten that

German submarines are prowling off the coast of Florida and South Carolina every night? They know that the Germans landed agents on Long Island. The situation is so dangerous that New York City, Philadelphia, Jersey City, and other towns on the East Coast are holding blackouts every night. Who is going to inform the civilian population of their duties and responsibilities during a blackout?" Taylor asked. "A civilian population cannot be welded in a few months into a people informed, equipped and ready to fight a total war except through highly organized and cooperative effort. Will power and patriotism alone will not do the job."[35]

Just as the police officers patrol our cities, so the labor leaders police the no-strike pledge, Taylor contended. And just as police need bullet-proof vests to protect them against assailants, so did the unions require protection—in this case from the federal government. That was the purpose of maintenance-of-membership proposed by the War Labor Board. "We placed armed guards with fixed bayonets around such natural resources as power plants, munitions factories, and dams. . . . A maintenance-of-membership clause may often be such a protective device which the War Labor Board has fashioned to safeguard the existence of another kind of natural asset—the trade union. . . . Who in the world are we going to turn to, except organized labor, to carry through this voluntary program of sacrifice on the part of the workers of this country?" Taylor linked the union leaders' demand for "union security" to the U.S. battle against the Axis powers. "With this protection, the union can be freed from the . . . eternal battle to preserve its existence against attack either from without or from within. It can be free to devote all of its energies to the job of licking Hitler and the Japanese war lords."[36] Taylor, Davis, and the Labor Board boys considered unions essential to modern capitalism, U.S. government, and democracy.

The union representatives on the board—George Meany, Matthew Woll, R. J. Thomas, and Tom Kennedy—were originally quite leery of the maintenance-of-membership plan, afraid that many workers, especially the new hires, would not pay dues. Their opinion changed after 91 percent of the workers at the International Harvester Corporation voted in favor of a contract that included a maintenance-of-membership clause guaranteeing mandatory membership for the duration of the agreement.[37]

Nonetheless, the corporate executives on the War Labor Board refused to concede. Although more liberal than most top company executives—that was why they were chosen by the administration—they thought of themselves as representatives of the business class in general, the vast majority of whom remained resolutely committed to the open-shop principle. In the Federal Shipbuilding and Drydock Co. case, which the board debated in March and April 1942, the four business representatives declared that they could not endorse any national policy that, in their words, "compels any unwilling employer to force an unwilling employee either to join or to remain a member of a labor union in order to play his part in winning this war."[38] In another NWLB case decided in April, the board's business spokesmen questioned "whether it is the function of this administrative board to impose upon an employer conditions which require him to discharge even a single employee because of a failure to maintain union membership."[39] "If, for some valid reason, a man wishes to withdraw from a union [at any time during the life of a contract], he should be permitted to honorably do so without losing his job," declared the most recalcitrant employer on the board, the president of Standard Knitting Mills of Knoxville, E. J. MacMillan.[40] "This [question] should be a simpler issue than wages for which to find a solution," Roger Lapham, chairman of the board of the American-Hawaiian Steamship Company, wrote in a memo to his fellow board members in February 1942. Yet "the truth is, of the two, it is the more troublesome because neither management nor labor seem[s] able to discuss it without an emotional pounding on the table."[41]

Although Taylor believed that "no man's freedom is abridged in any way by this clause," he made no headway, for the labor and business leaders on the board conceived "liberty" and "democracy" in utterly different ways.[42] The disparity became obvious when the large majority of the employees of the International Harvester Company voted to be represented by a union in the election supervised by National Labor Relations Board on April 15, 1942. "Roger [Lapham] puts a great deal of emphasis upon democracy," declared Bobby Watt, an AFL international representative temporarily serving on the board. "I think that the majority rule is the essence of democracy, and if you take that away[,] you have nothing left but chaos," Watts argued. Roger Lapham couldn't understand that. "I don't know if I quite get it," he responded. "I don't understand you [either]," agreed the president of Proctor & Gamble, Richard Deupree. To the union men, democracy meant majority rule. The corporate executives saw it as individual choice, including the freedom of every worker—even one dissenting employee—to refuse to join a union.[43]

Twelve days later, April 27, 1942, the NWLB voted by an eight-to-four margin to impose a maintenance-of-membership provision on Federal Shipbuilding & Drydock Company, a New Jersey subsidiary of U.S. Steel. There was a serious risk that U.S. Steel's chief executives would defy that decision. If they had, many other corporations would have followed their lead, forcing Roosevelt to either seize the shipyard or ask the conservative-led Congress to pass highly repressive labor legislation. Fortunately for the administration, the Allies, and the board's public and labor members, U.S. Steel management announced on May 8 that they would institute a maintenance-of-membership program at the New Jersey docks despite serious reservations.[44]

The board's ruling in the Little Steel case, the other highly controversial case, on July 16, 1942, favored the companies. In this case, the board set firm limits on increases in wage rates for blue-collar employees at Bethlehem Steel, Republic Steel, Youngstown Sheet & Tube, and Inland Steel. It also ordered those companies to add maintenance-of-membership provisions in their contracts with the Steelworkers union. Neither ruling was unanimous. The four union representatives on the board dissented on the wage issue; the four corporate representatives had dissented on the union security question.[45] Each side won in one case and lost in the other, and none of the eight representatives quit. The ruling ended a deadlock. The board subsequently applied the same maintenance-of-membership principle and similar wage-rate limitations to nearly all the cases on its docket.

* * *

The War Labor Board began with a small staff. "Do you know what the reputation of our Board is that I am most proud of? It is the most understaffed division in Washington," Taylor remarked on October 7, 1942.[46] He shouldn't have boasted, for that very week the president issued Executive Order 9250, which required every U.S. company and private employer, whether they negotiated with a union or not, to obtain approval from the NWLB before increasing their employees' wages. A backlog of grievance cases had already piled up at the board even before October 1942. Now "Form 10's," as the paper requesting permission to raise wages was labeled, flooded into their Washington, DC, office. The NWLB's staff could not handle the deluge. "I think this board has no concept yet of the extent of delegation that it has to do in order to make this thing operate. . . . I think we have to change. . . . We have been a tight little country club up to this time, where everybody knows every detail. . . . I think that the organization is going to spread," Taylor remarked in a November session.[47]

In late October, the board announced that it would set up ten regional offices, each headed by a full-time staff person representing the NWLB. The regional boards would be composed of labor, employer, and public figures, all of whom would be selected by the board's national office. This plan was not bold enough. Decentralization means "taking away from Washington the *whole* panel structure and setting it up in the backyards of the people involved," Bobby Watts of the AFL declared at a January 5, 1943, NWLB meeting. "I think [that creating] panels all over this Nation would give this Board [that is, the regional boards] teeth; I think it would give it roots; I think that it would . . . [give] an increasing number of employers and labor representatives . . . responsibility that they ought to have."[48]

By March 1943 the NWLB had established thirteen full-fledged tripartite regional war labor boards to cover the United States and its territories—headquartered in New York City, Boston, Philadelphia, Atlanta, Cleveland, Detroit, Chicago,

Kansas City, Denver, Dallas, San Francisco, Seattle, and Honolulu.[49] The regional boards handled nearly all dispute cases and wage applications except a handful of cases considered of national import. In this way, the National War Labor Board became the industrial-relations counterpart of the U.S. Supreme Court that Will Davis had envisioned at their first meeting in January 1942. And, although a union or company executive could in principle appeal a regional board's ruling, few did, and few of those appeals were accepted. The bulk of the decisions were made at the local level by the regional directors, who were chosen by Taylor, or the regional boards, arbitrators, or tripartite panels appointed by the reginal directors.

On July 1, 1943, the NWLB went further, giving the regional directors the power to force employers and unions to insert binding arbitration as the final step in their contracts' grievance procedures. "Maximum production during the war is a duty," Davis told the regional directors. The regional boards must "do everything possible to promote widespread utilization of arbitration as the final step in the grievance machinery."[50]

Taylor sent their most promising young staff around the country to organize the regional boards. Thus Saul Wallen was appointed chairman of Regional War Labor Board I in Boston, Theodore (Ted) Kheel was named chairman of Regional War Labor Board II in New York City, and Lewis (Lew) Gill, a Taylor protégé from Penn, was named chairman of Regional War Labor Board V in Cleveland. "I was scared to death," Will Davis remembered in 1955, "because there wasn't anybody [who] knew anything about these peculiar operations of the War Labor Board except the people who'd been through it. These were procedures that had never existed before. . . . So what we did was, we stripped ourselves of the young men who had been with us from the start . . . and who were really carrying on our activities and knew about it. . . . We sent these kids out."[51]

Davis and Taylor gave the regional chairmen the authority to select the public, employer, and union representatives in their area and recruit other young attorneys and economists as arbitrators, mediators, and researchers. Granted higher federal classification than the other regional board members, they rated the performance of their fellow board members and staff and had full responsibility for the regional boards' expenses.[52] It was a heady experience for professors and lawyers just a few years out of school. Taylor, Davis, Wayne Morse, and Frank Graham "brought us young guys up and they taught us a lot of things," Ben Aaron remembered. "And in private they might criticize some things we had done. But if we ever pulled anything off that was good, they'd praise us to the skies to the other elements on the board—the labor and management guys. And if any of them got down on us, the public members were in there protecting us every inch of the way. So we grew up in a highly protected atmosphere but we absorbed what these great men could teach us."[53]

"The thing that really caused me to be a *practitioner* was the War Labor Board," recalled John Dunlop, who focused on economic theory before being recruited by Taylor. "I held a number of different posts as Special Assistant to George Taylor and Will Davis. I was their representative on the Construction Board, the Wage Adjustment Board, and I commuted back to Boston as vice chairman of the Boston Board. I watched these people and developed the capacity and willingness to undertake the costs of managing and settling something."[54] George Hildebrand, a University of Texas associate professor of economics who was appointed wage stabilization director for the Regional War Labor Board in Denver, put it most succinctly: "The Board was our post-graduate training."[55]

In the latter part of 1944 and early 1945, the NWLB further decentralized, setting up eighteen additional tripartite boards, panels, and commissions focused on specific industries: national airplane frames, West Coast aircraft, West Coast lumber, automobiles, meatpacking, newspaper printing and publishing, nonferrous metal, shipbuilding, war shipping, steel, the telephone industry, northern textiles, southern textiles, the Detroit tool-and-die industry, transit, trucking, and construction. Each of these committees consisted of one or two public representatives, several union officials and high-ranking corporate executives for the industry, plus one or two arbitrators.[56]

Taylor moved his most prized staffers from city to city and post to post as emergencies arose, often appointing them to several positions simultaneously. Kerr was one example. An assistant professor of labor economics at the University of Washington before 1942, he became vice chairman of Regional War Labor Board XII in Seattle, public representative for Regional War Labor Board X in San Francisco, the San Francisco Board's wage stabilization director, public representative on the West Coast Airport Commission, and chairman of the Meatpacking Commission, which met in Chicago. Ben Aaron, Ted Kheel, David Cole, Sylvester Garrett, Nathan Feinsinger, John Dunlop, Ralph Seward, and Vernon Jensen were similarly favored.

* * *

The story of Regional War Labor Board III shows how the new system worked. Located in downtown Philadelphia, the board was responsible for a huge region, including the tobacco fields in Virginia, the Baltimore shipyards, chemical plants in Delaware, rubber-tire factories in Trenton, Radio Corporation of America, Campbell Soup, and the New York Shipbuilding Corporation in Camden, and the entire state of Pennsylvania, including the massive complex of steel mills and bituminous coal mines in and around Pittsburgh, the anthracite mines and clothing factories in and near Wilkes-Barre and Scranton, railroad towns like Reading, the locomotive, aircraft, and garment factories in Philadelphia, and General Electric (GE) and Westinghouse factories in Erie, East Pittsburgh, and Philadelphia.

To chair that regional board, Taylor chose Sylvester ("Syl") Garrett, an engaging thirty-one-year-old attorney who was a graduate of Swarthmore College and the University of Pennsylvania Law School. From 1938 until August 1941, Garrett served as an attorney at the National Labor Relations Board under William Leiserson. He next became chief counsel for the leather and apparel section of the Office of Price Administration. Taylor recruited him for the Pennsylvania Regional War Labor Board in August 1942.[57]

"Chairman George Taylor, who was the guy who really masterminded this regionalization, said, 'Syl, I'm going to give you a list of names in Philadelphia, Pittsburgh, Baltimore, Richmond where I'd like you to go and see key people in the community and get some ideas . . . to staff your operation,'" Garrett remembered. "I was supposed to put together a staff within two weeks." He headed for campuses. "I found Paul Guthrie at Randolph-Macon [College] way down there near Roanoke. Actually, my Disputes Director, Vernon O'Rourke, found him. I personally did find Charles Killingsworth who was an instructor at Johns Hopkins. We got him to work as one of our disputes panel chairmen. And he quickly established himself as first-rate.

"In Philadelphia, it was a cinch. I got Bill Loucks [an economics professor] at the Wharton School. Then I had Allan Dash and Bill Simkin already provided through their work with George Taylor. I got Frank Pierson [an assistant professor of economics] from Swarthmore, Howard Teaf [an associate professor of economics] from Haverford, Ray Buckwalter from Temple. . . . Eli Rock was a recent Yale Law School graduate. And all these people recruited among their academic friends. And in virtually no time I had a staff. That's a fact. I even got my old labor law professor from Penn [Alexander H. Frey] as one of my vice-chairmen." Garrett considered professors the ideal candidates for these jobs. "Where could you get people who by definition were supposed to be objective? Who had no axes to grind? Who had brains? Where were you going to get them except in academia? The colleges and universities were a gold mine!"[58]

Following Taylor's advice, Garrett met local union, business, and community leaders in the larger cities in his region in late 1942, seeking volunteers and suggestions for the Regional War Labor Board and the wage-rate panels. He asked the board's dispute director, Vernon O'Rourke, until that time an assistant professor of political science at Swarthmore, to scour western Maryland and Delaware for the same purpose. Eli Rock, the assistant dispute director, covered Erie, New Castle, Oil City, and Sharon in western Pennsylvania; and the Regional Board's public members canvassed Trenton, Scranton, Wilkes-Barre, Allentown, and Bethlehem. "By and large, the result of this intensive work was that our panel chairmen were people of real standing and recognized impartiality in their respective communities who had genuine interest in developing sound labor relations," Garrett recounted in 1946. He added, "Parenthetically, the recruiting campaign also enabled us to do a good deal of 'selling' of the War Labor Board program throughout the Region."[59]

By March 1943, three weeks after its official founding, Regional War Labor Board III staff had fourteen hundred Form 10s on their desks. They were appeals from employers urgently requesting permission to raise wages to avoid losing employees to other companies. Two to three hundred more were pouring in every week. The board could process only one hundred forms each week. How could they carry on without dismissing justified claims or fueling inflation? "That is a dangerous situation," remarked W. Horace Holcomb, executive assistant to the vice president of Baldwin Locomotive. "This situation cannot continue," Garrett agreed.

By early 1943, labor was so scarce in the country that employers were almost begging people not to quit. Lew Gill, the chairman of Region V, told Lloyd Garrison, NWLB's executive director and general counsel, about a small Ohio company that was turning out some essential military equipment. The owner "decided to go in for employees in a big way," Gill said. At that time semiskilled workers in a unionized factory in the North were paid an average of 75 cents per hour. "By virtue of some nifty setting of piece rates for unskilled and semi-skilled labor, the Company turned up with average hourly earnings of something like three dollars an hour. . . . One worthy citizen left his job as a bartender at $30 a week . . . and shortly received his first weekly paycheck of about $200." The fellow went to the paymaster saying that there must be a mistake but was assured that all was correct. "Some of the workers were so sheepish about their fabulous earnings on piece work that they deliberately slowed down in order to keep their pay within reason. An incentive in reverse," Gill remarked.[60] He told Garrett that the Cleveland board had set up tripartite panels consisting of one trade unionist, one employer, and one unaffiliated person, none of whom was a Regional Board V representative, to evaluate Form 10 claims, and that the Chicago and New York Regional War Labor Boards were doing the same. Although Garrett termed that step "drastic," after several meetings he decided to follow their example.[61]

Those panels could not operate in the dark, however, and the National Board's wage guidelines were fuzzy. The Philadelphians had to work out regulations themselves. Unfortunately, the wage systems at many of the companies in their region were intricate and often illogical, with some workers being paid considerably less or more than others for doing similar work in the same or a nearby facility. Several factors explained the phenomenon, including that companies had merged but not altered the pay systems; poor planning; and racial, gender, and ethnic prejudices. Garrett impishly awarded Roebling Steel Company of Trenton, which had eight thousand employees in two thousand job classifications "the honor of being the most unhealthy [wage system] . . . in the Region, with the possible exception of the Cramp Shipyard."[62]

Garrett and his staff had to be careful, for if they awarded a wage increase to one firm's employees, it could trigger new resentments. For instance, they had recently received a Form 10 request from a Philadelphia glass factory that produced blood plasma containers, an essential military item. The pay at the shop was relatively poor and the turnover was high. If the board approved the grievance, other workers in the same district might walk out, quit, or file their own grievances. But if the board did nothing, more workers at the glass shop would walk out, possibly depriving wounded marines of blood. If that problem wasn't enough, the Form 10 from the glass factory was near the bottom of the pile of requests.[63]

Leiserson had predicted that without wage guidelines "decisions . . . will appear . . . arbitrary and capricious."[64] Garrett now confronted exactly that problem. "It is perfectly clear," he told his fellow board members in March 1943, "that we are now faced with the necessity of getting together an encyclopedia on the various job classifications for the entire region, so that we will have these ranges to refer to whenever a particular inequality case comes up." He proposed that Regional Board III establish pay "brackets" against which applications for increases could be measured. The businessmen on the Regional Board bristled. "I agree with what you are aiming at, [but] I do not agree [that] you can establish the data," Horace Holcomb of Baldwin Locomotive retorted. Philco Radio vice president Harold Butler thought Garrett's idea made no sense. "It would be impossible. If we undertook to do it in just a square half mile from where we are sitting here, all of us would be working all of our time for the next three years, and we couldn't classify all those jobs because of the great diversity and great range."[65]

Allan Dash had just returned from his job as umpire for General Motors and the UAW to become vice chairman of the Philadelphia Regional Board. He asked whether Holcomb and Butler had a better idea. "If you do not, if you take no steps in trying to establish the data, then the attempt to apply this brake on inflation is impossible. That's what we've been doing, right and left, for the last three weeks, moving [rates at] these companies up, because they say they are low and claim an inequality. . . . What can we [do to] stop that? . . . [We're starting] the merry-go-round of inflation," Dash exclaimed. "This is the most important job that we've got for the war effort," John Zinsser, president of Sharp & Dohme, conceded. "There's no question about it."[66]

After an all-morning discussion that included off-the-record consultations, the majority of the Regional Board's members endorsed Garrett's wage-bracket proposal. There were six dissenting votes, presumably the six business representatives, although no names appear in the transcript. The businessmen continued to object even after the vote. "We don't believe that the necessity of getting by [i.e., reducing] our backlog [of cases] in any way justifies this Board to use half-baked information; and gentlemen, half-baked information is all you can get out of yardsticks," Holcomb remarked after lunch. Dash responded that other regional boards were conducting research to establish wage brackets. "They admit the procedure is rough; we admit it is rough; but it is something better than we are presently getting."[67]

Then Garrett, the chairman, intervened. "I'll admit that I'm not as well acquainted with these problems as all of the members of the labor and industry sides of the table," he began, deferring to the older men in the room. "My own feeling is that there are certain industries where we can get pretty definite information. . . . I'm thinking, specifically, of the garment workers; . . . the hotel and restaurant employees, the steel workers, and the tool and die machinists," he added. "Now, can't we reasonably expect to get some pretty definite information [there]?"[68]

Up to that point, the union representatives had remained quiet, but, prodded by Garrett, Alex McKeown, the president of the Full-Fashioned Hosiery Workers union, said that he could supply the data for piece rates for the garment industry not only in their region but throughout the entire country. McKeon and the AFL's regional representative then offered a motion to direct William Loucks, the University of Pennsylvania economist who was the region's wage stabilization director, to collect "all of the available information . . . [on] wages and ranges . . . in the various industries." After several more minutes, Holcomb of Baldwin Locomotive said that he would vote for that motion if they all understood that they were merely seeking information, not setting "benchmarks."[69]

The Regional Board appeared to be moving toward compromise when Professor Loucks intervened. Although he had thirty analysts, he would need more to gather and analyze the data. "This is going to take too much time," Garrett's law school professor Alexander Frey replied. Frey proposed that the board break itself up into panels of three—one trade unionist, one employer, and one professor. "With co-operative spirit," he claimed, they could cut down the backlog by quickly using the informal standards that they had employed over the past month. At that point, manufacturer John Zinsser objected. He proposed an alternative motion to authorize Garrett to go to Washington and obtain funds to hire more research analysts. The board immediately voted unanimously in favor of Zinsser's motion, ending that discussion. In the morning, the businessmen had strenuously objected to Garrett's plan; by the midafternoon they were his firmest backers.[70]

A week later, however, Horace Holcomb and the other businessmen threatened to not abide by the Board's "policy" decisions. They calmed down when Garrett assured them that no policy decisions would be made unless every member of the Board was present. After hearing from Garrett, the NWLB in Washington issued an order in November 1944 requiring the basic steel companies and the Steelworkers to form a joint wage-rate inequity negotiating commission consisting of representatives of management, the union, and NWLB staffers to thoroughly restructure their wage system. The commission formed, began their work, and continued after the war ended without the public members.

The board faced many other difficulties, including an August 1, 1944, "sickout" by eight thousand white drivers on Philadelphia's subways, elevated lines, buses, and streetcars to prevent eight African Americans from being upgraded from menial jobs in the maintenance department to motormen. "It's white against black! The colored people have bedbugs!" the strike leaders cried out.[71] The wildcat strike sharply reduced production at Baldwin Locomotive, Bendix Aviation, GE, Westinghouse, the Budd Company, Midvale Steel, and other companies making weapons and other material for the Navy and Army. Army and Navy officers and Regional Board staff went to the car barns, appealing to drivers to return, only to be jeered and booed. "The anti-Negro sentiment, especially in its present whipped-up state, and the cleverness of the leaders of the insurgent elements in capitalizing on that question, have resulted in the strike being completely out of the control of the CIO. The matter of principles, viz., the employment of Negroes on the lines, is one which cannot be compromised," Garrett reported to the NWLB.[72]

After hearing from Will Davis, the president authorized Secretary of War Henry Stimson to seize the Philadelphia Transit Company. Major General Philip Haynes sent five thousand troops to the city. He ordered the drivers to resume work or be fired and lose their draft exemptions. "We cannot kill any Germans or Japs with troops who drive transit vehicles in Philadelphia," Haynes declared.[73] With soldiers wearing steel helmets and carrying bayonets on every trolley, bus, subway car, and train, with all liquor stores in the city ordered closed by the governor, with all bars and restaurants ordered by the mayor to stop selling beer and liquor, and with the local NAACP and ministers urging black residents to "Keep your heads and your temper," the city remained relatively calm, unlike Detroit the previous year. The strike ended in a week.[74]

For all their travails, none of the members of Regional War Labor Board III ever quit or refused to obey the board's rulings when outvoted. The War Department's contracts with local companies facilitated compliance, as did constant reminders on the radio, in the papers, and on the newsreels about U.S. servicemen risking their lives in the Pacific, Italy, and France. Chaired by Garrett, Regional War Labor Board III stayed together throughout the war.

3

On Top of the World, 1946–56

> I was on top of the world, with greatly
> enhanced prestige in my own field and
> roseate hopes for the future.
>
> —Benjamin Aaron

WHEN THE WAR LABOR BOARD closed its doors in December 1945, Ben and Eleanor Aaron left Washington. Thirty years old, Aaron had just finished his brief stint as the board's final executive director. They headed back to Los Angeles, where he would begin arbitrating grievances for the aircraft industry, like he had done before for the board (see figure 4). Ben and Eleanor were staying with his sister and her family in Santa Monica, looking for a house, when he received a call from the War Department. General Douglas MacArthur, the Allies' Supreme Commander in the Far East, wanted him to join the Advisory Committee on Labor to draft new labor legislation for Japanese industry. Aaron would be given the assimilated rank of full colonel in the military government, with appropriate pay and privileges.

Ben Aaron was delighted, but hesitated for a moment: Eleanor was five months pregnant with their first child. When his sister and brother-in-law offered to help Eleanor, he accepted the offer on the condition that he could return home in three months.

The Advisory Committee on Labor was not very effective. "The whole trip had about it a touch of Hollywood atmosphere," recalled journalist Helen Mears, the only member of the Advisory Committee who spoke Japanese and was familiar with Japanese history and culture. Their plan to democratize manufacturing was thwarted by Japanese industrialists, the conservative government in Tokyo, and

FIGURE 4. Ben and Eleanor Aaron in Santa Monica after the war. Personal collection of Judith Aaron Turner.

General MacArthur, who was disturbed by the radicalism of the Japanese unions.[1] Nonetheless, the trip broadened Aaron's perspective on the world. Since he had had Japanese-Americans as classmates while in high school in San Francisco, he did not despise Japanese people, unlike most Americans of that era. He lamented the President's decision to drop the atomic bombs and declined an offer to fly over Hiroshima to see the rubble. Instead, he became engaged, to the limited extent that he could, with Japanese workers who were occupying factories in order to win concessions from their employers without ceasing work.

Aaron managed to get onto a military flight back in time for Eleanor's due date. Since there were no seats in the plane, he had to sleep on a canvas on the cabin's steel frame, with a marine's boots in his face. Fortunately, the pilot invited Ben to sit in the copilot's seat during the last leg of the flight to San Francisco. "The roomy leather seat seemed to me the quintessence of comfort," he recalled, "and the black, velvety night sky was illuminated by the light of countless stars. The radio was tuned to dance music from the mainland."

Aaron returned in early April. Their daughter Judith was born soon afterward. They found an apartment in Santa Monica, and Ben found himself in great demand. The Labor Department asked him to join a fact-finding board in San Francisco. UCLA asked him to join the faculty in their new Institute of Industrial Relations, and he began arbitrating grievance cases for North American Aviation,

Douglas Aircraft, the United Auto Workers, and the International Association of Machinists. "I was on top of the world," Aaron recalled sixty years later, "with greatly enhanced prestige in my own field and roseate hopes for the future."[2]

Ben Aaron's experience was not unique. All of the top War Labor Board vets began arbitrating grievances for unions and corporations. The federal government, state governments, and cities asked them to serve on labor-management committees. And most began teaching industrial relations courses and directing the new IR programs at universities. For Ben Aaron, John Dunlop, Clark Kerr, Pete Jensen, Syl Garrett, Ted Kheel, and other veterans of the board, the decade after the war were glory days.

* * *

During the 1960s and 1970s American labor historians argued that the major U.S. corporations and unions made a grand bargain after the Second World War in which General Motors and many other major unionized corporations agreed to generous wage and fringe benefits for the unions' members in exchange for the union officials' renunciation of any rights regarding production methods in the workplaces. Their thinking began to change in the 1980s, following President Ronald Reagan's firing of eleven thousand striking air-traffic controllers. Since then labor historians have taken the opposite tack, arguing that the major corporations never compromised with unions after that war. On the contrary, according to the new consensus, corporations worked continuously to undermine unions throughout the postwar era.[3]

Neither perspective is convincing overall. It is true that some major firms, for example, Thompson Products and Sears, Roebuck, developed strategies that successfully prevented unionization while others, most notably General Electric, abandoned their earlier cooperation with unions in the latter 1940s and fought hard to undermine organized labor.[4]

Most of the larger corporations, however, in the manufacturing, mining, and transportation industries and the building contractors' associations *did* reach compromises with unions during the 1940s, agreements that continued for many years afterward. Yet there was no "grand accord" at the summit of labor and capital. There never could be, in the highly decentralized environment of business-union relations in the United States, in contrast with the more consolidated systems in West Germany, Sweden, and Austria.

Rather, compromises were hammered out firm by firm after 1945. The unions and corporations reached settlements despite the reluctance of the corporate managers. Compromises can be partially explained by the Wagner Act, which required corporations to bargain in good faith with unions; the Davis-Bacon Act, which stipulated that all construction workers be paid the union rates; and the influence of President Harry Truman and his successors, who leaned on unions and management to settle disputes. Despite intermittent recessions, the U.S. economy boomed from 1940 all the way to the early 1970s. Unions remained relatively strong throughout the era, although there was a slow decline in the share of the workforce they represented.

However, economic forces, federal legislation, and national politics don't explain how and why the arrangements that emerged took the form they did, or how those arrangements endured for more than three decades. We cannot understand the postwar era without considering the part played by the Labor Board vets—who were now in the prime of their lives.[5]

* * *

The Labor Board vets' role in union-management relations after the war was charted in November 1945 at the labor-management conference in Washington that George Taylor organized and directed at the request of President Truman. No longer assured of cost-plus profits by contracts from the War Department, and aware that workers had acquired considerable power vis-à-vis foremen, supervisors, and even plant managers during the war, the corporation executives at the conference demanded that unions acknowledge "managerial prerogatives." They also refused to concede wage increases to unions unless the administration rescinded price controls. Yet American workers' earnings fell precipitously in 1945 as production for the military sank even as consumer-goods prices and rents rose. Challenged internally—A.F.L. affiliates versus C.I.O. affiliates, Communists versus anti-Communists, John L. Lewis of the United Mine Workers versus nearly all other unions—and harassed by conservative Congressmen, the press, and the surly Truman administration, the union leaders felt they had to win big wage increases for their members to maintain power.

The situation overseas was even more perilous. Despite the surrender of Germany and Japan, the survival of capitalism and democracy was by no means assured in Europe and Asia. On the contrary, Soviet troops occupied Poland and the eastern half of Germany, including half of Berlin. Communists controlled the Provisional Government of Poland in Lublin and had more seats than any other party in Czechoslovakia's National Assembly. A coalition of Communists and Socialists held three-fifths of the seats in the French Assembly; Marshal Tito's Liberation Front swept Yugoslavia's parliamentary election; and the Hungarian government signed exclusive trading rights with the Soviet Union despite remonstrations from the U.S. State Department. The French lacked coal to restart furnaces in their factories and heat their apartments. Looking ahead, the Communists had a good chance of winning the national elections scheduled in France and Italy in June 1946, and, after six years of war, Britain was exhausted.

The situation in Asia was no less daunting. Ho Chi Minh proclaimed Vietnam an independent nation in September 1945, even as France tried to reestablish colonial control. Mao Zedong's army was on the offensive against Chiang Kai-Shek's troops in northern China. One-hundred thousand Indonesians rose up against the returning Dutch colonialists. And although the U.S. ambassador in Manila claimed that the agrarian revolt in the Philippines was dead, the *New York Times* reported that if the envoys left "the airy corridors of Malacanan Palace and the gracious saloons of the grandees," they would find the rebels "armed and active."[6]

Like Franklin Roosevelt before him, Harry Truman needed cooperation between union and corporate leaders to reduce strikes, slowdowns, and other obstacles to production. Two days after the U.S. Army Air Force dropped its second atomic bomb on Japan, the President asked George Taylor to bring leading business executives and union officials to Washington for a conference, as he had done for Roosevelt after Pearl Harbor. The President's National Labor-Management Conference opened on Monday morning, November 5, 1945, in the U.S. Department of Labor's auditorium on Constitution Avenue NW, three blocks from the White House. The meetings continued throughout the month, pausing only for weekends and Thanksgiving. Thirty-six delegates and thirty-six alternates attended sessions in the gold-and-blue room. Union officials sat behind a long table on one side of the room, the corporate executives behind another on the opposite side, with the conference's chairman—Chief Justice of the Supreme Court of North Carolina Walter P. Stacey, a former railroad-industry arbitrator—in the front, surrounded by a profusion of ferns. One hundred reporters sat in the back, accompanied by newsreel operators.[7]

The conference participants included the presidents and board chairmen of the Pennsylvania Railroad, Consolidation Coal, U.S. Steel, General Motors, Monsanto Chemical, RCA, Hanes Knitting Company, Goodyear Tire, and other such corporations, each of whom was accompanied by an adviser. The presidents of the U.S. Chamber of Commerce and the National Association of Manufacturers, which represented medium-sized and smaller businesses, also sent delegates. An equal number of labor leaders were present, including the president and secretary-treasurer of the AFL, William Green and George Meany; the president of the CIO, Philip Murray; and the CIO's general counsel, Lee Pressman. Also on hand were the presidents of the United Brotherhood of Carpenters and Joiners, the International Brotherhood of Teamsters, the United Auto Workers (UAW), the United Steel Workers of America, the United Electrical, Radio & Machine Workers, the United Mine Workers, International Union of Mine, Mill, and Smelter Workers, the Bricklayers, Masons & Plasters' International Union, and other prominent unions.[8]

George Taylor served as conference secretary, sat on the Executive Committee, and chaired the Rules Committee. He appointed five of the Labor Board veterans—Clark Kerr, Ralph Seward, Saul Wallen, Bill Simkin, and James Healy—as secretaries for the other committees. Taylor held eleven press conferences, which he called "seminars," during the conference to clarify issues for the press and the public. "He is the only man in the whole works that knows what is going on," one participant remarked.[9]

"The whole world now needs the produce of our mills and factories—everything stands primed for a great future," President Truman declared at the opening session. "But," he added, raising his voice for emphasis, "situations and circumstances can change rapidly. Our unparalleled opportunity may not long remain open. We must have production—vast production. We must have it soon." Stable relations between unions and management are as essential now as they were during the war, he argued. "Our country is worried about its industrial relations. It has a right to be. . . . Under the patriotic pressure of a desperate war crisis, management and labor have performed a miracle of production . . . and yet as soon as controls were lifted, industrial strife began. Some of it was expected. . . . But . . . they never expected anything like the amount of strife which has been threatened," he continued.

Truman was referring to the UAW strike underway at General Motors, a wildcat strike by Greyhound bus drivers, a general strike in Stamford, Connecticut, a strike that had shut down 80 percent of cotton textile production in Maine, and a strike by the San Francisco machinists that was delaying the return of troops from the Pacific. Strikes were imminent at the Ford Motor Company, Chrysler, and Packard, the major steel companies, Westinghouse, General Electric, Goodyear Tire, Lockheed Aircraft, the railroads, and many coal mines. "Labor and management *must* work together to expand the economy of our Nation," the President told the delegates. "No realist can expect the millennium of a perfect no-strike, no lock-out era at once. But continued production and an expanding industry—unhampered as far as humanly possible by stoppages of work—are absolutely essential to progress. That is the road to security at home and peace abroad."[10]

Despite Truman's pleas at the opening session and in separate private meetings with business and union leaders in the Oval Office, the union presidents were unwilling to make concessions on wage increases and the company presidents demanded control of discipline at their worksites. "The Labor-Management Conference was a flop," *Time* magazine reported halfway through the parley. "Barring a miracle—by a group of men who had proved to be in no mood to perform one—it would soon fold up without offering the American public anything except its regrets."[11]

Time was mistaken, for there was one issue on which the delegates were "of one mind," as Taylor would have put it. Every delegate agreed that unions and corporations engaged in bargaining should add grievance and arbitration procedures for handling employees' complaints to their contracts. Indeed, Truman considered their accord on that point the linchpin of the conference. "If bargaining produces no results, there must be a willingness to use some impartial machinery for reaching decisions on the basis of proven facts and realities, instead of rumor or propaganda or partisan statements," he had declared at the opening session. "That is the way to eliminate unnecessary friction. That is the way to prevent lock-outs and strikes. That is the way to keep production going."[12]

The delegates called for grievance procedures "so clear" that no employee or supervisor could be confused. They recommended that larger firms adopt multistep grievance-resolution procedures, so that disputes could be settled at the lowest level possible, except in cases that raised broad questions of policy or contract interpretation. They advised company executives and union leaders to train their staffs in the grievance procedures. The goal of grievance and arbitration hearings should be "the achievement of sound and fair settlements," the delegates declared, "not the 'winning' of cases." They advised businessmen to consider the employees' grievances not as irritations but as valuable sources of information, a way of "discovering and removing the causes of discontent." Though urging union and management officials to resolve most grievances themselves, they recommended that they send difficult cases to an arbitrator. The delegates advised companies and unions to develop procedures for selecting arbitrators and to split the arbitrator's fee equally. Finally and most important, an arbitrator's decisions "should be accepted by both parties as final and binding."[13]

Some American firms and unions had established grievance and arbitration systems before the United States entered the war—mainly in the garment and railroad industries. Others set up these arrangements during the hostilities at the insistence of the NWLB. Still others added grievance and arbitration clauses to their contracts after the war ended. Except in the trucking industry, where the Teamsters frequently relied on mobsters rather than arbitrators to adjudicate differences, the vast majority of U.S. companies and unions engaged in bargaining adopted grievance and arbitration systems by 1950. And most companies and unions hired former War Labor Board staff for the job.[14]

* * *

However, agreement on the principle of grievance arbitration was only the beginning. The systems had to actually work. "Right there is the crux of the problems the United States faces today," George Taylor declared in a *Washington Post* column in October 1946. "We have adopted collective bargaining as a national institution—we have strong labor unions and large, established corporations—but we haven't yet learned how to make collective bargaining work. We haven't learned to solve problems instead of trying to win an argument. . . . If collective bargaining means anything people have to give as well as take."[15]

The first contracts signed in the steel, auto, rubber tire, meat-packing, glass, aircraft, maritime, trucking, electrical equipment, and lumber industries in the mid-1930s and early 1940s were only a couple of pages long. They committed the management to bargain with the union, specified wage rates, and established a grievance procedure, but did little more than that. They were "no more than a skeleton understanding," as Taylor commented in 1949.[16]

During the war, most firms and unions maintained their prewar contracts, since the War Labor Board decided wage rates, hours, and virtually all other matters. But after 1945, companies and unions negotiated new contracts every year or every other year. By the early 1950s their agreements became tangles of clauses and subsections addressing procedures for a wide variety of issues, including layoffs, recalls or work-sharing, contracting work out, job content, methods of operations, transfers between jobs, opportunities to choose shifts and machines, discipline, promotions, demotions, wage rates, incentive pay, merit increases, bonuses, work shifts, changes in schedules for individuals, call-in pay for unscheduled work shifts, waiting time, rest periods, preparation time, penalty pay, the "right" to overtime work, the obligation to work overtime, holidays, vacations, safety, rates of operation, workloads, and "union security," plus clauses requiring binding arbitration of unresolved grievances.

Complex agreements bred thorny disputes. Company and union negotiators spent weeks haggling over the terms, often not settling until late in the evening before a contract was about to expire. By then negotiators were dog-tired. Deals reached under such conditions were inevitably contradictory. However, negotiators' fatigue do not entirely explain muddled contract language. More fundamental was the nature of the disputes. Although company and union officials would, if pressed hard, yield on wage rates, both were loath to make concessions on discipline or modes of operation. The latter were the most difficult subjects for both the unions' members and top management, and concessions made in these areas were hard to recoup afterward. Moreover, a union leader who made such concessions was apt to be denounced and perhaps voted out of office, while his counterpart on the other side was vulnerable to attacks from higher-ranking executives, the company board, and stockholders.

Nonetheless, the unions and corporations had to reach contractual agreements of some kind. That hadn't been true earlier, when unions were weaker and the government less involved, but by the mid-1940s union power and pressure from state and especially the federal government made written agreements mandatory. Consequently, as Harry Shulman, the principal umpire for Ford Motor Company and the United Auto Workers, observed at the time, there was "an almost irresistible pressure to find a verbal formula which is acceptable, even though its meaning to the two sides may in fact differ." Alternatively, the two parties might sign agreements that were perfectly lucid but included incompatible clauses. Moreover, Shulman explained, "No matter how much time is allowed for the negotiation, there is never enough to think every issue through in all its possible applications, and never ingenuity enough to anticipate all that does later show up." Finally, although the issues in the contracts were complex and the provisions complicated, the language nonetheless had to be clear enough to be understood by the workers, the shop stewards, union business agents, the foremen, supervisors, and the clerks in the payroll office—the people most directly affected by the contracts—and, in many unions, the members who would vote on the proposed agreement.[17] "At General Motors as in every other arbitration situation I've ever been in, your real problem is never between the company on the one side and union on the other. It is between this language and the realities," Ralph Seward remarked after arbitrating grievances for nearly fifty years.[18]

* * *

Three cases—Harry Shulman with the Ford Motor Company and the United Auto Workers, John Dunlop with the building contractors and trades unions, and Sylvester Garrett with U.S. Steel and the United Steel Workers of America—show how the Labor Board vets managed to devise compromises during and after the war despite such difficulties.

Relations inside Ford Motor Company's factories were chaotic in the latter 1930s and early 1940s. While General Motors and Chrysler were signing contracts with the United Auto Workers, Ford employed mobsters and ex-boxers to ambush UAW organizers and threatened or sacked pro-union workers. Under pressure from the National Labor Relations Board and Henry Ford's wife Clara, the company finally signed a contract with the UAW in 1942. Power relations in the factories upended after that, as union committeemen took revenge on the goons. By 1943 conditions reached the breaking point at Ford plants, with frequent wildcat strikes, some involving thousands of workers; inter-union rivalry playing out in UAW locals, grievances piling up at the last step of the procedure, and collective bargaining dissolving. A three-day-long race riot in Detroit in June 1943 left thirty-four dead and more than four hundred wounded, with $2 million in damages to property. The rampage did not end until six thousand federal troops marched through the city. Navy Secretary Frank Knox and other members of the Roosevelt administration feared Ford would not be able to fulfill its contracts to produce tanks, planes, jeeps, and other goods needed by the armed forces. "The Union felt very keenly about the future at the Ford Motor Company, even to the point that some of us on the inside of the UAW felt that if the unauthorized strikes continued and if there was an inability of the parties to get along, it would ultimately end in the union at Ford destroying itself," recalled Monroe Lake, the UAW's former assistant national Ford director.[19]

It was in the midst of this emergency that Ford Motor Company and the United Auto Workers, prodded by the National War Labor Board, agreed to hire Harry Shulman as umpire to resolve their grievances, much as General Motors and UAW officials had done with George Taylor three years earlier. Shulman was a Jewish immigrant, born in the Czarist Empire in 1903. He grew up in Providence, Rhode Island, and graduated from Brown University and Harvard Law School. He subsequently clerked for Justice Louis Brandeis and became a professor at Yale Law School. In 1939 he was named Sterling Professor of Law there, succeeding William O. Douglas, who had joined the U.S. Supreme Court. Forty-years old, bespectacled, balding, short, modest but confident in his manner, and highly regarded for his intelligence, judgment, civility, and compassion, Shulman became the fulcrum holding the UAW and Ford Motor officials together.

During his first years in Detroit, Shulman heard as many as forty cases each day in his suite in the Penobscot Building, a forty-seven-floor skyscraper in Detroit's financial district. In the evenings he held court in the cocktail lounge on the high-rise's top floor. Shulman would chatter with the union and company men, discussing past cases, pending cases, and those rulings that, in his words, he had put under his desk blotter "to let them age and ripen" before releasing them. He advised the union and company reps about whether to file grievances on particular issues. He even discussed purely personal matters with them. "He acted as a kind of father confessor for everyone who came to see him," remembered Ben Aaron, who chaired the War Labor Board's Tool & Die Commission in Detroit in 1943.[20]

Shulman held hearings and chatted in cocktail lounges for three days every other week, returning to New Haven in between to teach his classes and write his arbitration awards. Between June 1943 and May 1954 he issued 284 "opinions," as he termed his arbitration rulings, for the UAW and Ford. These were single-spaced evaluations, ordinarily twelve to seventeen hundred words long, each dealing with one specific issue—for example, discharges for stoppage, transfers within a workplace, reclassification of a worker's job, assaults on foremen, time spent in checking tools, assignment of skilled tradesmen to other classifications, and vacation eligibility. In some instances, Shulman wrote opinions addressing similar grievances in two or more factories. Other rulings dealt with a single factory, most often one of the factories inside the River Rouge, the massive complex of plants in Dearborn, Michigan, where thousands of native-born migrants from the South and Midwest who had never before been in a factory suddenly found themselves working with local Detroit immigrants and Communists, Trotskyists, and Socialists vying for control of UAW Local 600.

Shulman normally began his rulings by summarizing the views of the aggrieved employees and the arguments presented by the union and management representatives. He would then evaluate the strengths and weaknesses of the contending parties' opinions, compare the case to similar cases that he had considered, and, finally, announce his decision. In addition to addressing the particular case in question, Shulman often made general observations about the parties' attitudes and their mutual relations. His rulings were printed and distributed throughout both Ford management and the Ford division of the union. Three times his collected opinions were bound together and privately published for the benefit of the union, management, and his successors. In addition to these relatively lengthy "opinions," Shulman issued several hundred memoranda—briefer, three-hundred- to six-hundred-word judgments that addressed specific grievances at one or more Ford Motor workplaces or settled points left unresolved in contract negotiations. He also issued 2,624 "decisions." These were typically one or two sentences long, and addressed one grievance or several related ones. The briefer pronouncements normally referred back to the bound opinions, which functioned as precedents in the Ford industrial jurisdiction.[21]

Shulman's opinions became the legislation to point shop-floor workers, union committeemen, foremen, supervisors, and higher-ranking management and union officers out of mayhem. "The arbitrator's opinion can help in rationalizing the agreement . . . and . . . foster . . . greater appreciation . . . of each other's views and needs," he declared in a lecture at Harvard Law School in February 1955. Perhaps because he grew up in very modest circumstances, Shulman was particularly sensitive to the people on the shop floor. "It is the rank and file [above all] that must be convinced," he argued. "The less that their private law [the UAW-Ford contract and the umpire's rulings] is understood by the workers . . ., the greater is the likelihood of wildcat stoppages or other restraints on productivity. . . . Consistency is not a lawyer's creation. . . . It is a normal urge and normal expectation. It is part of the ideal of equality of treatment," he maintained.[22]

Relations between Ford Motor and the UAW's Ford division stabilized after Henry Ford retired in 1946 and Harry Bennett, the vice president who had directed the company thugs, was dismissed. A new team of young engineers, mathematicians, and other professionals nicknamed the "Whiz Kids," most notably Robert McNamara, the future U.S. Secretary of Defense, was brought in to assist the new president, Henry Ford II, the twenty-nine-year-old grandson of the founder. Meanwhile, the UAW's new president, Walter Reuther, began to take control of the union's office, torn by political wrangling.

Shulman functioned like a chief justice at Ford Motor, to the dismay of Robert Campbell, the company's principal representative in arbitration hearings. "Shulman has always believed his jurisdiction should not be limited in any way," Campbell told an interviewer after he retired. "He has his own definite ideas of how the relationship of the parties should be conducted and has constantly attempted to 'master mind' the parties into his idea of 'ideal' management-labor relationship regardless of the restrictions imposed upon him by the Agreement. ... Shulman's method amounts to a one-man control of an operation ... establishing more policy than the parties."[23]

Despite such complaints, Henry Ford II and Reuther continued to rely on Shulman until he died in May 1955 at the age of fifty-two.

* * *

John Dunlop (see figure 5) acquired comparable influence with America's major construction contractors and building trades unions. Building contractors employed 1,982,000 Americans in 1947—5 percent of the U.S. private nonagricultural

FIGURE 5. John Dunlop at Harvard University in the early 1940s.
John T. Dunlop Papers, Harvard University Archives.

workforce.[24] At that time, more than 90 percent of those workers belonged to one or another of the building trades unions. There were nineteen different national building trades unions and nearly as many associations of contractors. Except for the Laborers' International Union of North America, the membership in AFL building trades union membership was almost entirely white. Jobs were obtained through family ties. The father was an electrician or a plumber, and he would train his sons. There were apprentice programs, but these too were confined to family or other members of the ethnic group. The same was true of the contractors.[25]

The principal source of conflict in the industry was not between the contractors and the unions, although such clashes existed, but between unions maneuvering against one another for work assignments. Also involved in decisions were local building trades councils, local contractors' associations, the National Contractors Association (which dealt only with union brotherhoods), the Associated General Contractors of America (which included both unionized and nonunion firms), the American Federation of Labor's Building and Construction Trades Department, and locals of several other AFL and CIO national unions that were not affiliated with that department but nonetheless had members on construction sites.

The Taft-Hartley Act, passed by Congress in June 1947 over President Truman's veto, outlawed the building trades unions' greatest sources of power: the secondary boycott and the closed shop. Specifically, the act prohibited one union from calling on other unions to boycott an employer who was refusing to recognize their rights and also made it illegal for employers to hire only union members at their work sites. These provisions threatened the building trades unions, up to that point among the largest and most powerful unions in the country. The National Labor Relations Board tried for a year to find a solution but failed, for the method of worker representation mandated by the Wagner Act—elections in workplaces—made no sense in the construction industry, where tradesmen moved frequently between job sites and contractors.

Consequently, officers of the building trades unions, contractors' associations, and the AFL's Building and Construction Trades Department began meeting in late 1947 to find a way to get around those clauses of the act. They turned to Dunlop, who had chaired the Wage Adjustment Board, a branch of the War Labor Board during the war, to mediate their often-contentious meetings. The negotiations led to the formation of the National Joint Board for the Settlement of Jurisdictional Disputes in early 1948. The National Joint Board, as it was usually called, consisted of eight men: representatives of the Brotherhood of Carpenters and Joiners and another large building trades union; representatives of the smaller, more specialized trades unions; representatives of the contractors, similarly divided between representatives of more general and specialized bodies; plus Dunlop, who was the chairman.

In addition to chairing the National Joint Board for the Settlement of Jurisdictional Disputes, Dunlop was an associate professor of economics at Harvard at the time, directed the Harvard Trade Union Program, and flew back and forth between Boston and Washington, DC, to serve various federal labor-management and wage regulation panels.

A dispute at a construction site in Los Angeles in 1951 is one illustration of Dunlop's role in the industry. A year earlier, Governor Earl Warren of California joined five hundred civic and business leaders and an array of Hollywood movie stars to celebrate the groundbreaking of the Statler Hotel in downtown Los Angeles. At thirteen stories high, the Statler would have 1,275 rooms. With fifteen conference and banquet rooms, the hotel would offer greater convention capacity than hotels in any other city west of Chicago. It would be the first hotel built in downtown Los Angeles since 1923 and, according to Statler executives, "the last word in hotels."

The mayor, the governor, the business community, and the unions were all delighted, until August 24, 1951, when sixty sheet-metal workers stopped working at the site. A subcontractor from New York was using seventy members of the International Association of Bridge, Structural and Ornamental Iron Workers to install the hotel's aluminum windows. However, the Sheet Metal Workers union claimed that the AFL Building and Construction Trades Department had awarded their union, not the ironworkers, the jobs of mounting 10-gauge or lighter metal and that the aluminum window frames fit into that category. Their sixty members at work on other jobs on the site protested the usurpation. On August 28 the Sheet Metal Workers began picketing around the construction site. Seventy percent of the eight hundred workers employed at the site immediately stopped work. Ignoring the Taft-Hartley prohibition against secondary boycotts, they refused to cross the sheet-metal workers' picket line, although, needless to say, the ironworkers continued to work, as did carpenters and truck drivers, apparently because of prearranged pacts among their officers.

Dunlop was in Washington, DC, that morning, meeting with the other members of the Wage Stabilization Board, a committee set up by President Truman to control wages during the Korean War. When he was informed about the boycott in Los Angeles, Dunlop stepped out of the meeting for a moment. He sent telegrams to the presidents of the Ironworkers and Sheet Metal Workers unions "advising immediately resumption of work." He promised both union presidents that the National Joint Board would thrash out the issue at their next meeting.[26]

The National Joint Board for the Settlement of Jurisdictional Disputes handled an average of five hundred such cases every year between 1948 and 1955, many of them quite thorny. "Who shall put in a metal ceiling? Who shall lay a lateral sewer pipe, and where does the main sewer end and a lateral begin? Who shall install metal windows? Who shall put up the backing to toilet accessories? All of these enormous questions might seem very trivial to someone who has not tried to erect a building," Dunlop drily remarked in 1955.[27] As the chair of the National Joint Board, Dunlop decided how disputes like the one at the Statler Hotel in Los Angeles were settled. He met in person with the other eight members of the Joint Board or, if time did not permit, called them over the phone, worked out compromises, and informed local building unions' business agents of their rulings.

"Dunlop always had enormous influence because Dunlop was a deal-maker," recalled Daniel Bell, who was *Fortune's* labor reporter in the 1950s. "He was a superb manipulator, a superb backstage operator."[28]

* * *

Sylvester Garrett acquired influence at U.S. Steel as great as Shulman's and Dunlop's at Ford Motor and the construction industry. (See figure 6.) "Syl," as Garrett was called, was a charming man of medium height, with big shoulders, a wide jaw, sparkling eyes, and buoyant smile. He looked a bit like Franklin Roosevelt and Garrett was also stricken by polio as a young adult, although not as devastatingly as the future president. Garrett was still able to walk, albeit with a limp and cane, and was so energetic that he climbed the peaks of Vermont's Green Mountains and New Hampshire's White Mountains every summer. As chairman of Regional War Labor Board III during the war, Garrett developed good relations with the Steelworkers regional directors, the union's general grievance negotiator, and the steel companies' executives in Pennsylvania.

After the NWLB closed, Garrett worked for the National Wage Stabilization Board for a year and then joined the Stanford University law school faculty. Garrett and his wife, Molly Yard, purchased a home in Palo Alto. On the side he served as coordinator of labor relations for Pittsburgh Plate Glass and Libbey-Owens-Ford, the largest glass manufacturers in the U.S.[29]

Syl and Molly might well have remained in Palo Alto had not the vice president of U.S. Steel, R. Conrad Cooper, and the president of the Steelworkers, Philip Murray, prevailed on him to move to Pittsburgh in 1952 to head their Board of Arbitration.[30] U.S. Steel and the Steelworkers had gone through two "permanent arbitrators" and eleven temporary arbitrators since 1946, and relations between the union and the corporation had degenerated. U.S. Steel and the Steelworkers officials had worked well with Garrett during the war. They hoped he could succeed where others had failed.

Few U.S. corporations had a longer or more violent history of opposition to labor unions before the 1930s than U.S. Steel. On March 2, 1937, in a move that startled the business community, the president of U.S. Steel, Benjamin Fairless, signed a rudimentary contract with the Steel Workers Organizing Committee, an amalgamation affiliated with the recently founded Committee for Industrial

FIGURE 6. Sylvester Garrett, chair, Regional War Labor Board III, 1956. Special Collections, Indiana University of Pennsylvania Archives.

Organization led by Phil Murray.[31] After a brief strike, Jones & Laughlin Steel, which, like U.S. Steel, had its headquarters in Pittsburgh, also signed a contract with the Steel Workers Organizing Committee. However, Republic Steel, Bethlehem Steel, and the other large steel manufacturers fought the union furiously. Those companies did not sign contracts with the Steelworkers union until 1941, when pressure from union agitation and federal agencies became too great to resist.

Relations between representatives of U.S. Steel and the Steelworkers became quite positive, even cordial, during the war, which was remarkable after their toxic history. The issue that brought the two parties together was their common desire to streamline the mammoth corporation's exceptionally complex wage-classification system. Employees at Carnegie Steel and U.S. Steel's other subsidiaries were divided into fifty thousand separate job classifications, with widely varying wages for similar work. At a time when most steelworkers were paid no more than $1 per hour, one worker in a coke oven, for example, might receive 10 or even 15 cents more than another performing the same job. Pay for scarfers in slab mills varied by as much as 38 cents. The same was true of other jobs in the mills. Several factors explained the huge differentials, including poor planning, uneven technological development, mergers, supervisors' favoritism, and prejudices against African Americans, Slavs, and Latinos. U.S. Steel, where 40 percent of the nation's steel was produced, was a consolidation of more than one hundred companies, some of which themselves had been products of mergers.

Nothing aroused (and still arouses) more resentment among employees than their belief that other employees were paid more than they were for the same job. The problem was rife at U.S. Steel and across the industry, and when the USWA finally won contracts, union and management were inundated with grievances.

"Chaos" was the word that Garrett used to describe the wage payment system at U.S. Steel in the early 1940s. The corporation's vice president for industrial relations, Wilbur ("Wib") Lohrentz, termed the situation "a real mess," while Gabriel Alexander, who arbitrated disputes for the Steelworkers and Great Lakes Steel Company, Crucible Steel Corporation, Jones & Laughlin Steel, and Armco Steel after the war, described it as "ghastly."[32] "It was really horrible back in the early '40s, the grievances you'd get. I saw lots of grievances which were demanding that we fire the General Superintendent," remembered Warren Shaver, a lawyer then serving as assistant to Wilbur Lohrentz. "We had thousands of them, really. We had 11,000 grievances in one year," he continued. "The thing was the *big* burden on our shoulders on both sides [that is, union staff and management] all these years."[33]

The USWA, U.S. Steel, and the NWLB arbitrators had a common interest in streamlining the wage system, as did the U.S. government, with its dependence on steel for military goods. "One guy would think he wasn't being paid as much as the next guy to him and he was working a lot harder," remembered Ralph Seward, who arbitrated grievances at Bethlehem Steel, the second-largest steel manufacturer. "They would come to me with a whole series of these things, and I had to figure out, 'Should I raise his wages or not?' But then you could see what happens, like a [pick-up sticks] game, you pulled out one little part of this thing and the whole thing begins to fall down on you!"[34]

Encouraged by Garrett, who at that time was chairman of Regional War Labor Board III in Philadelphia, the NWLB issued an order in November 1944 requiring the basic steel companies and United Steel Workers of America to form a Joint Wage Rate Inequity Negotiating Commission consisting of seven management representatives, seven union officers, and two NWLB staff members to restructure the wage system.[35] By that time government, corporate, and union officials all felt confident that the United States and its allies would defeat Germany and

Japan. The parties understood that restructuring the wage systems would take many years. So the Joint Wage Committee continued to meet without the public members throughout 1946, even though the union struck all of the major steel companies in January.[36]

In January 1947 the ten largest steel companies and the United Steelworkers of America announced that they were going to institute a plan to rationalize the industry's entire job and wage structure. They called the plan "the Fair Day's Work Program." The phrase harkened back to Charles Dickens's 1865 novel *Our Mutual Friend* ("They only ask for a fair day's wages for a fair day's work is ever my partner's motto") and Thomas Carlyle's 1843 account of Chartism, *Past and Present* ("A fair day's wages for a fair day's work: it is as just a demand as governed men ever made of governing. It is the everlasting right of man"), and had long been used by trade unionists in England and U.S. to justify their claims. The "fundamental principle . . . is that the employee is entitled to a fair day's pay in return for which the Company is entitled to a fair day's work," the committee announced.

To achieve this goal, company engineers, in consultation with union staff, would study 4,500 hourly-paid jobs, reduce them to 1,150 "benchmark jobs," and fit the new designations into one of thirty categories, each with its standard hourly rate. Then—and this would be an even bigger undertaking—they would evaluate all incentive jobs and the rates workers received to rationalize that system. The overall plan, which was entitled "job evaluation," was a postwar variation of Frederick W. Taylor's "scientific management" scheme with one big difference: the union's representatives would help to implement it. Many American companies and unions, not only in steel but in most other kinds of manufacturing, introduced job evaluation systems after the Second World War.

At that time Garrett was teaching law at Stanford and periodically flew to Pittsburgh to advise Pittsburgh Plate Glass and Libbey-Owens-Ford management about their labor relations policies. While on Grant Street one day, he ran into Earl Moore, a U.S. Steel executive. "He was gleeful," Garrett recalled. "'You're not going to believe this. The union has agreed to our inequity program! We're spending five cents more per hour but, believe me, it's worth it.' There was no question in his mind that this was a *tour de force*."[37] The arbitrators were also pleased, freed now of the tortuous grievance disputes that they continuously had to sort out. "Fantastic," said Seward, Bethlehem Steel's arbitrator. Looking back, Garrett, who was not involved in the Cooperative Wage Study but had proposed a rudimentary version back in early 1943, described the agreement as "as fine an accomplishment as we've ever seen in the history of collective bargaining, in terms of really dealing with a massive, nasty problem in a business-like way."[38]

The 1947 job evaluation accord had been negotiated in private by a handful of representatives of the parties, principally U.S. Steel's vice president for industrial relations, R. Conrad Cooper, and Elmer Maloy, a founder of the Steel Workers Organizing Committee. Neither local union officers nor lower-ranking company officials were consulted, let alone the workers who sweated in the mills. As Garrett remembered years later, "This was the first time that many of the other officers and the rank and file discovered that they were going to have a Fair Day's Work Program. And it quickly became apparent that there was a firestorm developing . . ."[39]

Letters, postcards, and petitions poured down on district offices and national union offices. The most vitriolic came from roll turners, whose jobs were put into the "C" category in a scale that ran from A to H. "I know that most committees were composed of craftsmen like yourself and millwrights who said 'roll turners always thought they were lords of the mill but that is changed now,'" one turner wrote Elmer Maloy. "The fact is that roll turners raised their own rates and maintained them above machinists' rates throughout the years until your gang came along and hit us on our backs." "I will point out to you that we are dues paying members," another wrote to the Steelworkers president Phil Murray, "and are not going to sit still for this gypping. Our idea of unionism always was that it meant organization for mutual benefit, not taking from one and giving to another."[40]

With the union's master contracts with U.S. Steel and the other large steel companies coming up for renewal in April 1947, the union officers' position became increasingly precarious. They had approved the Fair Day's Work Program; now they were "squirming, trying to do anything but go along," remembered Seward.[41] Chewed out by the members, the union's leaders backed off. Although the two parties' representatives met in February and March to consider the terms of the next contract, progress was slow. Union negotiators tried to secure a clause specifying that the employees' existing performance levels would be considered "a fair day's work," but management would not concede. They decided to institute the plan with or without union participation. "Each side was negotiating at arm's length on vital issues involving immense stakes for both," an outsider observed.[42] Relations between the negotiating parties, warm only a few weeks earlier, had become ice-cold.

Feeling abandoned by the union's negotiators, angry members started taking their problems into their own hands. Every year during the late 1940s and early 1950s, thousands of workers submitted grievances alleging wage discrimination by U.S. Steel management. Typical were complaints submitted by machinists employed at the Waukegan, Illinois, plant of American Steel and Wire Company, a subsidiary of U.S. Steel. One grievance maintained that "the out-of-line differentials that we were given while working on [the] Signode Strapping Machine are incorrect and does not represent a true picture of our old job." Another group of employees declared, "We hated the Fair Day's Standard rates installed on 2 MCO machines for Bronze and Copper," and demanded that "production standards be installed whereby we can maintain our average earnings without any superficial, temporary and inequitable help."[43]

If such matters strike some reader as small potatoes, millworkers had a different view. The majority had been employed in the steel mills for many years. They remembered foremen demanding bribes, help around their houses, or other humiliations in the early 1930s. Anyone who refused risked losing their jobs. That is a chief reason why the steelworkers so valued the union: the contracts' work rules protected their dignity. "As my father used to say, 'If the union didn't do anything else, it put an end to that,'" remarked Jack Metzger, a retired professor of labor relations whose father had been a molder in the U.S. Steel mill in Johnstown, Pennsylvania. "In my father's view of things, the very impersonality of the labor contract as a binding document was the foundation of his freedom and dignity, and a great deal of peace of mind as well," Metzger emphasized. "He believed in what was called then 'the sanctity of the contract.'"[44]

Yet the contracts negotiated after the war created new problems. For example, one section of the contract signed by representatives of Carnegie-Illinois Steel and the Steelworkers appeared to give the management the upper hand: it stipulated that "the Company retains the exclusive right to manage the business and to direct the work forces" and, furthermore, that the management "at its discretion" could establish new incentives. However, in the same agreement the company conceded that every job and classification in effect on the date that the contract was signed "shall continue in effect" unless the job was discontinued, its content was changed to the extent of one full classification, or the union's officials approved another change. Section 2-B of the 1947 contract proved to be the steelworkers' trump card. It read that "in no case shall local working conditions . . . deprive any employee of rights guaranteed under this Agreement."[45] Dispute over those sixteen words ultimately would later spark the biggest strike in U.S. history—the four-month-long strike of five hundred thousand steelworkers in late summer and autumn of 1959.

Between 1946 and 1951, U.S. Steel and the United Steelworkers of America went through thirteen arbitrators. By the latter date, the management was refusing to make any concessions to the union. The United States was at war in Korea, the President had established a Wage Stabilization Board, and the company's negotiators reasoned that if they made concessions, the Wage Stabilization Board would simply split the remaining difference. With a nationwide strike imminent, Truman seized ownership of the mills, only to have the U.S. Supreme Court rule that he had exceeded his powers.[46]

It was in the midst of the 1951 emergency that U.S. Steel and the Steelworkers officials asked Sylvester Garrett to take charge of their Board of Conciliation and

Arbitration. Representatives of both sides knew and respected Garrett. The union's lawyer, Arthur Goldberg, and U.S. Steel's attorney, Wilbur Lohrentz, promised Garrett that Ralph Seward, who was temporarily arbitrating their grievances, would issue a ruling that would ease the wage-classification mess before he took over. But Seward's award, issued in May 1952, only sharpened the differences. When Garrett arrived in Pittsburgh, he found that the union and management spokesmen were "worlds apart" in their understanding of the contract.[47] To get out of the morass, Garrett would have to proceed step by step, arbitrating a series of unresolved grievances, much as George Taylor and the National War Labor Board had done with the union security and wage-rates disputes in 1942.

One example was a dispute at the National Tube Division of U.S. Steel's complex at Loraine, Pennsylvania. In those mills, skelp was heated in huge furnaces and then shaped into pipes through a series of thirteen horizon stations. The corporation had invested $3 million to reconstruct two of the six mills in that complex of factories after the war. The newer plants were more productive; earnings for incentive workers rose appreciably. Employees in the older plant, whose earnings lagged behind, felt cheated, and they protested. It was a typical wage-inequality gripe. The union local asked the management to adjust the incentive rates so that paychecks for workers at the older mills would equal those at the new facilities. National Tube's management responded by conducting a time-study in 1949 and then announcing a new incentive system covering all six factories, including the new two ones where the workers had expressed no dissatisfaction. Among other changes, management proposed to reduce the size of work crews, eliminating some jobs and combining others. For example, a roll setter would become a roll setter–table attendant. The employees considered the new arrangement dangerous. "The skelp coming through the furnace was grabbed with a tong-like tool and pulled over a forming device which caused the edges of the skelp to come together and weld to form a pipe. It was desperately hot," Garrett remembered. "I knew it was hot because I stood here alongside that welder when I made my plant visit. Even though they had a huge fan blowing the heat away and a screen up to the welder's waist, it was still very, very hot indeed."

By custom, welders' jobs rotated: a man would work beside the roller for twenty minutes, rest for twenty minutes, and then pick up a light job for twenty minutes before returning to the roller in front of the furnace. The management planned to eliminate one employee; consequently, the remaining two would spend ten more minutes each hour sweltering in front of the roller. The local union officers protested; the local management proceeded regardless, and in November 1949 five workers filed a grievance. Because union and company representatives could not agree despite meetings at five levels from the shop floor to top offices, the wrangle was sent to Garrett.

Two questions were involved in this case. The first was whether management had the freedom—or "prerogative," to use the term used then—to cut the size of work crews and length of spell times, or in other such ways to change work rules without consent of the local union. In a twenty-seven-page-long award in which he discussed in depth the conflicted contract provisions pertaining to that question, Garrett ruled that management did not have such latitude. The second question was whether technological conditions had changed sufficiently in the mills to allow the management to override customary working conditions, a power clearly granted, in principle, in Section 2-B of the contract.

Garrett informed the management that he had not received sufficient information to answer the second question. Rather than requesting additional material, Garrett ordered the parties' grievance representatives to resume negotiations. But he added a codicil: if the Steelworkers and management negotiators could not settle within forty days, he would determine the matter himself. This attachment put the management in a quandary: if they didn't compromise with the union, Garrett might issue an intolerable ruling. It was a shrewd move intended to push the two parties toward resolution.[48]

Six months earlier, soon after becoming chairman of the Board of Arbitration and Mediation, Garrett had asked the Steelworkers president and U.S. Steel's vice president for labor relations to each appoint one person who would have the authority to speak for their respective parties as he drafted arbitration awards. "I went to Phil Murray first, and I said,

> "I'm afraid with these big incentive [wage] issues pending and your local working conditions cases pending, I can't handle this job unless I have direct access either to you or to someone you will designate for th[is] purpose with whom I can discuss any problem in complete confidence and know that this person represents you. I want to be able to talk about any policy question, any procedural question or any draft opinion with such an individual." I said, "Will you agree?" He said, "Sounds good to me, can you get John Stephens [of U.S. Steel] to agree?" I said, "I'll go up there this afternoon." I went up, talked to Stephens, and he agreed. . . . That's how I got "designated representatives."[49]

Stephens chose as his representative his legal counselor, Wib Lohrentz; David McDonald, who had become Steelworkers president after Murray's death in November 1952, chose Elmer Maloy, one of the union's founding figures. They were followed by attorney Warren Sheaver, for the company, and Ben Fischer, a socialist who helped organize the Aluminum Workers of America in the mid-1930s and then became an aide to Murray and McDonald, for the union. Garrett and the company and union representatives met regularly. Their sessions were informal and confidential, and they operated by consensus. Local union and management people would present their arguments to Garrett in grievance hearings. In turn, he would draft a ruling and then discuss it with Sheaver and Fischer and, on occasion, allow them to review the text. Garrett would consider their objections, make whatever alterations he considered appropriate, and then meet again with Sheaver and Fischer. The three men commonly would review the second draft line by line. Garrett would make final revisions and issue his opinion as if he were the sole author.

George Taylor had done the same thing in disputes in the Philadelphia hosiery and men's clothing industries during the 1930s. Taylor's protégés followed his example. "We wrote one draft," remembered Bill Simkin, who had replaced Taylor as the arbitrator for the Philadelphia men's clothing industry when his mentor went to Detroit to umpire disputes between General Motors and the UAW in 1940. In the late 1940s, Simkin became chief arbitrator for Bethlehem Steel and the Steelworkers. "We would take that draft," Simkin recalled in a discussion with Garrett four decades later,

> we would first read to them the introduction, and get them to talk about it and discuss whether we had gotten everything important in the introduction. We would read them [the draft] or give them copies . . . of the labor [local's] position and the [local] industry [i.e., management] position to see if we'd covered everything. They would comment on the draft, indicating any statements [that] we made that were gonna raise hell somewhere. And they would indicate varying degrees of acceptance, they would say, "Well, we don't quite like this but we understand you." We would not give them a copy of the opinion [itself] until we have extended, sometimes quite extensive discussion, and then sometimes—this is not too often . . . but sometimes, the answer would come out of that extended discussion from them!!

In other words, Simkin also guided the two sides toward meetings of the minds. "You're describing my clearance system, except that I would send them the whole draft first, then I'd meet with them," Garrett told Simkin. "Isn't that astonishing?"[50]

In working this way, Garrett was manipulating the local union and management people, not to mention the aggrieved workers in the mill. None of them knew that the arbitrator had cleared his decision and the language to put the higher-ups' minds at rest. Yet because he had done so, he was far more successful, at least temporarily, than the fourteen other arbitrators who had been employed by U.S. Steel and the Steelworkers between 1946 and 1951. "Over a period of time, arbitration became the instrument for writing the nitty-gritty of contracts," remarked Ben Fischer, the union's chief representative in arbitration.[51] Between 1952 and 1957, the number of unresolved grievances sent to Garrett by the international union and U.S. Steel declined by 90 percent. By March 1957, Garrett had only thirty-one grievance cases on his desk, the lowest level ever in his lengthy career with that corporation and union.[52] Contract negotiations also had mellowed in the decade after the war ended. In the 1946, 1949, and 1952 strikes, both the Steelworkers and the manufacturers fought hard over the issues of managerial prerogatives, whether the management would pay 100 percent of the cost of pensions, and the union shop. In 1956, by contrast, only three pennies separated the two parties, a difference that was split after a four-week walkout.[53]

Fundamental disputes over control of work processes persisted underneath the surface, exploding three years later in the biggest strike in U.S. history. However, that was not apparent yet, and Garrett had managed to foster a bond between Warren Sheaver and Ben Fischer firm enough to survive even the bitter battle, as will become clear in chapter 5.

* * *

Cooperation of the sort that Garrett, Shulman, and Dunlop nurtured depended on steady increases in compensation for the workers and increases in the prices that companies charged their customers. Yet only two of the Labor Board vets— Clark Kerr and Professor Sumner Slichter of Harvard University—discussed the correlation in any depth, and they both welcomed the resulting inflation.

Clark Kerr addressed the inflation issue in remarks at a meeting of the Industrial Relations Research Association at the end of 1951, just as a long confrontation between the major steel manufacturers, the Steelworkers union, and the Wage Stabilization Board was sharpening. "Severe direct controls wear out relatively quickly" and should be kept in reserve for true emergencies, Kerr argued. In his opinion, the federal government should permit mild inflation in wages and prices, "if other factors were favorable, since it would allow the raising of both costs and purchasing power per unit of product. . . . It would not, by itself, force a substantial inflation," he declared, adding "a mild inflation can make a contribution in drawing forth resources and satisfy the powerful groups in society, provided it does not get out of hand."[54]

Sumner Slichter was even less hesitant. Born in 1892, Slichter was a generation older than the Labor Board boys. A student of John R. Commons at the University of Wisconsin, Slichter served on the Commission on Industrial Relations of 1913–15 and subsequently taught economics at Princeton, Cornell, and Harvard and served as a public representative on Regional War Labor Board in Boston during the Second World War. Slichter advised Jean McKelvey on her doctoral dissertation and served as John Dunlop's mentor at Harvard. Kerr referred to Slichter as "our guru."[55]

In an article that appeared in *Harper's* magazine in August 1952, immediately after the conclusion of the steel strike, Slichter argued in favor of steadily rising inflation not only for the sake of labor-management peace but also to revive the economies of U.S. allies in Western Europe and Asia. "A stable price level . . . would handicap the United States in its effort to unite the free nations of the world against communism and to make these nations prosper so that communism cannot flourish within their borders. *At the risk of being called a dangerous and irresponsible thinker, let me say that in the kind of economy possessed by the United States a slowly rising price level is actually preferable to a stable price level,*" he declared. In 1957 and again in 1959 Slichter encouraged what he called "creeping inflation."[56]

Neither Slichter, Kerr, nor any other of the Labor Board vets ever imagined inflation getting out of hand.

4

Down-to-Earth Utopians

Class warfare will be forgotten and in its place will be
bureaucratic contest of interest group against interest
group. The battles will be in the corridors instead of
the streets, and memos will flow instead of blood.

—Clark Kerr, John Dunlop, Frederick Harbison,
and Charles Myers, 1960

JOHN DUNLOP WAS A DOWN-TO-EARTH GUY. It didn't matter whether he was
talking to the president of Harvard University or the president of Boilermakers
Local 29. He always assumed the same rough-and-ready manner. Nearly thirty
years after they had worked closely together on a Harvard faculty committee,
essayist Roger Rosenblatt still vividly remembered Dunlop's unique combination of common sense and sassiness. "Dunlop was fond of putting on country-
boy airs. If I used a phrase like *seriatim* in a sentence, or even a *status quo* or an
ad infinitum, he would scratch his head and ask, 'That's Latin, ain't it?'" Dunlop
was the Lamont University Professor, one of the most prestigious appointments
given to Harvard faculty, yet he acted like a farm boy when talking to Rosenblatt, a
twenty-nine-year-old Manhattan-born assistant professor of literature.[1] Although
the other Labor Board boys didn't put on country manners, they also were level-
headed men with no time for fancy words, ideology, or anything like that. Or at
least that was how they thought of themselves.

The truth was more complex than that. It is true that—like Dunlop, who
grew up on a pear ranch in Placerville, California, and a Presbyterian mission in
the Philippines—many of them came from out-of-the-way places such as Stony
Creek, Pennsylvania (Clark Kerr), Paw Paw, Illinois (Robben Fleming), the outskirts of Salt Lake City (Vernon Jensen), Blasdell, New York (Richard Lester),
Onawa, Iowa (E. Wight Bakke), Beaver Dam, Wisconsin (James Healy), and a

frontier settlement in Alberta (Lloyd Reynolds), where they changed the straw in the barn stalls, milked the cows, and fed the chickens and pigs before going to school or helped out at the family's hardware store, shoe store, or gas station—that kind of work.[2] Consequently, they weren't suckered in by Communists hawking the *Daily Worker* or Trotskyists preaching Permanent Revolution, unlike big-city kids whom they met in college. They were sensible young men, not attracted to inflammatory notions.

No value stood higher in the minds of Dunlop, Kerr, and the other Labor Board vets than being "realistic." "What would work among the 'bumps and grinds' of the real world; not what might work in the 'best of all possible worlds'" were the words Kerr chose to describe their mindset after the Second World War. *Rationalism, reason,* and *effectiveness* were other keywords in their vocabularies. They insisted that they had no ideological convictions of any kind—not Marxism, not progressivism, none at all. The industrial-relations field "became more unified in outlook and more neutrally professional," Kerr declared. "Reality is more complex than theory or ideology once supposed."[3]

That was why Dunlop used Harvard Business School's case-study method in his courses on industrial relations at Harvard. Rather than giving lectures, he would give students five- or ten-page-long descriptions of disputes between a particular business and a specific union, tell them to imagine that they were consultants to one side or the other, and then ask what advice they would offer. He wanted the students to grasp the complexities of the conflicts to prepare them for the real world. For the same reason, Dunlop and James Healy, another Labor Board vet, published a 511-page-long volume, *Collective Bargaining: Principles and Cases*, in 1953 and Clark Kerr and E. Wight Bakke compiled a 946-page-long collection of documents titled *Unions, Management, and the Public* in 1949, volumes used by industrial-relations professors throughout the country. "The bottom line they seek is fidelity to reality," read the caption that Dunlop, Kerr, Richard Lester, and Lloyd Reynolds chose for the photograph opposite the title page of a 1988 book on how they interpreted labor markets.[4]

This desire to shed ideology and be realistic came to dominate American intellectual life in the years after the Second World War, after an era in which progressive (and, to a lesser extent, socialist and Communist) thinking had held sway. It followed the jolt that U.S. GIs experienced upon seeing piles of corpses and emaciated survivors at Buchenwald and Dachau in spring 1945 (newsreels and photographs of which were shown in movie theaters and published in *Life, Time,* the *Saturday Evening Post, New York Times Sunday Magazine,* the *Boston Globe, Stars and Stripes,* and other big-circulation magazines and newspapers), the publication a year later of an English-language edition of Max Weber's essays "Politics as a Vocation" and "Science as a Vocation," with his message that the "fate of our times is . . . 'the disenchantment of the world'" and that "Politics is a strong and slow boring of hard boards . . . [that] takes both passion and perspective . . . in a very sober sense of the word," the advent of the Cold War, the downfall of progressive politics after Henry Wallace's ill-starred 1948 presidential campaign, and the rise of Senator Joe McCarthy in 1950.

These developments help explain the rise of modernization theory among political scientists and other social scientists during the 1950s, of consensus interpretations of U.S. history among historians, and of the turn to abstract expressionism by artists such as Jackson Pollack, who previously were committed to American Scene realism and Marxism. Influential theologians, sociologists, and historians, including Reinhold Niebuhr, Daniel Bell, and Richard Hofstadter, distrusted simplistic conceptions of "the people" and feared mass movements. The Labor Board vets were part of that trend. Indeed, they were near the vanguard, since they discovered as soon as they began to work with unions how heterogeneous and contrarian the real people were. "Optimism about the perfectibility of human nature has given way at best to skepticism; and more of the problems of man are now seen to be inherent directly in man himself," Kerr wrote in 1969, recalling their early years.[5]

Yet while the Labor Board vets insisted that they were objective and unbiased, their ideas about unions, management, law, the economy, and the future of the world, expressed in their voluminous writings, public lectures, and arbitration awards, amounted to an ideology in its own right. Indeed, it is hard to imagine why Labor Board vets such as John Dunlop, Sylvester Garrett, and Jean McKelvey (see figure 7) would have continued their work resolving grievance hearings, counseling union and management officials, and training young mediators and arbitrators to the very end of their lives if that had *not* been ideologically motivated. They suffered from infirmities and were financially comfortable. Yet they kept working regardless. What factors other than faith and ideology could explain their determination? Kerr's repeated insistence that "There are no utopian solutions which will bring universal industrial peace" unintentionally points to the answer.[6]

Although they would have winced if characterized this way, the Labor Board veterans were in truth utopians. Not utopians like the early-sixteenth-century German Anabaptist peasants led by Thomas Munzer or the Millerites in America in the early 1840s, who were convinced that the perfect world was imminent. Nor did they resemble the socialist followers of English cotton manufacturer Robert Owen, who created utopian communities in rural America in the early nineteenth century or the followers of Edward Bellamy, whose 1888 novel *Looking Backward, 2000–1887*, depicting a society based on cooperation, brotherhood, and

FIGURE 7. Jean T. McKelvey after the war. Kheel Center, Cornell University.

government-owned industries geared to human need, sold one million copies in the aftermath of the 1886 Haymarket riot in Chicago and violent strikes on the railroads the following year.

Rather, John Dunlop, Clark Kerr, and their colleagues belonged to the kind of middle-of-the-road reformers whom the German sociologist Karl Mannheim in 1929 termed "liberal-humanitarian utopians." Unlike Anabaptists and the Adventists, who were certain that Christ's second coming would transform the world at once, the Labor Board vets believed that the world could be re-formed rationally, over time, by thousands of steps ranging from grievance hearings and educating shop stewards and personnel managers to resolving high-profile union-corporate conflicts through mediation and federal commissions. Unlike the followers of Johann Georg Rapp, the German weaver and vine tender turned prophet who broke with the Lutheran Church and founded utopian farming communities in

Harmony, Pennsylvania, and New Harmony, Indiana, in 1805 and 1814, or the Branch Davidian followers of David Koresh, who perished in a fire at Mount Carmel, Texas, on February 28, 1993 after cutting themselves off from society to await Christ's arrival, Dunlop, Kerr, and the other Labor Board vets were fully engaged in world affairs. With a *mentalité* emanating that from the middle echelon of the social order, the liberal-humanitarian utopians pursued what Mannheim termed "a dynamic middle course" between the "ecstasy" of the oppressed chiliast and the "immediate concreteness" of the ruling conservative class, to "bridge the gap between the imperfection of things as they occurred in a state of nature and the dictates of reason by means of the concept of progress."[7]

Dunlop was not unaware of worker poverty in the 1930s. He and his brother hired migrant workers to pick fruit on the family's pear ranch. While in England in 1937 to study with John Maynard Keynes, he stayed with a textile worker's family in Manchester for a few weeks to see how they lived. He also met English trade union officials in London. Yet Dunlop was never engaged in politics, the labor movement, or other events of the 1930s, unlike radical students he studied with while at the University of California at Berkeley.[8] The same was true of Milton Derber, who succeeded Dunlop as director of research and statistics at the NWLB and became a professor of industrial relations at the University of Illinois after the war. Son of a traveling clothing and jewelry salesman, Derber earned his undergraduate degree at Clark University during the mid-1930s. A serious student fascinated by the New Deal and labor, he chose the University of Wisconsin for graduate school because of John R. Commons, Senators Robert La Follette Sr. and Jr., and the state's progressive reputation. But he never became personally involved with unions, strikes, or radical politics. "I was a student, period. I didn't get involved. It's not really my style," he recalled years later.[9]

Clark Kerr was the exception who proved the rule. As a Swarthmore undergraduate, Kerr became deeply committed to pacifism. He campaigned for disarmament and for the United States to join the League of Nations and submit disputes to the World Court in the Hague. He remained a pacifist for the rest of his life. He joined the Student League for Democracy, the youth branch of the Socialist Party, while at Stanford University in 1932–33. He rejected Communism, however, when he learned about the Bolsheviks' putting down the sailors' rebellion at Kronstadt in 1921. In fact, hostility to communism brought Kerr together with his future wife, Catherine (Kay) Spaulding. They were attending a peace conference in Los Angeles in 1934. A rumor spread that Communists were planning to take over the meeting. Clark and Kay were seated next to each other on the stage. She passed him a note, "Are you a Communist?" He wrote back, "No." "Nor am I," she wrote back. They were married on Christmas Day. By the mid-1930s, he had become a New Deal Democrat.[10]

Although there were some exceptions, the majority of the Labor Board boys had only limited or little knowledge about union-management relations before they were hired by the War Labor Board. Kerr studied California cooperative farms as a graduate student at Stanford and Berkeley—not labor unions, his great interest afterward. Richard Lester, who was appointed chairman of the NWLB's Southern Textile Commission, had concentrated on international comparative monetary policies before the war. Dunlop's dissertation, completed in 1939 and published five years later under the title *Wage Determination under Trade Unions*, was theoretical in nature.[11]

Ignorance proved to be a blessing, for they were not sidetracked when they were in college and graduate school by Marxist interpretations of economic relations or the law of diminishing marginal utility, which was the generally accepted principle of the theory of wages. The latter theory held that a business will pay a productive agent only as much as he or she would add to the firm's utility. Its proponents assumed that there was a single market in which all workers sought to maximize their advantage, and that all jobs were open to the person with the best bid: the result was a "going rate" for each occupation.[12]

When George Taylor and Will Davis sent their young staffers to industrial centers in 1943, they told them to find the "going rate" in the labor markets in each region and apply that rate at the companies with War Department contracts. But theory did not fit reality. After a couple of months working as wage stabilizer director for the Regional War Labor Board on the West Coast, Alaska, and Hawaii, Kerr decided that the law of marginal utility was fundamentally flawed. "The avalanche of wage data by occupations and by localities during World War II at first bewildered and then convinced War Labor Board economists . . . [that] in the absence of collective bargaining . . . [there was] no single 'going rate' but a wide dispersion," he recalled at American Economic Association's annual meeting in December 1949. "Abundant evidence now testifies that it would, in the absence of collusion, be almost more correct to say that wages tend to be *unequal* rather than the other way around."[13] Richard Lester was even more definite. After reviewing wage rates in a variety of jobs in southern textile mills, he concluded that that "perfect competition seems to be the exception rather than the rule."[14]

Unencumbered by Marxism, rejecting marginal utility theory, and indirectly influenced by John R. Commons (1862–1945), the University of Wisconsin institutionalist labor economist with whom many of their professors had studied, Kerr and Dunlop developed a new, institutional interpretation of U.S. labor, politics, and economics in the latter 1940s, although they shunned the term *institutional*, which had an old-fashioned Progressive connotation by then.

The U.S. economy had been utterly transformed since the late nineteenth century, the Labor Board vets believed. It no longer consisted of discrete individuals, as Alfred Marshall had imagined, but *institutions*—specifically, labor unions, corporations, and employers' associations. (They seldom referred to farmers or farm organization, despite the significance of agriculture in the U.S. economy. They also ignored consumers and consumer organizations.) And since workers always wanted high compensation and employers and stockholders demanded higher profits, conflicts were inevitable. "Industrial conflict cannot be eliminated and can be only temporarily suppressed," Kerr declared at a conference of sociologists in Belgium in 1953.[15]

Although conflict was inescapable, that was not necessarily bad, Kerr asserted. On the contrary, conflict—especially open conflict such as strikes—serve a valuable function. Having mediated scores of strikes, some of them quite fierce, Kerr likened strikes to the classic Greece tragedies in which retribution was followed by reconciliation. Strikes can be "constructive," Kerr maintained, for they can "result in the greater appreciation of the job by the worker and of the worker by management." It was not uncommon for productivity to rise after strikes, he believed. "The chance to rebel against the other party on occasion establishes the independence of the group and of the individual, makes acceptance of the surrounding social system easier," he avowed. Our objective should be "a golden mean," between unions and management, "some reasonable combination of conflict—even aggressive conflict—and co-operation," he argued in 1954. "Limited antagonism serves a social purpose."[16]

* * *

But only reasonable leaders can conduct reasonable conflicts. Consequently, the Labor Board vets devoted much of their efforts after the Second World War to educating union officials, company managers, and students who went on to assume positions in management, unions, and government offices. Many U.S. universities set up industrial relations programs (or "IR," as it was called then) in the 1940s, not only at land-grant universities, but at elite private universities, Catholic universities, and, in a few cases, liberal arts colleges. IR programs were established in the Northeast, in the Midwest, on the West Coast, and on Hawaii. IR programs were also set up in states where unions were fairly weak, but not absent—North Carolina, Oklahoma, Kansas, Nebraska, Alabama, and Virginia.[17]

Who could be better qualified for those programs than the Labor Board vets? The leading universities appointed veterans of the Regional or National War Labor Board staffs to direct their IR programs. The University of California, for example, appointed Clark Kerr as director of their Institute of Industrial Relations at Berkeley, and Paul Dodd, a UCLA economist who had been on the Regional War Labor Board in San Francisco and the NWLB, as director of their program at UCLA. The University of Illinois chose W. Ellison Chalmers, chairman of the

National War Labor Board's Shipping Commission to direct their Institute of Labor and Industrial Relations on their Urbana-Champaign campus. Sumner H. Slichter and John Dunlop established the Harvard Trade Union Fellowship Plan.

IR was a hot field in the mid- and late 1940s, attracting veterans who saw unions as a way to improve the world. When the half-million servicemen and women taking correspondence courses in 1945 were polled, "labor" ranked near the top of the subjects they would most like to study when discharged, trailing only engineering and accounting.[18] Cornell University created the most ambitious program. The idea originated in the latter 1930s when a rash of strikes and rising labor costs led some garment manufacturers to move their operations out of the Empire State. Fearing a mass flight of industry, the state legislature created a joint House-Senate committee to investigate the problem and recommend solutions. One of the committee's principal recommendations was to establish of a college where students who were planning to become personnel managers or join unions' staffs could study together. After considering bids from the University of Rochester and the University of Buffalo, the committee opted for Cornell University in Ithaca in the western section of the state. Not only would Cornell's association with the Ivy League give the program stature, but as a partially state-chartered institution, the school at Cornell would receive funding from the state government. Students preparing for careers in organized labor and management were more likely to respect each other if they met in Chautauqua County's lovely rolling hills rather than smoke-filled Buffalo, where unions were very strong, or open-shop Rochester, the committee argued.

The legislature christened the new institution the "New York State School of Industrial and Labor Relations," implying that unions and management would have equal influence. The new school offered baccalaureate, masters, and doctoral degrees with a faculty that would include professors of law, economics, history, political science, sociology, and psychology. Acknowledging the unions' great strength in the state, the legislature added three additional seats to Cornell University's board of trustees and asked union leaders to nominate trustees.

The school opened its doors on November 2, 1945, with two professors, 107 freshmen and sophomores, and 11 graduate students. CBS Radio broadcast Governor Thomas Dewey's convocation address nationally.[19] The students lived together in Quonset huts constructed during the war. Being older than the usual undergraduates and with careers in mind, "they were very serious students," recalled Jean McKelvey, and the faculty had "missionary zeal" for fostering peace between labor and management, remembered John (Jack) McConnell, a sociologist who had previously taught at NYU and served on the Regional War Labor Board in New York City.[20]

The California state legislature created IR programs at UCLA and UC–Berkeley at the urging of Governor Earl Warren, a liberal Republican who feared that strikes, the Bay Area's reputation as communistic, and Los Angeles's reputation as ultra-reactionary would discourage further investment in the state, which had boomed during the war. He was also competing for the 1948 Republican Party presidential nomination with Governor Tom Dewey of New York, who had already approved the IR school at Cornell. During the 1930s and the war, the California university system's extension program had provided some funds for the Pacific Coast Labor School, a left-wing program that trained rank-and-file unionists. The funding stopped once the Cold War began. The Institute for Industrial Relations would be an honest broker between labor and management, the governor reasoned.[21]

Chicago trade unionists provided the impetus for the IR program in Illinois. The leaders of Milk Wagon Driver Union Local 753 wondered why the University of Illinois didn't offer assistance to unions in the state, just as it provided aid to the state's farmers. At their urging, the Illinois State Federation of Labor passed a resolution in 1942 calling for a program at the University of Illinois that would provide "expert and detailed knowledge and advice . . . [so] that equality and justice be done for the workers" during and after the war. The University of Illinois's IR program opened in September 1946.[22]

The University of Wisconsin's Industrial Relations Research Institute was proposed in 1947 by Edwin Witte, the eminent economist who had drafted the report to the president and congressional committees for the creation of the Social Security Act and chaired the Regional War Labor Board in Detroit during the war, and Nathan Feinsinger, a highly regarded professor of law who served as associate general counsel and a public member for the NWLB. They recruited Robben Fleming, a promising young law professor who briefly worked on the NWLB's staff before entering the army, to direct Wisconsin's program.

Each of the IR programs approached the field in its distinctive ways. Harvard University considered its purpose to be training leaders in every field in the United States and the world. Consequently, Dunlop brought in promising mid-level labor officials who showed promise of national leadership. Since Dunlop's ties were mainly with the construction industry, the Harvard students were mainly from the building trades and other AFL unions. Each year ten national vice presidents, staff members, local officers, organizers, educational directors, editors of union papers, union organizers, and staff from the Boilermakers, the Molders, the International Brotherhood of Electrical Workers, other building trades unions, and other AFL unions such as the International Ladies' Garment Workers Union studied for a year at Harvard. Dubbed Trade Union Fellows, these men and handful of women not only took classes with Dunlop, Slichter, and James Healy but also participated in seminars in the business school across the Charles River. The goal was "to provide training for executive responsibility" for America's unions. The Trade Union Fellows lived and dined with the undergraduate and graduate students in Leverett House and Quincy House, allowing up-and-coming union leaders and future business and government leaders to network.[23]

Cornell's IR program had an extension program that offered classes in Albany, Buffalo, Binghamton, Auburn, Niagara Falls, Glen Falls, Utica, and Ithaca in 1946–47. Jean McKelvey, Jack McConnell, Pete Jensen, Lois Gray, and Maurice Neufeld taught extension classes such as Introduction to Industrial and Labor Relations, History of the American Labor Movement, Parliamentary Law and Effective Speech, Contract Negotiations and Collective Bargaining, Grievance Procedures, Mediation and Arbitration, Shop Stewards' Training, Personnel Staff Training, the Foreman's Role in Industrial Relations, and Current Trends in Labor Legislation. These classes met in union halls, YMCAs, and high schools. They were so popular in the mid- to late 1940s that the professors frequently had to give the same class twice each evening, from 5 to 6:15 p.m. and from 6:45 to 8 p.m.

The extension program at the University of Illinois's Institute of Labor and Industrial Relations offered eight- and twelve-week-long off-campus courses for shop stewards and local union officers with courses similar to those offered by Cornell, although they also occasionally taught job evaluation and time-and-motion study. During the summer, the institute offered weeklong classes on the Urbana campus for the Steelworkers, the Machinists, and the International Ladies' Garment Workers' Union. The Steelworkers sponsored the most ambitious program, with a four-year curriculum for business agents and officers of the union's locals.[24] The University of Illinois's Institute also organized classes on supervision, processing workers' grievances, collective bargaining, and increasing productivity for managers at six hundred companies in eighty Illinois communities.[25]

In addition to nuts-and-bolts off-campus courses for shop stewards, foremen, and supervisors, the IR programs at Cornell, Illinois, UC–Berkeley, UCLA, Rutgers University, and other universities developed courses and majors for undergraduate and graduate students. Undergraduates in the IR School at Cornell took courses in sociology, economics, political science, and industrial relations in their first two years. The juniors and seniors took specialized classes such as Union Organization and Management, Corporate Finance, Human Relations, Social Security, and Mediation and Arbitration. After class, the professors loaded the students onto buses and headed to Binghamton, Elmira, Buffalo, Endicott, and other nearby towns to tour factories and met with management and union officials. McKelvey dubbed that part of the curriculum "Bus 101." "Economics ought to be concerned not solely with the behavior of Ricardo's economic man but also with the customs, social habits, beliefs and activities of real human beings," she wrote in 1948. "Unless students are given an opportunity to learn something firsthand about actual union functions, how can they appraise the worth of the abstractions currently being circulated as true coins in the leading economic journals?"[26]

To introduce their students to what they proudly called "the real world," Cornell's IR school frequently invited outsiders to the campuses. In six weeks in 1948, the treasurer of the Eastman Kodak Corporation, the vice chairman of President Truman's Council of Economic Advisers, the U.S. representative to the International Labor Organization, the research director of the Textile Workers, the educational director of the International Ladies' Garment Workers' Union, and the personnel manager of the Easy Washing Machine Company spoke to students on the campus. They also arranged internships so that the students could see inner workings of the contending parties. During the summer following the freshman year, the students at Cornell's IR school worked in a union's office or traveled with union organizers. After their sophomore year, they worked with a company manager. After their junior year, the students worked in a public agency.

The Cornell students also watched union and company representatives negotiate contracts. Afterward, the students and professor discussed the issues and the negotiators' tactics. These observations normally occurred off campus. An exception was David Cole, the noted Paterson, New Jersey, mediator who chaired the NWLB's Northern Textile Commission, who taught for one year at Cornell's IR school. While there, he persuaded American Airlines and the pilots' union officials to conduct their negotiations in the front of his classroom. "And one day," McKelvey recalled, "the students said to Cole in their separate session, 'You know what the settlement's going to be, why are you waiting?'" This was October. Cole replied, "Well, that's what a mediator has to do, wait until the time is right."[27]

"Graduates of the School are likely to find themselves on opposite sides of the same table," Cornell University's president E. E. Day told the 1949 New York State CIO Convention. "We hope that they will. We expect they will," he continued. "If and when that time comes, and they are in responsible relationships to the contending parties, we expect something is going to happen to the nature of the negotiations. Not that all issues will be resolved; there will doubtless still be conflicting concerns and interests, but we confidently expect that at times there will be a larger measure of common understanding, common appreciation, common knowledge of what is involved in the pending issues. That is the goal of our program, and it is toward that goal that we are moving."[28]

* * *

The Labor Board vets did more than teach. They arbitrated grievances for companies and unions. They founded the National Academy of Arbitrators, an association of the top labor-management arbitrators who met annually to discuss mutual interests. They served on tripartite (union-employer-public) boards set up by presidents, governors, and mayors to avert or end strikes and contain inflation. They developed systems to regulate industrial relations for state and municipal employees and consulted privately with corporate and union leaders.

And they wrote prolifically. The Labor Board vets frequently contributed articles to the *Atlantic Monthly, Harper's*, and the *New York Times Sunday Magazine* and, in a few cases such as Jean McKelvey, to progressive journals such as *Labor and Nation*. They gave many papers at the American Economic Association and the American Sociological Association and published articles in top-ranked professional journals such as the *Quarterly Journal of Economics* and the *American Economic Review*. The IR professors at Cornell University produced and edited a new scholarly journal, *Industrial and Labor Relations Review*, in 1947. The IR professors at UC–Berkeley started another journal, *Industrial Relations*, in 1961. Finally, they published a profusion of books on every aspect of industrial relations. "So extensive has been the outpouring that it has become quite difficult for the academic student, to say nothing of the industrial relations man, to keep up," Edwin Witte muttered in 1948.[29]

In addition, they founded a society: the Industrial Relations Research Association (IRRA). The IRRA was a unique organization. Its membership was not composed of a single profession—unlike the American Bar Association or the American Economic Association. Rather, it brought together economists, attorneys, psychologists, professors, union officials, corporate executives, mediators, arbitrators, government officials, and members of the clergy to discuss pressing issues in industrial relations. They met annually between Christmas and New Year's Eve in one of the major industrial cities to discuss compelling issues affecting unions and management, especially in the United States but also elsewhere. The principal papers were published annually, originally edited by Jean McKelvey. Local IRRAs met monthly to hear a speaker or debate issues. Like Richard T. Ely, John R. Commons, and Jane Addams, members of the IRRA aimed to improve relations between labor and capital.

* * *

By the early 1950s, the War Labor Board vets were quite upbeat. "Our record is pretty good," John Dunlop declared at the 1952 winter meeting of the IRRA. Unlike Australians, Americans don't have to ration gas, he pointed out. The U.S. government isn't using troops to unload essential cargo, unlike Britain, or send troops into the mines to prevent flooding and destruction of property, as in France. Moreover, strikes were no longer violent in America, as they had been before. "We have had a great outpouring of words, but almost no blood," Dunlop declared.[30]

Clark Kerr felt sure that harmony had arrived in U.S. industries. Employers today "believe that industrial peace pays" and that concessions to unions, especially in wages, "were not as burdensome as once thought," he argued at the 1952 annual meeting of the American Economic Association. Moreover, union leaders have become "mature enough" to no longer need to fight for "institutional security," he continued. They now focus on wage demands, currently their members' principal concern.[31] "Maintaining industrial peace has not proved such a grave social problem," Kerr asserted in his address as president of the IRRA in December 1954. "Except for a few major waves of strikes, each of which had particular causes . . ., industrial peace has been the general order of affairs. Domestic tranquility has never been threatened. Man-days lost to strikes have not been a heavy social cost. Rather, the problem, over time, may become one of too great harmony."[32]

Sumner H. Slichter of Harvard University was even more confident. In an article in the *Atlantic Monthly* in October 1956, Slichter declared that the fifty years since 1900 had produced "a near revolution" in the economic and social structure of the United States. Traditional middle-class occupations had expanded more rapidly than other jobs, he believed. One out of five skilled workers and their families were able to live better than seven out of ten managers and business owners, and many blue-collar workers were enjoying the same living standards as professionals, technical workers, and administrators. A generation ago, Slichter noted, it was widely believed that technological changes, the rise of big business, and conflicts between social classes would slowly delete the middle class and class conflict would intensify. In fact, the opposite has occurred, he declared. "Class lines have been becoming more and more blurred, and the demand for moderation in public policies appears to be coming from all groups in the community."[33]

In retrospect, it is clear that Kerr, Dunlop, and Slichter had erred grievously, for while they and other Labor Board vets were helping to stabilize relations between unions and corporations in the Northeast, in the Midwest, and on the West Coast after the war, many of those corporations were beginning to build new factories in the southern and southwestern states in the 1950s, where labor costs were lower, unions were weak, and union-shop contracts outlawed.[34]

Their failure to recognize the problem is telling, since they had seen this process before, with their own eyes. Dunlop, Slichter, James Healey, and other Labor Board vets studied or taught in Massachusetts in the 1920s and the 1930s, when textile manufacturers began closing their operations, either declaring bankruptcy or relocating to the southern states. The same is true for George Taylor, Bill Simkin, and Allan Dash, who had worked with the silk hosiery union and companies in Philadelphia. They were hired precisely because many of those companies were moving out of Quaker City for low-wage, nonunion shops in Reading and other smaller towns. The same was true in New York State. The state government in Albany set up the ILR School at Cornell University to try to slow the movement of capital out New York State.

The Labor Board vets failed to recognize the vulnerability of the union-management system they had worked so hard to foster. Indeed, until Irving Bernstein published *The Lean Years: A History of the American Worker, 1920–1933* in 1960, none of the Labor Board vets wrote anything—nothing at all—about antiunion corporations or southern labor.[35] The Labor Board boys studied history in college. They included history in their anthologies. Dunlop often used historical evidence in his arguments and even taught labor history courses. Yet the Labor Board vets seemed to believe that history ended in their time.

* * *

With union-management relations apparently stabilizing in the United States, several of the Labor Board vets began to explore unions and industrialization in Asia, the Middle East, Africa, and Latin America.

"We are living in the single century of greatest economic change in the long record of mankind . . . world-wide industrialization," Kerr declared in his presidential address to the IRRA's meeting in December 1954. England was thoroughly industrialized by the end of the nineteenth century, he pointed out. Sweden, Germany, and the United States industrialized in the mid- and late nineteenth century, followed by Japan and Russia. The remainder of the world, however, remained largely agricultural as late as the 1930s.

Industrialization is now proceeding across the world, Kerr argued. By the end of the twentieth century, all but the most remote regions of the globe will be industrialized, he predicted. This will involve "a staggering volume of investment and at least an equally amount of social upheaval." We are living in a revolutionary era of a new kind, he continued. "The massive revolution of this era is not the revolution against the industrial system in its capitalist form, as Marx envisaged it, but rather a revolution in favor of industrialization in almost any form—provided only it is successful."[36]

We must investigate these developments, Kerr declared. He was inspired by Lloyd Fisher, a polymath whom he had appointed as director of the Wage Stabilization Board at the Regional War Labor Board in San Francisco in 1943 and to the faculty of the Institute of Industrial Relations at UC–Berkeley in 1946. Although originally a Marxist, Fisher's outlook changed after working as an assistant for Harry Bridges and Lou Goldblatt, the left-wing president and secretary-treasurer of the International Longshoremen and Warehousemen's Union. Fisher came to believe that "the center of labor [in the United States] is conservative or can soon become so, and the militancy and radicalism come from the periphery," as he put it in an August 1947 article in the *New York Times Sunday Magazine*. This insight was confirmed on November 2, 1948, when few workers voted for Henry Wallace, the Progressive Party's candidate for president, despite appeals from Harry Bridges of the Longshoremen and other union leaders friendly to the Communist Party. "We got more votes in Amherst than Lynn," the UE's international representative in Massachusetts Don Tormey dolefully recalled.[37]

Two months later, in January 1949, the Communists led by Mao Zedong conquered Beijing and established the People's Republic of China. The Chinese Communist Party and the People's Liberation Army were composed of peasants and led by intellectuals like Zhou Enlai, not proletarians. Fisher concluded that the previous interpretations of labor and socialism have "proved spectacularly in error. Propertied classes, the military and the revolutionary groups have all been far more decisive influences in most countries than 'working classes'—at least as represented by trade unions."[38]

Fisher was not able to pursue his ideas, for he was stricken with cancer in 1951 and died in February 1953 at the age of forty-one. Kerr and others, however, carried his thinking further. In November 1953, 115 IR professors and others from the State Department, the Labor Department, the Ford Foundation, and several other countries met at Cornell University for a three-day conference on human resources and labor relations in underdeveloped countries. Beside the Cornell IR faculty, Kerr, and Dunlop, the IR professors at the meeting included Charles Myers from MIT, Frederick Harbison of the University of Chicago, Walter Galenson from UC–Berkeley, and Robert Alexander from Rutgers University, among others. The conference discussed economic and social changes in underdeveloped countries, labor productivity in what they termed "backward" areas, ownership and managerial problems in underdeveloped countries, labor movements and organization around the world, the impact of the International Labor Organization and other agencies in India and Latin America, and future research.[39]

Kerr and his graduate student Abe Siegel gave the most important presentation. They dismissed the existing interpretations of labor, workers, and labor movements by Karl Marx, Sidney and Beatrice Webb, Joseph Schumpeter, Karl Polanyi, Selig Perlman, G. D. H. Cole, and others as moralistic and too focused on the Western world and capitalism. They called for a broader conception that would take in socialist and capitalist systems throughout the world. "Capitalism is after all not one thing but many," Kerr and Siegel declared. The same was true of socialism. "The socialism in Moscow, in South Wales, in Tel Aviv evidences almost as much variety as capitalism in Detroit, in Abadan, in Rome, in Dusseldorf." The central question, they argued, is not capitalism or socialism but *industrialism* in its diverse varieties. "What types of social structure are compatible with industrialization?" they asked. Who set the rules and how do they gain that power? What are the consequences of each of these social structures? And which are "transitory" and which will become stable and why?[40]

After rejecting the original request, the Ford Foundation approved a revised exploratory grant of $80,000 to Kerr, Dunlop, Charles Myers, and Frederick Harbison in 1952 to study labor problems in economic development outside the United States. Two years later, they received a $475,000 grant. At that point, they established the Inter-University Study on Labor Problems in Economic Development to sponsor research in Asia, the Middle East, Europe, Africa, and Latin America. During the following six years Kerr, Dunlop, Myers, and Harbison received $500,000 additional funding from the Ford and the Carnegie Foundations, or a total of $1,055,000—comparable to $9,328,000 today, the second-largest grant given to a social-science project in the country up to that time.

Will industrialism in one form or another succeed or will intense protests in some nations undermine the process in some countries? What factors "spell success or failure in getting over what they termed the 'radicalization hump'?" How will "rampant" nationalists such as Egypt's president Gamal Nasser and Communists such as Chairman Mao Zedong of China affect the process? How will relations between management, labor organizations, and governments evolve in the process? How important is university education for industrializing societies? These were among the questions addressed by Kerr, Dunlop, Myers, and Harbison and the professors and researchers whom they recruited in their twenty-year-long study.[41]

Kerr, Dunlop, Harbison, and Myers ultimately sponsored more than forty projects in thirty-five countries. Although top priority was given to research on India and the Middle East, particularly Iraq and Egypt, they also conducted or funded studies of Argentina, Brazil, Chile, Yugoslavia, Turkey, Indonesia, and sub-Saharan Africa. For comparison's sake, they also funded or conducted studies of advanced industrial nations—Japan, the Soviet Union, England, Germany, Poland, France, and Sweden. By the time it shut down in 1973, the Inter-University Study had funded work by ninety-five economists, sociologists, and political scientists. Although the majority of the research was conducted by faculty and staff at UC–Berkeley, Harvard, MIT, the University of Chicago, and Princeton, where the four principals were based, other projects were done by scholars at universities and research institutes in India, Beirut, Liverpool, Sweden, West Germany, France, Japan, Italy, and South Africa.[42]

Kerr, Dunlop, Myers, and Harbison wrote many articles and books themselves—some individually, some in pairs (Myers and Harbison focused on education and high-level manpower in India and Africa) and many as a foursome. They edited others. In addition, Kerr, Dunlop, Myers, and Harbison organized numerous international conferences on labor relations, human resources, and economic development around the world. Kerr, Dunlop, Harbison, and Myers were so enterprising that the Ford Foundation staff mischievously referred to them as the "famous Four Horsemen" who "knew no geographic bounds."[43]

Their work reached a fever pitch. Between December 21, 1958, and January 31, 1959, the four men, accompanied by the associate director of the Ford Foundation, Thomas Carroll, visited Rome, Athens, Istanbul, Beirut, Tehran, Karachi, Delhi, Calcutta, Jakarta, Singapore, Hong Kong, Tokyo, and Honolulu, concluding with a press conference at Kerr's ranch house in the Berkeley hills.[44] The five undertook the trip in preparation for the Inter-University Study's marquee book *Industrialism and Industrial Man: The Problems of Labor and Management in Economic Growth*, which was published by Harvard University Press in 1960. The book was subsequently translated and published in Persian, Arabic, Japanese, Dutch, Spanish, Italian, and German. They also produced abbreviated versions of their conclusions in articles for the *International Labour Review* and the *Harvard Business Review*.[45]

Among the most memorable were their trips to Eastern Europe and the four international conferences convened by Dunlop and noted Soviet economists that brought together economists from the United States, Western and Eastern Europe, and the Soviet Union between 1960 and the early 1970s. In the first week of September 1961, for example, John Dunlop and Professor Vasilii P. Diatchenko, who was vice chairman of the Presidium of the Association of Soviet Economic Scientific Institutions, chaired a conference in Lake Como, Italy, that assembled forty-two professors and others with equal numbers from the Soviet Union, Poland, East Germany, Czechoslovakia, Hungary, and Rumania on the one side, and the United States and Western Europe on the other, to discuss papers on measurement of productivity, international comparisons of productivity, wages and productivity, and technological, management, and organizational factors affecting productivity.[46] In September 1964, Kerr, Dunlop, and Walter Galenson met economists in Poland, Hungary, Czechoslovakia, and Yugoslavia. They were struck by the quality of the Communists' economists, their forthrightness in discussion, variation in situation of the Eastern European economies, and their common animosity toward Germany. Except for the Czechoslovaks and, to a lesser extent, the Hungarians, the economists in those nations seemed optimistic about the future but concerned about the U.S. intervention in Vietnam and quite apprehensive about the Republican Party's presidential candidate, Senator Barry Goldwater.[47]

In September 1966 almost forty economists, again equally divided between those from the Soviet Union and Eastern Europe and others from the United States and Western Europe, met for a week in Nice, France, to discuss modern trends in planning and markets under various economic systems.[48] These were among the first direct informal meetings among economists from the East and the West since the Russian Revolution. The meetings included highly eminent scholars, including Aubrey Silberston, the secretary-general of the Royal Economic Society, Alexander Nove of the University of Glasgow, Nobel Prize–winning Wassily Leontief, and the Soviet Academy of Economics chair of the Institute of Mathematical Economics, Nikolay P. Fedorenko, as well as Dunlop, Kerr, Harbison, and Myers. They met in the seminars, in the hallways, over drinks, and at dinners, with the aim of liberalizing the socialist economies and, implicitly, bridging the division between East and West.

As Kerr, Dunlop, Myers, and Harbison pursued these numerous projects, their perspective on labor and world affairs changed. Their research and interaction with trade unionists in the United States in the 1940s had convinced Kerr and his colleagues that, far from being radical as they imagined when they were young, workers and labor leaders were actually rather conservative. Workers romanticize the past and initially resist change. Over time, however, they accept the industrial order and seek gains within it. That had been the case in England and the United States, Kerr and his colleagues believed. Labor protests will be even less of a problem in the newly industrializing nations, the foursome were convinced.

Industrialization has become more "humanitarian" than it was in the era of Marx and Dickens, Kerr and his colleagues pointed out, and managers were now often professionally trained and taught how to cultivate a disciplined, productive labor force. "Today men know more about how to control protest," they argued. Worker protests lead management to institute more predictable and reasonable rules and regulations, checks and balances, and guarantees to workers. This led to "the 'constitutional' approach of authority over workers," a sort of balancing of forces in the economy and the society that Kerr termed "industrial pluralism." The proletariat is not revolutionary. Several years before Herbert Marcuse's 1964 treatise *One-Dimensional Man* excited New Left thinkers, Kerr and his colleagues were arguing that worker protests were "more the fruit of the past than the seeds of the future" and that worker protests "get organized, channeled, controlled."[49]

Like Lloyd Fisher, Kerr and his colleagues saw the managerial elite as the revolutionary force in industrializing societies. That had been true in later eighteenth-century England, just as it was in the mid- to late-nineteenth-century United States and Soviet Union between the world wars. They viewed the elites in the postcolonial India and in the People's Republic of China as the revolutionary force in those huge lands for the same reason. In each of these settings "the organization builder plays a crucial role," Kerr and his colleagues declared. It does not matter whether the builder is the owner of the business, a professionally trained manager, or a government official. In each instance, "the keystone is the arch of management." The "organization builder" sets the rules for the other members of management and the "tone of the organization." The Labor Board veterans considered management "a form of human capital . . . indispensable for successful industrial development."[50]

Kerr, Dunlop, Harbison, and Myers distinguished between five distinct "roads" to industrialism. The first was led by a "dynastic elite" drawn from the landed or commercial elites or, in some instances, a military caste (like the samurai in Japan), a religious hierarchy, a government bureau, or tribal chiefs. Their elites were held together by their commitment to the established order. There may be new people but the emphasis is on a "closed system in the aristocracy." The emphasis is on maintaining tradition, as in Saudi Arabia for decades. Members of these elites recognize the need for industry yet stress the essential element of the past during and despite change. Division often emerges in the dynastic elite. Industrialization will succeed "only if the 'realists' are dominant, strong, competent, and patriotic," Kerr and his colleagues argued. They pointed to Germany and Japan in the latter nineteenth and early twentieth centuries as exemplifying such realists.[51]

A second type of elite was the rising middle class, as epitomized in England and the United States during the Industrial Revolution. This sort of elite posited "progress" as the society's ideal. They did not assert a rigid ideology, tending instead to be pragmatic, but favored opportunity for the individual, laissez-faire government policy, and decentralization. This of course produced conflict, but rather than attempting revolution, the middle-class elite sought to obtain their objectives by degrees. There was no central planning under such leaders; rather, competition spurred growth. Under this system, new, "relatively classless" societies emerged, such as the United States, Canada, and New Zealand.[52]

The third type of elite has been led by revolutionary intellectuals who sweep away both the dynastic elite and the rising middle class. They claim to have a superior theory with a scientific understanding of history. They establish a monolithic, centralized state and attempt "a rapid forced march toward industrialism, and they mold education, art, literature and labor organizations to their single-minded purpose."[53] Although they were not specific, the authors were obviously thinking about Stalin and Mao.

The fourth and fifth kinds of elites were colonial administrators and nationalist leaders. The former may initiate industrialization in empires but are bound to fail, Kerr and his colleagues were convinced, for they place the interests of the imperial home over that of the colonies they rule. They are succeeded by military men, leaders of the independence movements, or younger local people sent abroad for education. "The members of this group are in a hurry—to deliver and deliver fast." They quote Gamal Abdel Nasser, who promised the people of Egypt "We shall march forward as one people who have vowed to proceed on a holy march of industrializing."[54]

The colonial elite are the most transient, Kerr and his colleagues wrote, shortly after the revolutionaries won independence for the Gold Coast in West Africa and named the free nation Ghana, or "Warrior King." Independence for Africans was imminent, led by nationalists or Communists. If dynastic elites prove ineffectual, they also will be succeeded by nationalists, revolutionary intellectuals, or communists. Even if dynastic elites govern well, Harbison and Myers reported, they will also change, as the hereditary elites recruit educated people from the lower ranks of society. No example was provided, but they appeared to have been thinking about the Shah of Iran, who oversaw a vigorous program of industrialization, but was subsequently overthrown in 1979 by Shiite radicals led by Ayatollah

Khomeini. The nationalist elites would inevitably change as well, for they had no clear economic agenda.

With colonial, dynastic, and nationalist elites each unstable, the world was virtually certain to transmute into either middle-class societies or ones led by communist revolutionaries. Yet these kinds of social systems will also change, Kerr, Dunlop, Harbison, and Myers predicted. Middle-class systems are stabler than any other, they believed, unconsciously describing themselves, "partly because the middle class is also the mediating class in society and makes its adjustments a little at a time rather than in dramatic bursts." Over time, businesses become larger, management separates from ownership, workers' organizations acquire influence, and the state assumes functions such as regulation of labor-management conflict, providing minimum levels of employment, assuring equality of treatment and opportunity. "The middle class still rules, but less obviously so; and the markets are still major instruments for making decisions, but they are no longer so open."[55]

The communist states will inevitably change, Kerr, Dunlop, and their colleagues predicted. National minorities will demand a voice in those states. The military and scientists in communist nations will make demands of the state. As workers acquire greater skills, they also will make demands of the state. Although none of these groups will aim for state power, they will come to share authority within their sphere as revolutionary fervor diminishes. Moreover, a new generation of leaders will take power, "more professional, more bureaucratic . . . further removed" from revolutionary aims and thought. They viewed reform-minded Communist Party leaders such as Nikita Khrushchev as transitional because revolutionary ideology lacked a program for an advanced industrial ideology. Rigid ideologically, such communists were not capable of handling diversified production rather than basic industries such as mining and steel manufacturing. "The wolves give way to the watchdogs," the Four Horsemen predicted. Communist systems represented a transitory stage in history, Kerr and his colleagues believed. "It is communism that withers away," they declared more than twenty years before Ronald Reagan made the same prediction to Prime Minister Margaret Thatcher and the the British Parliament in 1982.[56]

Kerr and his colleagues expected "pluralistic industrialism" to ultimately prevail throughout the world. Industrialism would replace agriculture as the "dominant mode of production." Authority would be "concentrated," but individuals would be free to choose their workplaces and an extraordinary diversity of goods to purchase. Contrary to Marx's prediction that workers would become unskilled, skill levels would increase. The managed would have to cooperate with managers. Higher education would be widespread, research increasingly significant. Industry would come to resemble the university, with responsible, independent faculty. Professional groups would acquire higher prestige, and a "new equality" would emerge as nearly all are well educated. This in turn would foster "consensus in society." Harsh exercise of state power would no longer be needed to hold societies in balance. On the contrary, education would lead to more demands for liberty, and as the educated compare their nation to others, progress would proceed across the world. Kerr and his colleagues expected the state to become more, not less, powerful, with responsibility to maintain a steadily increasing rate of growth and provisions for public health, transportation, and recreation. As citizens would become more educated and enjoy greater leisure, the state would become responsible for ensuring an attractive physical environment. The state would be the largest employer in society. The state would itself not, however, be fully unified. There would be checks and balances, including means to ensure public approval of state policies. "This is industrialism at work, centralizing and decentralizing at the same time; creating areas of control and areas of freedom."

As for labor, they predicted that workers would be increasingly mobile, and paternalistic factory management would fade away. People would identify more with their occupations, particularly if it required strict training to enter. Occupational and professional associations would negotiate with the enterprises and the state. Virtually all members of society would belong to such associations, which would ensure efficiency, access to positions, "comparable incomes," and codes of ethics. The associations would penetrate the government regulatory agencies. Groups would "jockey over the placement of individuals, the setting of jurisdictions, and the level of decision-making. Although classes will weaken, organized occupational groups will continue to dispute with each other." They foresaw "the forming of alliances, the establishment of formulas, the half-evident withdrawal of support and of effort, the use of precedents and arguments and statistics," as they saw in their own universities. "Persuasion, pressure, and manipulation will take the place of the face-to-face combat of an earlier age. . . . It will be less between the broad program of capital and labor, and of agricultural and industry; and more over budgets, rates of compensation, work norms, job assignments," they declared. There would no longer be great conflicts in societies. Instead, there would be innumerable disputes over relatively insignificant matters. In their most memorable words, the Four Horsemen declared, "Class warfare will be forgotten and in its place will be bureaucratic contest of interest group against interest group. The battles will be in the corridors instead of the streets, and memos will flow instead of blood."[57]

Like Marx and Engels in 1848 and Francis Fukuyama in 1989, Kerr, Dunlop, Myers, and Harbison envisioned one end for humanity. They foresaw "pluralistic industrialism" around the globe from the United States to Brazil, Russia, China, India, and Africa. They were more specific than Marx and Engels in their description of that world. Kerr and his colleagues foresaw a rate of technological change so rapid, or a single innovation so dramatic, that we "may make such a quantum jump that the whole industrialization process will be altered." They imagined professional management and the spread of higher education in all societies. They also predicted a workforce "dedicated to hard work, a high pace of work and a keen sense of individual responsibility for performance of assigned norms and tasks."[58] In exchange for the hard work, humans in the future will enjoy a higher standard of living, more leisure, and more education. "This will be the happy hunting ground for the independent spirit. Along with the bureaucratic conservatism of economic and political life may well go a New Bohemianism in other aspects of life," the Four Horsemen calmly prophesied, not imagining the chaos that would erupt at their universities soon afterward.[59]

From one angle we could see Kerr, Dunlop, and their colleagues as simply ethnocentric, projecting the late 1950s United States—specifically Berkeley, Cambridge, and Princeton—onto the rest of the world. From another perspective, the Four Horsemen were following Marx's prediction that the most advanced capitalist nation provides the template for the others, yet, like Marxists, they greatly underestimated the power of religion and nationalism in industrializing nations.

"The age of utopias is past," Kerr, Dunlop, Myers, and Harbison declared, to be succeeded by an "age of realism" in which no one can expect perfection.[60] At a time when such popular futurist novels as Ray Bradbury's *The Martian Chronicles* (1950), Neil Shute's *On the Beach* (1957), Eugene Burdick and Harvey Wheeler's *Fail-Safe* (1962), and Robert Heinlein's *Farnham's Freehold* (1964) depicted nuclear holocaust and a post-apocalyptic world, Kerr, Dunlop, and their colleagues were meeting with their Soviet counterparts, discussing how to increase productivity in industries, and downplaying differences between the socialist and capitalist systems. They foresaw convergence, all societies moving toward the same end. "The industrial society knows no national boundaries; it is destined to be a worldwide society," they declared in 1960.[61]

Seemingly far-fetched when first advanced, their prediction briefly appeared close to realization in the latter 1980s, when Deng Xiaoping assumed power and Ronald Reagan and Mikhail Gorbachev met in Reykjavik to negotiate a treaty to abolish nuclear weapons. Although those plans were not fulfilled, by 2000 tens of millions of young women and men were leaving their peasant families in rural Chinese provinces for new lives and opportunities in cities. Chinese professionals flocked into McDonald's and Starbuck's in Shanghai, Beijing, and other cities. The managers of state-owned factories in the People's Republic laid off millions of industrial workers. Labor unions waned not only in the United States but also in Western Europe, and professional employees no longer could look toward lifetime careers at one firm. Thus Kerr, Dunlop, Myers, and Harbison's vision of the future outside the United States appears farsighted, even as they failed to understand what was happening to labor and management in their own country.

5

War and Peace in Steel, 1959–72

> Some conflicts, even bitter ones, have contrib-
> uted materially to industrial peace and efficiency.
> —John T. Dunlop

IN SPRING 1959, SYLVESTER GARRETT prepared drafts for his rulings on four grievances filed by the United Steelworkers of America Local 4889 against the management of U.S. Steel's Fairless Works, a finishing facility near Philadelphia (see figure 8). Employees at that mill turned cold-rolled steel produced in U.S. Steel's Clairton, Irwin, and Edgar Thomson works into galvanized sheets, which were in turn sold to appliance and auto manufacturers and construction contractors. The management reduced the number of employees in work crews at the facility in 1957 and, when the 1958 recession ended, they rehired fewer workers than had been employed there at the time of the layoffs. The practice was occurring not only at the Fairless Works, but throughout U.S. Steel, at other steel companies, and in other industries in the late 1950s, and the number of grievance cases filed by workers rose rapidly.

Garrett was tentatively planning to accept the union's argument in the case filed by chemical technicians who had been forced to perform duties of test preparers in addition to regular work. He intended to reject grievance in a second case in which the management had removed one of the four pump tenders. He planned to tell the union and management officials to reconsider the other two grievance cases about lubrication system tenders and workers in the billet yard of the Rolling Division on the basis of his analysis of the first two disputes.[1]

He gave one copy of his drafts to Ben Fischer, the Steelworkers' principal specialist in grievance cases and aide to the union's president. He gave the other

FIGURE 8. Sylvester Garrett, chief arbitrator, U.S. Steel and United Steelworkers of America, 1960s. Photo by Ted Russell/The LIFE Images Collection via Getty Images.

copy to Warren Shaver, U.S. Steel's vice president for labor relations. Garrett asked Fischer and Shaver to look over the drafts. Did either of them have problems with his findings? His explanations? Specific points or terminology? Garrett had followed this procedure since 1952, when he was first chosen as the principal arbitrator in grievance cases for U.S. Steel and the steelworkers. He had been following his mentor, George Taylor, who used the same approach in the Philadelphia silk hosiery and garment factories in the 1930s.

The technique helped resolve many of the problems that bedeviled relations between the Steelworkers and U.S. Steel since the Fair Day's Work Program was first introduced in April 1947. By 1957 the number of grievance cases on his docket had dropped by 90 percent and relations between Shaver, Fischer, and Garrett had become quite amicable.

It was different this time. Rather than questioning Garrett's reasoning or challenging his conclusions, as he had done at various times in the past, Shaver brought the drafts to his boss, R. Conrad Cooper, U.S. Steel's executive vice president for personnel relations. Cooper decided to use Garrett's preliminary rulings to drum up support among the major U.S. steel manufacturers in a campaign to eliminate what they called featherbedding. The result was a 116-day long strike—the biggest strike ever in U.S. history and one of the most consequential.

Although labor historians, other labor specialists, and elderly residents of Hometown, Braddock, Johnstown, Gary, and other steel towns are familiar with the momentous 1959 steel strike, many don't realize that it was prompted by the management's reaction to an arbitrator's decision. Even fewer recognize that the strike was resolved, in part, by another arbitrator, George Taylor. Nor that John Dunlop, James Healey, Charles Myers, and other Labor Board vets responded to the strike by proposing a plan to restructure the industrial relations in the steel industry to prevent epic industrial actions in the future and protect the union. Or that Garrett, Taylor, David Cole, and several other Labor Board vets worked for the next dozen years to help build tighter bonds of cooperation between the Steelworkers' union leaders and steel management than had existed before 1959. Or, finally, that the agreements encouraged by the Labor Board vets ultimately weakened the steel companies, the Steelworkers union, union members, and their communities.

* * *

As explained in chapter 3, relations between the steel companies and the Steelworkers had become more amicable by the mid-1950s. Beneath the surface, however, pressures were mounting that threatened that harmony. The source was not the union officials, who achieved their principal objectives during the decade after the war: significant wage increases for the members, noncontributory pensions, paid vacations, time-and-a-half for overtime, time-and-a-quarter for Sunday work, cost-of-living protection against inflation, mandatory union membership, and dues automatically deducted from paychecks. By the mid-1950s, the union leadership had become satisfied, indeed, overly content. Nor were challenges emerging from the union's members or unionized workers generally who—with one important exception, African-American workers—had also become fairly contented, did not expect much more from the union, and feared any more strikes.[2]

Rather, demands for change came from corporate headquarters. Labor costs increased more rapidly than consumer prices in the decade-and-a-half after the war ended, especially in industries in which unions were solidly established. Between 1945 and 1959, average hourly wages rose more than 200 percent in auto manufacturing and the building trades. In steel production, blast furnaces, coal mining, and railroad transport they rose 260 percent.[3] Employers not subject to foreign competition—for example, building contractors—could usually absorb such increases, but it was harder for auto manufacturers and other companies facing foreign competition as European manufacturing revived in the mid- to late 1950s. The U.S. share of world exports fell by almost one-fifth between 1953 and 1959.

Consequently, corporate profits lagged. "There is no doubt that since 1956 corporate profits after taxes have behaved badly—as a rate of return on net worth or on sales, as an absolute amount, or as a share of national income," George Hildebrand, professor of economics and industrial relations at Cornell University and former wage stabilization director of the RWLB in Denver, remarked in 1963. "Our economy is in serious economic difficulties for which there is no easy answer," Hildebrand declared.[4]

These problems were particularly acute in the steel industry. Incorporated at the beginning of the twentieth century, U.S. Steel, Bethlehem Steel, and Republic Steel continued to burn pig iron in open-hearth furnaces as late as 1965 rather than investing in the far more efficient basic oxygen furnaces, as Japanese and West German steelmakers had done after the war with U.S. aid from the Marshall Plan. As wages and benefits for U.S. steelworkers rose, foreign steel manufacturers were able to undercut domestic manufacturers. Imports of steel to the United States began to exceed exports by the end of the 1950s. In addition, the steel manufacturers' major customers—the auto and can manufacturers and major construction contractors, began to use aluminum, copper, reinforced concrete, fiberglass, plastic, and even wood in their products. With labor costs and competition increasing, the steel companies' after-tax profit rates fell from an average of 12.5 percent of stockholders' equity between 1955 and 1957 to 7.2 percent in 1958 and 8 percent in 1959. Moreover, although the public and union members could not believe it was true, the largest steel manufacturers—U.S. Steel, Bethlehem Steel, and Republic Steel—were the *least* profitable in the industry. Indeed, steel was less profitable than other U.S. manufacturing industries.[5]

Political factors also motivated top management. Liberal Democrats triumphed in the congressional and gubernatorial elections in November 1958. The AFL-CIO's Committee on Political Education had targeted sixteen U.S. senators for defeat that year; nine of them lost and two others chose not to run again. The incoming U.S. Congress will be "much more Democratic than the last ... [and] much more beholden to the power of labor," James Reston of the *New York Times* predicted the day after the election. Since Dwight Eisenhower could not run for a third term, corporate executives feared that a pro-labor Democrat would capture the White House in 1960. Yet the unions' leaders were on shaky grounds too, for conservative newspaper commentators and televised hearings of Alabama Senator John McClellan's Select Committee on Improper Activities in Labor and Management had exposed mob influence in the Teamsters, the International Longshoremen's Association, and a half-dozen other unions in 1957, 1958, and 1959, with impacts not only on those unions but on the reputation of organized labor in general.[6]

During the mid- to late 1950s, older corporate presidents and board chairmen such as Benjamin Fairless at U.S. Steel who had made accommodations with unions retired. The boards of directors of many major firms appointed younger, more pugnacious chief executives such as Roger Blough, who undertook a vigorous effort to convince Congress, the press, and the public that wage increases and federal support of unions were the cause of consumer inflation. Inspired by General Electric (G.E.) vice president Lemuel Boulware, the new executives recruited new vice presidents to devise new strategies to defeat unions. In addition, corporations lobbied Congress and state legislatures for bills to outlaw the union shop and organizational picketing and outlaw unions from donating to political campaigns. They developed programs in more than 125 communities to establish a better business climate—that is, one more receptive to the investment and less friendly to unions.[7]

Nineteen fifty-nine "was a rough strike year, the worst strike year since the all-time high in 1946," a prominent San Francisco business executive remarked in May 1960. Although there were no more strikes in 1959 than the three preceding years, strikes that were called lasted on average three times as long. Unions struck the big farm-equipment manufacturers—Caterpillar Tractor Company, International Harvester, and Deere Manufacturing; three of the four large tire manufacturers—B. F. Goodrich, U.S. Rubber, and Firestone; two of the four major meatpackers—Swift & Company and Wilson & Company; the three major copper-mining firms—Phelps Dodge, Anaconda, and Kennecott; and also General Electric, Bell Telephone, the Pennsylvania Railroad, Pratt & Whitney Aircraft, Allis-Chalmers Manufacturing, the major elevator manufacturers, the Hollywood film studios, and coal operators in Kentucky. In addition, unions struck the Atlantic and Gulf Coast docks, Bethlehem Steel's shipyards, Standard Oil of Indiana's refineries, and Pittsburgh Plate Glass. If that were not enough, aircraft workers walked out at Eastern Airlines, American Airlines, Trans World Airlines, Northwestern Airlines, and Capitol Airlines terminals on Thanksgiving weekend and on Christmas weekend, the airlines' most profitable dates. "Bargaining is still a very grim, relentless, difficult operation. . . . Everybody is outraged. . . . Everybody is indignant," David Cole remarked in May 1960.[8]

The steel strike was the most significant of all. As A. H. Raskin, the *New York Times* labor reporter, wrote at that time, the steel manufacturers became "the ball carrier for major sections of management in a general fight to get rid of alleged 'featherbedding' and other forms of manpower waste . . . [and] recapture the upper hand in bargaining."[9] Total employment costs per man-hour at U.S. Steel rose an average of 8.1 percent every year between 1940 and 1956 while shipments of steel rose at the rate of 2.7 percent per year compounded annually, declared Conrad Cooper, the corporation's executive vice president, in a meeting of the Society for Advancement of Management's Pittsburgh chapter in 1958. "Simple division tells us that employment cost per man-hour rose three times as fast as did product output per man-hour. It also tells us that employment costs per unit of product rose slightly more than five per cent per year compounded annually. In other words, employment cost per unit of product rose more than five per cent each year for 16 years. These are the facts," Cooper maintained. "These trends have to be stopped."[10] "It is time to call a halt to 20 years of inflationary excesses that have placed the steel industry under a serious competitive handicap," Cooper declared during the 1959 strike. A year later, he told a House of Representatives labor subcommittee that the union "is the moving force toward pricing steel workers in this country out of their jobs."[11]

In the past, the steel manufacturing corporations had preferred to bargain separately, while the Steelworkers' leaders pressed for industrywide bargaining. In 1959 the companies reversed course, forming the Steel Companies Coordinating Committee to negotiate with the union. The committee consisted of presidents and executive vice presidents of U.S. Steel, Bethlehem Steel, Republic Steel, Jones & Laughlin Steel, Inland Steel, Youngstown Sheet and Tube, Armco Steel, Great Lakes Steel, Kaiser Steel, the Colorado Fuel and Iron Corporation, Wheeling Steel, and Ludlum Steel. Those twelve corporations produced 87 percent of the steel produced in the United States in the 1950s, with U.S. Steel alone producing approximately 40 percent of the industry's total. Conrad Cooper chaired the Coordinating Committee's four-member negotiating team.

The steel executives were in a stronger position than the union in 1959, for employment in the industry had been falling for eight years, except for nonunion supervisors, whose numbers climbed. The recession in 1957–58 hit the industry particularly hard, with two hundred thousand steelworkers out of work and three hundred thousand others on short hours.[12] Even workers with high seniority were laid off for four, five, even six months, and unemployment soared in black neighborhoods of Chicago, Gary, Pittsburgh, and Birmingham. While business improved in early 1959, the union members' top priority in the 1959 negotiations remained job security, not wage increases, while the companies were incensed about having to raise wages in 1958 in accordance with the contract despite the slump.

If the steel executives had demanded only concessions on wages or on fringe benefits—the Steelworkers' leaders almost surely would have found a face-saving way to meet their terms or would have concluded the strike after gaining little. According to polls, a majority of the union's members were opposed to striking again, convinced that increases gained through strikes were wiped out by consumer price increases. After four nationwide steel strikes since 1946, the Steelworkers' president David McDonald also did not want to call another one.[13]

All that changed in the first week of June when Sylvester Garrett informed Warren Shaver and Ben Fischer that he was going to rule against the management's free hand in the crew-size grievance cases.[14] Up to that point, the management committee had refused to consider wage increases. Now Cooper changed tactics. If the union would accept new language in Section 2-B—specifically, "Nothing in this contract shall prevent management from improving the operating efficiency of its plants," the Steel Companies Coordinating Committee was willing to concede modest increases in incentives and hourly wages.

Section 2-B originated back in 1947. Although the evidence is not absolutely clear, the clause apparently was drafted by Lee Pressman, general counsel for the CIO and the Steelworkers from their founding until he was dismissed by Philip Murray for backing Henry Wallace and the Progressive Party in the 1948 presidential campaign. The companies' negotiators hadn't imagined the clause would constrain managers in the mills. On the contrary, the fourth subsection of Section 2-B expressly declared that "The Company shall have the right to change or eliminate any local working condition if, as the result of action taken by Management . . ., the basis for the existence of the local working conditions is changed or eliminated."[15] Cooper, who was vice president for engineering at U.S. Steel at that time, later insisted that Section 2-B "had no bearing on Management actions to change crew size, spell time, and workloads."[16]

The third subsection of Section 2-B, however, stipulated that "Should there be any local conditions in effect which provide benefits that are in excess of or in addition to the benefits established by this Agreement, they shall remain in effect for the term of this Agreement, except as they are changed or eliminated by mutual agreement." Moreover, the fourth subsection specified "that when . . . a change or elimination is made by the Company any affected employee shall have recourse to the grievance procedure and arbitration."[17]

Unlike automobiles, rubber tire, and other industries, steel was not produced on assembly lines or through other continuous processes. Instead, employees in steel mills were organized into crews and, as Sylvester Garrett remarked in a conversation with Ralph Seward, the former arbitrator for Bethlehem Steel, "men can't work together continually without a sort of rules and habits developing." Those practices were learned on the job, from others already in the mills. They had informal histories and, as Garrett put it to Seward, "they were part of the job. They were part of the way men worked. And they were a terrific psychological importance to the employees. . . . They had economic importance and security importance, but they were part of what the men understood by their working conditions."[18]

The arbitrators whom the steel corporations and United Steelworkers hired to resolve grievances interpreted the "local working conditions" clause in Section 2-B-3 in the 1947 U.S. Steel-Steelworkers contract liberally. They were born and raised in the Progressive era, often in Progressive families, and graduated from liberal colleges such as Swarthmore. Like Louis Brandeis, who considered the U.S. Constitution as a "living document" that must be understood in light of the current day, the Labor Board vets interpreted the union-management contracts as dynamic. In their minds, the phrase "local working conditions" referred to the size of work crews, assignments of duties, workloads, overtime and seniority procedures, paid lunch periods, contracting out of work, and virtually all other aspects of work. Saul Wallen, chairman of Regional War Labor Board I in Boston during the war and a noted professional arbitrator in Boston afterward, considered working conditions in existence before a contract was signed as a "silent document" that remained in effect unless explicitly outlawed.[19] "I think management has some rights . . . [but] if there is a [existing] plant practice or a variety of other circumstances, I cannot agree with a principle that [it] always be stated in the agreement," Simkin remarked in conversations with Garrett.[20]

In the opinion of Saul Wallen, Bill Simkin, and other top labor-management arbitrators, Garrett was on solid ground in his reading of the U.S. Steel-Steelworkers contract. Section 2-B explicitly prohibited any change in existing working conditions unless the management introduced new machinery or the union approved. An engineer's time-and-motion study showing that certain employees were unnecessary or that cutbacks would make the plant more competitive did not necessarily justify a reduction in the size of work crews or new work assignments in the arbitrators' minds. After the Fair Day's Work Program was instituted in 1947, union members filed thousands of grievances to preserve existing working conditions. If the cases went to arbitration, Garrett and the other Labor Board vets frequently ruled in favor of the union. Alternatively, they would send the grievance back to the management and union officers to reconsider, as Garrett did in two of the Section 2-B grievance cases in spring 1959. As historian James Rose observed, "The quickest and cheapest method management had used for reducing labor costs—cutting jobs without changing production methods or technology—was no longer available."[21] Section 2-B became the steelworkers' trump card.

When Conrad Cooper learned that Garrett would not give the management complete freedom to reduce crew sizes, he decided to go all out. His determination was not surprising. Born in Beaver Dam, Kentucky, in 1902, fifth son of eight children of a coal miner who operated a small colliery, Cooper was four years old when the family moved to South Dakota, making part of the trip in a covered wagon. The family lived in a sod house; his father was a cattle rancher. Self-supporting from the age of fourteen, Cooper became the star center at the University of Minnesota's football team, a team that stopped Red Grange, the legendary running back for the University of Illinois's Fighting Illini and later the Chicago Bears. He was also the university's heavyweight boxing champion, rode broncos in rodeos, and considered becoming a professional in the National Football League or going into the ring before finally becoming an engineer at the Charles E. Bedaux Company (1929–37), Wheeling Steel (1937–45), and U.S. Steel (1945–68).

Cooper's team had blocked Red Grange. How could they not stop David Mc-Donald and the Steelworkers? Contemporaries described Conrad Cooper as intelligent, poised, handsome, inflexible, and extremely determined. "Extremely competent if you can stand that kind of completely ordered mind," Seward remarked. "A very tough character. . . . Coop never gave up," recalled Garrett. "He was not a compromiser; everything was black and white for him," commented R. Heath Larry, Cooper's successor as U.S. Steel's vice president for personnel services, who had a wilier style.[22]

U.S. Steel's management had tried to wash their hands of Section 2-B in 1952. But because the United States was at war in Korea, they had to present their case to the National Wage Stabilization Board. In his testimony, Cooper argued that if Section 2-B were not eliminated, "featherbedding practices of untold magnitude . . . [would] shut off major sources of improved productivity." Wilbur Lohrentz, an attorney on the staff of U.S. Steel's vice president John Stephens, claimed that Section 2-B fostered a "restrictive, technical, legalistic attitude that led to a complete dehydration of labor relations, a paralysis of 'precedents' and steel plants full of 'sea lawyers.'" These arguments failed to convince the Wage Stabilization Board, whose members—Nathan Feinsinger, Harry Shulman, John Dunlop, Clark Kerr, and George Taylor—were all Labor Board veterans.[23]

Nineteen fifty-nine would be different, the steel management felt sure. They knew their demand that the union surrender Section 2-B would provoke a strike but figured the union would concede within two months. The Steelworkers had no strike fund, many of the union's members were still in debt from the previous year's layoffs, they were anxious about the future, and David McDonald, the union's president, was unpopular. He almost lost the 1956 election to a little-known rank-and-filer named Donald Rarick after McDonald raised union dues. Only once had any steel strikes lasted more than seven and a half weeks. That was the 1919 strike, a total rout for the workers, as the older men knew.[24]

At 12:01 a.m., July 15, 1959, half a million members of the United Steelworkers of America went on strike, shutting down nearly all steel mills in the United

States and Canada. It was the fifth industrywide steel strike since 1946 and was more brutal than the others. It lasted far longer, 116 days, for the management and union were fighting over a principle that they both considered crucial, and not, as in the other postwar strikes, over wages or other forms of compensation that were more open to compromise. "Each side in steel is almost fanatically convinced of the moral rightness of its own position," A. H. Raskin of the *New York Times* commented. Finally, like Carnegie Steel's lockout of the Amalgamated Association of Iron and Steel Workers in Homestead, Pennsylvania, in 1892 and the great 1919 steel strike, the 1959 steel strike represented more than a conflict in that single industry. "The steel companies and the United Steelworkers of America have become standard-bearers of what amounts to class warfare, low voltage, non-violent, but none the less destructive for industrial democracy and an economy calculated to serve the consuming public, as well as its dominant power blocs," Raskin remarked on November 29.[25]

Although Cooper was sure that the union would concede, he was wide off the mark. The attack on Section 2-B galvanized the previously disaffected, sluggish union. As Jack Metzger explained in *Striking Steel*, his moving recollection on his father, a union griever at the Bethlehem's Johnstown, Pennsylvania, works, "Cooper's strategy—a long strike focused on work rules—had mistakenly tapped into the Steelworkers' strength in 1959. Work rules were something about which rank-and-file workers tended to be inflexible. To effectively fight back the company's demands required a sturdy conservatism rather than a utopian idealism. And even the psychological dynamics of a long strike played into the 'I don't eat shit for nobody' machismo of workers with more than two decades of unionism under their belts."[26]

The strikers remained out through July, August, September, October, and early November, surviving on whatever savings they had, vegetables from their gardens, donations from family, cereal and other food distributed by the union locals and churches, odd jobs, and contributions from the International Ladies' Garment Workers and the United Auto Workers. Locally owned banks were loath to insist on mortgage repayments, local storekeepers were often willing to extend credit, and, since the union had pull in Harrisburg, Columbus, Springfield, and other state capitals, many strikers received unemployment checks or other welfare aid.

In late October, General Motors had to shut down assembly lines, harming their suppliers, dealers, and employees. Construction halted on the St. Lawrence Seaway and Manhattan skyscrapers, and the U.S. Army quartermaster was sending urgent messages to the Defense Department. As other manufacturers ran short of steel, the national unemployment rate rose.

In early November, the Justice Department obtained a Taft-Hartley injunction for an eighty-day cooling-off period, despite the union's appeals all the way to the

U.S. Supreme Court. The workers returned to work on November 7. Yet the court injunction could not defeat the union, for the workers were clearly willing to walk out again after eighty days passed. In fact, the injunction strengthened the union by riling up the members and allowing them to stock up food. With congressional and presidential elections less than a year away, the Eisenhower administration could not appear to be siding with steel companies. With the president's approval, Vice President Nixon leaned on U.S. Steel's Roger Blough to settle. Warned that "people of the country will not tolerate another massive struggle of this type in the steel industry" and that the overwhelmingly Democratic Congress would pass legislation requiring compulsory arbitration and government wage-fixing if the strike resumed, the steel companies conceded. The contract they signed on January 5, 1960, included a 41-cent-per-hour wage and benefits increase over thirty months, life and health insurance entirely paid by the companies, and substantial improvement in pensions for retirees. Section 2-B stayed in the contract.[27]

* * *

By the time the strike ended, the majority of Americans had become annoyed by all the antagonists, especially the unions. What does collective bargaining produce, many asked, other than heated speeches, wage-driven inflation, and stoppages that prevented other Americans from making their living? "We are only the sheep that go to the shearing yet the Legislature has left us without a shepherd," moaned one Los Angelena in February 1960 after a strike stopped the city's pitiable public-transport system. *New York Times* columnist Arthur Krock dismissed Eisenhower's call for regular meetings between labor and management outside the bargaining table, saying it would "leave totally undisturbed the legalized power of a nation-wide union to paralyze the economy indefinitely."[28]

The Labor Board vets firmly disagreed. The beauty of the American system of industrial relations, in their opinion, was its heterogeneity. Each industry, each company, and each union was distinctive. Each required different arrangements, as was appropriate for the vast size of the continent and the diversity of its industries. Each contract reflected the union and employer's distinctive characters. The various proposals raised in the press and the Congress, such as a ban on industry-wide bargaining, an extension of antitrust laws to cover unions, labor courts, or new federal or state labor legislation would make matters worse, as Taft-Hartley injunctions demonstrated, in the opinion of George Taylor and John Dunlop.

Yet it did not make sense, they agreed, for companies and unions to negotiate contracts every third year, meeting round-the-clock as the contract deadlines approached, and at the end sign contracts that were certain to include inconsistent provisions. Something had to be done to protect the collective-bargaining system, they knew.[29]

As so often before, George Taylor pointed the way forward. In early July 1959, a week before the steel strike began, Taylor gave an interview to *U.S. News and World Report*, a business-friendly weekly. "Is there any practical way to avoid big strikes that threaten the country with a national emergency?" the reporter asked. At that time, the sole method available under federal law was for the president to appoint a board of inquiry, and, if it reported that the strike would cause a national emergency, have the attorney general obtain a Taft-Hartley injunction to stop the strike for eighty days. But that course of action merely angered unions without assuring settlements.

Taylor proposed an alternative: use arbitration to resolve contract disputes, much like the grievance procedure. "I think that, if parties to a dispute negotiate for a long period and still do not settle the issues between them, then there is an obligation on the two parties to agree between themselves to set up an arbitration board," he told the reporter. Back in the 1920s, when he was hired to umpire grievances for the Full-Fashioned Hosiery Workers of America and the Hosiery Manufacturers Association in Philadelphia, few believed that arbitrators could settle grievances, he said. Yet by the end of the Second World War, arbitration of unsettled grievances had become the norm in America.

Why not adopt the same approach for contract disputes in steel and other fractious industries? "A procedure of this kind would be democratic so long as the parties themselves specify the issues to be settled and accept the procedure for settling those issues," Taylor declared. Voluntary arbitration of unresolved contractual differences was long overdue, he suggested. "The serious thing that is happening in this country, I feel, is the loss of public confidence in what I call decentralized, private decision making in private industry in labor disputes and price determination. . . . It is time to be socially inventive."[30]

U.S. News waited until mid-October to publish its interview with Taylor. A week earlier, October 9, 1959, Dwight Eisenhower asked Taylor to chair a three-member board of inquiry into the causes of the strike. Taylor accepted on the condition that he be allowed to mediate, not merely conduct an inquiry. Taylor and the other mediators met with the union officials and corporate executives for six days to no avail. "The board cannot point to any single issue of any consequence whatsoever upon which the parties are in agreement," they informed the president. The Justice Department proceeded to obtain a court injunction to stop the strike.[31]

The board of inquiry nonetheless opened the way for new forms of cooperation in the steel industry, for one of the twelve integrated steel companies—Kaiser Steel—responded positively to Taylor's suggestions that the management and union set up committees consisting of representatives of labor, management, and the public to devise plans to prevent future strikes: in other words, create modern equivalents of the National War Labor Board for their industry.[32]

Kaiser Steel was unique among America's twelve integrated steel manufacturers. It was much more up to date than the others, having been established by Henry Kaiser, father of the current chairman Edgar Kaiser, during the Second World War to produce steel for vessels built in Kaiser's shipyards. It was relatively small, producing 2 percent of the nation's steel in its one mill in Fontana, California, forty-five miles east of Los Angeles. Ranked ninth among America's steel companies, the firm had 7,500 employees, employees who were, on average, younger than those in the steel mills in the Midwest and the East, and fewer of their employees were on incentive pay than at the older steel companies. Kaiser Steel was geographically isolated (there was no other basic steel mill west of the Mississippi). Their factory complex was more modern than the others. Kaiser possessed its own coal and limestone mines and also an iron mill, so they could resist pressures from U.S. Steel, which owned the bulk of the nation's iron ore mines. There were fewer long-established work rules at the Fontana mill and, unlike U.S. Steel, Republic Steel, and Bethlehem Steel, they didn't have a decades-long history of animosity and strike breaking. In fact, some of the activists who led the Dues Protest movement in Pennsylvania against David McDonald in 1957 quit their jobs afterward to go to work at Kaiser Steel. Finally, unlike the eastern companies, Kaiser Steel produced aluminum, making it more vulnerable to pressure from the Steelworkers union, which also bargained with Alcoa. These factors, plus the Kaiser family's liberal perspectives, enabled Taylor to pry the company off the Steel Companies Coordinating Committee.[33]

On October 26, 1959, Edgar Kaiser and Steelworkers president David McDonald announced that they had signed a two-year contract. Under the contract, the management agreed to increase wages and fringe benefits for its blue-collar employees by 22½ cents per hour over the next eighteen months, to meet with the union local's representative to discuss changes in work rules, and to establish a tripartite "Long-Range Planning Committee" to develop a formula for "'equitable sharing' of the fruits of industrial progress." This committee would consist of Edgar Kaiser and two Kaiser Steel vice presidents; David McDonald; the Steelworkers general counsel Arthur Goldberg; the union's West Coast district director; and George Taylor, John Dunlop, and David Cole, much like the National War Labor Board. Taylor was named chairman of the committee. The Long-Range Planning Committee would not handle individual workers' grievances. Kaiser Steel and the steelworkers already had an arbitrator. Rather, it would develop a plan to prevent future strikes. "I think the industry must take a step to solve what is going on. The country cannot stand this continual period—[where] we run up to a deadline and then we have a strike," Edgar Kaiser declared on NBC's *Meet the Press* television show on Sunday, November 1.

The nine-member tripartite committee began work on March 9, 1960, with lunch and a meeting at Kaiser Steel's office in Manhattan. They discussed how they could develop a long-range plan for equitable sharing of the fruits of industry and how the workers at Kaiser Steel could be as well informed as the members of the board of directors about the company's costs, prices, and other information. They also discussed revising the grievance procedure, changing the incentive system in light of the new technology, and establishing better communications between workers and management.[34]

Taylor, Goldberg, and McDonald saw the Kaiser Plan as a model for the entire industry. But CEOs at the other steel corporations were not persuaded. They had older workforces and higher labor costs. Having seen Garrett rule against U.S. Steel in the Section 2-B arbitration cases, they were unwilling to cede further authority to Labor Board vets. "The steel firms are old hands at checking bad decisions of such people," *Iron Age* commented. "They didn't trust arbitrators and they got stuck in that groove and they wanted to stay [that way]," Garrett later remarked.[35]

Yet the management at U.S. Steel, Bethlehem, and the others major producers could not continue unchanged. They took a beating during the strike. The management's strategy was predicated on the assumption that the market for their product was guaranteed. They were wrong, for foreign steel manufacturers and domestic producers of alternative material were beginning to capture segments of the market. Moreover, corporate profits in steel were even lower in 1960 than before the strike. They remained low for the next three years. By the first week of January 1961, the U.S. steel industry was operating at merely 38.6 percent of its capacity, the lowest level since the 1930s except during strikes. The Steelworkers' top officials also were worried. Although the union won the strike, its funds were depleted and the membership had shrunk after layoffs began in spring 1960.

Neither the union nor the management could afford another fight like the one they waged in '59, "one of the most costly ventures of any labor union," as I. W. Abel, the Steelworkers' secretary-treasurer, remarked. They had to develop a system "in which the parties could seek to solve problems, rather than seek to announce and defend positions or 'clobber the opponent,'" U.S. Steel's vice president R. Heath Larry remarked in September 1963.[36]

As a result, although Conrad Cooper and the other steel executives rejected the Kaiser Plan, they were willing to cooperate with the union's leaders in developing a system for larger steel companies similar to Kaiser's. The contract that the union's and corporations' executives signed on January 4, 1960, included a pledge to set up the Human Relations Research Committee to "plan and oversee studies and recommend solutions of mutual problems." According to the contract, the Human Relations Research Committee would be chaired by two persons of "outstanding qualifications and objectivity," one chosen by the union, the other by the corporations. The companies and union also pledged to create a committee on local working conditions with a neutral chairman, which would make recommendations by November 30, 1960.[37]

Although the Local Working Conditions Committee dissolved after a few meetings, the Human Relations Research Committee carried on.[38] It consisted of two executives from U.S. Steel, one each from Bethlehem and Republic Steel, Steelworkers' top three elected officials, and the union's general counselor Arthur Goldberg. When Goldberg was chosen by president-elect John F. Kennedy as secretary of labor, he was replaced by Marvin Miller, a shrewd economist who had served as a hearing officer for the Regional War Labor Board in Philadelphia during the war, but, unlike the other Labor Board vets, went to work for unions afterward. Since the corporate executives were leery of the arbitrators, Conrad Cooper persuaded David McDonald that they should appoint themselves as the committee's cochairmen. Thus the Human Relations Research Committee consisted of the same men who negotiated the contracts in 1956 and 1959–60.

But it was not top union and management officials who did the work of the Human Relations Research Committee, but rather Marvin Miller and lower-ranking union and management staff—mainly lawyers, economists, and other professionals based in the companies and the union's headquarters. They formed a number of subcommittees, each of which also had eight members—four from the union and four from the companies, including executives from Armco, Youngstown Sheet & Tube, and other steel manufacturers in addition to U.S. Steel, Bethlehem, and Republic Steel, which already had seats. The subcommittees met more than two hundred times between 1960 and 1964, reporting their findings to the Human Relations Research Committee.[39]

The subcommittees addressed questions essential to the workers in the mills, the union committeemen, higher ranking union officials, and management: the grievance procedures, wage incentives, seniority, medical insurance, job training, racial discrimination, job classification manuals, overtime and vacation scheduling, work assignments, and the contracting out of work. If they reached consensus, they would bring the proposal to the Human Relations Research Committee. If that committee approved, the language would be inserted into future contracts. George Taylor was not appointed to the committee, but the subcommittees were following his suggestion and Marvin Miller kept him informed.

The Human Relations Research Committee had several basic ground rules. "First," Miller explained, "the parties have agreed that all activities—studies, notes, discussions, data, recommendations, etc. will be privileged, unpublished and restricted to use only by the parties. Secondly, that all activities of the Human Relations Committee will be on an uninhibited basis. . . . Any member of either group is completely free to make any suggestion or comment, propose any plan or study, submit any data, testimony, or statistical information without fear or being bound by a commitment." Nevertheless, the subcommittees had clear agendas laid out ahead of their meetings, so that neither party had "an unlimited hunting license," added U.S. Steel vice president R. Heath Larry.[40]

After a while, the Human Relations Research Committee dropped the word *research* from its name, for they were negotiating, not merely seeking information. Without abandoning their existing contracts, the Steelworkers union and the eleven steel companies were moving away from countdown bargaining and, in the words of David Feller, who succeeded Goldberg as the Steelworkers' general counselor, were "slowly working their way to a 'permanent' contract": an agreement without any fixed termination date that either party could reopen at any time.[41]

A memo for the subcommittee on grievance procedures written by Marvin Miller and Ben Fischer suggests how the subcommittees worked. Although Sylvester Garrett had managed to sharply reduce the unresolved grievances on his desk by 1957, the number of grievances burgeoned during the 1958 and 1960–61 recessions, when thousands of workers were laid off or switched to other jobs. There were so many grievances that the length of time required to settle cases doubled between 1957 and 1961. Originally intended to serve as a way to quickly address workers' complaints and thus prevent strikes, the grievance procedure was becoming increasingly slow, expensive, and ineffectual.[42]

Miller and Fischer suggested that the subcommittee on grievance procedures obtain current and past statistical data, including the number of grievances submitted, how they were handled at each stage, and their eventual disposition. They also suggested that the subcommittee meet with the leading labor-management arbitrators in the country, including Garrett, David Cole, and Bill Simkin, the former arbitrator for Bethlehem Steel who had recently been appointed director of the Federal Conciliation and Mediation Service. They wanted "frank, off the record appraisal of our problems" in those meetings, Miller and Fischer wrote. The subcommittee should investigate the grievance procedures at well-managed corporations in other industries, such as International Harvester, General Motors, and Ford and meet with their management and union leaders as well as their arbitrators. They should also compare grievance procedures in various steel plants to find which succeeded. Finally, they ought to conduct experiments on new forms of grievance procedures in one plant to see which might be best.

The subcommittee followed their lead. Although grievance procedures had barely changed since the Second World War, as the editor of *American Metal Market*, a trade journal, remarked in March 1961, the steel industry and the union "are about to open an offensive against the growing accumulation of worker complaints, more formally known as grievances."[43]

The 1959 strike taught top management in Pittsburgh that they couldn't batter the union into submission. They had major problems to confront: domestic and international competition, inflation, "featherbedding," protests from civil-rights organizations and black steelworkers, and, by the end of the 1960s, legal and political objections from environmentalists. To deal with these and other issues, they had to cooperate with the union, especially its quite capable staff. As Conrad Cooper conceded in October 1961, "There is no room for conflict. It may be later than we think."[44] By working with Marvin Miller, Ben Fischer, and other union staff members, the steel companies' officers and staff revised grievance, arbitration, and seniority procedures, created an interplant job opportunities program, and job classification. "We started with hostile mistrust on both sides. We ended with understanding," remarked Miller, who, as his subsequent performance as director of the Major League Baseball Players Association made clear, was hardly afraid to confront truculent bosses.[45]

In December 1962 George Taylor announced that the Kaiser Steel Long Range Sharing Committee—the nine-member committee of three representatives of the United Steelworkers led by Marvin Miller, three representatives of Kaiser Steel led by the chairman of their board Edgar Kaiser, and three public representatives, John Dunlop, David Cole, and Taylor—had reached unanimous agreement on a plan to provide secure employment for the employees at Kaiser Steel and share the benefits of increases in productivity. The Kennedy administration considered the proposal so significant that the president discussed it in detail with the members before it was publicly announced. Under the plan, which was approved in a secret ballot election by the union's members in January 1963, the company replaced the individual incentive and hourly wages with a group incentive—the group in this case being the entire mill workforce.

Under the plan, Kaiser Steel's engineers would measure "total production costs" in the mill in 1961. If workers and management subsequently cut production costs by any means—whether by workers' output, better materials, or any other factor—the gain would be divided up, with 32.5 percent going to the employees. That was not peanuts. In the first thirty-five months after the plan was adopted, Kaiser's employees received an average of nearly $43 every month. "It used to be unheard of to sell a $500 color television set. In November and December we sold 269 of them," a furniture store in Fontana told a reporter in March 1964.[46] Under the plan, wages for workers at Kaiser would never fall below the rates negotiated by the Steelworkers for comparable work at the other steel companies. It would also provide "protection against automation," at least in principle, by promising to transfer rather than lay off workers whose jobs were eliminated by the production-cost declines. Moreover, the plan reinstated the cost-of-living allowance for Kaiser Steel workers, a valuable provision that David McDonald had surrendered in his negotiations with other steel companies in 1962. Finally, Section 2-B remained in the contract at Kaiser. The company's chairman, Edgar F. Kaiser, told the press that it would be less expensive to keep the clause than provoke resentment among their employees, as the other basic steel companies tried to do in 1959. Under the plan, the management could, however, change work rules if Taylor, Dunlop, Cole, and Steelworkers representatives on the committee agreed.[47]

* * *

The Labor Board vets did not limit themselves to Kaiser Steel. In early 1960, John Dunlop, Jim Healey, Fred Harbison, and Charles Myers, in consultation with George Taylor, Clark Kerr, David Cole, and others, sketched out a plan to deal with future problems of the U.S. steel industry.[48] Dunlop and his colleagues feared that the steel strike might have "most serious consequences for the American labor movement." The Congress and the public were increasingly unfriendly to unions. The federal government had intervened forcefully twice since the Wagner Act: first, with the Taft-Hartley Act of 1947, then Landrum-Griffith a year ago, they noted. The protracted steel strike might lead Congress to enact additional laws: Perhaps a mandatory vote by the employees before unions can strike, compulsory arbitration, labor courts, or tribunals as in Australia and New Zealand. Or the federal government might decide contract terms in the basic industries.[49]

That sort of talk worried the Labor Board vets who favored more traditional U.S. forms of unions and collective bargaining. Yet they realized that the advent of automation, structural unemployment, and the higher cost and greater delay in the grievance procedure were threatening those older ways. They also were concerned about issues beyond the workplace, including the increasing cost of medical care and hospitalization, alcoholism, and, more generally, "problems of the aging, the youth, and the women."[50]

The Labor Board vets proposed "separate, informal, exploratory conferences between the heads of the steel union and the steel industry with a select group of leading university professionals in the field of industrial relations"—presumably themselves. They would start by meeting with a few "carefully selected" union representatives such as astute staffers like Marvin Miller. Afterward, they would meet with leading corporate executives. The purpose of these meetings was "to probe into the underlying reasons for the hostility and misunderstanding" between steel management and the steel union. They wanted to "develop . . . a general framework for future problem-solving relations . . . with[out] government intervention or control."[51] Unless union and corporate leaders find "other and better ways" of resolving their entrenched fears, mistrust, and opposition, Congress was likely to establish tribunals. "Then, voluntary bargaining would perish. . . . Time is of the essence."[52]

The election of Kennedy as president and his nomination of Arthur Goldberg, the Steelworkers' skilled lawyer, as U.S. Secretary of Labor offered the Labor Board vets a chance to pursue those ideas. Goldberg had worked with the Labor

Board vets ever since 1948, when he succeeded Lee Pressman as general counsel of the Steelworkers and was an ardent supporter of Kennedy for the Democratic presidential nomination. At his urging, Kennedy announced his Presidential Advisory Committee on Labor-Management Policy. Co-chaired by Secretary Goldberg and Secretary of Commerce Luther Hodges, the committee consisted of seven prominent corporate presidents, seven top union leaders, and seven "public representatives," specifically George Taylor, David Cole, and Clark Kerr. The goal was to reestablish consensus between unions and corporate leadership.[53]

The Presidential Advisory Committee on Labor-Management Policy met regularly for five years. They debated national policy on automation and technological advance, economic growth and unemployment, inflation, wage and price policy, and collective bargaining. Despite conscientious efforts, the differences of opinion between the corporate leaders on the one hand and the union leaders and the public representatives on the other were so great as to preclude any sort of corporatist-style collaboration between labor unions and corporations across the U.S. economy.[54]

But the Labor Board vets did make headway in the steel industry. The 1962 contract signed by U.S. Steel and the Steelworkers incorporated Sylvester Garrett's 1959 rulings on local working conditions into the new agreement. As Ben Fischer of the Steelworkers commented later, "Over a period of time, arbitration became the instrument for writing the nitty-gritty of contracts."[55] In 1965, Secretary of Labor Willard Wirtz, Senator Wayne Morse of Oregon, and Bill Simkin, the chairman of the Federal Mediation and Conciliation Service, who were all Labor Board veterans, mediated the steel negotiations. The union had not won a wage increase since 1960. I. W. Abel had just defeated David McDonald in a close contest for the union presidency. And the steel business was booming again after four slow years. The Steelworkers were determined to win improvements in the 1965 negotiations. Yet profits in the industry remained lower than in other industries and, with the number of U.S. forces in Vietnam increasing, President Lyndon Johnson was determined to prevent a strike and inflation.

As the contract deadline neared, Johnson asked Abel and Conrad Cooper to extend the agreement negotiation for a week. He sent Air Force One to Pittsburgh to pick up the negotiating teams. Abel readily accepted the invitation. Cooper declined, preferring U.S. Steel's own airplane. When the negotiators arrived at Andrew Air Force Base, they were whisked by an army helicopter to the White House lawn and the Oval Office, where Johnson warned them not to be headstrong. The steel executives and union leaders then began meeting with Wirtz, Simkin, and Morse. Johnson put them in a grungy room in the basement of the Executive Office Building, a block from the White House, with broken air conditioning, stale sandwiches, and clamor from the street so loud that they could hardly hear each other. After seven days, they finally conceded to the president and reached a compromise settlement on the eve of Labor Day. Cooper, Abel, and the others wanted to rush away, but Johnson insisted that they stay until he announced the settlement on television.[56]

Meanwhile, Sylvester Garrett, Ralph Seward, and other Labor Board vets continued to serve as the principal arbitrators for the Steelworkers and the major steel manufacturers. They handled every sort of worker grievance, which became more numerous in the absence of strikes. Wage rates remained an extremely thorny area as consumer prices rose in the latter 1960s. The majority of steelworkers were paid according to the amount of work they produced, yet incentive rates continued to vary in unpredictable ways despite the 1947–48 Fair Day's Work Program. In the 1968 contract negotiations, the Steelworkers demanded that the minority of workers who were paid by the hour—such as maintenance workers, crane operators, and laboratory technicians—also receive incentives. Although the Steel Industry Coordinating Committee rejected the demand, they did agree to let an arbitration panel consisting of Garrett, Simkin, and Seward decide the issue. In August 1969, the panel issued an order that extended incentive coverage to an additional sixty-five thousand steelworkers. The Steelworkers president I. W. Abel hailed the ruling, saying "this decision will mean millions of dollars for our members." R. Heath Larry, vice chairman of U.S. Steel and head of the Steel Industry Coordinating Committee, was less pleased, complaining that the ruling "can have serious impact on the employment costs of the companies."

Since incentive rates varied between the eleven companies and within each mill, the panel's ruling lacked specifics. Garrett, Simkin, and Seward simply ruled that the companies provide incentives for no less than 85 percent of all production and maintenance workers at the companies and at least 65 percent at each firm associated with the Coordinating Committee. By the following summer, all of the major steel companies except U.S. Steel accepted those terms. Prodded by Garrett, U.S. Steel agreed in June 1970 to let him settle their disagreement. Garrett issued his ruling in November of that year. It provided incentive pay for ten thousand more production workers at U.S. Steel, bringing up the total covered by incentives at that company to 91 percent of the total production employees, with $5 million in retroactive pay. U.S. Steel accepted the order. The *Wall Street Journal* complained that the decision would raise costs for auto manufacturers. "The overriding aim of arbitration is labor peace and, in most cases, that means peace at something close to labor's price."[57]

* * *

In December 1972, the Steel Industry Coordinating Committee and the Steelworkers' top officials decided to finally adopt George Taylor's recommendation that they submit unresolved contract disputes to arbitration. They called the new arrangement the Experimental Negotiating Agreement (ENA). Under its terms, the steel management and union teams would begin negotiating about the next contract no later than February 1, 1974. If they were unable to resolve their differences by April 15, the Impartial Arbitration Panel, composed of three public members—Sylvester Garrett, Ralph Seward, and Benjamin Aaron—would resolve whatever issues remained up in the air. By these means ENA would prevent a strike in the industry for at least three more years. The union's six-hundred-member Basic Steel Conference ratified the agreement in January 1973.

The decision to rely on arbitrators to settle contractual disputes represented a radical departure from past practices and principles for both the union and the corporations. Nothing has been more sacred to American trade unionists than their right to call strikes. To a far greater extent than in Europe, American unions rely on strikes as their principal source of power. Yet the president of the Steelworkers, I. W. Abel—son of German and Welsh immigrants who joined the Steel Workers Organizing Committee in 1936; became president of the union local at the Timkin Roller Bearing Company in Canton, Ohio; marched in the bloody Little Steel strike in Mahoning Valley in 1937; represented labor on the Regional War Labor Board in Cleveland; and served in leadership posts in every industrywide strike after that—voluntarily surrendered the steelworkers' right to strike.

In the same way, no principle has been historically more inviolable in the minds of America's corporate executives than "management's right to manage." Yet R. Heath Larry, the U.S. Steel lawyer who succeeded Conrad Cooper as the chairman of the Steel Industry Coordinating Committee, gave up the right to write contract terms to a panel of Labor Board vets whose arbitration triggered the 1959 steel strike in the first place.

The union and corporate leaders ceded these powers because the alternatives were worse. Foreign manufacturers made inroads into the U.S. steel market during the 1959 strike. Every three years after that, when risk of another steel strike arose, German, French, English, Italian, and Japanese steel manufacturers made further inroads into the U.S. market. During 1971, imports reached a record height of 18.4 percent of the U.S. domestic market—an increase of 1,700 percent since 1957 despite quotas implemented by the Johnson and Nixon administrations at the urging of Abel and the chief executives of U.S. Steel, Republic Steel, and Bethlehem Steel.[58]

In the mid-1960s, the steel companies' labor costs began to rise again. Conrad Cooper rationalized U.S. Steel's defeat in 1959 by pointing out that the wage increase the union won in 1960 was half the increase the union won in 1956. Wage and fringe benefit increases remained modest in 1962 and 1963. Once the economy improved in the mid-1960s, however, and Abel replaced McDonald, the union was able to win substantial wage increases, eroding profit margins. The corporations responded by scrapping the last of the Bessemer furnaces, reducing the number of open-hearth furnaces, and buying additional Basic Oxygen Furnaces. They also set up a joint union-management productivity committee in the mills. Nonetheless, the rate of return on equity in primary U.S. steel firms were merely 4.3 percent in 1970 and 4.5 percent in 1971, less than half the rate in all U.S. manufacturing at that time and the lowest in the steel industry since at least 1950.[59]

I. W. Abel began thinking about using arbitration instead of strikes after spending that long week in the basement of the Executive Office Building in Washington, DC, in September 1965. If the president of the United States was unwilling to allow the union to strike, why not allow the arbitrators to settle their contract disputes, he thought to himself. It would be best for the union, he reasoned. Abel knew from firsthand experience the costs that strikes imposed on the union and on its members. As secretary-treasurer of the Steelworkers in 1959, he had to deny funds to needy members' families. Well aware of the cost of imports and competition from domestic firms that produced substitutes for steel, Conrad Cooper proposed the Experimental Negotiating Agreement in the 1967 contract negotiations. Abel agreed, but the union's district directors refused to go along. They changed their minds in 1972, after imports reached unprecedented heights and the Steel Industry Coordinating Committee made greater concessions.

The ENA signed in 1972 guaranteed annual increases of a minimum of 3 percent for all steelworkers, maintained Section 2-B and the cost-of-living allowance (COLA). The latter was especially important, as price of consumer prices kept rising. The union's locals were given the right to call strikes over local issues if approved by the international union president. Finally, the contract provided a $150 bonus for the union's members.[60]

Although Ed Sadlowski, the impassioned young director of the Steelworkers district in South Chicago and Gary, denounced the ENA in his 1977 campaign for Steelworkers presidency—as did radical students, radical professors, and outside critics—many others were relieved. The young local union president of USW Local 2644 of Bethlehem Steel in Johnstown, Pennsylvania, saw the ENA as "the preservation of thousands of jobs—and the preservation of the industry as well." "It's very nice for us," the purchasing agent for a major machine builder in the Midwest said. "Everybody singing out of the same hymn book for once, the old idea of mutual benefit is back." "If this thing works as it looks like it will[,] we won't need to stockpile. It'll be a relief," a spokesman for General Motors, the world's largest steel buyer, declared.[61]

The Labor Board vets were delighted. They saw the ENA as the culmination of their efforts in America's most essential industry. "A great idea," Sylvester Garrett told the *Wall Street Journal*. He conferred with Abel and Heath Larry as they reached the details of the agreement. "They've got their feet on the ground . . . their heads in the clouds." The ENA will prevent the Steelworkers and companies from falling off the cliff, Garrett declared after the union's delegates approved the plan. "What we have done is to create a different precipice for ourselves. If we go over the edge this time, we won't fall into a strike—we'll fall into impartial arbitration." The ENA, Garrett declared, revealed "sophistication and a realistic approach to practical problems by both parties."[62]

This was their hope in 1972.

6

When the Meek
Began to Roar

Public Employee Unionism
in the 1960s

What happens to your precepts of representative
government if the legislature has to conform to
collective bargaining? These are terrible problems.
I don't think you can solve them simply with
muscle, and by being kinetic. A whole new set of
concepts has to be worked out. It won't be, you
know. It's going to be a mess for a generation.
—George W. Taylor, 1967

UNTIL THE 1960S, the Labor Board vets worked entirely in the profit-making
sector of the U.S. economy. This was not due to a lack of interest in unions among
government employees. But for many years governors, mayors, and state legislatures were even more hostile than private employers to organization of their
employees. Governor Calvin Coolidge's terse rejection of Samuel Gompers's
appeal for sympathy when Boston's poorly-paid police officers went on strike in
1919 ("There is no right to strike against the public safety by anybody, anywhere,
any time.") resonated throughout union officialdom. "It is impossible to bargain
collectively with the government," George Meany declared when the AFL and
the CIO merged in 1955. The principal exception—the Communist-led United
Public Workers of America—was expelled from the CIO in 1949, harassed by
New York City mayor William O'Dwyer and the U.S. House of Representatives
Committee on Un-American Activities, and soon disintegrated.[1]

Circumstances changed for the labor movement and the Labor Board vets during the 1960s, as government employment expanded exponentially; government resistance against unionization of their employees waned; schoolteachers, sanitation workers, and other government workers began to organize locally; new unions for public employees emerged; older ones revitalized; and the Teamsters and other unions previously based entirely in the private sector won contracts with government agencies.

Consequently, Presidents John F. Kennedy and Lyndon Johnson, Governor Nelson Rockefeller, and New York mayors asked the Labor Board vets to handle conflicts in the public sector. At the request of Governor Rockefeller, a committee of Labor Board veterans chaired by George Taylor drafted legislation for the peaceful resolution of disputes in the public sector in New York State in 1966. Revised and adopted a year later, the Public Employees' Fair Employment Act— popularly termed the Taylor Act—was passed and signed in Albany and became a guide for employment relations throughout the Empire State and a model for other states.

The Labor Board vets hadn't paid much attention to companies' profit margins when they were working in the private sector. Their top priorities during the Second World War were to prevent wage inflation and to stop strikes. After the war ended, they helped union and company officials resolve disputes. Rising labor costs, defense of managerial prerogatives, and company profits were burning matters for corporate leaders, but not the mediators and arbitrators.

But, when George Taylor, David Cole, John Dunlop, and other NWLB vets began working in the public sector, they became quite concerned about how increases in wages and benefits for government employees would affect the budgets of the public schools and other government bureaus. It wasn't the salary increases per se that troubled them so much as the way those decisions were made and the consequences for democracy. The Labor Board vets always thought of themselves first and foremost as protectors of the public interest. "The real question is whether the threat of a strike [by public employees] is the way to allocate public funds," George Taylor told a reporter in 1967.[2] "How can a city perform its functions effectively if a major part of its budget is authoritatively determined by the decisions and policies made by 'outsiders'?" he asked in 1972.[3]

George Taylor, David Cole, John Dunlop, and other NWLB vets had developed good working relationships with union leaders in the steel industry, the airlines, the railroads, and the building trades—indeed, virtually every other private-sector industry they worked with. They had a much harder time dealing with Albert Shanker of the United Federation of Teachers, Victor Gotbaum of District 37 of the American Federation of State, County, and Municipal Employees, and leaders of the other government workers' unions that emerged during the 1960s."We *have* changed our minds," Cole admitted.[4] Their thinking about the impact of unions on public funding and their reaction to the new union leaders revealed conservative qualities in their values and actions that were not as apparent earlier in their careers.

* * *

The Labor Board vets first became involved with public employees in January 1961, when the Board of Education of the City of New York appointed a committee of five prominent citizens to advise its members how to implement collective-bargaining policy for teachers. The committee included David Cole, the Paterson, New Jersey, attorney who served on the Regional Board War Board II in the Second World War and went on to mediate disputes in the steel industry, on the waterfront, in the atomic energy industry, and with the merger of the AFL and CIO in the latter 1950s; George W. Taylor; and Walter Gellhorn, a noted professor of law at Columbia University who had served as chair and vice chair of the Regional War Labor Board II.[5]

The Board of Education was prompted by a one-day strike undertaken by several thousand teachers two months earlier. Despite the strength of unions in New York City, the public school teachers had never gone on strike before. Schoolteachers were generally regarded as timid. "Teachers are constitutionally and by training conservative, long suffering, almost submissive. . . . It is not possible to imagine a motion to strike . . . by a majority of teachers," *The New York Teacher*, the house organ of the Teachers Union in the city and an affiliate of the AFT, remarked in the 1920s.[6]

There was one exception. In 1946, public school teachers did go on strike in San Francisco; St. Paul; Buffalo; Norwalk, Connecticut; Pawtucket, Rhode Island; and Wilkes-Barre, Pennsylvania. Unable to keep up with rising prices during the war and watching blue-collar unions winning large wage increases by walking out, teachers in those cities followed their neighbors' example, often successfully. In other cities teachers who threatened to strike received salary increases. All this was done without organization, for the American Federation of Teachers (AFT) was weak and the National Education Association (NEA) was firmly opposed to walkouts.[7] After teachers struck in Buffalo, the state legislature passed one law that raised salaries throughout the state and another, the Condon-Wadlin Act, that outlawed strikes by state employees, required the school board to fire any employees who violated that law, and prevented pay raises for three years for any striker who was rehired. Washington, Nebraska, Missouri, Pennsylvania, Michigan, Texas, Ohio, and other states also enacted antistrike laws at that time.[8]

Teachers in New York were largely quiescent throughout the 1950s. Yet factors were at work during those years that encouraged teacher militancy in the 1960s.

One was monetary. Although teachers' salaries improved after 1946, wages for unionized carpenters, masons, electricians, plumbers, and other union members who lived in the same neighborhoods as teachers rose much more rapidly. Moreover, while most teachers in the early twentieth century were women, many men entered the field in the 1950s—so many, in fact, that they constituted the majority in high schools and junior high schools in New York City by the early 1960s. Although high school teachers had historically received higher salaries than elementary school teachers, the New York Board of Education equalized teacher salary in the early 1950s—irritating high school teachers who had specialized fields of knowledge and often master's degrees. Furthermore, the composition of the teacher corps had changed. Although the large majority of teachers in New York in the early twentieth century were mainly Christians, Jews became the majority of New York City's teachers by the 1950s. Quite of few of the teachers were children of union garment workers who had grown up in ardent pro-union, socialist households. Finally, the emergence of the civil-rights movement in southern cities in the 1950s and early 1960s inspired unorganized New York City teachers to act for themselves too.

On January 3, 1959, six-and-a-half months before the epic steel strike, seven hundred teachers in New York City's evening high school program pledged to quit their jobs unless their pay was raised more than 100 percent before classes resumed four weeks later. The students in the program were adults and teenagers who had dropped out of the regular high schools. They attended classes twice a week, three hours each evening, in sixteen of the city's high schools. Their teachers received $12.25 each evening, much less in terms of real wages than their counterparts in the 1930s.[9]

The night-school teachers' mass resignation in February 1959 heralded a new attitude. The protest was organized by the High School Teachers Association (HSTA), a local group not connected to NEA or the AFT. The HSTA's lawyer had suggested resignation to sidestep the Condon-Wadlin Act. Most of the members of the HSTA were older, fairly conservative men, but the officers—Roger Parente and Samuel Hochberg—were more progressive politically. They viewed the threat of mass resignation by evening school teachers as a lever to organize the daytime high school teachers. "This is different from the usual teacher threat in that these people mean business," Parente told the reporters. Superintendent of Schools John Theobald was unfazed. "I am sorry they feel that way, but as long as they do, they can go ahead and quit," he offhandedly remarked to reporters.

The threat to resign was a shrewd tactic, for almost all of the evening school teachers also taught during the day. They weren't putting their regular jobs at risk and, if the ploy succeeded, they could next demand salary increases for their daytime jobs. Indeed, the HSTA was demanding an increase of $1,000 in salary for teachers in the regular high schools in the midst of the evening school protest.[10] And the protest proved far more effective than Superintendent Theobald imagined. So many teachers picketed or called in sick that the Board of Education had to shut down fifteen of its sixteen programs after the second evening.[11]

The strike continued for four weeks. The teachers returned at the end of February, having won promises of increases beginning July 1. A year later, the HSTA merged with the New York Teachers Guild to form the United Federation of Teachers (UFT). Although their combined membership was fairly small, the HSTA had fervent supporters in the high schools, as the Teachers Guild did in the junior high schools, and the Teachers Guild had a charter with the AFT, which was affiliated with the AFL-CIO. Thus, the new union could receive support from Harry Van Arsdale, president of the powerful Central Labor Council of New York, and Walter Reuther, director of the AFL-CIO's Industrial Union Department. Moreover, although the president of the UFT, Charles Cogen, was cautious, the second tier of leadership—David Selden, Roger Parente, Samuel Hochberg, and especially Albert Shanker—were capable of acting and eager to do so.[12]

In a rally at St. Nicholas's Arena in Manhattan in late March 1960, fifteen hundred voted to authorize a strike if necessary to gain higher wages and other benefits. A month later, four hundred of the union's delegates issued a series of demands to the Board of Education: a collective-bargaining election, across-the-board salary increases, $1,000 increases for promotions, 50 minutes of free time at the lunch hour for elementary school teachers, ten sick days per year for full-time substitutes, and deduction of union dues from teachers' paychecks. The union leaders threatened a strike of unlimited duration beginning on May 17, 1960, a day that Governor Rockefeller had designated as Teacher Recognition Day, unless the "substantial progress" was made to a "satisfactory agreement" with the Board of Education on these issues.[13]

The school administrators and the union's leaders maneuvered for the next half-year—spoiling for a fight, then hesitating, back and forth. Finally, the UFT called for a strike on November 7, 1960, the day before the Nixon-Kennedy presidential election. The union promised to picket every public school in the city. The superintendent of schools called on parents to send their children regardless, promising that the principals and nonteaching staff would ensure their safety. At that time, the Board of Education employed 38,932 teachers. According to the *New York Times*, at least 5,942 teachers failed to appear at work, or 15 percent of the total—almost certainly an undercount, since principals asked substitute teachers to replace those who struck.

New York City had a vigorous working-class culture in those days. Fully 34 percent of the teachers were absent in the elementary and junior high schools at the Battery and on the Lower East Side. At least one-fifth were absent on the West

Side of Manhattan, East Bronx, and South Bronx. An average of 19 percent were absent at the academic high schools, with much higher levels at the prestigious Stuyvesant High School and the Bronx High School of Science. Students walked out of school en masse at several high schools. Some elementary school students refused to cross teachers' picket lines. Although the UFT had not convinced the majority, the strike nonetheless startled the Board of Education, Mayor Robert Wagner, and city bigwigs, including the *New York Times* editors who denounced the teachers' "outlaw strike" as "illegal, unjustified . . ., a damaging disservice to the interests of all teachers, and an example of bad morals to the youth of our city."[14]

The Board of Education's Advisory Commission of Inquiry held three day-long public hearings in March and April, where Taylor and Cole discovered how fragmented the city's teachers were. New York City teachers belonged to nearly one hundred sorts of associations—divided by city boroughs, teaching subjects and levels, religious faith, and politics. Twelve separate organizations hoped to represent the teachers in meetings with the Board of Education—not only the UFT and the NEA, but also the Teachers Union, which had originally linked to the Communist Party; the Catholic Teachers Associations of the Diocese of Brooklyn and the Archdiocese of Manhattan; the Secondary School Teachers Association; the Elementary School Teachers Association; the Substitute Teachers' Association of Greater New York; Council of Attendance Teachers; the Assistant Attendance Teachers' Association; and the Doctorate Association of New York Educators.[15]

Representatives of the largest of these organizations, the UFT and the NEA, had utterly different conceptions of the "teacher." Speaking on behalf of the UFT, attorney David Feller repeatedly compared teachers to highly skilled union members. That is why, he argued, teachers in the high schools, elementary schools, and junior high schools should all be in the same bargaining unit. "It is bad enough in an industrial plant where you have separate crafts. I hardly need talk about flight engineers or pilots or stewards to bring the point home that the public interest is in favor of the broadest possible representation in this area." Eric Rhodes, director of the NEA's New York office, could not have objected more forcefully. "It is a sad day for teachers, when a group purporting to bargain for teachers refers to teaching as a craft and not a profession. I think this would be shocking and revolting to the vast majority of the teaching profession."[16]

Many teachers had only the foggiest notion of collective bargaining back then. That was true of some of the union leaders as well. "As a matter of fact, I was none too sure myself of how to go about it," David Selden, top staffer for the UFT, later conceded. For that reason, the commission's first recommendation, in its May 17, 1961, report to the Board of Education, was to send a letter to all employees in the New York public school system licensed by the superintendent of schools answering the question "What Is Collective Bargaining?" The commission would ask teachers whether they wanted to be represented in a single group or, alternatively, in separate subdivisions—for example, as elementary school professionals, secondary school professionals, daytime teachers, evening-school teachers, counselors, school psychologists, school nurses, and the like. They proposed that the Commission of Inquiry itself, not the Board of Education, be in charge of the referendum. The commission also proposed excluding supervisors from the referendum, at least temporarily. This plan "should lead to a formal collective bargaining election later this year," Taylor, Cole, and their colleagues declared. If, however, the referendum revealed a convincing judgment against collective bargaining, further steps toward a bargaining should be postponed "for the time being."[17]

Taylor and Cole hoped that this plan could improve the teachers' salaries and working conditions while containing costs and preventing strikes. They expected the UFT to win a majority of the votes and, although there is no mention of it in their papers, they almost certainly assumed that they would be appointed to mediate between the UFT and the Board of Education.

If the Board of Education had approved Commission of Inquiry's proposal, perhaps their hopes could have been realized. After all, the UFT's president Charles Cogen was prudent, the federal government was only beginning to provide funds for local schools, and interracial relations in the city were still fairly calm. None of this was certain to continue, however, and, in retrospect, their hopes appear unrealistic, even fanciful. Unionization of entirely new workers have historically been tumultuous in the United States. That was true for shoemakers in the 1830s, railroad craftsmen after the Civil War, coal miners in West Virginia in the 1890s, garment workers in the early twentieth century, and, of course, steel, auto, and many other workers in the 1930s and 1940s. Why should it have been different when government employees organized? Moreover, the times were changing in the United States in the early 1960s, most obviously in Greensboro, North Carolina, and other southern cities—but not only there. Could New York City be exempt?

In any case, the commission's plan was cut short even before it began, for the Board of Education refused to accept its recommendations, prompting the normally unperturbed George Taylor and his colleagues to resign in protest.[18]

* * *

The next Labor Board vet to become involved was Theodore (Ted) Kheel, who was appointed by Mayor Robert Wagner to serve on a three-member mediation panel in the UFT and the Board of Education's contract negotiations in September 1963. Born in Brooklyn in 1914, a graduate of DeWitt Clinton High School, Cornell University, and Cornell Law School, Kheel joined the staff of the National

Labor Relations Board in 1938 and was appointed chairman of Regional War Labor Board II in Manhattan in 1942. In 1946 he was appointed deputy director of New York City's division of labor relations; a year later he was named director. In 1948 Kheel resigned the government office, turning to private mediation. He mediated disputes between the Transit Workers Union and New York's seven private bus companies. Afterward he became, in the words of labor journalist Steven Greenhouse, "the go-to guy for mayors, labor leaders and business executives during the post–World War II era." Kheel mediated an average of a thousand cases every year for more than thirty years. So the mayor naturally turned to him when the UFT and the Board of Education's contract negotiations deadlocked in early September 1963.[19]

As Taylor and Cole anticipated, the UFT defeated its rivals in an election to become the bargaining agent for teachers with the Board of Education in December 1961 and won its first contract, a one-year agreement, in June 1962, after a one-day strike in March. When the union leaders pressed for larger increases in summer 1963, the president of the Board of Education replied that no additional money was available and, if that changed, the funds would be directed to students' needs, not teacher salaries. The union responded by threatening to strike for a third time even though the Condon-Wadlin Act had been amended to ensure punishment in the event of a walkout.[20]

The collision was averted at the last moment when the mediation panel devised a compromise accepted by the Board of Education and the union that included salary increases, better grievance procedures, the right to hold union meetings in the schools, principals required to notify teachers about any complaints, and the right of counsel for teachers at hearings.[21]

Some of the conflicts in New York City that Kheel mediated were quite protracted—most famously, the 114-day-long newspaper strike in the city in 1962–63. Others, like the teachers' 1963 contract, were quickly resolved. Regardless, Kheel always took charge. "I walk into every negotiation and the first thing I say is that I'm *not* there to make recommendations. I *promise* not to make recommendations. And, of course, from that moment on I'm actually making recommendations."[22]

In this respect, he was following the approach of George Taylor. But in personality and stage presence, Kheel could not have differed more. He was a bon vivant fond of fashionable suits, sports cars, and fine food. At various times, he owned a stake in the fine French restaurant Le Pavillon in Manhattan, and wine bin No. 1 at both the Rainbow Room and Windows on the World. His correspondence includes a letter from a Playboy Club bunny thanking him for his help in trying to help her and the other women unionize. He gloried in being the center of the stage. "These crisis situations are where Teddy gets his kicks," one Labor Board vet remarked. "Some men look at Gina Lollobrigida and are set aflame.

Kheel gets the same reaction by exposure to a really tough strike situation—one that involves big stakes for the community and also presents a novel or a difficult problem. He just can't bear to be out of that kind of thing, no matter how painful or exasperating or time-consuming it gets."[23]

* * *

In late August 1965, Mayor Wagner appointed Kheel, George Taylor, and David Cole to mediate the United Federation of Teachers' contract negotiations with the Board of Education. By that point the UFT had already acquired thirty-three thousand members and a zealous president, Albert Shanker, a socialist, former junior high school science teacher, and fervent advocate of teacher unionism. The Board of Education had a new president as well, Lloyd K. Garrison, who had served as chief counsel for the National War Labor Board in the Second World War and as chairman in late 1945. Great-grandson of the fearless abolitionist William Lloyd Garrison, Garrison had been educated at St. Paul's School in New Hampshire, Harvard College, and Harvard Law School. Committed to social reform, he had been an officer of the Urban League, chaired the original National Labor Relations Board in 1933, and served as dean of the law school of the University of Wisconsin. A longtime member of the American Civil Liberties Union, Garrison defended Langston Hughes, Arthur Miller, and Robert Oppenheim when they were charged with disloyalty to the United States.

Al Shanker was in Los Angeles attending the AFT's national convention when the mayor appointed Taylor, Cole, and Kheel. He agreed to mediation but warned that this "does not necessarily mean that the issues will be resolved without a strike." Shanker set September 10 as the deadline for an agreement. If the union and the Board of Education did not have a written contract by then, he vowed, the union would go ahead with its plan to strike on Monday, September 13, the opening day of school. If there was a strike, he predicted, 40 thousand of New York's nearly forty-eight thousand teachers would walk out.[24]

Superintendent of Schools Bernard Donovan was no less firm. The UFT's demand for $100 million in salary increases was "unrealistic," he declared. The Board of Education had offered $8 million for the upcoming year, and $8 million more a year later, and the board could not go further. "I don't think the Board of Education or I, as Superintendent, believe that even the teachers want us to buy peace at the expense of the children," Donovan told the press.[25]

The negotiators met the mediators daily for two weeks, each side conceding a tad while trying to pressure the other to yield more. "Both sides are conscious of the need not to disturb the school program," David Cole maintained. "This is collective bargaining at work," Kheel claimed. The union's top negotiator, Jules Kolodny, was not as optimistic. He admitted that they had made some progress but added that "time is growing short and many fundamental issues remain unresolved."[26] The two negotiating teams reached agreement on every issue except salary increases one day before the deadline. The mediators then proposed $40 million in salary and benefit increases over two years as a settlement, an amount the union and board representatives accepted. "It was a remarkable achievement, involving some of the very best collective bargaining I have ever seen," George Taylor told reporters. "I have never felt better about our school system than I do now. It is in extremely capable hands on both sides of the bargaining table," Kheel declared.[27]

Lloyd Garrison was less upbeat. Despite his sympathy for unions and liberal causes, he feared the contract's long-term consequences. Although relieved that a strike and the ensuing animosity had been avoided, "the board views with grave misgivings the heavy mortgaging of the future," Garrison declared. "No one knows what the board will receive from the city and the state next year, and Federal funds cannot be used for increased teachers' salaries and so will not relieve the strain."[28] Developments in the next decade would justify Garrison's misgivings.

* * *

Although the public schools opened on time, the city was brought to a halt three and a half months later, January 1, 1966, when the Transit Workers Union (TWU) and the Amalgamated Transit Union went on strike against the Transit Authority, the agency that operated New York's subways and buses. The TWU's long-time president Mike Quill spurned the Transit Authority's offer of a $25 million wage and benefit increase, terming it a "peanut package" and refusing even to issue a counterproposal. This was a first strike by the TWU since 1932. Since five million New Yorkers took the subway or a bus to work and school—three-quarters of them coming into Manhattan from the outer boroughs—the city's commerce and schools came to a standstill.

The newly inaugurated mayor John Lindsay advised city residents to prepare for "untold hardships." The transit commissioners warned of a "catastrophe" if a fire occurred and the streets were clogged. Thirteen thousand firemen were ordered to appear at their stations in uniform for the duration. Twenty-one hospitals set up a rally bus system. Mike Quill was not afraid. The old Irish trade unionist had a close relationship with the former mayor, Robert Wagner, but despised Lindsay, a white, Anglo-Saxon, Protestant, Yale-educated, patrician Republican who campaigned on a promise against "power brokers." Quinn needed to impress his increasingly African American and Puerto Rican membership. "I don't think a strike for two weeks would be a catastrophe. London withstood the *blitz*," he snorted. Four days later, Quinn and eight other union leaders were arrested for defying a court injunction. "The judge can drop dead in his black robes and we would not call off the strike," he declared before going to jail.[29]

The strike lasted twelve days, sharply curtailing transit and commerce throughout the region and beyond. Over the following weeks, opinion makers advanced various proposals to prevent similar disasters in the future. U.S. Senator Jacob Javits and Representative Ogden Reid of New York introduced bills to give the president power to deal with disputes such as the New York transit strike. UAW president Walter Reuther called strikes like that one that paralyzed New York City "obsolete" and argued that the wage standards in private industry be used as a measuring rod of fairness for civil-service workers. In a press conference at the University of Wisconsin, Nathan Feinsinger, a former member of the National War Labor Board, proposed applying the 1926 National Railway Labor Act to intrastate transit. "New York's brush with catastrophe indicates the urgency of acting now," the *New York Times* declared.[30]

Governor Nelson Rockefeller, a liberal Republican with a record of cooperation with union leaders, had decided on a plan before the others spoke. On January 15, three days after the transit strike ended, he announced that he was appointing a special panel of "national leaders in the field of labor relations" to recommend legislative proposals to protect the public against the interruption of essential government services while also protecting the rights of public employees. Rockefeller selected John Dunlop; David Cole; George Taylor; E. Wight Bakke, the director of the Labor and Management Center at Yale University; and Frederick H. Harbison, director of the Industrial Relations Section at Princeton University, for the panel. Notably absent was Ted Kheel, who not only was considered too close to New York mayors but supported the right to strike for all public-employee unions except the firefighters, police officers, and prison guards.

Every member of the panel had served on the War Labor Board, and they had worked together on industrial-relations issues for years. Rockefeller appointed Taylor as chairman of the Governor's Committee on Public Employee Relations. Cole and Dunlop proved to be the other most influential members. "Millions of residents of New York City and its suburbs have just gone through the most devastating experience and have suffered personal hardships and economic losses through no fault of their own. . . . I am determined that this should never happen again," the governor declared.[31]

* * *

Rockefeller asked the Taylor Committee to recommend legislation within sixty days. The committee held public hearings for two days in early March. This allowed representatives of the Chamber of Commerce, unions, and others to speak publicly.[32] The hearings were a mere formality, however, for Taylor, Cole, Dunlop, Bakke, and Harbison had already consulted privately with the people whom they deemed essential and had been mulling over the issues even before the strike ended. The committee had its first group meeting on January 29, two weeks after their appointment, where they exchanged ideas, developed a plan, and distributed writing assignments. They met periodically throughout February and March, critiquing each other's drafts.

"We are not accustomed to 'labor troubles' in this area," David Cole remarked, using an expression that harked back to the late nineteenth century. The public-employee union membership had quadrupled since the mid-1950s, Dunlop noted, and successful strikes were proving to be the best organizing devices, regardless of the law. "The meek have begun to roar," Cole replied.[33]

Taylor, Cole, Dunlop, Bakke, and Harbison had worked with union leaders for years at every level, AFL and CIO unions, the railroad brotherhoods, and left-wing unions expelled from the CIO. Except for John L. Lewis of the United Mine Workers during the war, they rarely had problems with union leaders, regardless of their politics. But Al Shanker of the United Federation of Teachers and Victor Gotbaum of District 37 of American Federation of State, County and Municipal Employees, were different—zealous, crude, and unrelenting. "Shanker speaks for *LABOR*. HEADY. . . . At the vortex of incompatible contentions & conflicts. . . . Public employment is a new area in which labor unions play a role—a late starter but Wow!" Cole wrote in his notes.[34]

There is a "diminishing respect for the public welfare," Taylor, Cole, and Dunlop complained. There were pressures on unions and management in the private sector that prevented the contending parties from demanding too much, but "extortionate conditions [won't] drive government into bankruptcy," Cole wrote in his notebook during the 1966 transit strike. "This presents a serious danger to the public as well as an irresistible temptation to leaders of public-employee organizations," he added. The UFT was competing with the NEA. "The leaders [are] fighting for status. Muscle [is] admired. . . . Disruption, shock [are] OK. . . . Punishment to the public is now an *objective*—a complete change [from the past]."[35]

"How [to] get respect for law?" the Labor Board vets wondered. The public—that is, the government—has the authority, but the government "hesitated to use its full power or strength." Journalists and other public opinion-makers view conflicts between the government employee unions and government agencies as modern versions of industrial relations of the past. Such thinking is mistaken, the Labor Board vets believed. They considered employee relations in the public sector "basically different." Therefore, the practices of the private sector, especially its "evil features," should not adopted "blindly and ritualistically" by the public sector, they believed. They realized that industrial relations in the public sector were at an early stage. Nonetheless, they had to figure out what could be most constructive "and what is undesirable or harmful and why."[36]

In the past, they remarked, government employees did not have the right to organize, elect union representatives, or bargain with government agencies. Civil-service commissions determined job classifications, salaries, pensions, sick leaves, and the like. Employee organizations existed, it is true, but strikes were banned by law, public opinion, and often by the employee organizations themselves. Consequently, employee organizations were "kept in the position of petitioners." They lobbied, with the implicit threat of political reprisal if the politician in question was not receptive. Postal employees did so at the federal level. Teachers' groups and other civil-service associations did the same at the state level.

But the situation has changed, the committee members groused. "Teachers, heretofore compliant and law-abiding, have been discovering new muscles." Teachers are going out on strike every September, they remarked. The strikes "arouse strong emotions." Yet, unlike owners of private companies, mayors, and school boards are not "free to make final agreement." Only state legislatures or city councils set taxes. Teacher strikes consequently undermine the sovereignty of school boards. "These disputes . . . interfere with services which have always been thought to be inviolable." Public-employee strikes are "notorious." Cole sighed. They trigger distress but not resistance. On the contrary, the most aggressive public-employee unions are "apt to be pattern-setters." And they are effective, since unlike business owners, mayors, and school boards cannot move their schools to other locations or lock out the teachers.[37]

"Who represents the public?" Taylor, Cole, Dunlop, Bakke, and Harbison asked. Since the war, they had been employed by unions and employers to resolve grievances. They received excellent compensation from their work. This led arbitrators to think primarily of their employers' and the unions' interests. It was different when they were hired by Governor Rockefeller for the Committee on Public Employee Relations. "*Somebody must speak up in defense of the public welf[are] & interest*, however unpopular this may be in the labor fraternity," David Cole remarked.[38] "Is a *good* settlement only one extracted from an exhausted and bloody opposition?" he continued. "Won't such settlements lead to a morose and resentful opponent determined to get even—with no period of constructive stability or tranquility? Extortion and destructiveness cannot possibly be regarded as sound criteria for determining wages and working conditions[.] Otherwise, what happens to all the techniques for . . . improving co-operation[?] . . . Can complex and difficult technical and social problems be handled by reliance solely on force?"[39]

These opinions led the Taylor committee to declare that public-employee unions, regardless of their nature, should be allowed to call a strike. In this regard, they were at odds with their former colleague, Ted Kheel, who insisted that nonessential government workers should have the right to strike. "Confining no-strike laws to vital government service is meaningless," Dunlop replied. What government work is not essential? If school crossing guards struck, what would happen to the children? When teachers strike, students and their families suffer, especially poor families. Nonessential workers do not strike, Dunlop remarked. They don't have leverage. Strikes are called or threatened by employees in the most essential offices—the schools, the sanitation departments, the bus drivers, the hospitals, the prisons, the fire departments, the police departments—the people on whom the whole public depends. Employees in these facilities deserve the right to organize, the Taylor committee agreed. They should be represented by unions, negotiate agreements, sign contracts, submit grievances, obtain mediation and arbitration—every aspect of collective bargaining except the right to strike.[40]

The first step, Taylor and his colleagues advised, was to recommend repeal of the Condon-Wadlin Act. Not only was the law ineffective, for the legislature had repeatedly rescinded the penalties after strikes ended but it penalized individual workers rather than the unions and union leaders who had called the walkouts. The Taylor committee preferred legislation that guarantees government employees the right to unionize while providing effective alternatives to strikes.

But what is an alternative to strikes? David Cole thought the government should deny or withdraw recognition and dues checkoff for unions that called strikes. John Dunlop had a different idea. He made an analogy with the garment industry where prices and compensation are set before the season begins. It was not like that for the public-employee unions that sought salary and benefit increases and other changes in working conditions *after* the budgets were decided by the city and state governments. That pattern created enormous problems. The new labor law, Dunlop argued, should steer the unions toward lobbying and campaigning for pro-union candidates—what he called "the political route." If the law was written that way, the parties "will devise something" to attract union support. "Decisions regarding the available money must remain a political issue," Dunlop maintained. This argument convinced Wight Bakke. Strikes by public employees are "bad," he declared, because they provoke public disapproval without "interfer[ing] with profits"; in this case, taxes. "We should therefore require employees to rely on stepped up political activity," Bakke said, remarking that postal employees have done well in the political arena without striking.[41]

Dunlop was prescient. The plan that they recommended helped end strikes in the public sector for forty years from the mid-1970s until the mid-2010s, even as the public unions continued to grow. But the change did not occur overnight. The public-employee unions' turn from striking to politicking took time.

* * *

The Governor's Committee on Public Employee Relations report, issued on March 31, 1966, called for the repeal of the Condon-Wadlin Law and passage of new labor legislation for New York State. The new legislation would (1) give public employees the right to organize and be represented by associations; (2) require the state, local governments, and other political subdivisions in New York to recognize, negotiate, and sign written agreements with employees selected by a majority of their employees; (3) continue the ban on strikes by public employees and provide strict penalties for violations; (4) create a system of mediation, fact-finding, and legislative action to settle impasses; (5) create a public employment relations board to put into effect the new system.[42]

Although collective bargaining including the right to strike has been recognized "as an essential democratic right" of employees in the private sector of the U.S. economy since 1935, "the right of public employees to strike has never been recognized by the public, legislature, or by the government in the United States," the committee observed. There are good reasons for this distinction, in the opinion of Taylor and his colleagues. Private employers "have countervailing rights": they could lock out their employees, go out of business, or, although the committee didn't mention it, relocate their operations. No comparable constraints operate in the public sector, the committee argued. "It is the budget, rather than the market place, which constrains collective negotiations in public employees." For that reason, disputes between government administrators and public employees should be resolved politically, as part of "the budget-making processes," rather than in the streets, they argued.[43]

The committee urged the legislature to create the Public Employment Relations Board (PERB), which, like the National Labor Relations Board, would certify units of representation. Since New York State comprised 62 counties, 932 towns, 553 villages, 62 cities, 1,199 school districts, and hundreds of other political subdivisions, the committee encouraged the state legislature to permit legislative bodies of local governments to create their own local PERBs.[44]

Inspired by Dunlop, the committee argued that the principal conflicts in the public sector emerged because the government administrators and public-employee unions had failed to reach agreements before the budgetary deadlines mandated by law. Therefore the new legislation should require government administrators and the union to conduct their negotiations well before the budgetary deadline for submitting their budget to the legislature. If they are unable to come to an agreement sixty days before the deadline, the PERB would appoint a mediator to meet with the parties. If mediation fails, the PERB should appoint a three-member fact-finding board who would be representatives of the public. This board would hear the contending parties' arguments collect appropriate statistical data and could make requests on its own initiative. A majority of the fact-finding board would be required to submit a recommendation no later than fifteen days before the submission of the legislature's budget deadline. The final stage would be legislative action on the budget or other policy.[45]

The committee argued that this plan would be the best method for resolving disputes in the public sector. "Fact-finding requires the parties to gather objective information. . . . An unsubstantiated or extreme demand from either party tends to lose force," Taylor and his colleagues maintained. "It is ultimately the legislature and the political process which has to balance the interests of public employees with the rest of the community, to relate the compensation of public employees to the tax rate, and to appraise the . . . quality of public services . . . to the aspirations of public employees," they concluded.[46]

The committee proposed penalties for public employees who defy the new legislation that would be more effective than the 1947 Condon-Wadlin Act. They began by broadening the definition of *strike* to include "any concerted work stoppage or slowdown by public employees for the purpose of inducing or coercing in the terms or conditions of . . . employment." They urged the legislators to give greater power to the judiciary to issue injunctions to stop strikes and increase the penalties for violators. Moreover, the injunction should be imposed *before* the strike begins. The existing civil service law that provides for reprimand, fines, demotion, suspension, or dismissal for participation in a strike or slowdown, in proportion to the extent of the misconduct, should be maintained. Furthermore, the State of New York should follow the federal government's insistence that "employee organizations which seek recognition must agree not to assert the right to strike against the government." Unions already recognized in the state would continue to receive dues checkoffs, but the PERB should have the power to cancel such rights after a hearing if the union's members went on strike. The committee rejected calls by Ted Kheel and others to grant the right to strike for nonessential government workers.[47]

The committee's proposals were not directed only at unions. They "strongly urged" government agencies at all levels to devise methods for handling employee grievances, including arbitration on a case-by-case basis, much as private companies and unions had done during and after the Second World War. They urged the state and all local governments and political subdivisions "to recognize, negotiate with, and enter into written agreements" with employee organizations. Aware that some government bureaus will refuse to negotiate with duly-recognized employee organizations on the grounds that the subjects were under the exclusive control of legislative bodies, they encouraged the legislature to pass a statute that clarified which subjects were "open to negotiations in whole or in part . . . and which are for determination solely by the legislative body."[48]

Over the previous decade, the committee noted, the number of government employees had increased by close to 50 percent in the State of New York—from 409,000 to over 609,000. At that rate, there would be more than one million state government employees in New York by the latter 1970s. The City of New York already has more employees than U.S. Steel or Standard Oil, Taylor and his colleagues pointed out. Public employees are increasingly joining unions. Yet "there is as yet no counterpart in state and local government to the Vice-President of Industrial relations in private industry." Union pressure forced business corporations to hire more competent personnel managers and industrial relations vice presidents during the 1940s. New York State and its cities, counties, and towns must do the same now, the committee argued. They also recommended training programs for the public-employee unions, like the Labor Board vets did in private industry during the Second World War. They also urged the state government to recruit qualified mediators and fact-finders. Finally, the state must facilitate grievance procedures to improve the exchange of information and ideas between union representatives and government administrators. "Despite many complexities, we believe it is both feasible and desirable to develop a system of effective collective negotiations in the public service," the Taylor Committee declared. "This can be achieved in a manner which is consonant with the orderly functioning of a democratic government." Still, the systems used in private industry can't be duplicated in the government sector: "New procedures have to be created."[49]

* * *

Militant public-employee union leaders blasted the Taylor Committee's proposals. "Condon-Wadlin tried to bludgeon the unions to death and failed; the report would try to bleed them to death to make sure they don't function," exclaimed Victor Gotbaum, executive director of District Council 37 of the American Federation of State, County, and Municipal Employees, which had sixty-two thousand members in New York City. The president of the New York State AFL-CIO advised the legislature to reject the Taylor Committee report, saying that it did "violence" to the principle of collective bargaining, was "union busting," and that the "few improvements . . . are insubstantial and are only meant to disguise the anti-labor restrictions."[50]

But the Civil Service Employees Association of New York State, which had 137,000 members, supported Taylor's proposal, as did Harry Van Arsdale, the president of the New York City Central Labor Council, and Peter Brennan, the president of the New York City Building Trades Council. A committee of the New York City Bar Association supported the proposed legislation, as did the majority leader of the Republicans in the state senate, although with reservations in the latter case because the PERB would weaken elected officials in dealing with government employees. Governor Rockefeller, who was running for reelection in November and was planning to run for president in 1968, was reticent at first. He didn't want to alienate the unions, but he subsequently spoke in support of the proposed legislation.[51]

The state senate and house leaders in Albany reached a compromise in April 1967. The Public Employees' Fair Employment Act retained the principles of the Taylor Committee, with modest revisions in the penalties. The compromise legislation included a fine of $10,000 or one week's dues, whichever was less, on any union whose public-employee members stayed on strike; denial of checkoff dues for a maximum of eighteen months after the strike; a flexible system of penalties for individual strikers. A major provision was that it did not require PERB approval of the New York City's labor laws. Instead, there was an assumption of equivalence with state and city labor laws—a major concession to the city's public-employee unions. The legislators and the governor reached agreement at 4 a.m., after thirty hours of meetings. When asked what the new legislation should be called, the governor replied, "the Taylor Law." "This is one law where the legislators didn't fight to have their name on it," George Taylor quipped.[52]

Governor Rockefeller called the Taylor Law "a milestone in employer-employee relations in the state" with "tremendous implications nationally." Leaders of the public-employee unions hardly concurred. "This is an infamous bill that will stiffen the [union leaders in the] city's posture," declared John DeLury, president of the Uniformed Sanitationmen's Association. He promised to set up a strike fund. The Taylor Act "relegated public employees to second-class citizenship," the Uniformed Firefighters Association declared. "No law is going to take away our right to strike," shouted Victor Gotbaum.[53]

The union leaders were correct. The number of strikes, slowdowns, sick-outs, and other job actions by teachers, garbage collectors, postal workers, bus and subway drivers, nurses, hospital aides, firefighters, police officers, and other public employees swelled in the late 1960s not only in New York City but in Chicago, Philadelphia, St. Louis, Kansas City, Fort Lauderdale, Albuquerque, San Francisco, and smaller cities too.

New York City's unions were the brashest of all.[54] At 11 p.m. Thursday, January 25, 1967, 6,000 members of the Teamsters Local 237 employed in public housing quit work over a pay dispute, leaving almost 500,000 residents—mostly elderly residents and single mothers on welfare and their children—without hot water or heat. On May 11, 700 laborers and truck drivers employed in the sewer division of the city's Department of Public Works went on strike to protest the elimination of seventy-five jobs. In February 1968, 3,500 members of Local 272 of Teamsters Garage Employee Union struck for a week, temporarily leaving 190,000 New Yorkers, mainly in midtown Manhattan, without a place to park their cars.[55]

Such walkouts became common in the city. Most significant was the strike called in September 1967 by the United Federation of Teachers demanding major salary increases, a reduction in class size in schools in disadvantaged neighborhoods, more professional assistance in those schools, and the power for teachers to remove disruptive students from their classrooms. This was the first strike affecting every one of the city's public schools. "There will be no teachers. There will be no schools," the union's president Albert Shanker warned. Superintendent of School Bernard Donovan was more hopeful, predicting that most of the teachers would "put their professionalism ahead of their unionism" and report to work. The superintendent was mistaken. The vast majority of white teachers did respect the strike call. The 1967 teacher strike lasted for fourteen days, with the union winning major concessions from the school board despite the Taylor Act. The strike aroused anger, which persisted long after the strike concluded. Puerto Rican organizations, the New York City NAACP, and the African-American Teachers Association charged that the strike demands were racist. Of the city's 58,000 teachers, 12,000 refused to strike, and the walkout did not improve relations between the union leaders and the superintendent and his staff.[56]

Four months later 10,000 New York City sanitation workers, members of the Uniformed Santitationmen's Association, went on strike for nine days, demanding a $600 wage increase, a Monday-through-Friday workweek, time-and-a-half for Saturday work, double time for Sunday work, 10 percent differential for night work, and, not least, a one-year contract instead of the expired three-year agreement. As days passed, one hundred thousand tons of refuse mounted in city streets. The piles of trash were greatest in South Bronx, Central Harlem, the Lower East Side, and Brownsville and Bedford-Stuyvesant in Brooklyn—the most crowded sections of the city. Residents set hundreds of fires at night to eliminate the garbage, creating the danger of a firestorm. Firemen were put on fifteen-hour shifts. Major John Lindsay asked for the governor to send the National Guard, which only increased union leaders' support for the sanitation workers. "The older members remember when the National Guard meant strikebreakers—there is a loathing for strikebreaking," remarked Moe Iushewitz, secretary of the New York City Central Labor Council. In the meantime, the sewers were "getting clogged," the New York City health commissioner reported. "We are getting reports of backing up.... If ... waste gets on streets and basements ... we have threat of typhoid and dysentery."[57]

* * *

The teacher and sanitation strikes prompted Nelson Rockefeller to reestablish the Governor's Committee on Public Employee Relations. He asked the committee to reexamine the Taylor Act. Taylor and his colleagues blamed the tripartite Office of Collective Bargaining of New York City (OCM) set up by Mayor Lindsay on September 1, 1967, for the problems plaguing the city. "There is no requirement for finality," Taylor told Arvid Anderson, the OCM's chair, in spring 1968. "The common denominator in the teachers' and sanitationmen's strikes ... was an ambiguity—a no man's land—over jurisdiction of PERB and OCB," Dunlop declared. Anderson did not agree. He told Dunlop and Taylor that he was against stiff penalties, that the law's insistence that the unions and public agencies have to submit their positions fifteen days before the legislature decides its budget was "ridiculous."

Anderson's argument did not persuade the Taylor Committee, which told Anderson that "the City's industrial relations problems are both the cause and effect of its budgetary problems."[58] "Are we willing to accept defiance from *muscle unions*?" David Cole asked when the committee met privately. He was referring to unionized garbage collectors, laborers, and truck drivers in the Department of Public Works sewer division and to schoolteachers, all of whose work was so strategically placed that they could strike regardless of the law. "The more critical the service[,] the greater the muscle," Cole remarked.[59]

Taylor, Dunlop, Cole, Bakke, and Harbison stood their ground. In a report submitted to the governor in June 1968, they attributed the February sanitation strike to the New York City's Office of Collective Bargaining, which, they argued, did not have a system for final determination of disputes between public unions and employers comparable to the PERB, as required under the Taylor Act. It was different in the rest of the state, where hundreds of first-time negotiations between employee and government "have been peacefully concluded," they declared. About two-thirds of the nine hundred thousand public employees in New York State are now represented by employee organizations, the committee asserted, and a "growing number" of those employee organizations "have signed—as a condition for receiving recognition or certification—affirmations that they do not assert the right to strike against the government." From the committee's point of view, the problem lay not in the Taylor Act but in New York City's Office of Collective Bargaining.

In mid-October 1968, Nelson Rockefeller and the chairman of the PERB, Robert Helsby, brought together almost the entire *dramatis personae* for three days of debate on the Taylor Act and the relations between public-employee unions and state and local governments. Six hundred fifty men and women attended the Governor's Conference on Public Employment Relations. They met at the Hilton Hotel in midtown Manhattan. In addition to Governor Rockefeller, George Taylor, David Cole, and John Dunlop, the speakers included UFT president Albert Shanker; Uniformed Sanitationmen's Association president John DeLury; the presidents of the American Federation of State, County and Municipal Employees and the Service Employees' International Union; Senator Thomas Laverne, the Republican majority leader in Albany who had a critical role in shaping New York State labor law; and Justice Arthur Goldberg, who as secretary of labor in the Kennedy administration had persuaded the president to issue an executive order that permitted federal employees to join unions.

They met in a tense atmosphere. On Sunday evening, March 30, President Lyndon Johnson had startled the American people by announcing that he did not intend to run for reelection. Four days later, Dr. Martin Luther King Jr., who had gone to Memphis to support striking sanitation workers, was murdered by a sniper while standing on the balcony of the Lorraine Motel. The assassination generated rage and riots in more than a hundred cities, large and small. Two months later, on June 5, Senator Robert Kennedy, who had just won the California primary and was expected to capture the Democratic nomination for president, was assassinated by a Palestinian refugee. Despite not entering any of the primaries, Vice President Hubert Humphrey secured the Democratic nomination for president at the party's convention in Chicago in late August while Chicago police slugged antiwar protestors in the streets. Humphrey campaigned against the Republican nominee Richard Nixon and Governor George Wallace of Alabama, the candidate of the American Independent Party.

The Patrolmen's Benevolent Association of New York City threatened a sick-out shortly before the Governor's Conference was to convene. The Uniformed Firefighter Association was engaged in a slowdown, the Uniformed Sanitation-men's Association was threatening to strike again, and the United Federation of Teachers went on strike again to protest the dismissal of white teachers from schools in the Ocean Hill-Brownsville section of Brooklyn—the teachers' fourth strike of the year. Shanker, John DeLury of the sanitation workers union, and Lillian Robert and Robert Fuller of the American Federation of State, County and Municipal Employees were sent to jail that fall for violating the Taylor Act.[60]

Every union speaker at the Governor's Conference condemned the legislation for not allowing any public employees to strike, not even those whose work was not indispensable; for assigning the state legislature and city councils the ultimate authority for the settlement of disputes; and for being excessively rigid. Mediators also criticized the law. Justice Goldberg, who had years of experience in negotiations as counsel for the Steelworkers and was at that moment trying to mediate between the sanitation workers union and the city, said he preferred "a wide latitude for collective bargaining until the ultimate moment" when the legislative body could perhaps intervene "on some ad hoc basis."[61]

The law's sharpest critic was so harsh that he was excluded from the meeting. That was Ted Kheel, the former chairman of the New York Regional War Labor Board and long-time New York City mediator. Three days before the Governor's Conference, Kheel sent a pointed thirteen-page critique of the Taylor Act to Robert Helsby, chairman of the PERB and cochairman of the meeting. He gave a copy to reporters the next day, Saturday, October 12, so that his remarks would be quoted in Sunday papers, so as to attract maximum attention. "The impasse and penalty provisions of the Taylor Law have failed," Kheel told Helsby, "and there is no reason to believe that further experiment . . . will make them work effectively." Kheel called the law "schizophrenic," attempting to simultaneously forbid strikes yet sponsor "an 'ersatz form' of collective bargaining." This was the same sort of "unilateral determination" of relationship embodied in the now-repudiated Condon-Wadlin Act of 1947, according to Kheel. Despite the supposed changes, public officials can still reject fact-finding recommendations, as John Lindsay did in the February 1968 sanitation workers' strike. Dunlop argued disputes should be handled by the state legislature or a legislative committee. Why, Kheel asked? They were hardly objective decision makers. He challenged the Governor's Committee claim that relations in the public sector are different from those in the private sector. It is impossible to write a law that could uproot "with one stroke" all customs that working people and employers "have found normal and natural for generations." Kheel thought that the cooling off mandated in the 1947 Taft-Hartley Act was preferable to the Taylor Act.[62]

Normally cool-tempered, Taylor refused to accept Kheel's rebuke. "It would be regrettable—even deplorable—if a continued concentration upon the strike issue, by some unions and by a few 'experts,' should stifle an orderly forward development of the movement toward more rational relationships everywhere," he replied at the conference. Let us suppose their vision of the future came into being, he asked. What would we have in New York City, the New York State, and the United States? One strong labor organization would demand big increases in compensation and other benefits. Other strong unions would be impelled to equal or even win more. The most powerful unions would leapfrog while those with less sway would fall further behind. The government wage structure would become "very lop-sided," Taylor exclaimed. "The right to strike would . . . be extended to public employees . . . in the worst possible way. . . . What is termed a 'practical' approach [in the private sector] is quite impractical as far as the public interest is concerned," Taylor maintained. The "employer" is ultimately not the school board, the sanitation department, or other government offices, but the state legislature, the governor, and the judiciary. If some unions acquire extraordinary strength, what happens to the rest of the budget? Public employees' rights must be recognized, Taylor acknowledged, "but without a rough-shod infringement upon the fundamental rights of everybody else."[63]

After the conference concluded, Rockefeller asked Taylor's committee to propose amendments to the law for the state legislators to consider when they convened in February. Taylor, Cole, Dunlop, Bakke, and Harbison recommended changes in the law that would have required New York City's Office of Collective Bargaining to adopt procedures "substantially equivalent" to those approved by the PERB in other municipalities in the state. Doing so would "provide for equitable treatment of public employees on the merits of their claims," they declared, "rather than on their ability or lack of ability to bring the public to its knees."[64]

The Taylor Committee's proposals did not satisfy the Republicans, who captured majorities in the state Assembly and Senate in November 1968. A Gallup Poll taken in March 1968 showed that nearly six out of ten Americans thought that teachers had the right to unionize, but an equal number believed that they should not be permitted to strike. Opposition to strikes was greatest in the northeastern United States, where the public-employee unions were strongest. Americans who did not belong to unions were most strongly opposed to teacher strikes, but even union members were divided about teachers' strikes. Similar opinions existed for unions and strikes by nurses.[65] These polls were taken before the United Federation of Teachers conducted a strike in May 1968 and three more strikes in September and October. The teachers' strikes that kept children of the school, the sanitation workers' strike that left mountains of debris on city street, fuel-oil strikes that left families cold during the flu season, and the strikes in the four state mental hospitals—these and other stoppages enraged many voters and, consequently, state legislators. "The Neanderthals are in command; the whole attitude is 'hand somebody his head,'" one Republican legislator told the *New York Times* labor reporter A. H. Raskin.[66]

The amendments to the Taylor Law enacted in spring 1969 protected state employees from unfair treatment by their managers and compelled the state and cities to bargain in good faith with unions, while also imposing higher penalties on unions that defied the law. The greatest change, however, was the reinstatement of mandatory punishment for individual strikers. Under the new law, any employee who went on strike would lose two days' pay for one day off the job. Some Republicans proposed loss of pay for workers engaged in slowdowns, but abandoned the plan when one legislator sarcastically asked, "How are you going to tell when they are slowing down?"[67]

Taylor had warned union leaders that strikes by teachers, sanitation workers, and other public employee were bound to backfire. He told reporters that he considered the amendments "unduly harsh." Labor relations in the public sector in New York State had fallen into "a cycle of futility" with powerful unions conducting illegal strikes, which in turn incited tougher legislation.[68]

* * *

When the Labor Board vets became involved, public-employee unions were fragile and relations between administrators and employees were regulated by civil-service procedures fashioned in the Gilded Age. In the mid- and late 1960s, George Taylor, David Cole, John Dunlop, Wight Bakke, and Fred Harbison designed a system that led to the unionization of 90 percent of New York State's public employees by the early 1970s, with procedures for resolving the strikes and other disputes between the unions and administrators. The system did not end strikes in New York City, other cities in the state, or the public schools, as Rockefeller promised the public. If anything, the law encouraged union militancy, as its union critics promised. Another decade of conflict and economic catastrophe would have to pass before stabile relations between unions and administrators emerged in New York State and other state and city governments.[69]

The Labor Board vets went on to other projects after the amendments to the Taylor Law were passed. John Dunlop was appointed dean of the Faculty of Arts and Sciences at Harvard University. David Cole handled other disputes, beginning with the Metropolitan Opera and the American Federation of Musicians in New York City before chairing the National Commission for Industrial Peace in the Nixon administration. Fred Harbison returned to his work on manpower development in Africa. Wight Bakke served on the National Manpower Policy Task Force on engineers and scientists and coauthored a book on student activism. George Taylor returned to the Wharton School and advised the Nixon administration on its wage-price controls.

Even as they moved on, Dunlop, Taylor, and Cole knew that problems remained ahead in the public employment arena. "Competition escalation of pension benefits is likely to be very expensive," Dunlop predicted at the Governor's Conference on Public Employee Relations. Taylor foresaw "a run on the bank" for higher and higher wages and benefits at state and municipal services. "I think the public, certainly a good part of the thoughtful public, is becoming a little fed up with strikes in major industries and in the more essential services . . . where the strike was never designed to play a part. After all, the strike is an attack on the pocketbook, isn't it?" David Cole asked in 1974.[70]

During the 1970s, those conflicts came to a head.

7

"How Can We Avoid a Columbia?"

The Student Revolt, 1964–71

The campus has replaced Haymarket Square
and the Embarcadero.

—Clark Kerr

I am convinced, as I have been for a long time, that
we must understand the politics of dissent, and that
we must play the game with considerable skill.

—Robben Fleming

THOUSANDS OF STUDENTS gave Clark Kerr a standing ovation when he walked onto the stage of the University of California's Berkeley Greek Theater at eleven in the morning, December 7, 1964. Kerr undoubtedly appreciated the applause even though he and the chairman of the Political Science Department had packed the amphitheater with fraternity and sorority students predisposed to the administration. He had had a rough time that fall, attacked by a student rebellion of a force unprecedented in the history of American higher education.

Kerr was fifty-three years old at that time. He had been the president of the University of California, the largest university in America and one of the most prestigious, since 1958, after serving for six years as chancellor at Berkeley, the university's flagship campus. When Robert Sproul announced in 1957 that he planned to retire after thirty years as president of the university, the board of regents planned to appoint as his successor UCLA's "football-puffing" chancellor, Raymond Allen, previously the president of the University of Washington. To confirm their opinion, the regents asked top university administrators across the country for their suggestions. Their response was almost unanimous, "You already have Clark Kerr at Berkeley."[1]

By the early 1960s, Kerr was considered the most influential university president in the United States. *Time* magazine put him on their front cover in October 1960, three weeks before the presidential election, under the banner "Master Planner." In his first six years presiding at the University of California, he had developed a plan to enlarge California's public university system and link junior colleges, state colleges, and research universities. He had decentralized the university's administration, planned three new campuses at San Diego, Irvine, and Santa Cruz, increased funding for the humanities and the social sciences—the principal weak area at the university when he assumed office—and procured funds for increasing facilities and faculty to accommodate the baby boomers. Kerr and his wife Catherine lived with their children in their exquisite ranch house in El Cerrito, in the hills over Berkeley.

The protests began in the third week of September. On October 1 university police drove into Sproul Plaza, in the center of the campus, where a former student, Jack Weinberg, was staffing a recruitment table for the Congress of Racial Equality, in violation of university regulations. When the police put Weinberg into their car to drive to headquarters and book him, someone cried out, "Sit down!" Several hundred students promptly circled the vehicle. They kept the police car encircled for thirty-one hours until Kerr negotiated a temporary truce. Neither side was satisfied with the terms, however, and protests, counterstrokes, and discord continued for the next two months. Over Thanksgiving break, the chancellor, Edward Strong, sent letters to four students who had led the original sit-in, ordering them to attend a hearing for the illegal activity. The letter angered many students, who demanded that the charges be dropped. When the administration refused, eight hundred students and other activists occupied Sproul Hall, the main campus administration building and were arrested at 3 a.m. the next morning, in the largest arrest in the history of the state of California.

The confrontation was a distressing experience for Kerr, who had been a radical student himself at the University of California at Berkeley thirty years earlier, had denounced repressive political policies of the university administration as a young professor during the McCarthy era, and, once he was appointed president, had urged the regents to loosen the constraints on political speech on the campus.[2] Kerr was a lifelong pacifist and an ardent supporter of democracy in unions and equal rights for African Americans. He traveled to Vietnam for eight days in 1967 and afterward drafted a statement cosigned by noted intellectual, university, corporate, and religious leaders appealing to President Lyndon Johnson to deescalate the fighting in that war. "This is an effort by a moderate group to place a position before the country that we think it badly needs," Kerr declared at that time.[3]

Yet he was utterly out of tune with *mentalité* of the students protesting in Berkeley in 1964, and he was afraid of how conservative Californians would react to the student protests—quite justifiably so, as it turned out. The conflict between the student radicals and Kerr continued until January 1967, when California's new governor, Ronald Reagan, who had campaigned on the pledge to "clean up that mess at Berkeley," fired the University of California president, an act foreshadowing his dismissal of the striking Professional Air Traffic Controllers in August 1981. "I left the presidency just as I had entered it—fired with enthusiasm," Kerr joked in public, although intimates said the termination hurt him badly.[4]

But Kerr did not walk away from the world of higher education. On the contrary, he was immediately appointed chairman and director of the newly established Carnegie Commission on Higher Education, which he decided to locate in Berkeley. He also maintained his faculty post at the Institute of Industrial Relations at the university. Over the next decade, Kerr's commission produced more than a hundred studies on how to finance higher education in the United States; politics in the academy; issues facing university presidents; student protests; the future of science, social science, and medicine in universities; faculty unions; and related issues.[5]

As student protests spread east, trustees at other prestigious universities appointed other Labor Board vets as their presidents, chancellors, and top deans. John Dunlop was chosen as dean of the Faculty of Arts and Sciences at Harvard University. Robben Fleming became chancellor of the University of Wisconsin at Madison and president of the University of Michigan. John McConnell became president of the University of New Hampshire. Richard Lester became dean of the faculty at Princeton University. Other universities appointed the Labor Board vets' protégés as presidents and top deans. Thus Derek Bok, a law professor who had coauthored a study of the place of organized labor in society with Dunlop, was named president of Harvard University. William Bowen, a labor economist, became president of Princeton University. Michael Sovern became president of Columbia University. Arnold Weber was appointed president of the University of Colorado and Northwestern University. Harold Enarson became president of Ohio State University. Edwin Young was appointed dean of the College of Arts and Sciences at the University of Wisconsin at Madison. And George Shultz became dean of the Graduate School of Business at the University of Chicago, where he advised their provost how to handle the student revolt there.

Who could be better qualified to handle student radicalism, trustees reasoned, than the industrial relations professors who had dealt with unions, strikes, and worker grievances for years? But the industrial workers and radical students were hardly alike. The workers of the 1940s and 1950s were adults, often married with children, well organized, resolute, and sharply focused in their objectives: the

right to bargain collectively, fair treatment on the job, protection of jobs, and better compensation. The students of the mid- and late 1960s were younger, intense,
frequently hotheaded, and occasionally violent and they had bolder objectives,
some of which the university administrations could not satisfy even if they wanted
to: end of university contracts with the Defense, Army, and Navy Departments,
end of recruitment on campus by Dow Chemical and other companies whose
products the U.S. armed force used in Southeast Asia, terminating the Reserve
Officer Training Corps (ROTC), student power, Black Power, Women's Liberation, U.S. withdrawal from Southeast Asia, and world revolution. "At present in
the United States students—middle class youths—are the major exploited class,"
the influential anarchist Paul Goodman wrote in January 1965, in the aftermath of
the Sproul Hall arrests in Berkeley. "Negroes, small farmers, the aged are rather
out-caste groups; their labor is not needed and they are not wanted. The labor of
intelligent youth is needed and they are accordingly subjected to tight scheduling,
speedup, and other factory methods. Then it is not surprising if they organized
their CIO. It is frivolous to tell them to go elsewhere if they don't like the rules,
for they have no choice but to go to college and one factory is like another."[6]

Kerr botched the job. "We fumbled, we floundered, and the worst thing is I
still don't know how we should have done it. At any other university, the administrators wouldn't have known how to handle it any better," he remarked to Abe
Raskin, the New York Times labor reporter in February 1965.[7]

Over time, however, the other Labor Board vets did find ways to handle the
student upheaval. They consciously avoided mistakes made by Kerr and other
university administrators. Drawing on their experience in industrial relations,
they did not ask for police, state troopers, or the National Guard to drive students out of buildings they occupied. Instead, they negotiated for endless hours
with the radicals and, after compromises were reached, installed new systems
of "governance" to resolve future conflicts on their campuses, systems that were
ultimately adopted by administrators by nearly all American universities.

* * *

Ironically, Kerr had anticipated the student revolt, although he thought that the
students would rebel against the faculty, not against him and the chancellor. He
made the prediction in Godkin lectures that he delivered at Harvard University in
April 1963. Named for E. L. Godkin, the renowned post–Civil War editor of *The
Nation*, the annual Godkin lectures were delivered by Lord James Bryce, Walter
Lippmann, Gunner Myrdal, Justice Robert Jackson, Senator Paul Douglas, Lord
C. P. Snow, and other luminaries. The selection of Kerr as the lecturer in 1963
suggests the stature he had acquired by that time. He chose as his title "The Uses
of the University." Harvard University Press published Kerr's lectures later that

year. Now in its fifth edition, *The Uses of the University* became a staple in graduate schools of education and a primer for university administrators.

"The university started as a single community—a community of masters and students," Kerr declared in 1963. "It may even be said to have a soul in the sense of a central animating principle." American universities changed profoundly, however, during the industrial age. After the Civil War, they began to assist farmers and companies by conducting research and establishing agricultural extension programs and schools for engineers and, later, corporate executives. During and after the Second World War, universities became far more ambitious. "The university is being called upon to produce knowledge as never before," Kerr remarked. It was no longer a "university" but a "multiversity." State and privately endowed universities have been "performing services for practically every constituency that requested it," the President's Commission on Campus Unrest observed in June 1970.[8]

Kerr was the most articulate advocate of the multiversity. Yet he recognized their detrimental impact on undergraduate education. Swarthmore College had only five hundred students when he entered in September 1928. There were no academic "departments" at the college, simply broad areas of inquiry. He decided to focus on the social sciences. The classes were small and relations between students and professors close. He thrived in this environment, graduating with high honors, a Phi Betta Kappa key, and three athletic letters and was elected president of the senior class. Admitted to Columbia University's law school, Kerr decided to spend the summer in California, spreading the message of international peace to the West Coast where the Quaker's American Friends Service Committee lacked organization. Kerr found the Golden State so exciting that he decided to postpone law school and instead applied for a master's degree in economics at Stanford University.

Unlike the students who applied to mammoth universities during the 1960s or any college today, Kerr encountered no bureaucratic obstacles when he applied to graduate school. "In those days things were kind of informal," he recalled sixty years later. "I just went to the registration line—I hadn't applied—and said I'd like to apply to be a graduate student, and I got referred to the registrar himself. He says, 'Where did you go to college?' I say, 'To Swarthmore.' He says, 'What's your record there?' I say, 'Well, I got high honors.' He says, 'You're admitted.'"[9]

Before the Second World War, the leading private universities still considered educating undergraduates their highest priority. Jacques Barzun, Columbia University's noted professor of literature, earned his bachelor's degree at that university during the mid-1920s. He termed his education in the arts and sciences at that time as "informal." The faculty "set up as many small discussion groups (colloquia, seminars, preceptorials) as possible." The professors did not abandon lectures. In fact, the number of lecture classes and their sizes increased during the 1920s at

Columbia and other universities, a prelude to the great expansion that occurred after the Second World War. But "they let lapse the *formality* of lecturing.... One might say that in the university old-style the split between its two functions of imparting and creating knowledge was bridged by the duty of all [members of the faculty] to teach undergraduates."[10]

Education was not so different at the best public universities, recalled Robert Nisbet, who earned his bachelor's and doctoral degrees in sociology at the University of California at Berkeley between 1932 and 1939 and then was appointed as an instructor in their Sociology Department. Before the United States entered the war, teaching introductory classes was considered a prize awarded to the most highly respected senior faculty, Nisbett recalled.

The universities changed during the Second World War. The faculty were asked to teach algebra, trigonometry, or precalculus if they remembered high school mathematics, or, if not, to develop other courses related to war for cadets being trained on the campus. Nisbet put together a course on Thucydides's history of the Peloponnesian War.[11] Other Berkeley faculty received funds from the War Department. J. Robert Oppenheimer and Ernest Lawrence, physicists at UC-Berkeley, played key roles in the building of the first atomic bombs at Los Alamos, New Mexico. Philosophy professor Edward Strong—whom Kerr appointed as chancellor at UC-Berkeley in the early 1960s—was named supervisor the Lawrence Radiation Laboratory at Berkeley, an experience that may help explain his stern response to the student protests in 1964.

Although federal funding to the universities declined briefly after V-J Day, it resumed when the United States began to confront the Soviet Union in 1947. The Department of War was renamed the Department of Defense. The National Science Foundation, the Atomic Energy Commission, and other federal agencies were created, and these and other bureaus began to pump millions and later hundreds of millions of dollars into universities, the bulk of it going to twenty-five large schools that were reconceived as "research universities." In the process, he observed, the century-old distinction between land-grant institutions such as Ohio State University and privately funded universities such as Yale University blurred. They all became, in Kerr's words, "Federal Grant Universities."[12]

As money poured in, the universities became mammoth. By 1962, the University of California had operating expenses of nearly a half-billion dollars and nearly one hundred million more on construction. It employed more than forty thousand men and women, more than IBM, "and in a far greater variety of endeavors," noted Kerr. In addition to its six campuses (and the three new ones scheduled to open in 1965), the university maintained facilities in more than a hundred locations, including agricultural and urban extensions across the state, experiment stations, and projects in nearly fifty foreign countries. The university had three thousand professors, including seven Nobel Prize winners (six of them at Berkeley), and listed nearly ten thousand courses in its catalogs. It owned ranches, apartment buildings, vineyards, movie studios, and seven oceangoing ships. It had connections with virtually every kind of industry in California and with nearly all level of government. "Over 4,000 babies were born in its hospitals" in 1962, Kerr exclaimed. "It is the world's largest purveyor of white mice. It will soon have the world's largest primate colony." Harvard resembles the University of California, Kerr told his audience. "And Harvard and California are illustrative of many more."[13]

By 1963, the University of California had 70,000 undergraduates and nearly 30,000 graduate students on its campuses at Berkeley, Los Angeles, Davis, Santa Barbara, Riverside, and San Francisco, plus 200,000 more in extension programs. According to the Master Plan develop by Kerr in 1960, enrollment at the University of California would rise to 214,000 undergraduates by 1970. Kerr insisted that none of their campuses enroll more than 25,000 students. Several other universities were even larger: 30,000 at the University of Wisconsin's Madison campus in 1963; 40,000 students at the University of Minnesota and at Ohio State University.

These developments transformed undergraduate life. Until the midtwentieth century, the bulk of the students enrolled at prestigious universities and colleges in the United States came from economically well-off, white, old-line Protestant families. It was an era when students at Andover, Choate, and other preparatory schools chose colleges, not the other way around. If student body was somewhat more diverse at the top state universities like UC-Berkeley, Michigan, and Wisconsin, it was a difference of degree, not kind. Sports were the students' greatest interest and the majority of students lived in fraternities and sororities that excluded African Americans, Jews, and other minorities.

The composition of the student body changed between 1945 and 1960 and even more so during the 1960s. The 1944 GI Bill provided funds for veterans from working-class and lower-middle-class families and gave them the opportunity to attend universities, including private as well as public institutions, for the first time. The U.S. Congress passed similar legislation during the war in Korea. Meanwhile, rising prosperity of the 1950s enabled young people from modest backgrounds to attend college. This meant that a large number of Catholic youth, who had previously gone straight into the workforce after high school, dropped out earlier, or attended Catholic colleges, were attending public institutions. The number of African American students attending previously all-white universities north of the Mason-Dixon Line began to rise slowly, and the private universities removed the quotas on Jewish students and began to appoint Jews to their faculties. These developments were a prelude to the transformations of the mid- to late 1960s, when elite private universities undertook a concerted effort to draw in African Americans students, many more Jews were added to the faculties, and all-male colleges like Harvard and Amherst became coeducational.

Classes for undergraduates began increasingly large and impersonal. According to sociologist Neil Smelser, the student body at Berkeley increased 80 percent between 1953 and 1964, but the number of faculty was enlarged by merely 18 percent. Even that statistic understates the change, for by the early 1960s approximately one-sixth of the tenured faculty at Berkeley—the professors whom the chancellor considered "stars"—had half-time teaching appointments, typically one class per semester, sometimes less. Roughly one-fourth of the faculty in the social sciences and the humanities were on sabbatical or on leave at least half of each year. As a result, undergraduates received much of their instruction from graduate students or junior faculty. Students in the humanities and social sciences were particularly short-changed. The undergraduates might well have felt "that they were being invited into an elite institution only to be educated mainly by second-class teachers," remarked Smelser, who was brought into the chancellor's office in early 1965.[14]

"Recent changes in the American university have done them [the undergraduates] little good," Kerr conceded in 1963. Not only did graduate students and young professors do most of the teaching, but professors were hired for their research potential, not their ability to teach. Moreover, knowledge was constantly being divided into smaller segments until it became unintelligible to undergraduates. "The undergraduate students are restless," Kerr observed. "If the faculty looks on itself as a guild, the undergraduate students are coming to look upon themselves more as a 'class'; some may even feel like a 'lumpen proletariat.'"[15]

* * *

The history of radicalism at Berkeley reaches back to the late 1910s, when rents skyrocketed in the Russian Hill section of San Francisco, prompting poets, musicians, and other bohemians to move across the bay. They settled in rooming houses and garden cottages south of the campus. Tuition was free, rents cheap, the weather mild: what could be finer? In 1934 longshoremen led by Communists led a general strike in San Francisco. During those same months, Upton Sinclair was campaigning for the Democratic nomination for governor on a platform called End Poverty in California. In October the student council at UCLA announced it would hold an open forum to discuss the election. The provost, a well-connected Republican named Ernest C. Moore, responded by suspending the student council's president and four other council members, charging that they were trying to convert the campus into "a hothead of Communism." In April

1935, students at Berkeley and UCLA held one-hour "strikes," signing the Oxford Pledge that they would not go to war if the nation was attacked and demanding the end of mandatory enrollment in ROTC.

As UC-Berkeley acquired a reputation in the East as "more Communist than Stalin," the board of regents imposed strict limitations on political speech by UC students and faculty, controls that were stiffened during the McCarthy era. No outside speakers were permitted to speak on campus without the prior approval of the university president or his representative, or unless invited by a professor for a specific class. University facilities could not be used for partisan political activities of any kind. Local law enforcement agents and antiradical organizations such as the American Legion began to spy on campus radicals. And, starting in 1950, every professor and all other University of California employees were required, as a condition of hiring and continued employment, to take an oath swearing that "I am not a member of, nor do I support any party or organization that believes in, advocates, or teaches the overthrow of the United States government, by force or by any illegal or unconstitutional methods."[16]

Kerr and other UC faculty protested the oath, but the students generally remained silent at that time. The mood on the campus began to change, however, by September 1958, when Kerr was inaugurated as president. Josef Stalin died in 1954, succeeded two years later by Nikita Khrushchev, who denounced Stalin's crimes and subsequently permitted modest reforms. In 1957 Ghana became the first freed colony on the continent of Africa, and African Americans in Montgomery, Alabama, began their arduous but ultimately successful boycott to sit anywhere on the city's buses. Meanwhile, students whose parents had participated in the antiwar or union demonstrations of the 1930s or marched against General Francisco Franco were entering UC-Berkeley and comparable universities and colleges. In 1958 a small group of politically radical students at UC-Berkeley organized a slate to challenge fraternity and sorority dominance of the student government. After four African American college students sat in at a lunch counter at the Woolworth's in downtown Greensboro, North Carolina, on February 1, 1960, protest against discrimination against African Americans in public places spread across the South. In the next eighteen months more than seventy thousand men and women participated in civil-rights demonstrations. They were followed by protests against racial discrimination in housing and jobs in San Francisco, Oakland, and Berkeley. The execution of Caryl Chessman for rape at the state penitentiary on San Quentin Island in San Francisco Bay on May 2, 1960, aroused widespread protests from radicals in the Bay Area, including some UC-Berkeley students. Ten days later, small groups of Berkeley students and others protested when the House Un-American Activities Committee held hearings in San Francisco. In 1961 communists and other Bay Area radicals organized a Fair Play for

Cuba Committee to support Fidel Castro's new revolution. That same year, the U.S. Supreme Court began to broaden the lawful definition of free speech to include literature previously deemed pornographic.

Kerr began to lift restraints on political dissent on the UC campuses in that atmosphere. He did not drop all the tethers, however. That was not Kerr's style and he would have encountered considerable opposition from the board of regents and state legislators if he had. Instead, he moved cautiously. In October 1958 restrictions were lifted on speeches on campus by political candidates. After the opening of a new student union in September 1959 outside Sather Gate, the south entrance to the campus, Kerr obtained permission from the regents to transfer a 26-by-40-foot spot at the end of Telegraph Avenue to the City of Berkeley so the political radicals could continue to solicit support from students and others entering the campus there. In 1960 the Associated Students of the University of California, the official student society financed by mandatory student fees, was granted permission to invite visitors to speak on any subject as long as they did not claim to speak on behalf of the association. In June 1963 the ban against on-campus speeches by Communists was lifted.[17] In recognition of these changes, the American Association of University Professors presented Kerr and the board of regents the Alexander Meiklejohn Award "for outstanding contribution to academic freedom" in April 1964.[18]

Kerr's liberal reforms, however, clashed with other actions that he took during those same years. In 1959 his office published a series of regulations on student behavior. In his memoir *The Gold and the Blue*, Kerr described the rules as "mostly old," a codification of the various edicts issued by the regents or the administration during Robert Sproul's period in office "or where new, liberating." He conceded that, when "brought together, this large body of existing rules looked like . . . a new set of rules . . . and oppressive." Radical students termed the regulations "the Kerr directives" and questioned his right to issue such orders. "In a democratic society, the source of authority for such regulations is rightfully derived from the society's constituents, which in this case . . . are the students and not the university administration," two students declared in *The Daily Cal* in 1960.[19]

In February 1964 members of the Congress of Racial Equality, including UC-Berkeley students, entered Lucky's supermarkets in San Francisco, Oakland, and Berkeley, filled their shopping carts to the top, put the groceries in front of the cash register, and walked out, disrupting business. They were demanding the supermarket hire more African Americans. When the management of the swank Sheraton-Palace Hotel in San Francisco refused to sign an agreement to hire a specific number of African Americans, the Ad Hoc Committee to End Discrimination began a series of demonstrations in March, including picket lines outside its doors, sit-ins, a "sleep-in" in the lobby, and performances by the acerbic African

American comedian Dick Gregory. Nearly nine hundred people were arrested at the Sheraton, many of whom were UC-Berkeley students. In April, 226 demonstrators, the majority high school and college students, occupied Cadillac, Chrysler, and Lincoln-Mercury dealerships, again demanding the managers hired more African Americans. Sixty demonstrated were arrested for singing, chanting, or sitting in the cars and the showroom floors. According to Donald Mulford, a conservative Republican state representative whose district included Berkley and Oakland, 412 students were arrested in eight demonstrations between 1960 and spring 1964. He called on the board of regents to expel any student who was arrested twice.[20]

The political temperature became even fervid that summer. Several UC-Berkeley students, among them Mario Savio, who had been involved in job protests in the Bay Area during the spring, joined the Student Non-Violent Coordinating Committee's project to help rural African Americans register to vote in Mississippi. On July 15, 1964, the National Republican Party, meeting in San Francisco's Cow Palace, nominated the blunt conservative Senator Barry Goldwater as their presidential nominee. Three weeks earlier, Goldwater had voted against the Civil Right Act, an act that outlawed discrimination in employment and public accommodations, authorized the attorney general to institute suits to desegregate public schools and other public facilities, and provided some protection for voting rights. On August 3 came the news that three young civil-rights activists—Michael Schwerner, James Chaney, and Andrew Goodman—had been murdered in Philadelphia, Mississippi, prompting thirty-five Berkeley students to organize a sit-in in the U.S. attorney's office in San Francisco. Four days later, August 7, the U.S. Congress passed the Gulf of Tonkin Resolution giving President Johnson free hand to "take all necessary steps" that he considered necessary to fight the armed forces of the National Liberation Front and North Vietnam, prompting several UC-Berkeley professors to sign a statement published in the *Chronicle of Higher Education* condemning U.S. government action in that region. Finally, on September 10, 1964, Brad Cleveland, a former UC graduate student, wrote a thirteen-page open letter to Berkeley undergraduates calling for "AN OPEN, FIERCE, AND THOROUGHGOING REBELLION ON THIS CAMPUS." His letter was stapled to a booklet distributed by the radical student group SLATE, which evaluated teachers and courses.[21]

In July 1964 a reporter from the *Oakland Tribune*, a daily owned by the former Republican U.S. senator Bill Knowland, a fervent Goldwaterite, contacted the UC public information office asking why the administrators were permitting the University of California students to recruit demonstrators at the corner of Telegraph Avenue and Bancroft Way to picket the Republican convention. Wasn't that university property? Vice Chancellor Alex Sheriffs's staff discovered that the reporter was right. At Kerr's request, the regents had agreed to transfer the property to the city, but the transfer had never occurred.

In a series of meetings between mid-July and mid-September, Vice Chancellor Sheriffs, Chancellor Strong, and their staffs decided to halt political activity in front of the campus, as the regents' 1935 edict required. The November election was looming with a ballot that included not only the presidential contest but a proposition to repeal California's fair housing act. Classes were about to resume. Badgered by local conservatives, they decided to act. It was best to act right away, they reasoned, to prevent the radicals from making an uproar on the campus. Sheriffs and Strong told the dean of students, Kathryn Towle, to send a letter to the presidents of all the student organizations on the campus informing them that, effective September 21, money raising, recruiting, and other political activity would no longer be permitted on the strip of university property at Bancroft Way and Telegraph Avenue near the south entrance to the campus. More in touch with students than the higher-up administrators, Towle considered their decision unwise. She did not, however, appeal to Kerr, who normally did not speak to administrators at her level. Instead, she followed orders and sent the letter to the presidents of the student organizations.[22]

Clark Kerr was abroad with his wife and children at that time. While UC-Berkeley students were risking their lives in Mississippi and picketing the Cow Palace, he attended seminars and conferred with researchers as part of the multimillion-dollar Inter-University Study on Labor Problems in Economic Development project that he directed with John Dunlop, Fred Harbison, and Charles Myers. As a result, he did not know what was happening at home. He had delegated all authority to the university's vice president, Harry Wellman, whom he trusted. He occasionally read copies of the *International Herald-Tribune* that American tourists left in hotels and on benches. Otherwise, he mainly relaxed, putting current events out of his mind and taking measure of his first six years as university president. He took a side trip to the Greek islands with his family and a college friend and his family and participated in seminars in Yugoslavia, Czechoslovakia, Poland, and Moscow where American economists discussed hopeful new economic developments in eastern Europe. He concluded the two-month trip with two weeks of intense seminars in Hong Kong and Tokyo. "Student activists' tempers were at a boiling point," he wrote shortly before his death in 2003, but "I had been away for two months and was not fully aware of this."

When Kerr returned on September 15 and learned of Strong and Sheriffs's decision, he recognized their error. Sather Gate had been Berkeley's "Hyde Park" for thirty years, maybe more—the one place where radical students and others could proselytize. Kerr was a radical himself when he was young and was more tolerant of dissenting opinions than Sheriffs and Strong. Kerr hurried to Chancellor Strong's office the next morning, September 16. He later claimed it was the only time in his eight years as UC president that he intervened so directly in a chancellor's affairs. He advised Strong to retract his proposal. A decade older than Kerr and more conservative politically, the chancellor was ham-fisted in intra-university politics and stiffened whenever challenged. He refused to back down and received full support from Sheriffs.

"I then made my big blunder," Kerr wrote in his memoir. "I should have told him that I would have to declare his action null and void . . . or, at least, that I would have to postpone action on the Towle letter until the next meeting of the Board of Regents." Kerr attributed his error to fatigue. He had flown for twenty hours the previous day. He had not adjusted to Pacific Coast time and was overwhelmed by the backlog of work on his desk. It also would have been awkward for Kerr to overrule his subordinate since he had initiated the university's decentralization plan.[23]

Although this may be true, the explanation for his error lies deeper than that. From his youth, Clark Kerr had feared conflicts and confrontations. This characteristic helps explain why he was so attracted to the Society of Friends, which makes decisions through consensus. Kerr's attitude was paradoxical. He hated fights yet spent hours meeting with contentious trade unionists and company officers. His skills and commitment made him an effective, if perhaps angst-ridden, intermediary.[24] But operating by consensus was hardly the best approach for a chief executive. Kerr conceived of his principal task as president of the greatest public university in the United States to be *mediation*. "The president in the multiversity is leader, educator, creator, initiator, wielder of power, pump," he remarked in his 1963 Godkin lectures. "He is *also* officeholder, caretaker, inheritor, consensus-seeker, persuader, bottleneck. But he is mostly a mediator." Trained as a labor economist, he viewed the world as consisting of competing economic groups—a system he termed "industrial pluralism." A university also consisted of competing groups—the faculty, the alumni, the blue-collar staff, the white-collar staff, the student body. Kerr saw his job as president to be reconciling competing interests and simultaneously improving the quality of the university's product: research and education.

When Chancellor Edward Strong—who had been a professor at Berkeley when Kerr was a graduate student—refused to accept his advice, the university president backed down. He hadn't anticipated Strong's reaction. And although Kerr had spoken on more than one occasion in support of freedom of speech and political activities for students off and on campus, he was more conservative in the address he delivered at the University of California at Davis on May 5, 1964, after the sit-ins at Lucky supermarkets and the Sheraton-Palace Hotel. "The students, individually or collectively, should not and cannot take the name of the university with them as they move in religious or political or other non-university activities; nor should they or can they use university facilities in connection with such affairs," he declared then. Those remarks may have been intended to protect the university from attacks by conservative California politicians. But Chancellor Strong and Vice Chancellor Sheriffs used his statements to justify their decision to shut down the political agitation in front of Sather Gate in September.[25] "This was all wrong," Kerr admitted in his memoir. "I should not have accepted Strong's refusal. . . . I should have acted decisively."[26]

The result was the biggest eruption of protest in the history of the Berkeley campus up to that point. Dean Towle sent her letter not only to the left-wing student organizations—Campus Women for Peace, University Civil Liberties Committee, University Friends of the Student Nonviolent Coordinating Committee, and Young People's Socialist League—but also to the University Young Democrats, the University Young Republicans, and the Cal Students for Goldwater.[27] The administration intended to prevent *all* student groups—liberals, conservatives, and socialists alike—from distributing flyers at Telegraph and Bancroft, or anywhere else on campus. None could sell buttons, raise money, or recruit members. It is hard to imagine a more disastrous move by a university administrator at that time.

The diverse political clubs at Berkeley came together in a United Front, a term from the 1930s left. Within a week, they called it the Free Speech Movement, a name that linked the student protests to the civil-rights movement and to the First Amendment of the U.S. Constitution. Over the next nine weeks, the FSM, as the Free Speech Movement was quickly dubbed, conducted a long series of demonstrations and another sit-in on the campus, all intended to flout regulations until the university's policies were changed. Kerr made repeated concessions to the students, only to backtrack, most egregiously when the administration initiated new disciplinary action against Mario Savio and three FSM leaders over the Thanksgiving break. Finally, on Wednesday, December 2, 1964, approximately 760 students and a handful of local nonstudent radicals occupied all four floors of University Hall, the main campus administration building.

Governor Edmund (Pat) Brown was in Los Angeles at a dinner that evening. Kerr called the governor there, urging him not to act rashly. He asked Brown to come to Berkeley in the morning and negotiate with the students. Brown refused. Although a politically liberal Democrat, he was a former state attorney general opposed to negotiating with lawbreakers. Brown had supported himself in law school by working in his father's cigar store and waiting on tables. He had backed Kerr for years and was tired of his inability to rein in the demonstrators. The governor decided to use the state police. At 3 a.m. the next morning, Thursday, December 3, Chancellor Strong walked through the building with a megaphone informing the students that they must leave immediately or face arrest. All but a handful chose to stay. At 3:15 a.m., several hundred state police, acting under orders from the governor, entered Sproul Hall and began to remove the protestors.[28]

Imitating the civil-rights demonstrators in the South, the student protestors tossed out any pocket knives or other implements that might be considered weapons and, when approached by state police, lay limp. When officers picked up protestors, the others sang "We Will Not Be Moved!" It took thirteen hours, until midafternoon, for the police to complete their job. They stood on both sides of the stairwell, tossing the young men and women down. They were not gentle. The officers dragged students to the basement, which served as a holding cell. They papered over the new building's glass staircases so that outside observers could not see what was happening. The police photographed the students, carried them to police vans, and took them to Santa Rita jail, a minimum-security prison where Japanese-American citizens had been held two decades before. Thousands of other students and scores of professors stood outside Sproul Hall as this proceeded, horrified.

On Thursday afternoon, December 3, hundreds of Berkeley faculty, many of whom had been apathetic before the mass arrest, met, passed a resolution condemning the governor's action, and raised money to bail out the students. The next day, December 4, thousands of UC-Berkeley students boycotted classes to protest the arrest. Kerr tried to regain faculty and student support by canceling all classes on Monday morning, announcing a university-wide meeting at the Greek Theater. During the weekend, he met with the chairmen of the academic departments, who crafted a set of concessions that they hoped would satisfy the bulk of students yet not alienate the regents.

Kerr and the chairman of the Political Science Department, Professor Robert Scalapino, an expert on the Japanese labor movement, acted like theater directors. They put the department chairmen in chairs behind the podium, as in commencements and convocations. Fraternity and sorority brothers and sisters, generally cool to the FSM, would fill the seats in front of the stage: that is why Kerr received an ovation. Faculty would sit behind and on both sides of the more traditional students. The students who had occupied Sproul Hall were arraigned at nine o'clock Monday morning in the Berkeley Community Theater, the sole city facility large enough for the hearing. Arriving last for the campus meeting, the activists crowded into the back of the arena, although a handful of them sneaked to the front.

Professor Scalapino opened the meeting. He outlined the compromise proposed by the department heads and afterward introduced Clark Kerr, who promised that these provisions would be implemented immediately. The radicals moaned at some of the particulars, yet concessions had been made and Kerr had reason to hope that they could be isolated again.

Just as he was concluding the meeting, Mario Savio, the magnetic twenty-one-year-old philosophy major whose words inspired the Free Speech Movement, jumped onto the stage to speak. He had asked Scalapino and Kerr for permission before the program began but had been denied. Mounting the stage regardless, Savio grasped the mic to speak, only to be seized by three campus police (figure 9). Two officers took his arms, the third grabbed his necktie. As an expert on strikes, Kerr knew that the presence of uniformed police would enrage the students and faculty. He specifically told his staff to keep law enforcement officers away from the meeting, to no avail. "All hell broke loose," remembered Jo Freeman, the leader of University Young Democrats, who was nearby. "Kerr stood there," she recalled, "dazed and dumbfounded, watching his carefully constructed scenario fall apart. The audience rose and cried out, aghast." After protests from the chairmen of the philosophy and speech departments, Savio was allowed to return to the podium. Rather than delivering the speech that he had in his jacket pocket, he simply called on the students to reconvene for a FSM rally in Sproul Plaza at noon. "Clear this disastrous scene," he shouted.

The scene was photographed and reported everywhere, on television and in newspapers from coast to coast and beyond. Dorothea Lange and Paul Taylor had been thrilled when Kerr was appointed chancellor. Now they were appalled. "Clark Kerr will never get out from under that image," Lange predicted. "The student demand for total campus amnesty had been met, but it all went for naught," Kerr admitted later. "The crowd had seen Mario Savio dragged from the scene, and that was all it remembered. It was an accident that looked like fascism."[29]

* * *

The UC-Berkeley Academic Senate met the next morning, Tuesday, December 8. They passed a resolution accepting in full the FSM's demand for unqualified right to hold rallies, raise money, and recruit members for groups anywhere on campus, even if the group supported activities that were illegal off campus. The faculty vote was 824 ayes to 115 nays. An amendment introduced by sociologist Lewis Coser, a refugee from Nazi Germany, which would have outlawed calls for violence, was overwhelmingly defeated. Unqualified free speech would reign. When the meeting ended, students lined both sides of the sidewalk outside the hall applauding the professors' action. The clapping continued until the last professor left. "For a brief moment," recalled constitutional law professor Robert H. Cole, "the Good, the True, and the Beautiful seemed to some of us both one and real."[30]

Yet no calm emerged. Instead, battles intensified on the Berkeley campus in the ensuing months and subsequently spread to universities in the Midwest and the East Coast. In retrospect, the FSM's original call for the right to agitate at the entrance to the campus seems remarkably innocent. Their most articulate voice

FIGURE 9. Berkeley police arresting Mario Savio at the Greek Theater meeting, UC–Berkeley, December 7, 1964. Photo by Nat Farbman/The LIFE Picture Collection via Getty Images.

was Mario Savio, son of a New York machinist, a former altar boy and philosophy major, who had transferred to Berkeley from a Catholic college in the Bronx. He had spent the summer in Holmes County, Mississippi, dangerous terrain, going from farmhouse to farmhouse trying to persuade African American men and women to register to vote. Savio returned to sheltered California only to find that freedom of speech was prohibited at Berkeley. "In Mississippi an autocratic and powerful minority rules, through organized violence, to suppress the vast, virtually powerless majority," he told the students on December 2 before they entered Sproul Hall. He likened Kerr's administration to the racist white registrar in Mason County. "In California [too], the privileged minority manipulates the university bureaucracy to suppress the students' political expression. The 'respectable' bureaucracy masks the financial plutocrats; that impersonal bureaucracy is the efficient enemy in a 'Brave New World.'"[31]

Like Tom Paine, Mario Savio was a rebel whose vision of the future drew on an idealized past. Kerr wanted the university "to serve the needs of American industry; it is a factory that turns out a certain product needed by industry or government. . . . It is a bleak scene, but it is all a lot of us have to look forward to," Savio exclaimed in his speech in front of Sproul Hall.[32] He idealized small, empathetic institutions like Swarthmore College, which Kerr attended when he was an undergraduate. Writing in *Harper's Magazine* in 1966, after he was expelled from the University of California, Savio declared that "we want an end to the system of lecture courses, grades, and course units, to be replaced by instruction in small seminars and tutorials, with the quality of students' work evaluated at length in writing rather than by assignment of a number or letter grade." Savio blamed the state government for preventing students from receiving the kind of education they needed and deserved. "The California legislature's appropriations were 'niggardly,'" he declared. "Given the economic facts of life, each faculty member must choose to be primarily a teacher or primarily a researcher; there is not enough time to do both jobs adequately." "WE WANT A UNIVERSITY!" read one of the protesting students' leaflets.[33]

If measured in sheer intelligence, Kerr was the most impressive of the Labor Board vets. Unlike George Taylor, Sylvester Garrett, and John Dunlop, however, he lacked the ability to steer quarreling people to compromise. As Robert Cole, who was not hostile to Kerr, wrote in retrospect, "The campus administration's . . . arbitrary and erratic pattern of using discipline to snatch defeat from the jaws of victory repeatedly revitalized the FSM . . . while alienating many of those faculty who only wanted the administration to keep the peace."[34] Robert Sproul, Kerr's predecessor at the University of California, was far more effective with people. Kerr, by contrast, was aloof, as suggested by the fact that he chose to do most of his work at home, using drivers to bring carts full of memos and reports back and forth daily between his home office in El Cerrito and secretaries in his office on campus. By the time that he became president of the university, Kerr had almost no contact with students. Even his high-ranking administrator lacked contacts with students until after the FSM, exactly contrary to the advice that the Labor Board vets gave to employers.

In addition, Kerr had to contend with the John Birch Society and other conservatives. Although founded in Massachusetts, the right-wing society was strongest in Orange County, south of Los Angeles. Enraged about U.S. Supreme Court decisions on pornography, school prayer, racial integration, and other issues and the U.S. government's cooperation with the Soviet Union, the Birchers put bumper stickers on their cars and passed around petitions calling for the United States to withdraw from the United Nations, the removal of fluoride from tap water, and the impeachment of Chief Justice Earl Warren, the liberal former California governor who was Kerr's original sponsor at UC-Berkeley. The conservative Republicans and followers of John Birch won seats on local school boards and town councils, and succeeded in electing conservatives sympathetic to their views to seats in the state assembly and senate and the U.S. House of Representatives. In June 1964 they had roused sufficient support to help defeat Governor Nelson Rockefeller in the California Republican Party's presidential primary—and win the Republican Party's presidential nomination for Senator Barry Goldwater. In 1965 conservatives assumed the leadership of the California Republican Party. In November 1966 they helped elect the likable former actor Ronald Reagan as governor.[35]

Kerr's attempt to walk between conservative regents and the FSM failed. By spring 1965, protests at Berkeley were more raucous than in the fall, with some radicals raising banners stamped F.U.C.K., an acronym for "Freedom under Clark Kerr."[36] With an arbitrator's grit, Kerr managed to remain in the University of California presidency longer than his counterparts at Columbia University and Harvard University when their offices were occupied. But Ronald Reagan campaigned for governor on a pledge to "clean up that mess at Berkeley." (See figure 10.) On January 20, 1967, Kerr was fired by the board of regents. Mrs. Randolph Hearst, a member of the board, said that he was fired "for lack of administrative ability."[37]

"To make the multiversity work really effectively," Kerr remarked 1963, "the moderates need to be in control of each power center, and there needs to be an attitude of tolerance between and among the power centers, with few territorial ambitions."[38] By that criterion, Kerr had failed. More time had to pass and more adroit Labor Board vets had to be appointed before the student revolt could be contained.

* * *

The FSM emerged before most Americans were aware of the extent of U.S. involvement in the war in Vietnam, before Lyndon Johnson sharply increased U.S. troop levels and approved sustained bombing of cities and trails in North Vietnam, and before the first major confrontations between U.S. and North Vietnamese forces. Johnson ran for office in November 1964 as the peace candidate. In 1965, however, increasing numbers of American young men were drafted and mass marches against the war began. State troopers attacked Martin Luther King's march from Selma to Montgomery, Alabama, and bigoted whites bombed the homes of African American families who had moved into their neighborhoods in Chicago. In 1966 the Student Non-Violent Coordinating Committee and the Congress of Racial Equality adopted the cry of "Black Power" and expelled white members. Jobless and underemployed young African Americans men confronted police and attacked white-owned stores in many U.S. cities in the mid-1960s, including Harlem and Philadelphia in 1964, Watts in Los Angeles in 1965, Detroit and Newark in 1967, and more than one hundred cities large and small after the assassination of Dr. Martin Luther King in April 1968.

FIGURE 10. Clark Kerr at press conference during his confrontation with Governor Reagan, January 1967. Photo by Ted Streshinsky/The LIFE Images Collection via Getty Images.

The student revolt spread across the country during those years, with students seizing administrative buildings. They demanded that the administrations end ROTC programs, stop on-campus recruiting by the armed forces and corporations like Dow Chemical that produced military goods, and sever contracts with the Defense Department. They also demanded the establishment of Black Studies programs, the hiring of additional African American faculty and administrators, and major increases in enrollment of African American and Latino students. When the administrations did not meet all of the students' demands and the war in Vietnam continued, the conflict intensified. During the last week of April 1970, three thousand antiwar protestors rallied at Boston Commons and then marched to Cambridge, where they set fires at a bank and in the streets and broke almost all the windows facing Harvard Square. It took three hours for the combined police forces of several towns to regain control. When President Richard Nixon announced on May 1 that combined U.S. and South Vietnamese forces had entered Cambodia to destroy Communist sanctuaries and students were killed at Kent State University in Ohio and Jackson State College in Mississippi, the student movement exploded. At the University of Wisconsin in Madison, students put goggles over their eyes, donned bandannas soaked in baking soda and egg white to ward off tear gas over their foreheads, tied strings to gauze-covered Dixie cups over their mouths so that they could breathe, and then picked up pipes and cherry bombs to fight local police. "We must strike and strike hard—into the community and on our campus to turn the tide now raging so viciously against us," the student paper declared in a front-page editorial. The campus revolt climaxed at 3:42 a.m., August 23, when four young men—two of them university students and two local radicals—detonated a bomb inside the University of Wisconsin building that housed the Army-Math Research Center. A postdoctoral student, father of three children, died; three others in the building were injured. The Army-Math Center itself was not harmed. Except for the atomic bomb detonated in New Mexico on July 16, 1945, it was the largest bomb exploded inside the United States up to that date.[39]

"Why do you want to be a College President? It takes the hide of a hippopotamus," Yale University's president James Angell wrote a friend in their Psychology Department who had been offered the presidency at a Massachusetts liberal-arts college. By 1970 more than two hundred seventy universities and colleges—including such prominent institutions as Harvard University, Stanford University, the University of Wisconsin, the University of Illinois, Amherst College, Wesleyan University, Bryn Mawr College, Rutgers University, Purdue University, Brandeis University, Brown University, Oberlin College, Hunter College, Rice University, Carleton College, Claremont College, Dartmouth College, Hampton Institute, Northwestern University, the University of Pennsylvania, the University of Massachusetts, and the University of Texas—were looking for new presidents.[40]

In the seventeenth and eighteenth centuries, colonial American colleges were led by Protestant pastors. In the late nineteenth and early twentieth centuries, the leading universities and colleges selected professors of science and philosophers as their presidents. In recent times, trustees frequently appoint professors of economics as university presidents. During the 1960s, Clark Kerr later recalled, "They wanted us."[41]

* * *

Few university presidents, if any, were more successful in handling the student revolt, and none had greater influence in reshaping systems of governance in the universities than Robben Fleming, who served as chancellor at the University of Wisconsin at Madison from 1964 to 1968 and president at the University of Michigan from 1968 until 1979. Born in 1916, Fleming was a native of Paw Paw, in rural northern Illinois. His father operated a dance hall until illness forced him to close his business. He died while Robben was still in high school, leaving the family impoverished. Fleming nonetheless became valedictorian of his high school class, worked his way through Beloit College, was elected president of the student body during his senior year, and earned a law degree at the University of Wisconsin. While at Madison, he studied with Lloyd Garrison and Nathan Feinsinger, noted mediators, attorneys, and members of the National War Labor Board.

Although Fleming was only on the Labor Board's staff for merely five months before being drafted into the army, Feinsinger invited him to direct the University of Wisconsin's new Industrial Relations Center when he returned in late 1945. During the Korean War, Fleming served as executive director of the National Wage Stabilization Board, which was chaired by George Taylor, with Feinsinger, Dunlop, and Kerr among its public members. After the Wage Stabilization Board, Fleming was appointed a professor of law at the University of Illinois and director of the Institute of Industrial Relations, a larger industrial relations program. He arbitrated labor-management disputes throughout these years and was elected president of the National Academy of Arbitrators. His 1965 book *The Labor Arbitration Process* became the standard text in the field. In 1964 the president of the University of Wisconsin asked Fleming to return to Madison and become chancellor at that campus.

Fleming had not anticipated demonstrations at the University of Wisconsin. Nevertheless, like UC-Berkeley, the University of Wisconsin had a tradition of student radicalism dating back to at least the 1930s and, after the Johnson administration committed more resources to the war in Vietnam, faculty and students organized teach-ins on the campus. In February 1967, the Students for a Democratic Society (SDS) occupied Bascom Hall, the century-old heart of the campus, which housed the office of its president. They demanded that the administration no longer allow the Dow Chemical Corporation, manufacturer of the antipersonnel agent napalm, to interview students for jobs. City police arrested eleven students blocking the hallway of the business school. SDS responded by calling a mass demonstration that evening in protest.

Fleming met with the dean of students. "I was concerned about having them in jail when the evening meeting took place because I knew this might make them martyrs in the eyes of other students," he recalled. "Joe [the dean] suddenly said, 'Why don't we bail them out?' I thought this was a great idea and, since I had just received a substantial check for writing a chapter in a book, I said I would put up the money. The necessary arrangements were quickly made. . . . The bail was something in the neighborhood of $105 each. I paid with a check, and the students were released. Both Joe and I then went to the rally that night in the Bascom Hall auditorium that held several hundred people. Some of the SDS people talked, and both Joe and I then talked. The SDS people were puzzled as to just what to do. It was hard to castigate the university, or us, in view of fact that we had we bailed out the students."

The radicals were outfoxed by the silver-haired chancellor—who, they declared, began as the "Prince of Arbitrators" but had become the "tarnished Knave of Manipulators." Fleming never received the bail money that he paid for the detained students, but he probably was not bothered, for news of his feat raced among administrators and trustees at universities through the Midwest. He was soon offered the presidencies of the University of Minnesota and the University of Michigan. Fleming opted for Ann Arbor. When he left, the radicals' weekly paper *Connections* sardonically wished him well in a poem entitled "The Romance of Robben Head."

> Here endeth the painful tayle of
> Phlegmatic Robben Head—a chess piece
> Snatched by fateful digits from our board,
> and placed in another game.
> He will find, we fear, that to rule one's own
> Kingdom is an even more ignoble task than that which he now relinquishes.[42]

As the bard had warned, Fleming confronted greater challenges at Michigan but proved equal to the test. The best example of his agility is the way he responded to the "Action Teach-In" organized by the Ann Arbor Committee to End the War. The forum met on Friday and Saturday, September 19 and 20, 1969. Critics of U.S. policy in Vietnam had held teach-in meetings at many universities in 1965 near the beginning of the antiwar movement. The aim at the time was to inform students about the war and U.S. government policies. The teach-ins and the televised hearings of the Senate Foreign Relations Committee chaired by Senator J. William Fulbright of Arkansas spread the antiwar sentiments on the campuses and liberal segments of the public. Antiwar parade sponsored by an ad hoc Spring Mobilization Committee attracted somewhere between one hundred twenty-five and three hundred fifty thousand marchers in New York City and fifty thousand more in San Francisco. Fifty-five-thousand protestors marched on the Pentagon on October 21–22, 1967, and were met by lines of troops with fixed bayonets. Consensus about the war broke down, as the antiwar Senator Eugene McCarthy of Minnesota garnered 43 percent of the vote in New Hampshire's Democratic presidential primary on March 12, 1968, and Senator Robert Kennedy joined the race for the nomination on March 16. Two weeks later, President

Lyndon Johnson announced that he would halt bombing in North Vietnam and would not run for president again.

By the summer of 1969, the political situation in the nation had changed. With Johnson out of office and newly elected President Richard Nixon reducing U.S. forces in Vietnam, the antiwar movement lost momentum. The September 1969 "action teach-ins" were designed to revitalize students. Hence the title "action." The forum began on Friday evening, with a keynote speech by Rennie Davis, SDS's national community-organizing director, who had been indicted by the Justice Department for "conspiracy to incite riots" at the Democratic Party convention in Chicago the previous summer. Davis had just returned from Hanoi, where he met with North Vietnamese officials. Several workshops were offered after the teach-ins, chaired by leaders of the Clergy and Laymen Concerned about Vietnam, New Mobilization, the Fort Jackson Eight, the Vietnam Moratorium Committee, and local activists. The topics ranged from the fall campus campaign against ROTC to an early October antiwar action in Chicago and a planned Washington "death march" to a peaceful antiwar petition campaign in Michigan. The biggest event would be the national moratorium and strikes planned for October 15. Organizers envisioned a nationwide work stoppage for one day in October, two days in November, three in December, and so forth until the United States pulled out of Vietnam. U.S. Representative John Conyers of Michigan and Professor Howard Zinn of Boston University would give speeches on Saturday, followed by workshops for "those who see the war simply as a byproduct of a more central societal ill." The Ann Arbor committee put out bold flyers like one titled "VIETNAM—TIME'S UP!" Organizers expected considerable attention from newspapers, radio, and television for these events.

A group of University of Michigan faculty active in the antiwar movement asked Fleming, who had publicly announced his opposition to U.S. participation, to attend and speak after Rennie Davis. They thought that, if he spoke, "it might help us contain violent anti-war activities" on the campus that fall. "There are pros and cons to doing it," Fleming told his executive staff. "If I speak, I have already told them I will talk as a moderate who is opposed to the war and thinks we ought to get out of it, but who will say unkind things about the fascist left. This will probably draw booing from the audience. . . . On the other hand, the subject is urgent, the gamble that we can take the leadership and place it in the hands of the moderates rather than the extremists is attractive, and I personally feel deeply on the subject."

Fleming took the chance. Although his appearance on the platform will be "construed . . . in some quarters . . . as anti-government," he wrote the regents, others rightly see him as a moderate opposed to both the war and violence on campus. The university's regents would be coming to campus on Wednesday evening and conclude their meetings on Friday afternoon. They were welcome to attend Friday night's forum. He didn't tell the regents that he had an ace up his sleeve: he had known Rennie Davis, the keynote speaker, since the SDS organizer was a little boy. Fleming and Rennie's father, economist John C. Davis, worked together in 1951, when Fleming headed the staff of the Wage Stabilization Board and John directed the staff of Truman's Council of Economic Advisers. Fleming and his wife had been friends with Davis and family ever since then. When Rennie Davis arrived in Ann Arbor, he stopped by Fleming's office. Neither of them publicly acknowledged the visit or their friendship: had that information leaked out, Rennie's reputation would suffer. But the forum was less contentious as a result.[43]

In his speech at the forum, Fleming declared that the U.S. invention in Vietnam was a "colossal mistake." Contrary to his original plan, he did not denounce "the fascist left." He simply remarked that he "happens not to agree with the views held by the radical left." Fleming offered a series of arguments about why it was a major mistake for the United States to fight in Vietnam. They included the U.S. "obess[ion] with the idea that communism was a monolithic evil" and the expense of the war and the "spiritual costs." Fleming also talked about the unequal effects of the war on society. Many high school students "whose I.Q. warrants continued study do not attend" college because their families were poor "while others, with less capacity do because their parents are able to send them. . . . There are racial overtones here which only serve to exacerbate the injustices which flow from that cancer in our larger society."[44]

The next morning, Fleming asked members of the faculty who had held positions in Washington to review his speech and offer suggestions. The university publications office produced a handsome nine-page pamphlet of the revised text. Then the press relations office sent copies to the presidents of every college and university in the United States and the media. Although some Michigan residents denounced his actions and the *Detroit News* said that "the U. of M. no longer offers a forum in the search for truth," the response was overwhelmingly positive. The president of a major Michigan bank asked Fleming to send him five hundred copies, promising to give them to every member of his staff and the presidents of every major bank in the nation. "Huntley-Brinkley apparently used almost five minutes of my Viet Nam speech and this may stir up considerable interest," he told one of his vice presidents. "Do we need to be concerned about members of the President's Club? Should the *Alumni* magazine print it so the alumni will know what I actually said? Will you see that all of the deans get a copy, please? Allan Whiting, over in Political Science, told me in advance that he was going to use it in the Westinghouse [radio] network and that he would get it into the *New York Times*. You might talk to him. . . . P.S. What about our Congressional delegates?"[45]

Robben Fleming viewed his speech at the teach-in and the ensuing publicity as part of a larger attempt to contain the protestors and maintain stability at Ann Arbor. During the third week of April 1968, the SDS chapter at Columbia University, which had about 150 members, and the campus Student Afro-American Society, which was even smaller, ignited a rebellion of approximately seven hundred to one thousand students, who occupied one administration building, held three administrators hostage for twenty-hour hours, and then occupied three other buildings. On the sixth day of the protest, more than one thousand New York City police officers stormed the campus, clearing the buildings in a violent, chaotic confrontation. Afterward, students called a strike that shut down the university. "Basically, the sit-in and strike of April and May gave us a chance, to express the extreme dissatisfaction we feel at being *caught up in this 'system,'*" the Columbia Strike Coordinating Committee declared in late 1968. "We reject the gap between potential and realization in this society. We rejected our lives in this university and our future lives in business, government, or other universities like this one. In a word, we saw ourselves as oppressed, and began to understand the forces at work . . . for our oppression. We saw those same responsible for the oppression and colonization of African Americans and Puerto Ricans in ghettos, and Vietnamese and the people of third world." This was their answer to the question of why students from privileged families put the pictures of Che Guevara and Malcolm X on walls of their dorm rooms and raised red flags in "liberated" buildings. The nomination of Vice President Hubert Humphrey at the Democratic National Convention ended electoral politics, in their opinion, while "the Chicago Police Department provided an alternative—to fight. . . . The struggle goes on. Create two, three, many Columbias, that is our watchword!"[46]

As president of the University of Michigan, president of the Association of American Universities, chairman of the National Association of Land-Grant Universities' Committee on Student-Faculty-Administrative Relations, a member of the American Council on Education's Special Committee on Campus Tension, and in testimony to a committee with the same name appointed by President Nixon after the murders of students at Kent State College and Jackson State University, Robben Fleming led the way for reform of American university relations, much as he and the more senior Labor Board staff had done in industry during and after the Second World War. "I am convinced, as I have been for a long time, that we must understand the politics of dissent and that we must play the game with considerable skill," Fleming told the chairman of American Council on Education's (ACE's) Special Commission, Sol Linowitz, in October 1969. Linowitz was chairman of the board of the Xerox Corporation and a trustee of three universities.[47] Other members of the ACE's committee included the former president of Brandies University, chancellors of UCLA, Vanderbilt University, and Clark College, the executive director of the National Urban League, a former president of the American Bar Association, four university professors of law and philosophy, four officers of student organizations, a university trustee, and Bill Moyers, who was publisher of *Newsday* at that time.

While acknowledging the impact of the U.S. war in Vietnam on the universities, the committee called for "overdue reforms" inside universities and colleges. The committee visited more than fifty campuses and conducted dozens of interviews. Students were disturbed by "hypocrisy" and "corruption" in American society, especially as manifested in the war, and found universities and colleges unresponsive to the problems of society and indifferent to students' needs, they reported. Among other proposals, the committee recommended student participation in curriculum policies, formalization of disciplinary proceedings, specific channels through which students could register grievances, greater accessibility of university presidents and professors to students, explanations of university plans and policies to their constituencies, more diversity on boards of trustees, and the development of specific strategies for handling campus disturbances by college presidents.[48]

Fleming worked energetically to address those issues at Michigan and contain protests on the campus. A talk that he typed out himself for a September 18 meeting of the University of Michigan regents, "How Can We Avoid a Columbia?," reveals much about his thinking. "There is no absolutely certain way" to avoid a debacle such as the one that occurred at Columbia, Fleming wrote in his notebook. There is "very great unrest" among the students about the war, race, and poverty. The radical students did not cause the unrest: it arose from genuine problems in the country. "There are some revolutionaries on campus," he planned to tell the regents, "and I am convinced that there is left-wing money flowing into the effort. But it is a mistake to think that this is the root of the problem. Radical left-wingers are so few that they are successful only when they can ally with others on a given issue. The real tragedy of Columbia was not necessarily the agony of that eviction. It is the aftermath which has split the faculty and student body so terribly. [We h]ave to remember that [fact] when you weigh [our responses to] external vs. internal criticism."

"Any hopefully successful" policy, Fleming believed, involved three ingredients: First, the administration must isolate the revolutionary students. "This we have so far done," he would tell the board. Second, they had to retain the loyalty of the great majority of students. "This we have done," he noted. Third, we must "hold the faculty with us. . . . This [too] we have done." Like a good father, Fleming would listen to upset students and would give them freedom within limits. We "must be willing to spend endless hours talking" to students and others on the campus. "This we are doing." But we have to "make it very clear that we will not tolerate certain kinds of conduct" and "work out an advance plan to use the police if necessary . . . [and] "have rules and regulations and an enforcement machinery. . . . This we have [also] done."[49]

Fleming planned to tell the regents that he would not under any circumstances permit students to occupy a building for an extended period of time, as Grayson Kirk had done at Columbia. This was the "lesson" that he and administrators at other universities drew from the report prepared by Archibald Cox, the Harvard law professor and industrial-relations expert whom the Columbia trustees brought in for advice after the disaster at their university. Instead, Fleming, his staff, and a handful of selected faculty members prepared a plan to use force if necessary. They engaged local photographers to take pictures of students occupying buildings to facilitate identification. They compiled a list of laws under which students could be indicted and considered which courts and which judges would be more supportive. The campus police force was small, as was the Ann Arbor city police force. That was a problem. They could turn to the county sheriff's officers, the director of the university's Center for Research on Social Organization, sociologist Albert Reiss, told Fleming. But "I shudder at the thought of how the latter group would behave. . . . Frankly, I doubt whether we could get an effective force of 1,000 men (which is hardly enough for a Columbia type situation) from the state police or a combination of state and local police," Reiss continued. The only alternative was the National Guard; they would probably do the best job. "If we must move, we must move rapidly and effectively."[50] Fleming decided to contact the governor.

But the "real danger is not violence, vandalism, hostages, seizures of building etc.," wrote Fleming. "We can and will deal with that without any timidity. *The real problem is likely to be a peaceful, non-violent sit-in. If we use the police to throw them out we will lose the majority of the students and the majority of the faculty. If we don't[,] we will get a good deal of public criticism.* This is the real problem we need to talk about."[51] This conviction—the belief that radical students acting peacefully put administrators in a double-bind—led Fleming to decide against using force even if provoked. He acted with such restraint that the FBI's Detroit office called him "meek" and asked their Washington office for permission to use "dirty tricks" such as fake letters to trustees and state legislators to force him out of office, as the FBI had done at UC-Berkeley.[52]

University presidents had never before dealt with protests comparable to those that swept the country in the 1960s. Consequently, Fleming and the other Labor Board vets drew on their previous experience in industry to reorganize American universities' systems of governance.

Fleming came up with a plan for Michigan that consisted of a complaint referee, a University Trial, and a University Court of Appeals. At first glance, the plan looked like the civil judiciary system, but with important differences. As critics on the campus complained, Fleming provided no "trial by one's peers." In fact, there would be no trials at all. Instead, Fleming proposed "a dispute-resolving" plan. Under the plan, a student or faculty member who felt that a violation of University Council Regulations had occurred would submit the accusation to the complaint referee, a lawyer not on the University of Michigan payroll. The referee would provide a list of trained arbitrators for the parties to choose from. The arbitrator "would have the function of finding of fact, determining guilt or innocence, and imposing sentence, if any. Neither of the parties could appeal arbitrator's decisions except on grounds of arbitrariness or capriciousness."[53] After the April 1968 upheaval at Columbia University, Michael Sovern, a law professor who specialized in labor relations and conflict resolution, was appointed chairman of Columbia's new Executive Committee of the Faculty to respond to grievances and repair relations among the faculty, students, administrators, and the neighborhood. Sovern developed a system similar to Fleming's. He received much praise for this work and in 1970 was named dean of the Columbia Law School and president of the university in 1980.

In 1968 the National Association of Land-Grant Universities created its Committee on Student-Faculty-Administrative Relationships, chaired by Fleming, that consisted of two university presidents, two chancellors, one university vice president, and a professor of sociology. They conducted an in-depth study of "university governance" at twenty-five universities—public and private, secular and religious, predominantly white and predominantly African American. In its final report, Fleming's committee singled out the University of New Hampshire—whose president was John McConnell, former dean of Cornell's School of Industrial and Labor Relations, accomplished labor-management arbitrator, and veteran of Region II of the National War Labor Board—for its highest praise, as did the *Chronicle of Higher Education*, the new weekly journal for university administrators. McConnell had set up the unicameral University Senate at New Hampshire. It consisted of thirty undergraduates, thirty faculty, twelve administrators, and five graduate students as members who would confer separately before meeting collectively. The University of New Hampshire's University Senate resembled the National and Regional War Labor Boards—representatives would speak for their constituencies rather than as individuals; they would meet and bargain and then consult with the university's president and trustees. "Ideally, the three major groups in a University—faculty, students and administrators—work together toward a set of clearly identified educational goals," the university senate's leaders remarked. "We had long sessions and discussions, many of them pretty personal and heated, but, nevertheless, were resolved in a fashion that kept things on a reasonably even keel," recalled McConnell. "I was grateful for my industrial relations background."[54]

In the winter of 1969–70, teaching assistants started to organize unions at the University of Wisconsin–Madison, the University of Michigan at Ann Arbor, Purdue University, and Indiana University, another component of the student revolt. The research universities could not have continued without their labor, yet, as the President's Commission on Campus Unrest confessed, they were "generally underpaid and overworked . . . necessarily inexperienced, often distracted by the demands of their own degree programs, not infrequently unprepared to give even minimally adequate instruction, and in some instances deeply disillusioned."[55] The TAs organized first and most effectively at Madison. The Teaching Assistants Association (TAA) of Madison wanted more than better compensation or less work. They wanted a voice in courses' content, reading assignments, and pedagogical techniques. The TAA called a strike in March 1970, after nine months of unproductive negotiation. The TAA claimed that attendance in the college of arts and sciences was down by 70 percent. Radical students formed a committee to support the TAA; drivers for the campus bus service, who belonged to the Teamsters, respected the TAA's picket lines. The TAA's president, Bob Muehlenhamp, was arrested for allegedly attempting to prevent a truck from making deliveries.

The dean of the College of Arts and Sciences at Wisconsin at that time was Edwin Young, a professor of labor economics and labor-management arbitrator. Nathan Feinsinger, the professor of labor law who served on the War Labor Board, volunteered to mediate between the TAA's representatives and the dean. Unlike administrations at other universities, which have strenuously fought against teaching assistant unions, Ed Young was willing to negotiate with the union about the length of their contracts, job security, workload, class size, evaluation of teaching performances, access to employee files, grievance procedures, and a health plan—in other words, every aspect of a standard union contract. He adamantly refused, however, to discuss the TAA's demand for a share in designing classes. "The price of relinquishing authority for education is too dear," his aide told the *Chronicle of High Education*. "We cannot bargain over what courses are taught. If we accede, we would have an exodus of qualified faculty members," declared Young. "The issue of who controls educational planning is the rock which must be cracked before the strike can be settled," Feinsinger told the *Chronicle*. The Labor Board veterans viewed unions' "bread and butter" demands as legitimate but drew the line on "ideological issues."[56]

On March 20, 1970, the same week that the TAs struck at Madison, an African American student group named Black Action Movement (BAM) began a student strike at Ann Arbor. "It was the most difficult I had to face because it was a racial matter and the feelings were intense," Fleming wrote later. (See figure 11.) BAM's demands—"I always insisted on using the term *requests*," said Fleming—were similar to those being made by African American students at other campuses.

FIGURE 11. **Robben Fleming in late night meeting with Black Action Movement leaders, March 1970. Jay Cassidy photographs, Bentley Historical Library, University of Michigan.**

They demanded that the university raise the African American students' proportion of the student body from 3.5 percent to 10 percent within three years, demanded financial aid to African American students, a Black Studies program, a center for African American students, and an increase in the number of African Americans on the faculty and in the administration, particularly the admissions office. "Open It Up or Shut It Down" was BAM's slogan. "I knew from my experience in the labor field that one of two things had to happen" if the administration's didn't concede, wrote Fleming: "Either the strike would fail for lack of support, or it would become disruptive." When some students and professors continued their classes, white radicals supporting BAM started running through the campus, breaking up classes, throwing stink bombs, destroying furniture in the library, and shoving library books onto the floors.

Fleming did not call the police. Instead, he met with the board of regents for sixteen hours and then negotiated a settlement with BAM's leaders. That latter session also ran for sixteen hours. In effort, Fleming mediated between the regents and BAM. "At 4:00 a.m., when our conversations seemed stalled," he wrote in his memoir, "one of their [BAM's] spokesmen said that he had to make a telephone call," recalled Fleming.

> It seemed to me an unlikely time . . ., but he went to the adjoining room where there was a telephone. In a few minutes he came out and announced that I had a call. I knew this could hardly be true at that hour, but I didn't know what he had in mind.
>
> He came in the room with me, and when the door was closed, he said, in a perfectly calm and friendly voice, "We've got to get this thing over with. What is the best offer you can make?" I repeated what we had been saying, "We will set 10 percent as our *goal*, we will provide the financial aid to make this possible if the student has need, and we will do the other things we have already told you about. Beyond that I cannot go, nor do I think the Regents will go further." He said, "All right, let's go back in the other room. I will ask you the same question, and you give the same answer. Then I will say that we must consider it until morning. We will then meet at 10:00 a.m. in this room to end it."
>
> We returned to the bargaining table and went through the required conversation. They then left, as did I, and I was sure that the break I had been waiting for had finally come. We met the following morning for the formal agreement.

In addition to setting 10 percent African American enrollment as a goal, the agreement promised to increase the number of recruiters of undergraduates in the Admissions office to nine, hire additional graduate-student recruiters, and new staff members specifically charged with recruiting African American faculty. Moreover, Fleming promised to hire a staff person to recruit Mexican American students and that the university would enroll a minimum of fifty Mexican American students by fall 1971, to create a university-wide appeals board to rule on the adequacy of financial-aid grants for students, and to create the Center for Afro-American Studies. Fleming and the regents refused to accept four other of BAM's demands: amnesty for strikers, a black student center, tuition waivers, or collection of fees from students for a scholarship named for Martin Luther King Jr.

The cost of this compromise was much higher for Fleming in terms of public opinion than the agreement arrived at during the Action Teach-In in September

'69. Vice President Spiro Agnew denounced Fleming as a "marshmallow" who had "buckled under to a few squads of kid extortionists." He received quite hostile letters from older white University of Michigan alumni and other Michigan residents. The university's budget was affected as well. "Some [other] things will be cut and they will be valuable," Fleming told reporters, "but these decisions will be left to the deans." Fleming retained the backing of university regents, however, who were willing to stomach hostile public opinion to keep the university stable.[57]

Through skill and good fortune, Fleming managed to contain the upheaval at the University of Michigan. Although there were large protests on the campus later, including building occupations, the situation never became as chaotic as at UC-Berkeley, the University of Wisconsin, or Columbia University. The contrast is more remarkable since SDS's founders—Tom Hayden, Al Haber, Carl Oglesby, Richard Flacks, and others—were University of Michigan students and SDS was founded at Port Huron, Michigan, not far from Ann Arbor. Fleming seemed so liberal that the local FBI sought permission to use dirty tricks to force him out of office, but he stood absolutely firm in areas of labor policy that he considered precious—in this case, sympathy strikes, much as Nathan Feinsinger and Edwin Young at Wisconsin refused to compromise on the issue of course content. During the BAM strike at Michigan some faculty canceled their classes as a statement of solidarity. After the strike was settled, Fleming issued a "No Work, No Pay" edict: professors who stopped teaching would receive no salary that month. A number of full professors, including some who opposed BAM, tried to dissuade Fleming, but failed. He would not tolerate sympathy strikes.[58]

* * *

On Wednesday, April 9, 1969, three hundred radical students and friends led by SDS's Progressive Labor faction seized Harvard's University Hall, the 154-year-old building at the center of Harvard Yard, where the files and offices of Harvard College deans were located. The students forced the nine deans out, locked the door with chains, and issued six "nonnegotiable" demands, including expulsion of ROTC from the campus and rollback of rents of university-owned housing units in Cambridge. Franklin Ford, the dean of the faculty, used a bullhorn at 4 p.m. to warn the students to leave or face criminal trespass charges. Although a third of the students did leave, almost two hundred remained in the building. Rejecting the advice of several deans, Harvard University president Nathan Pusey decided to call in the police and state troopers to remove the radicals. Shortly before 5 a.m. on Thursday, April 10, the dean of Harvard College gave the students five minutes to leave or be arrested. "Pusey Must Go! ROTC Must Go!" the students chanted back.

Four hundred police officers—half of them from the police departments of Cambridge, Somerville, and Boston, the other half Massachusetts State Police—

swarmed into Harvard Yard wearing helmets and carrying clubs and shields. They pushed and dragged away 120 Harvard and Radcliffe students who had camped outside University Hall to protect their classmates inside. Then, using sledgehammers, chain cutters, and a battering ram, the police broke into University Hall. Many of the troopers had removed their badges to avoid retribution. One hundred eighty-four people, of whom 145 were Harvard and Radcliffe students, were arrested, charged with criminal trespass. One student suffered a broken back; two suffered concussions; another, a broken ankle; and forty-four more were treated for contusions, lacerations, abrasions, and other minor injuries. The student radio station had placed microphones inside University Hall. They played tapes of the assault, including screams and cries repeatedly over the next several days, while the *Crimson* put photos of the bloodied students on its first page.[59]

As Robben Fleming warned, Pusey's decision to use force united the students behind the radicals and sharply divided the faculty into two factions—conservatives who backed the president's decision and others, who backed the radicals. The majority of older faculty and alumni held Nathan Pusey in high regard, in part because he had refused to cooperate with Senator Joseph McCarthy in the 1950s. Most of the students and more recently hired faculty, however, regarded him as rigid and small-minded. "After the bust, there was basically no legitimate authority in the university," Samuel Huntington of the Government Department remarked.[60]

Consequently, power on the Harvard's campus passed from the administration to the faculty, which elected a special committee to review and act on the affair. John Dunlop was elected to the Committee of Fifteen and almost immediately became its most influential member, according to essayist Roger Rosenblatt, who at the time was a twenty-eight-year-old assistant professor of English and was also elected to the committee. Rosenblatt distinguished Dunlop from James Q. Wilson of the Government Department, who was also on the committee. Wilson was determined to "beat down the radicals" and made no bones about it, Rosenblatt said. His attitude offended moderates on the committee. Dunlop was "more clever, more roundabout, and he appeared to be more flexible," Rosenblatt believed. Dunlop's appearance and physique conveyed his position. "He was neither a handsome nor an unhandsome man; neither tall nor short, fat or thin." Dunlop seemed to "have willed" his body to make himself invisible. (The same could be said of Clark Kerr.) Dunlop always wore the same clothes: a blue blazer, gray slacks, and a bowtie. He had spare black hair combed back. "He spoke in a raspy, plaintive voice that betrayed no particular emotion. He moved like an old athlete—which he was, having played on Berkeley's tennis team under the great coach Don Budge." Fifty-five years old at that time, he reserved his strength until needed. Dunlop was "on everybody's side and on nobody's side." He was "indefatigable," Rosenblatt remembered, often working until 2 a.m. but always back in his office at 7 in the morning. Dunlop joked that his greatest gift as a negotiator was behind him: "he had a hard, strong ass, and he could outsit other negotiating parties in labor disputes."

The most contentious issue facing the special committee and the faculty was punishment for nine students charged with leading the occupation. Although liberal faculty members elected Rosenblatt to this crucial committee, Dunlop managed to win his support, even affection. Without telling Rosenblatt, Dunlop had persuaded the other committee members that only the popular young liberal English professor could execute this politically dicey task. At the Committee of Fifteen's last meeting before the faculty met, Dunlop agreed to defend the rationales for the various levels of punishment for students; Wilson would explain the decisions about particular individuals (whose names, however, remained anonymous). The remaining issue on discipline was to present the Resolution on Rights and Responsibility. "When Dunlop asked, 'Roger, will you do it?' I knew the fix was in."[61]

In September 1969 Pusey asked Dunlop to serve as acting dean of Faculty of Arts and Sciences. In January 1970 he gave Dunlop a long-term appointment to the post. Dunlop was also named Lamont University Professor, one of the six University Professors free to work and teach in any part of the university. "Forceful, self-confident, canny, he became the czar of the interregnum," Morton and Phyllis Keller wrote in their history *Making Harvard Modern: The Rise of the American University*.[62] He assumed the chair of the new University Committee on Governance established by the Harvard Corporation, a kind of a "constitutional convention." Dunlop put top priority on making plans for institutional reform, plans that the next president would implement. The University Committee consisted of students and faculty members from each of the university's nine faculties, two members of Harvard's Board of Overseers, one member of the Harvard Corporation, a Radcliffe trustee, one alumnus, and Dunlop; in other words, representatives of the various constituencies in the university. The Committee on Governance produced a series of reports on faculty and student "rights and responsibilities" (the same term used in industrial relations after the Second World War), the organization and functions of the university's governing boards and the president's office, Harvard's finances, the nature and purposes of the university, and procedures for selecting Pusey's successor. Dunlop and his committee reported that Pusey's tiny staff had been inundated by routine. They recommended major transformations: the creation of vice presidents for finance, administration, development, and government and community relations as well as a provost or chancellor who would oversee academic affairs. It was essential, the University Committee on Governance asserted, "to staff and perform properly the neglected [service] function" of the university."[63]

Dunlop's four years as dean were difficult. The arts and science faculty met twelve times in the spring of 1969 and ten times in spring 1970, unlike the four or five times normally, with four hundred, even five hundred faculty attending, three or four times as many as usual. Professors were denounced for their comments. A bomb exploded at the top of the Center for International Affairs in fall 1970. The ROTC building was attacked.[64] Nonetheless, Dunlop gained respect from nearly all the faculty by the end of his term. "Even his opponents on the Faculty capitulated out of respect for his skillful blending of energy, manipulation and unorthodoxy," the *Crimson* reported. "He took over a splintered Faculty in 1970 and in the next several years skillfully knit the deeply-rooted divisions back together, sending independent-minded reformers either into disarray or scurrying for the center."

Although more than three hundred men and women applied or were nominated to succeed Pusey as president of Harvard, the presidential search committee soon narrowed the list to two: Dunlop and Derek Bok, the dean of the law school, who was seventeen years younger and coauthored *Labor and the Community* (1970) with Dunlop. Conservative Harvard faculty members backed Dunlop, the liberals favored Bok. Dunlop spoke highly of Bok when he met with the search committee. Although Dunlop cared deeply about Harvard University, he was a problem solver, not an executive, and his greatest love was labor relations. He was not yearning to be the university's president. Dunlop continued as dean of the Faculty of Arts and Sciences for eighteen months after Bok assumed office to help his young friend. The *Crimson* reporter watched Dunlop in his curtain call at his final faculty meeting on Valentine's Day 1973. "As Faculty members and observers ambled into the University Hall faculty meeting," the elegant room on the second floor, originally a chapel, with tall windows, high ceiling, crystal chandeliers, and oil portraits of Harvard's past presidents crowding the walls that the SDSers had occupied four years before, they saw Dunlop seated, as usual, to the right of Bok, "trading quips with passers-by and periodically bursting into fits of laughter, always casting a canny eye about the room to reassure himself that everything in *his* Faculty was in order."[65]

* * *

In retrospect, the Labor Board vets stand out as performing a crucial part in the history of American higher education. They led the universities from older, informal forms of administration that had functioned well until the 1930s but flagged as time passed and collapsed in the mid- to late 1960s and led them to a new, more professional, more effective system of management governed by law and economics professors whom they had mentored. In his paper "Industrial Relations and University Relations" at the Industrial Relations Research Association's annual meeting in December 1968, Clark Kerr predicted this develop-ment. In the 1940s, the War Labor Board and its staff resolved disputes between corporate managers and unions. In the 1960s the same staffers, now twenty-five years older, developed comparable systems in universities. "The popular fears of 1964 and 1968 may turn out to have been as excessive in university relations as those of 1886 and 1919 were in industrial relations in the United States," Kerr declared. "Peacekeeping machinery was set up in industry. Now it is emerging on campus—from grievance handling to settlement of organized disputes. It is no more possible to produce B.A.'s with billy clubs than 'coal with bayonets.'"[66]

8

A Whole Different Ball Game, 1968–81

Instead of pointing to the sky, today's players should
be pointing to Marvin Miller.

—Jim Bouton, 2009

The departure of John T. Dunlop as Secretary of Labor
puts into mothballs the most ambitious experiment
ever undertaken in this country to establish a shadow
cabinet of top-level leaders in industry and labor
as advisers to the Federal Government in shaping
national economic policy.

—A. H. Raskin, February 1976

IN 1965 ROBIN ROBERTS called George Taylor at the University of Pennsylvania. Roberts was the veteran star pitcher for the Philadelphia Phillies. "He had the best fast ball I ever faced," Hall of Fame slugger Ralph Kiner recalled. When he grew older and lost velocity on his pitch, Roberts's finesse enabled him to continue to strike out many of the best hitters.[1] He had been elected to a committee charged with finding a full-time executive director for the Major League Baseball Players Association (MLBPA). He had read stories in the Philadelphia papers about how Taylor mediated labor-management disputes and so asked the professor whether he could help the ballplayers.

Taylor told Roberts that he was going to a labor convention the following week and would think about who would be best for the baseball players. He first called Lane Kirkland, George Meany's executive assistant at the AFL-CIO headquarters, who wasn't interested. Then he thought of Marvin Miller, chief economist for the Steelworkers. He knew that Miller was no longer happy at the union and thought he'd be ideal for the players. When the two met soon afterward at a meeting of the Kaiser Steel Long-Range Planning Committee in California, Taylor asked Miller whether he had ever heard of Robin Roberts. "Of course. Who hasn't?" replied Miller, an avid baseball fan. Taylor explained why he had asked and suggested that he call the famous pitcher.[2]

Marvin Miller grew up in the Flatbush section of Brooklyn in the 1920s and 1930s. He became politically radical during the Great Depression and majored in economics in college. Unable to join the armed forces because of a severely lame arm, he spent the war years as a hearing officer in the disputes division of the Regional War Labor Board in Philadelphia. It was a "marvelous job" that taught him how to handle "everything, every issue you can imagine," he recalled.[3] Unlike other Labor Board staffers, however, Miller didn't continue in mediation and arbitration after the war or return to teaching. He did not have an advanced degree, he did not want to be a professor, and he was close to the Communist Party. Miller's wife, Terry, ran for the New York State Assembly on the Progressive Party slate in 1948, and he held a succession of union staff jobs in New York City after the war only to be sacked repeatedly for his politics.[4]

Fortunately, he got a call in 1950 from Otis Brubaker, the research director of the Steelworkers, who he had worked with during the war. Brubaker needed an economist in his office. Miller jumped at the opportunity and kept quiet about his politics. He remained at the Steelworkers headquarters in Pittsburgh for fifteen years. After the 1959 steel strike, he became a top aide to the union's president, David McDonald, and a principal member of the Kaiser Steel Long-Range Planning Committee. The committee of union and management representatives and George Taylor, John Dunlop, and David Cole created a plan that offered worker compensation beyond the union-negotiated wages in exchange for an increase in productivity.[5]

McDonald lost the union presidency in a close vote in 1965. Although the Steelworkers' new president, I. W. Abel, promised to keep Miller on the staff, Miller was not convinced his job was secure. He had a family to support and began looking for other work. The Carnegie Endowment for International Peace offered Miller a post as director of a study of how collective bargaining techniques might be used in international relations. John Dunlop offered Miller a visiting professorship at Harvard University, with a light teaching load and excellent benefits. Then Robin Roberts approached Miller about becoming executive director of the Baseball Players Association.

The latter option was the most enticing. To be sure, there were considerable drawbacks. The MLBPA had been founded a decade earlier by representatives of the sixteen baseball teams and was primarily concerned with retirement pensions. The team owners covered the association's expenses. The modest pensions came from a share in the revenues from the annual All-Star Game. Earlier attempts to unionize the baseball players had failed, and MLBPA leaders like Bob Friend and Bob Feller were adamantly opposed to unions and collective bargaining. Robin Roberts was the son of a Welsh coal miner forced to leave for the United States after Britain's disastrous 1921 Black Friday strike. He had a college degree and, unlike the majority of players, was critical of the team owners. But even he sought firm assurance from Miller that the association would not call strikes.

A Milwaukee magistrate named Robert Cannon had been serving as the MLB-PA's legal consultant without compensation up to that time. Cannon was friendly with the team owners and hoped to someday become commissioner of baseball. When the player representatives decided that they needed a full-time executive director, they had offered him the post first. If Cannon had accepted, the team owners would have paid his salary. But the judge insisted on terms that the committee were unwilling to meet, and so, at the urging of Robin Roberts and fellow pitcher Jim Bunning, they turned to Marvin Miller.[6]

I. W. Abel told Miller he was crazy to take the job. Ben Fischer and Miller's other friends on the Steelworkers staff said the same, but Miller rejected their advice. As a member of the Steelworkers' staff, Miller had no personal interaction with members of the mammoth union, and the Steelworkers' district directors disliked Miller and the other staffers at the Pittsburgh headquarters.[7]

The situation he entered with the Major League Baseball Players Association couldn't have been more different. There were only six hundred players in the two leagues at that time. Miller would be able to get to know every single one of them, both stars like Hank Aaron, Sandy Koufax, Willie Mays, and Bob Gibson, and little-known players who especially needed union support. Forty-eight years old when Robin Roberts called, Miller had risen as high in the Steelworkers bureaucracy as possible, with his lack of experience in the mills. Yet he wanted more. He loved baseball and, although he was no longer a communist, he still had radical dreams. What could be more alluring than the opportunity to revolutionize the national pastime?

Miller nonetheless faced many difficulties at the new job. First, his nomination would have to be approved by the baseball players and by the coaches and managers, who also belonged to the MLBPA. Yet few of these men knew anything about unions. They were mostly high school graduates from small towns or the countryside, thankful to be paid to play in the Major Leagues. The team owners generally took a paternalistic attitude toward the players. Some would hand out a $50 or $100 bill when a player made a fine play and would cover the expenses if a member of a player's family had an unexpected large medical expense. But, when they were displeased, they would deny players privileges, and they bought and sold the players like livestock. The owner of the Pittsburgh Pirates, a real-estate magnate, named one of his racing horses "Roberto," after Roberto Clemente, the team's great Puerto Rican outfielder. When Miller went to the training camps in Arizona to meet the members, several team owners told managers and coaches that he was a corrupt union boss. Others called him a Bolshevik. They asked the managers and coaches to lean on the players to vote against him as director. With a few exceptions, the press was also overwhelmingly against Miller and the MLBPA. If all that was not enough to deter him, the association would have no staff except Miller and hardly any funds.

Miller managed to overcome these and other hurdles. Within several years, he organized one of the strongest labor unions ever in U.S. history. He was fortunate to be appealing to the players in spring 1966—the crest of the civil-rights movement, when Americans were increasingly willing to question authority. He surprised the players by not being a thug or a Bolshevik but a short, well-dressed, soft-spoken fellow who carefully considered the players' questions, answered everyone, and attempted to help them with their problems. The lack of staff proved to be advantageous as well. Miller visited every team in spring training or during the season and he encouraged the players to visit him in the association's office, which he moved from Milwaukee to Manhattan, readily accessible to both American Leaguers (who played in Yankee Stadium in the Bronx) and National Leaguers (who played at the Mets' Shea Stadium in Queens).

The Players Association would never have succeeded, despite Miller's skill, if the team owners hadn't been arrogant millionaires who knew nothing about labor relations and expected players to bow to their wishes. "The owners were a loose amalgam of highly individualistic entrepreneurs, who are the worst people in the world to deal with labor. They're impatient, egocentric, and exasperating to represent. Most of them had never worked inside structures where cooperation with other strong personalities was required. They were thus very poor at cooperating in the face of unified opposition," commented Bruce Johnston, U.S. Steel's vice president for labor relations.[8] "It was incredible. This was a labor-relations scene from the thirties in the mid-sixties," remarked Richard Moss, the young lawyer whom Miller hired from the Steelworkers' staff as the Players' Association's legal counsel.[9]

Miller moved deliberately. In February 1968 the association signed its first basic agreement. Its provisions included an increase in the minimum salary from $7,000 to $10,000; a joint committee to study the reserve clause, which legally obliged players to sign with the same owner indefinitely; and outside arbitration of unresolved grievances. In November 1968 the MLBPA signed an agreement with Topps Chewing Gum, the major marketer of cards with players' names, photographs, and statistics. Until then the chewing gum company would sign agreements with every player in the minor leagues for pennies, compensation that increased only modestly if the player entered the major leagues. The new agreement not only substantially increased annual payment to the players but provided royalties to the association, a measure that, along with other licensing agreements, over time produced a sizable strike fund for the association.[10]

In December 1969 the St. Louis Cardinals star centerfielder Curt Flood objected to being traded to the Philadelphia Phillies. He and his family had been living in the Gateway City for years, he was developing a reputation as an artist, and he considered the Phillies a racist team. "After twelve years in the major leagues, I do not feel that I am a piece of property to be bought and sold irrespective of my wishes," Flood declared. "I believe that any system which produces that result violates my basic rights as a citizen and is inconsistent with the laws of the United States and of the several states." When Commissioner of Baseball Bowie Kuhn refused to intervene, Flood asked the MLBPA for support. Miller warned Flood that the U.S. Supreme Court had protected the major league organizations in earlier cases, that the owners had extraordinary financial resources, and that consequently he was not likely to succeed. When Flood persisted, Miller asked his good friend Arthur Goldberg, the Steelworkers' former legal counsel and former U.S. Supreme Court justice, to represent Flood. They won at the U.S. District Court in May 1970, only to have the U.S. Supreme Court uphold the reserve clause and antitrust exemption of baseball in a 5–3 decision in June 1972.[11]

The Players Association and the Major League owners signed a second basic agreement in May 1970 that raised the minimum salary to $12,000, recognized the MLBPA as the exclusive bargaining agent for the players, reduced the maximum salary cut allowable in one year to 20 percent, and established the right of players to be represented by agents in bargaining. Most significant, the contract established a tripartite arbitration panel, with an impartial arbitrator sitting between the owners' and players' representatives to interpret disputes about the meaning of the contract. Although the team owners did not want to surrender power to an arbitrator, their chief negotiator—John Gaherin, who had years of experience bargaining with East Coast railroad unions and New York City transit and newspaper unions—favored grievance arbitration. In the midst of the Curt Flood litigation, the owners wanted to look fair. Gaherin and Miller persuaded them and the baseball commissioner that transferring "nickel and dime" cases to an independent arbitrator would be in the best interest of the sport.

Finally, on April 1, 1972, after overwhelming authorization votes, the baseball players went on strike. (See figure 12.) It was the first strike ever conducted by professional athletes in U.S. history. The issue was funding of the players' pensions. The initiative came from the players themselves, not Miller, who was afraid it might fail. He was wrong. The players hung on, and the owners conceded after thirteen days.[12]

185

FIGURE 12. Marvin Miller talking to Reggie Jackson on eve of the first baseball strike, March 31, 1972. Bettmann via Getty Images.

* * *

The English historian E. P. Thompson once declared that social movements have a life cycle of about six years. Unless they have an impact within that "window of opportunity," they have little effect on the larger society or politics.[13] Thompson's estimate was spot on. A handful of players wanted to turn their association into an effective union. Through a fluke, they avoided hiring a judge sympathetic to the owners or a conservative union bureaucrat. Instead, they recruited a highly skilled, hard-hitting union professional. Marvin Miller managed to win contracts that impressed the uninformed players. Meanwhile, a highly respected African American centerfielder was willing to risk his career to insist that the team owners or the federal courts recognize the players' rights. Within six years, virtually all the players were willing to strike despite public ire. The second contract stripped the baseball commissioner of power over traditional collective bargaining issues. Instead, power passed to experienced labor-management arbitrators.

The first arbitrator whom Miller and the owners' negotiator appointed was Lewis Gill. A protégé of George Taylor, Gill had chaired the Cleveland Regional War Labor Board during the war and subsequently mediated disputes for Bethlehem Steel and the Steelworkers; the public schools, police, and firefighters in New York City; and unions at United Airlines and Greyhound Bus. When the owners fired Gill for voting against them in an arbitration case, they appointed David Cole, whose previous work had included mediating disputes in the New York subways and waterfront, the steel industry, and the merger of AFL and CIO unions and had directed the Federal Mediation and Conciliation Service.[14]

When the owners fired Cole for voting against them in another case, the parties appointed Peter Seitz, another accomplished lawyer-arbitrator. Seitz had served as director of industrial relations for the Department of Defense, sat on an American Arbitration Association panel that recommended reform of New York City's labor laws, and arbitrated disputes between the National Basketball Association and the Basketball Players Association.[15]

Seitz issued two rulings that transformed the baseball industry. The first, announced on December 16, 1974, freed the Oakland A's star pitcher Jim "Catfish" Hunter from his contract with the team's owner, Charles Finley. Hunter had signed a contract earlier that year that specified that $50,000 of his salary for the season would be paid into an annuity administrated by his insurance company. When Charles Finley, who had made his fortune in insurance, realized that this expenditure could not be deducted from the club's taxes, he refused to pay. At Marvin Miller's urging, Hunter filed a grievance. As arbitrator, Seitz ruled that Finley had violated the contract, a decision that made Hunter a free agent. The result prompted frantic bidding by teams to snatch the pitcher. Two weeks later, Hunter signed a five-year $3.75 million contract with the New York Yankees. Suddenly baseball players could see how much their skills were worth on an open market.[16]

The climax to this story came in the following year, winter 1975. Andy Messersmith, a star pitcher for the Los Angeles Dodgers, and Dave McNally, a pitcher for the Montreal Expos, had played the entire season without a signed contract and filed a grievance claiming that they should be free agents the following year. The owners countered that the contracts that the pitchers signed in 1974 gave them rights to the players indefinitely. Miller argued that the reserve clause, as traditionally interpreted, was illegal. The decision lay in the arbitrator's hands.

Seitz decided that, if he had to choose, he would cast his vote with Messersmith, McNally, and the MLBPA. To avoid chaos, however, he urged the owners and Miller to negotiate a compromise and offered to mediate. Miller and the players consented, but the owners said no. They assumed that, if they lost in arbitration, they could win on appeal in the federal courts. Consequently, on December 23, 1975, Seitz issued the ruling that overturned baseball's reserve clause. Claiming that the decision would do "irreparable harm to baseball," the owners appealed to the federal district court in New York but failed, the judge upholding the arbitrator's ruling. The owners did not realize that since the U.S. Supreme Court's rulings in the Steelworkers trilogy in 1960, federal courts had consistently upheld arbitrators' rulings, unless they were extraordinarily capricious.[17] "I am not an Abraham Lincoln signing the Emancipation Proclamation. Involuntary servitude had nothing to do with this case. I decided it as a lawyer and an arbitrator," Seitz told reporters at a news conference after the decision was issued. "The decision does not destroy baseball," he added. "But if the club owners think it would ruin baseball, they have it in their power to prevent the damage."[18] Seitz's remarks in this instance were typical of the Labor Board vets, who would downplay the significance of their decisions.

The owners fired Peter Seitz the next day. Regardless, his ruling stood. In 1976 the baseball owners and the MLBPA negotiated new contracts that provided partial free agency for the players. The most marketable players attracted agents who negotiated multiyear contracts worth millions and, in some cases, tens of millions of dollars. Within a decade, even the lowest-paid players were receiving $500,000 a year—five times what Hank Aaron and Willie Mays, the highest-paid stars, were receiving when Miller was hired. But free agency meant more than money. It also gave players leverage with the teams' owners and general managers. Although Robin Roberts deplored Miller's militancy, he acknowledged the Labor Board vet's value for the players. "Through his work, ballplayers for the first time attained dignity from owners," Roberts later remarked.[19]

In 1991 Marvin Miller wrote a memoir about his life and work. He chose as a title *A Whole Different Ball Game: The Inside Story of the Baseball Revolution*. His account provides a vivid picture of developments in professional baseball between 1966, when Miller was hired, and 1991, when he retired. He called the transformation a revolution. Yet, as Miller certainly knew, conditions for the ballplayers' brethren in construction, manufacturing, shipping, mining, and other industries worsened during those very same years, with real wages stagnating or declining, benefits cut back, and union membership plummeting. In other words, labor and management saw not one revolution in 1970s and 1980s, but two. Or, more precisely, a revolution and a counterrevolution, with Labor Board vets at the epicenter of both.

* * *

The 1970s marked a critical juncture in U.S. labor history and for the Labor Board vets. The decade followed the most prosperous era in U.S. history. The gross national product more than tripled in the United States between 1941 and 1973, not counting inflation.[20] Labor productivity increased at a rate of 3.2 percent on average every year between 1950 and 1973.[21] And U.S. manufacturers, shippers, and other industries dominated world markets outside the communist world for a generation. Partially as a result, U.S. corporations' profits swelled, netting an average of $18,200,000 every year between 1947 and 1968 after languishing during the 1930s and receiving only modest returns during the world war. Most large corporations did far better than that.[22]

The postwar era was a boom time for unions as well. In large part because of the National War Labor Board's policies, union membership rose from 10.2 million in 1941 to 14.3 million in 1945. Union membership continued to rise after the war ended, unlike the years after the First World War, when U.S. unions suffered devastating defeats. The union share of the nonagricultural workforce in the United States reached a peak of 34.7 percent in 1954. Although the proportion declined afterward, unions nonetheless represented almost 27 percent of the nonagricultural labor force in the United States as late as 1972—a much higher proportion of the workforce than before the Second World War or since the 1970s.[23]

Compensation for union members also improved considerably after the Second World War. Hourly rates for union carpenters, for example, quadrupled between 1947 and 1973, twice the rate of increase of consumer prices during that period. The same was true for newspaper printers, local truck drivers, and transit workers represented by unions.[24] Average hourly earnings for male workers producing machinery in twenty-one mainly unionized cities more than tripled between 1947 and 1973—not including premium pay for overtime, work on weekends, late shifts, and holidays.[25] Workers in auto and truck factories did even better, with annual weekly earnings rising nearly 500 percent in that quarter-century. Moreover, as a result of the Labor Board's policy of not counting pensions as wage increases, many corporations introduced pension systems for their employees during the Second World War for the first time. Although monthly pensions were originally quite modest, after the war they rose three times as much as wages in the steel, rubber tire, and auto industries.[26]

Prosperity did not guarantee harmonious relations, as the steelworkers' 116-day-long strike in 1959 to defend their members' work practices made plain. Nonetheless, sizable profits and increasing productivity helped the Labor Board vets to persuade company and union negotiators to reach compromises in many instances. "The cheapest thing in any contract is money," New York City's premier mediator Ted Kheel remarked in 1965.[27]

But prosperity could not continue forever. Like Britain and most other industrial nations, the United States began to experience economic problems in the late 1960s. Americans endured four recessions in little more than a dozen years: 1970–71, 1975–76, 1980, and 1982–83, each harsher than the preceding one. Labor productivity fell in the United States in early 1973, kept falling for at least two more years, and remained much lower than in most other industrial nations through the remainder of the decade. Consumer prices, which had been stable in the early and mid-1960s, began to rise in 1966 and acquired momentum as time passed, doubling by 1978 and tripling by 1982. Prices rose even more rapidly in oil, construction, and medicine.[28] Finally, the number of strikes in the United States, the number of workers involved in the strikes, and the number of days lost in those stoppages all increased sharply between the mid-1960s and the mid- to late 1970s. The strike wave peaked in 1970, including wildcat strikes called by radicals in the National Association of Letter Carriers, the Miners for Democracy, and the League of Revolutionary Black Workers and authorized strikes by unions in other industries.[29]

A new term entered the English language in the early 1970s—*stagflation*, that combination of inflation and stagnation that liberal economists had not foreseen and could not explain.[30] By 1975 nearly 8 million Americans were unemployed—or 8.5 percent of the labor force, the highest rate since 1941.[31] Conditions became so distressing that *Time* magazine's editors asked "Can Capitalism Survive?" on the two hundredth anniversary of the publication of Adam Smith's *Wealth of Nations*.[32]

High inflation and stagnation were not the only problems alarming Americans at that time. In fall 1973, the Organization of Petroleum Exporting Countries sharply increased oil prices, and Arab members of the cartel imposed an embargo on oil shipments to the United States and the Netherland in retaliation for their aid to Israel during the Yom Kippur War. The embargo and price increases triggered shortages of gasoline, long lines at gas stations, blockages of interstate highways by angry independent truckers, and the murder of at least one gas station owner. In May 1974, in the wake of the Watergate scandal, the Judiciary Committee of the House of Representatives opened hearings to impeach President Richard Nixon. As the hearings proceeded, support for the president plummeted. Nixon was forced to resign on August 9, 1974—the first president of the United States to do so. In late April 1975 North Vietnamese forces attacked Saigon. They moved so fast that U.S. ambassador to South Vietnam Graham Wilson and his staff had to clamber into a helicopter on the roof of the U.S. embassy to escape. Frightened South Vietnamese aides tried to escape by holding on the copter's wheels, only to fall into the sea—a ghastly end to the first war that the United States had ever lost.[33]

The Labor Board vets were not daunted. They had wrestled with tough problems throughout their careers and, except for the Free Speech Movement, usually managed to come through. That is why every president of the United States since Franklin Roosevelt called on them during emergencies. And, in the early 1970s, the Labor Board vets seemed to be succeeding again.

The Nixon administration started to address labor issues with the construction industry. Construction produced roughly 10 percent of the gross national product and in 1970 employed three-and-a-half million workers—nearly all male and overwhelmingly white—in every part of the United States. That was twice as many workers as were employed in food and related industries, three times as many as in steel manufacture, six times as many as in mining.

Moreover, construction was the most strike-prone industry in the country, with carpenters, plumbers, masons, electricians, and other building trades walking off the job five times as often as other U.S. workers. The industry and its work-force were highly decentralized, with eighteen building trade unions divided into 10,000 locals, and many of the industry's 870,000 contractors were too small to withstand a strike. Nearly all the construction workers on major projects belonged to unions in the late 1960s; only half the residential projects were built by union-ized contractors. Nonetheless, hourly wages for workers in the building trades had risen 33 percent more than wages for U.S. workers generally since 1965 and rose at twice the rate of other workers' wages since January 1970.[34]

Business critics blamed the local unions' business agents for the building trades' unusually large wage gains. The *Wall Street Journal* ran a front-page story about Frank Sonsini, the business agent of Local 32 of the Bricklayers' Union in Newton, Massachusetts, as a case in point. The local had jurisdiction over Newton, Welles-ley, Needham, and Dover, Massachusetts—roughly 250 square miles. Sonsini was always comparing the wages for his bricklayers with those in nearby towns, in Bos-ton, and around the country, the *Journal* reported. The bricklayers' locals would "leapfrog," each using nearby masons' gains as the minimum increase for their next agreement. The business agent had close relations with his local's members. He distributed work assignments, collected dues, and met with workers informally on the job and in bars. "Frank Sonsini is clearly a powerful man," the business daily reported. "The members approach him only when summoned, and when he talks they listen carefully. Fifty-nine-years-old with a snappy fedora atop his balding head, sometimes he acts as a father confessor, sometimes as a bantering buddy, sometimes as a counsel and sometimes as disciplinarian. To most members, he speaks English; to some Italian. . . . Frank operates like a king," says an admiring colleague. Thanks largely to Mr. Sonsini's tough bargaining—and a strike along the way—their pay of $7 an hour was almost double their wage of 1960.[35]

Fortune magazine decried "the unchecked power of the building trades." Rich-ard Nixon called it a "crisis situation." He turned to John Dunlop to handle the crunch. Eight times since 1943, Dunlop had been appointed by presidents or selected by union leaders and contractors as chairman of construction industry boards, beginning with the Wage Adjustment Board of 1943–47 and including the National Joint Board for Settlement of Jurisdictional Disputes of 1948–57, the Atomic Energy Labor Relations Panel of 1948–53, and the Missile Site Labor Commission of 1961–67. He was on the phone almost every day with presidents of the national building trades and contractors' associations and commuted weekly between his office at Harvard and Washington, DC.

On September 22, 1969, President Nixon established the twelve-member Construction Industry Collective Bargaining Commission to curb wage inflation and cut back the number of strikes in the construction industry. The committee had the same structure as the Labor Board: four officers of the building trades unions, four leaders of the contractors associations, and four representatives of the public, with Secretary of Labor George Shultz and Dunlop as chair and secretary, respectively. The commission had the power to intercede in disputes at any construction site in the nation. They would develop a procedure for a thirty-day cooling-off period before a union could call strike or a contractor lock out workers, and pressured unions and contractors to hire more African Americans and other minorities in skilled jobs.

In a press briefing, Shultz explained that construction workers had been walking off the job four times as often as other American workers since January and that their wages and fringe benefits were rising at twice the rate of other workers. "It damn well better be a fruitful commission," exclaimed John Stastny, a Chicago-area home contractor who was vice president of the National Association of Home Builders and a member of the commission. "It's not just the home builders who need help, but the people—especially the middle class which is getting the biggest chops of all. . . . The construction industry has been bleeding for people for a long time."[36]

The Construction Industry Collective Bargaining Commission was a prelude to the wage and price controls that Nixon imposed on the entire U.S. economy in August 1971 and to other committees, programs, and departments chaired by Dunlop, by other Labor Board vets, and by Shultz to reduce inflation and unemployment, prevent strikes, and increase productivity over the next several years. On March 29, 1971, the president issued Executive Order 11588, which established a twelve-member tripartite committee chaired by Dunlop to control wages and resolve disputes in the construction industry. At first, the construction stabilization committee approved almost all the wage increases it reviewed, some as high as 18 percent for the year. Unlike his counterparts in the Labour Party in Britain, Dunlop did not believe that regulators on committees should use their authority to rectify inequities among workers. He was unwavering on that point. There are traditional differentials in the construction industry, he argued. Masons were traditionally paid more than painters, who in turn received more than laborers. One of the evils of inflation, Dunlop believed, was that it disrupts such distinctions and in the process generates resentment and protests. Consequently, the committee's initial decisions were intended to restore previous differentiations.[37]

In early July 1971, however, Dunlop declared "unacceptable" a pact that would have increased the pay of Philadelphia painters by 51 percent over two years. Painters had historically been paid less than masons, electricians, plumbers, and other skilled tradesmen. Their relative status should remain the same, was Dunlop's opinion. After that, his committee sent many contracts in the Philadelphia-area construction industry back to the unions and companies for renegotiation. "The work of this board has been quite good," William Dunn of the Association of General Contractors told the U.S. Senate's Committee on Banking, Housing, and Urban Affairs in November 1971. "If you can get something down from 18 to 12 percent, that is not perfect, but it is good," Dunn said. "And we didn't have a freeze to help us."[38] Under Dunlop's leadership, the Construction Industry Stabilization Committee was able to reduce first-year settlement increases in the construction industry from 17.6 percent in 1970 to 6.9 percent in 1972 and 5 percent in 1973, with comparable reductions in wage increases in renewed agreements. "The industry may be getting out of the morass," Dunlop told the *New York Times*.[39]

* * *

There were comparable developments in the steel industry. In August 1971 the Steelworkers signed three-year contracts with the major steel companies. Leaders of the union called the agreement the best that they had ever won. Then top management at U.S. Steel, Bethlehem Steel, Republic Steel, the Armco Steel Corporation, and Youngstown Sheet & Tube promptly announced price increases averaging 8 percent on practically all their products. Those increases were also unprecedented. "Contract Seen Hurting Steel Firms, Economy and Eventually Union; Big Price Rise Is Just First Result of Costly Accord; Some Mill Closings Likely; Joblessness & Profits Plunge," the *Wall Street Journal* declared.[40]

The Steelworkers and the major steel corporations were following a pattern adopted in early 1946 and maintained afterward: a strike or threatened strike produced wage increases followed by price increases. By the late 1960s, however, the practice had become counterproductive. Fearing a strike, the companies would build up huge inventories before the union contract was scheduled to expire, which forced management to hire more workers, pay time-and-a-half and double-time wages, and deploy old Bessemer furnaces. After the new contract was signed, management would lay off thousands and not call them back until inventories shrank. In the interim, the companies had to pay the laid-off workers through supplemental unemployment benefits, a benefit won by the union in the mid-1950s.[41] In 1971 the companies laid off workers even before new contracts were signed.

When a strike date was impending, foreign suppliers and smaller domestic competitors captured business from U.S. auto, railroad, aerospace, and appliance manufacturers and the major construction contractors—the major steel corporations' principal customers. "They are desperately afraid of the strike date," Ben Fischer, assistant to the president of the Steelworkers, remarked. "Not a strike, but strike *date*. They are desperately concerned about it."[42]

To prevent the cycle from happening again, the Steelworkers president I. W. Abel, the union's legal counsel, Bernie Kleinman, and Fischer began meeting secretly with R. Heath Larry and Warren Shaver of U.S. Steel soon after the 1971 contract was signed. The result was the Experimental Negotiating Agreement, a no-strike compact announced in February 1973. According to the agreement, management and the union would begin negotiations for the next contract—the 1971 contract would expire in August 1974—much earlier than before. If they had not reached a compromise by June 1974, the union and corporate officials would ask their arbitrators to write the next contract.

From the point of view of the steel companies, a beneficial aspects of the Experimental Negotiating Agreement was that it undercut their smaller domestic competitors—the thirty-five U.S. steel companies known as the Gotham Group (because they met at the Gotham Hotel in New York) who agreed to sign union contracts with wages and benefits identical to those signed by the largest steel manufacturers. The Steelworkers president I. W. Abel called the Gotham Group "me-too" and "coat holders." The no-strike agreement turned the bargaining world topsy-turvy, weakening smaller competitors while strengthening the big companies.

In April 1973 Richard Nixon issued an executive order establishing the tripartite National Commission for Industrial Peace to encourage corporations and unions in other industries to follow the steel industry's model. To chair the commission, he appointed David Cole—-the Paterson, New Jersey, arbitrator who had served on the War Labor Board, directed the Federal Conciliation and Mediation Commission, and mediated the merger of the AFL and CIO unions. Dunlop and Shultz were chosen as the other public members. The union representatives included the presidents of the Steelworkers, the Teamsters, the United Auto Workers, and the AFL-CIO. Management representatives included top executives of the Bechtel Corporation, First National City Bank, U.S. Steel, and General Motors.

New kinds of labor agreements were appearing everywhere in spring 1973. In March the nation's largest railroads made a tentative agreement with the unions on a new contract three months before the next contract deadline. It was the first time in the history of the railroads that a new contract was settled ahead of time without a threat of a strike. In April the maritime workers' union, which had conducted several major strikes in recent years, was about to settle on an agreement with management in the industry to resolve conflicts through arbitration. Similar agreements were in the works at the U.S. Postal Service, on the docks on the West Coast and Hawaii, in the Hawaii public schools, and at San Francisco newspapers. "From here on there will be very few if any national emergency disputes that will lead to strikes. It's been a long time coming and now it's for real," W. Willard Wirtz, U.S. Secretary of Labor in Lyndon Johnson's administration and a Labor Board vet, remarked at the end of April.[43]

Dunlop was even more optimistic. "The years 1970 to the present have had a better tone in the relationships between labor and management than any time since World War II," he declared at a seminar that he gave in December 1974 for clients of the Capital Guardian Trust Company, a \$1 trillion Los Angeles–based financial services company with offices around the world. "The British government is imposing a three-day work week and importing coal because of the National Union of Mineworkers' long strikes. We don't have anything like that here," he told the investors. Dunlop expected 1975 "to be a relatively light year in terms of labor problems."

At the end of the seminar, investors asked Dunlop what the best form of economic policy making for the government would be. "A central and fundamental question for the future," Dunlop replied. There was a sharp divide between foreign and domestic economic policy, he continued. One department is responsible for wheat exports, another for decisions about the price of wheat. There was little coordination and the decisions could be contradictory. The Council of Economic Advisers is poorly structured, Dunlop declared. Economic policy requires both "doers" and "analysis-advisors." Yet the current chair of the council, Alan Greenspan, focused only on the latter. Dunlop also disparaged Congress, saying that it was "poorly organized" for economic policy. What is needed, Dunlop told the financiers, is "a significant reorganization" before or after the 1976 election: "an executive agency pulling together economic analysis, motoring the economy, preparing options for executive decision[s] and seeing the agencies carried out those decisions."[44]

* * *

Although he shied away from the term *corporatist*, which, in the aftermath of Mussolini, had fascist overtones, Dunlop was trying to promote liberal corporatist-style arrangements to regulate wages, benefits, and economic policy in U.S. industries similar to those established in Sweden in the 1930s and in Austria and West Germany after the Second World War.[45] He had yearned for such an arrangement ever since he entered public life. The Wage Adjustment Board, which he cochaired between 1941 and 1947 (see chapter 2), was a committee of top union and business leaders certified by the Roosevelt administration to regulate all disputes and issues in the construction industry in the United States.[46] He saw that system as a model for the entire U.S. economy. "There seems to me to be no escape from the conclusion that in a world of powerful economic groups—unions, managements, farmers—-there must be attempts at coordination of the interests of these groups," Dunlop declared at the first meeting of the Industrial Relations Research Association in 1948. "One need not be optimistic about the prospects of these interest groups co-operating in the public interest," he continued. "Yet political and economic stability requires the Administration in power to take an active part in developing working compromises among these major interest groups. There must be created a mechanism for the discussions. Some advisory board to the President, and to the Council of Economic Advisers is in order. There is no other way to effectuate a working compromise in a society of dominant interest groups."[47]

Dunlop returned to the subject in his presidential address to the Industrial Relations Research Association in December 1960. "Our national industrial relations suffers from excessive legislation, litigation, formal awards and public pronouncements," he complained. He saw the AFL-CIO merger as a shotgun marriage, with the various unions in the two federations not working with their counterparts at the national or district levels, despite the confederation. National Association of Manufacturers and Chamber of Commerce leaders speak contemptuously about the labor movement, even as the corporations in those associations work effectively with unions. Politicians are even worse. "Fewer and fewer members of the Congress can be equipped to understand the technical issues. . . . Formal compromises in words assure unending litigation. . . . The long view has been lacking." Leaders of industry and labor have "to place much greater reliance upon the development of consensus."

Dunlop spent the academic year 1956–57 at the International Labor Organization's chief office in Geneva writing his renowned work *Industrial Relations Systems*. While there, he traveled to Sweden and West Germany, where he saw labor and manufacturers' associations working together to reach agreements. "If the confederation level of American management were engaged in collective bargaining, as is the SAF in Sweden, the actions of American enterprise management and policy pronouncements of the N.A.M. and Chamber might be more consonant," he remarked in his 1960 presidential address to the Industrial Relations Research Association. Can Americans cooperate in the same way? he asked his colleagues. "The method of consensus is admittedly difficult to apply. It is so much easier simply to pass another law, or issue another decision or another resolution. The achievement of consensus is often a frustrating process since it must triumph over inertia, suspicion, and the warpath. It is slow to build. But it is clearly the most satisfying and enduring solution to problems." Consensus building will require "leadership devoted to mediation among followers, a leadership which seeks to explain problems and seek solutions rather than merely to impose a solution by sheer power or to rail against a decision from without."[48]

The crisis of the 1970s seemed to provide the opportunity for corporatist regulation of the U.S. economy. Consequently, the Labor Board veterans wanted to repeal or amend the Landrum-Griffith Act, the law passed by Congress in 1959 in the wake of the exposure to organized crime in the Teamsters, International

Longshoremen's Association, and several other unions. The law weakened not only mobsters but law-abiding union leaders, they believed. By 1966, 10 percent of all proposed contracts were voted down by union members. In early January 1967, Secretary of Labor Willard Wirtz called the frequent rejection of contracts "very, very dangerous for collective bargaining." In an October 1966 speech, Dunlop said that it was time to give up "some of the exaggerated views of union democracy expressed in the spirit of the Landrum-Griffith Act." He proposed that international union officers should have the power, as a matter of public policy, to sign contracts without ratification of the members. As worker militancy intensified in the early 1970s, even more proposed contracts were rejected, and more union officers were voted out of office. In one session of the National Commission for Industrial Peace, Shultz asked, "Shouldn't we see whether we can agree on recommendations for modifying Landrum-Griffith?" "In '70 the building trades with the Labor Department worked up a document criticizing Landrum-Griffith. I have a copy," Dunlop replied. "Perhaps we could suggest Landrum-Griffith be re-examined for labor-peace purposes?" David Cole, the committee's chair, remarked.[49]

AFL-CIO president George Meany was thinking along the same lines. In September 1973 the AFL-CIO Executive Council announced that they planned to consolidate their organization, reducing the number of regions from sixteen to seven and to create a new executive position, the director of organization and field services, to facilitate cooperation with industry and government. The director would not only coordinate the federation's nationwide operations but also supervise its state labor federations and city labor alliances. If this position had been created, it would have been the first major change in the structure of the AFL-CIO since the federations merged in 1955. The idea of a director of organization was first conceived in 1955. It was envisaged for Walter Reuther, the president of the United Auto Workers, who was president of the CIO until it merged with the AFL. But Reuther never took the position, and the AFL-CIO had remained a loose collection of organizations. According to Paul Hall, the president of the Seafarers International Union who chaired the committee that planned the reorganization, the head of the new department "is expected to wield exceptional power in the labor movement," turning the AFL-CIO into "a more effective federation . . . [that] will have far-reaching consequences."

The AFL-CIO Executive Council offered the job of director not to the president of one of the major unions, as one would expect, but to W. J. (Bill) Usery, a trade unionist who had become a top-ranking union-management mediator. Born and raised in Georgia, Usery rose to become the International Association of Machinist's special representative to the President's Missile Site Labor Commission. Dunlop, who chaired that commission, considered the machinist "absolutely first rate." At the recommendation of George Shultz, President Nixon appointed

Usery as the assistant secretary of labor for labor-management relations in 1969. In March 1970 he helped to resolve the eight-day postal workers' strike by persuading the president to name a blue-ribbon commission whose members would be acceptable to both parties. Usery subsequently was appointed to the National Commission for Industrial Peace and named director of the Federal Mediation and Conciliation Service. The AFL-CIO Executive Council told Usery that he would be a strong candidate for the AFL-CIO presidency when eighty-one-year-old George Meany retired.[50]

Even Richard Nixon momentarily flirted with corporatist notions. In January 1973 he asked George Meany and Teamsters president Frank Fitzsimmons to designate union representatives who would serve as assistant secretaries of the Departments of Defense, Commerce, and Housing and Urban Development and hold subcabinet positions in all the other cabinet departments. This was part of the president's broader plan to construct what was called a New Republican Majority. He invited more conservative figures in the labor movement to dinners at the White House. He sent Secretary of State William Rogers and Secretary of the Treasury George Shultz to the AFL-CIO Executive Council meeting at Bal Harbour, Florida, in February. He appointed William (Pat) Brennan, the conservative chairman of the New York City Building Trades Council, as Secretary of Labor. And, with the support of Meany, the president appointed Dunlop as the new director of the Cost of Living Council. "Mr. Nixon's wooing of labor is one of the most breathtaking political romances of modern times," the *New Republic*'s columnist TRB declared. The *New York Times* editors were aghast. "It is one thing for the President to select people from either labor or industry on the basis of his conviction that each individually has the requisite of competence to fill a key post. It is quite another to go to the National Association of Manufacturers, the AFL-CIO or the American Farm Bureau Federation and, in effect, to bring them into Government as unelected organizational partners in establishing policy," they protested. "This smacks of syndicalism on the model of Mussolini's Italy or Peron's Argentina."[51]

* * *

Nixon's attempt to bond with labor leaders and build a working-class majority backfired, alienating establishment Republicans as the U.S. economy descended into the worst economic troubles since the Great Depression and Congress moved toward impeachment.[52] In the first quarter of 1974, the real gross national product declined at an annual rate of 5.8 percent, productivity tumbled at an annual rate of 5.5 percent, the consumer price index shot up 3.7 percent in three months, and the wholesale price index, which signaled impending consumer prices, reached an annual rate of 24.8 percent. The economy continued to decline for the next twelve months, reaching a trough in March 1975. The Dow Jones industrial average fell by more than 20 percent in 1974 despite inflation. The total value of all stocks on the New York Stock Exchange declined by nearly 30 percent.[53]

One might expect the deteriorating economy would ruin John Dunlop's reputation. After all, he had not only served as secretary of the Construction Industry Collective Bargaining Commission, chair of the Construction Industry Stabilization Committee, and chair of the National Commission on Productivity in the Nixon administration. He also had been director of the Cost of Living Council from January 1973 until the agency terminated on April 30, 1974, and he was the only member of Nixon's administration who had urged continuation of wage and price controls.

Yet that did not happen. On the contrary, President Nixon, President Gerald Ford, and the Democratic congressional leaders all continued to hold Dunlop in high regard. He was forceful and shrewd. He had ties to influential corporate executives, bankers, and building contractors. And no one in Washington or anywhere else had better connections with top leaders of organized labor than the bow-tied Harvard professor. When George Shultz announced in March 1974 that he planned to resign as secretary of the treasury in May, Dunlop was one of two candidates considered as his successor. Although Nixon ultimately selected William Simon, a conservative bond trader who had become deputy secretary of the treasury and "energy czar," President Ford appointed Dunlop as coordinator of the President's Labor-Management Committee in September 1974. This committee of eight corporate and eight union leaders was to meet regularly and offer recommendations to the president about federal economic policy.[54]

In January 1975 President Ford asked Dunlop to become U.S. secretary of labor. He was reluctant. Secretaries of labor have not historically been powerful figures in presidential cabinets, and after leaving the Cost of Living Council, Dunlop had returned to Harvard to teach. He had begun serving as an economic policy adviser for the Saudi Arabian government and was arbitrating contract disputes for the unions and contractors building the oil pipelines in Alaska, both lucrative activities. But ever since the war, Dunlop had felt a duty to serve. He told the president that he would join the cabinet if he could also serve on the Economic Policy Board—which met with the president almost every day to formulate, coordinate, and implement national economic policies—as well as heading the Labor Department and chairing the President's Labor-Management Committee. Ford readily agreed.[55]

Dunlop took the oath of office in the East Room of the White House on March 18, 1975. "I am very, very pleased to welcome the new Secretary of Labor," President Ford remarked on that occasion. "His career is distinguished by the ability to innovate and generate cooperation, to solve disputes, and to break through the

FIGURE 13. John T. Dunlop testifying before U.S. Senate Labor and Public Welfare Committee, February 1975. National Archives.

most difficult of situations. . . . I am told John has come to Washington . . . 1,600 times since 1938. Welcome to 1600 Pennsylvania Avenue, on your 1,601st visit to the Nation's Capital. There are plenty of things to do here, John." In reply, Dunlop promised to foster "understanding, persuasion, accommodation, mutual problem solving, and informal mediation" between labor and business. The U.S. industrial relations system was "not created by intellectual visionaries, nor invented by the government in 1935 or in 1947," he declared. "Its strength is its provision of maximum substantive decisions by private parties and minimal governmental intervention procedurally. . . . It is my hope that business, labor, and government, working together, can address the immediate problems of the Nation while having a deep appreciation of our longer run necessities and opportunities, not only for the economy as a whole but individual sectors . . . and regions as well."[56]

Dunlop was fully up to the task. Sixty-one years old, he worked sixteen hours a day or more seven days a week. He would arrive at his office by 7 a.m., having already scanned four or five newspapers and the White House news summary. He would work through the day and then amble to a nearby bar or restaurant, where he would sit in the back for a drink date, a dinner date, and an after-dinner date.

Dunlop would return to the efficiency apartment he rented in a modest hotel by midnight but often resume work, then return by 7 a.m. the next day. He always wore a gray suit or a blue suit and a bow tie. But there was nothing clerical about his demeanor. He was combative in cabinet meetings and, as a *Boston Globe* reporter remarked, would curse union and business negotiators "in language more suited to the Boston docks than the Cambridge classrooms."[57]

As secretary of labor, Dunlop put his highest priority on chairing the president's Labor-Management Committee, a sixteen-member committee that President Ford established on September 30, 1974, at Dunlop's request. The committee consisted of the chairmen of eight of the largest and most influential corporations in the United States and the world—General Motors, General Electric, U.S. Steel, the Bechtel Group, Mobil Oil, First National City Bank, Alcoa, and Sears, Roebuck—and eight of the most influential American union leaders, including the presidents of the AFL-CIO, the United Auto Workers, the International Brotherhood of Teamsters, and the Steelworkers. Dunlop served as coordinator, just as he had done for years in the construction industry. The president asked the committee to give him "man-to-man and face-to-face" counsel on economic matters. The committee met once a month on Saturday mornings behind closed doors. Staff members were excluded and the agenda was flexible. Dunlop consulted with its members between sessions. The topics included national energy policy, housing, federal spending and taxation, financing public utilities, unemployment, and labor-management committees in the private sector.[58] "In a world of powerful economic groups—unions, managements, farmers—there must be attempts at coordination of the interests of these groups," Dunlop had argued at the Industrial Relations Research Association in 1948. Finally his hopes were being realized.[59]

The Labor-Management Committee presented a series of proposals, each of which President Ford embraced. For example, although the president had declared that inflation was "domestic enemy number one" in his first address to Congress and had called for a one-year 5 percent surcharge tax on corporations and upper-level individuals to reduce the federal budget, the committee urged him to reverse course. They recommended a quick, temporary $20 billion tax cut for working-class and low-income taxpayers to spur spending and larger tax credits to businesses to stimulate acquisition of new factories and equipment. The president presented that idea in his January 1975 State of the Union address. On March 30, the Democratic majorities in Congress passed legislation for $22.8 billion in tax cuts, even more than the Labor-Management Committee had requested. In fall 1975 Dunlop convinced the president to extend the tax cuts for another year, to the dismay of Secretary of the Treasury Simon.[60]

Dunlop's committee convinced the president to support larger tax credits for utilities and stretch out the requirement to install pollution controls to ease construction of two hundred nuclear and one hundred fifty coal-fired power plants over the next decade. To garner support, Dunlop arranged for a visit to Capitol Hill by the AFL-CIO's George Meany and top executives of General Motors, U.S. Steel, and Sears, Roebuck. "I think Congress would listen to them," he hazarded.[61] After consulting with the committee, Dunlop developed a plan with Secretary of Housing Carla Hills for federal subsidies for construction of apartment buildings for low-income residents—a plan that attracted few investors but would create thousands of jobs for the building trades and contractors and improve living conditions for impoverished workers.[62] He put together a team of attorneys, economists, and accountants from the Justice Department, the Labor Department, and the Internal Revenue Service to determine whether prosecutors could win cases against the Teamsters' Mafia-controlled $1.3 billion Central State Pension Fund.[63] He also arranged for President Ford to meet with the president of the International Longshoremen's Association Teddy Gleason, George Meany, and Lane Kirkland to end the longshoremen's boycott of wheat sales to the Soviet Union, an agreement that guaranteed that half the ships carrying the grain would be U.S. vessels.[64]

Dunlop tried to change the regulation of employment practices in the United States during his brief tenure at the Labor Department. In 1940 the department had administered 18 regulatory programs, he pointed out. By 1960, the number had expanded to 40. By 1975 the number had soared to 134 distinct programs, most important those generated by the 1970 Occupational Safety and Health Act, the 1974 Employee Retirement Income Security Act in 1974, the 1964 Civil Rights Act, and the 1968 Consumer Credit Protection Act. The members of Congress who wrote the legislation were mainly lawyers, not business executives, trade unionists, economists, or mediators, he argued in the November 1975 report "The Limits of Legal Compulsion," which was distributed at the top levels of the White House. To get regulatory legislation passed required telling alarming stories of badly injured people, and, inevitably, "simplistic thinking about complicated issues." But designing and administering a regulatory program is "an incredibly complicated task," and ensuring compliance is even harder. He gave the example of the Office of Safety and Health Administration, which employed 1,200 people to inspect conditions in 5,000,000 workplaces. How could they possibly ensure safety in all those workplaces? And how could owners keep up with the regulations issued by OSHA?

The administration agencies instituted since the 1960s generally can't recruit and keep the most qualified college graduates, he argued, thinking of his own students. The rule-making process did not include mechanisms to develop conciliation and cooperation among the conflicting parties. On the contrary, they trigger conflicts between the contending groups and "weak and ineffective" remedies for the people whom the policymakers aimed to help. Moreover, the new programs sometimes have unintended consequences harmful to the people that the policy wonks hoped to aid. The current system of regulation "is inherently contentious and acts to maximize antagonism between the parties," Dunlop declared.

Dunlop believed that the parties involved should be directly involved in drawing up relevant regulations, much as unions and employers reached compromises in negotiations over contract clauses. Although doing so would require modification of OSHA and ERISA, it may be the most efficient way to achieve the program's objectives, he argued. "Trust cannot grow in an atmosphere dominated by bureaucratic fiat and litigious controversy: it emerges through persuasion, mutual accommodation and problem solving."[65]

* * *

Finally, Dunlop tried to persuade the president and Congress to change federal legislation regulating the construction industry. Under the 1935 Wagner Act, workers in every sort of industry except agriculture and domestic work were allowed to join unions, strike, and, on occasion, call a boycott of their employers. However, the 1947 Taft-Hartley Act outlawed secondary boycotts. In other words, Congress prohibited a union that has a dispute with one employer from pressuring another business to stop selling, or buying from, the first employer. This provision had a devastating impact on the building trades unions, where many different business contractors worked side by side. One example occurred in Denver in 1949. One contractor there subcontracted the electrical work on a building to a nonunion subcontractor. The other subcontractors on the site had agreements with unions. Consequently, the Denver Building Trades Council put up a picket line around the site, leading all of the tradesmen at the site except the electricians to walk off the job. A week later, the general contractor brought in a new, unionized subcontractor to do to the electrical work. The discharged subcontractor filed a charge with the National Labor Relations Board, charging that he and the general contractors were distinct businesses and that the other workers were conducting a secondary boycott in violation of the Taft-Hartley Act. The National Labor Relations Board was convinced by that argument, as was the U.S. Supreme Court in a 1951 ruling.[66]

The national building trades unions began calling on Congress to enact what they called common situs legislation, which would allow members of any building trade union to call on the other tradesmen employed at the same site to walk out in support of their demands. Since the building trades unions had political clout, Presidents Eisenhower, Kennedy, Johnson, and Nixon and their labor secretaries all supported the proposed act, but none of those administrations made the legislation a high priority.

Dunlop pushed much harder on this issue than his predecessors when he became secretary of labor. He had devoted much of his career to working with the building trades unions and contractors. By the early 1970s, however, "open shop" construction companies that did not recognize unions and "double-breasted" construction companies that had both unionized and nonunion branches were undercutting the building trades unions. The nonunion contractors were particularly strong in the South and the Southwest, areas that were booming economically, and in residential housing. In addition, 150 major corporations led by Alabama-based Blount Brothers Construction and Roger Blough, the former chairman of U.S. Steel, formed the Construction Users' Anti-inflation Roundtable to undermine the building trades unions.[67]

When price and wage controls ended on May 1, 1974, large segments of the construction industry, particularly the unionized sections, "reverted to the former malaise of widespread stoppages, whipsawing negotiations, disregard for productivity, excessive increases, and to a decline in the respect for leadership from national union and contractor groups alike," Dunlop declared. Although unemployment rates in construction remained high, there were more than four times as many strikes in May 1974, the beginning of the construction season, as in the same month a year earlier, and wages soared. In the San Francisco Bay area, for example, plumbers and steamfitters won an 18 percent hourly wage increase that month, despite a sharp fall in housing starts. There is "no way" to stop it, the *New York Times* economics columnist Leonard Silk wrote, adding that Dunlop was "sick at seeing his efforts go down the drain."[68]

Dunlop persuaded President Ford to support common situs legislation in Congress (S. 1479, H.R. 5900), which would "give to employees in the construction industry the same rights now enjoyed by industrial workers . . . to publicize by peaceful picketing the fact that either the principal or his agent-ally is engaged in a labor dispute with his employees."[69] Dunlop drafted a second, complementary act to create the twenty-five-member Construction Collective Bargaining Committee. The committee would consist of ten representatives of the construction industry, ten representatives of the building trades unions, and five neutrals headed by the Secretary of Labor. It was intended to pinpoint problematic areas in pending contracts and mediate between contractors and unions. The act would also require local trade unionists to obtain permission from the national trade unions before calling strikes.[70] Dunlop had tried for years to move bargaining away from the local level, where business agents played contractors off against each other, to the regional or, ideally, the national level, where terms of settlements could be tempered. As he remarked in a June 1975 Senate hearing on common situs, "I want the record to be clear that my interest over these 30 years in working in labor relations in this industry has been always on the side of trying to establish orderly procedures."[71]

* * *

If the Labor Board vets' hopes, most earnestly expressed by Secretary Dunlop, had come to pass, the economic system in the United States might have evolved differently than it actually did in the latter twentieth and early twenty-first centuries. More union-management contracts would have been negotiated across each industry at the national level, as they were in West Germany and Sweden, rather than at the local level or between discrete firms. Representatives of unions and corporations might have had much greater input into government regulation of working conditions, health, safety, and race and gender relations. The chairs of the largest corporations and the presidents of the most influential unions, along with the president of the AFL-CIO, would have met quarterly to discuss national economic policy with the president of the United States, who in turn would have urged Congress to implement the union and corporate officials' proposals. The unions' share of the labor force might have stabilized, rather than continuing to fall further. More federal spending would have been directed to investment in utilities and upgrading of harbors, roads, and other infrastructure. Other industries might well have followed the model of the steel industry, with union and corporate negotiators reaching agreement months before contract deadlines or letting arbitrators decide the terms of their agreements. If this had all happened, major companies like Bethlehem Steel might not have gone bankrupt, fewer manufacturing jobs would have been lost to other nations, and U.S. incomes might not have become as radically unequal as they did by the early 21st century. Ultimately, the United States could have moved toward a liberal corporatist form of governance of the sort that emerged a generation before in Western Europe.

Of course, Dunlop's dreams were not realized. The unions' share of the labor force and its political influence plunged after a succession of industrial and political defeats in the late 1970s and the 1980s. Working-class incomes stagnated. Industries were deregulated. Major manufacturing companies went bankrupt. Many others moved much of their operations to Mexico, China, or other nations, while imports of appliances, other electronic goods, automobiles, clothing, and steel soared. Labor leaders lost virtually all their power in national economic policy. And far from tending toward corporatism, free-market ideology came to dominate both political parties.[72]

Although the Experimental Negotiating Agreement survived for a dozen years, U.S. Steel ceased investing in steel manufacturing. Instead the corporation bought the Marathon Oil Corporation, changed its name to USX, and, in 1986, locked out the steelworkers until the union consented to wage cuts and changes in work rules. A *Pittsburgh Post-Gazette* cartoonist described the new scene in the steel industry perfectly: A group of executives in pin-striped suits celebrated the purchase of the oil giant, as a big "USX" sign floated above. Underneath it, a big-shouldered steelworker says, "I think we're the 'EX'!"[73]

W. J. Usery declined the AFL-CIO Executive Council's invitation to become their director of organization and quite possibly succeed George Meany. Instead, he continued as director of the Federal Mediation and Conciliation Service. He was later appointed secretary of labor and then left government service to found a consulting firm advising businesses on employer-employee relations. The National Commission for Industrial Peace that David Cole had chaired withered, in part because it was underfunded and understaffed but also because it was so closely tied to Richard Nixon, who was in deep trouble by the spring of 1974. "If we are a success, then it would be a victory for the Administration. There are some people who would not see any Administration win anywhere," one public member of the commission remarked.

In 1973 chief executives of 150 major corporations, led by the incoming and outgoing heads of General Electric, the heads of AT&T, Alcoa, and the retired chairman of U.S. Steel, joined together in a new alliance, the Business Roundtable, which advanced their interests in politics. The Business Roundtable was the most ambitious initiative to undermine unions and reduce government regulations since the American Plan of the 1920s.[74]

Finally, on December 22, 1975, President Ford vetoed the common situs bill. Ford had supported common situs in the spring of 1975 out of loyalty to Dunlop. But, by the summer, opposition to the bill went beyond opposition from open-shop contractors and became a battle cry for political conservatives. Right-wing agitators Terry Dolan and Richard A. Viguerie, aided by the National Right-to-Work Committee, started a letter-writing campaign to defeat the legislation. The White House received 625,000 anti–common situs letters and telegraphs, many more than Ford received after he pardoned Richard Nixon. Only 6,400 wrote in favor of the act. The *Wall Street Journal* and William F. Buckley took up the cause, as did the National Association of Manufacturers. More than thirty-five senators, representatives, and governors asked the president to drop his support, as did the undersecretary of commerce, James Baker. Dozens of other newspapers, including the *New York Times*, published hostile editorials. An opinion poll showed that 68 percent of those questioned opposed the common situs bill. So did 57 percent of the union members who were polled.

Ronald Reagan, who was preparing to challenge Ford for the 1976 Republican presidential nomination, condemned the bill as a threat to workers who did not want to join unions and to the health of the U.S. economy. Local Republican leaders followed his lead, warning that they would desert the president unless he vetoed the bill. Ford remained quiet during the congressional debate, hoping it would die there. When the House of Representatives and the Senate, both of which had large Democratic majorities, approved the bill in the second week of December, the president decided that he had to switch or lose the nomination to Reagan. He was almost certainly correct. Yet Dunlop was also correct when he warned the president that the action would hurt his chances of being reelected in November.[75]

Dunlop resigned as secretary of labor on January 14, 1976—the first member of a presidential cabinet to resign on a matter of principle since William Jennings Bryan in 1915.

His defeat in the common situs fight was part of a larger failure of attempts by cooperatively minded bankers, industrialists, and top labor officials like Felix Rohatyn of Lazard Frères, Irving Shapiro of DuPont, and Lane Kirkland of the AFL-CIO to introduce industrial policies in Washington to protect U.S. manufacturing and jobs in the mid-1970s.[76] Despite these defeats, Dunlop continued to express hope for union-management cooperation even after Ronald Reagan fired the unionized Air Traffic Controllers in August 1981. "It is *not* a major new era and that I am willing to sign my name to," he told a *Business Week* reporter in 1982, in the midst of the sharp recession.[77]

He was wrong. The defeat of common situs was more than a defeat for the building trades unions and John Dunlop. It signified the end of the system of conflict management in manufacturing, transportation, construction, and metal mining forged by the National and Regional War Labor Boards during the Second World War. Mediated by George Taylor, Dunlop, Sylvester Garrett, David Cole, Ben Aaron, Bill Simkin, and other arbitrators, the system survived disputes for a quarter-century after the war. It could not, however, survive the 1970s: the high inflation, low productivity and low (real) profits, frequent strikes and wildcat walkouts, rebellions against union leaders, high unemployment, declining real wages, greater foreign competition, the Business Roundtable, the environmentalists, consumer activists, and the galvanized conservative movement.

9

George Shultz at the Negotiating Table

Trust is always the coin of the realm.
—George Shultz, 2015

OF THE INNUMERABLE GRADUATE STUDENTS whom the Labor Board vets taught during their careers, only one was as brilliant, fervid, and thick-skinned as their tutors. That student was George P. Shultz, who enrolled in MIT's Industrial Relations program in September 1945 while still a major in the Marine Corps. He earned a doctorate in economics and became a star in Industrial Relations and a compatriot of John Dunlop, Clark Kerr, Charles Myers, and George Taylor. In 1969 Shultz joined the Nixon administration, where he served as the secretary of labor, director of the Office of Budget and Management, the secretary of the treasury, and counselor to the president. He returned to Washington in 1982 as the secretary of state in the Reagan administration. As secretary of labor, Shultz used the conflict-resolution techniques that he learned from his mentors to help institute affirmative-action programs in construction, steel, and then all American industries and end the racially segregated public school systems in the southern states. As secretary of state, he drew on his mediation experience to help end the Cold War.

In the three decades since leaving government, Shultz has spoken out repeatedly on the mounting risk of nuclear war. He also has proposed new ways to address climate change, the national debt, refugee policy, and the failure of the war on drugs, among other issues.[1] In January 2018, at the age of ninety-seven, Secretary Shultz traveled from his home in California to Washington, DC, to warn the Senate Armed Services Committee about the threat of nuclear war. "President Reagan thought nuclear weapons were immoral, and we worked hard to get them reduced," he told the senators. "I fear people have lost that sense of dread, and now we see everything going in the other direction. The more countries have nuclear weapons, the more likely it is that one is going to go off somewhere."[2]

Yet Shultz was not a clone of his mentors. Far from it. While the Labor Board boys were Democrats who favored wage and price controls, Shultz was a Republican leery of government intrusion into markets. He supported George W. Bush for president in 2000, and over the years repeatedly called on U.S. and western European leaders to use armed force against the Serbian president Slobodan Milošević, Iraqi president Saddam Hussein, and other odious foreign powers.

* * *

To understand the Labor Board vets' most influential protégé, one has to look back to his family heritage, his upbringing and education, his experience during the Second World War, and his work in industrial relations and other areas before he entered government. Shultz's maternal grandparents were Presbyterian missionaries who crossed the Mississippi, the Great Plains, and the Rocky Mountains to build a church for the Shoshone in eastern Idaho. The couple perished there, leaving behind their four-year-old daughter Margaret. The young girl was adopted by her maternal aunt Margaret, for whom she was named, and her husband George Pratt, an Episcopalian minister for the All Souls Church in Manhattan. "Uncle George and Aunt Margaret were like grandparents to me," Shultz recalled in his memoir *Turmoil and Triumph*. "We would often go to Uncle George's church on Sundays, and afterwards we would have lunch at their New York apartment. As a small boy, I didn't particularly enjoy this, but I liked them."[3]

Shultz's father Birl Shultz was a Quaker who grew up on a farm in Indiana. A good athlete, he won a scholarship to attend DePauw University, where he played football and earned a bachelor's degree. He taught history and served as the principal of a high school in Indiana for several years and then earned a doctorate at Columbia University. At Columbia, Birl Shultz studied with the renowned Progressive historian Charles Beard, who was also a Hoosier, a Quaker, and graduate of DePauw. He wrote his doctoral thesis on the appropriation process in the New York state legislature and edited with Beard a collection of documents surveying state referenda and initiative legislation. Shultz's father went on to found the New York Stock Exchange Institute in the wake of the deflationary depression of 1920–21. The institute sought to improve the stock exchange's employees' and members' understanding portfolio management and investment management. His 1942 book, *The Securities Market and How It Works*, received wide readership and was translated into Spanish, Japanese, and Mandarin.[4]

Thus George Shultz inherited missionary zeal, a progressive mindset, market expertise, dedication to research, and a passion for football. He was born in midtown Manhattan in 1920. When he was three years old, the family moved to Englewood, New Jersey, a small city easily accessible to Wall Street. In his junior year, he transferred to the Loomis School, the prestigious boys' boarding school in Connecticut, where he played varsity basketball, tennis, and football. He entered Princeton University in 1938, determined to make the Princeton Tigers football team. "When the early practice time came . . ., I was in great shape. I knew I impressed the coaches and had a crack at making the team." But he was whacked hard in an early scrimmage, his left knee badly injured. Consequently, he was asked to be coach of the freshmen backfield. "It was . . . my first teaching experience."[5]

Shultz majored in economics and public affairs at Princeton. As a child of the Great Depression, he was drawn to "what I thought of as the real side of the economy." He spent the summer between his junior and senior years in Tennessee, conducting research for his senior thesis on the Tennessee Valley Authority (TVA). He read files at the TVA's headquarters in Knoxville and boarded with a farm family in the western North Carolina hills. Shultz's thesis shows a sensitivity to the common people often lacking in economic studies. "The family took me in but initially was very slow to give me real answers to my questions." When his hosts asked him for help filling out a form for the TVA, he realized that farmers were giving bogus figures to the government office in order to receive fertilizer. This led him to conclude "that if you are going to get people to talk candidly, they have to trust you, and trust takes time to develop."[6]

When Japan attacked Pearl Harbor, Shultz tried to enlist in the U.S. Army Air Corps and the Royal Canadian Air Force only to be rejected for nearsightedness. Consequently, he completed his thesis, received his baccalaureate, and signed up for the U.S. Marine Corps. (See figure 14.) He went through office training at Quantico, Virginia. "When the sergeant handed me my rifle, he said, 'Take good care of this rifle, this is your best friend, and remember one thing: never point this rifle at anybody unless you're willing to pull the trigger,'" Shultz recalled decades later. "I told that story to President Reagan, and we were very careful we didn't make empty threats. . . . And there is another side of the coin to the boot camp wisdom, which is be known as a person who does what you say you're going to do. That way, people can deal with you, they trust you."

Commissioned as a second lieutenant, Shultz received artillery training in New River, North Carolina, and then was shipped to the Pacific, where he was engaged in several battles and promoted to captain and then major. "I consider myself a Marine today," he declared in a 2015 interview. While back in Hawaii between operations for rest and for the reforming of the battalion, he met an Army nurse named Helena ("Obie") O'Brien. They corresponded after he returned to the front and reunited afterward. They were married in 1946 and raised five children.[7]

FIGURE 14. Lieutenant George P. Shultz in the Pacific, 1944. Hoover Institute Library.

After V-J Day, Shultz was sent to the Boston Navy Yard. Since the Marines had little work for him, he was allowed to take courses in economics at MIT. This proved to be a pivotal experience. It was the ideal place and time to study union-management relations. The MIT faculty included labor economists Douglass V. Brown and Charles Myers, who served on the Regional War Labor Board in Boston during the war; Joe Scanlon, a former president of a Steelworkers local in Ohio whose "Scanlon Plan" for union-management cooperation attracted considerable attention in the 1940s and 1950s; and economists Paul Samuelson and Robert Solow, future winners of the Nobel Prize. "Lessons learned from that experience go so deep. How to apply economics to practical problems; how to think about the ebb and flow and the condition and timing of negotiations; how to understand the workings of an organization," Shultz reflected years later.[8]

After receiving his doctorate in 1946, Shultz was asked to join the MIT faculty. His first published books were studies of union-management cooperation, part of a series on the causes of industrial peace sponsored by the National Planning Association. This was a time when strikes shook many parts of the United States every year. Yet many firms and unions were resolving disputes with relative ease. Shultz and his collaborators investigated a dozen cases of cooperation. They concluded that full acceptance of the union by the management, strong, reliable unions that believed in private ownership, mutual confidence between the parties, and avoiding legalistic approaches to solving problems produced peace at those firms and unions.[9] Shultz went on to produce pioneering studies on wage pressures on management; management introduction of computers; automation; and a union-management program to assist laid-off workers at a meatpacking plant in Dallas.[10]

While teaching at MIT during the Stevenson versus Eisenhower campaign, "I found myself liking Ike," Shultz later recalled. As a senior staff economist at the Council of Economic Advisers, "I simply drifted into being a Republican."[11] He also became a consultant to President John F. Kennedy's Advisory Committee on Labor-Management Policy, chair of a Department of Labor task force on the operations of the Federal-State Employment Services, and a member of the governor of Illinois's Committee on Unemployment. In addition, Shultz served as George Taylor's right-hand man on the committee appointed by the secretary of labor to investigate the causes of the 1959 steel strike and recommend changes in policy. He chaired a task force on manpower issues that focused on the Labor Department for Richard Nixon's 1968 presidential campaign.

Shultz left MIT in 1957 to become a professor of industrial relations at the University of Chicago. Five years later, he was appointed dean of the Graduate School of Business at Chicago. While there, he became a close friend of Milton Friedman, the renowned free-market economist.[12] Although he was more empirically minded than Friedman, Shultz respected him immensely. He came to agree with Friedman that union practices cause inflation, a marked departure from Dunlop, Kerr, and Sumner Slichter. Like other Republicans, he believed that the federal government intervened far too often in strikes. Although he remained close to Dunlop, Kerr, Myers, and his other mentors, Shultz sought Friedman's advice once he entered government.

* * *

In 1968 Shultz was elected president of the Industrial Relations Research Association. In his presidential address, Shultz urged the members to make the question of race and employment as their top priority. The Labor Board vets had previously avoided racial discrimination questions. There were exceptions, to be sure. Sylvester Garrett acted forcefully to help break the strike called by white transit workers in Philadelphia to stop promotion of black workers in 1944, for example. As president of the National Urban League in the latter 1950s, Ted Kheel urged employers to hire more African Americans. But the Labor Board vets were appointed to arbitrate grievances by two parties, unions and companies, many of which excluded blacks and other minorities or confined them to the lowest-paying, most dangerous jobs. Privately, the Labor Board vets might have been disturbed by such behavior, but they rarely if ever challenged it. If they had done so, they probably would have been fired, as Peter Dietz was by the ball team owners, for arbitrators worked at the pleasure of the union and the employer.

Racial discrimination in employment can no longer be tolerated, Shultz declared. He pointed to "the appalling unemployment experience of black teen-agers" that "may be increasingly carried forward into their years as young adults." The most important sources of information about jobs are informal, he argued. African Americans are highly concentrated in neighborhoods where they interact mainly with other unemployed youth. Consequently, special measures—"measures that tap into the grapevine"—must be deployed to inform potential employees in those parts of cities about job openings. This issue was "more acute" because a large proportion of the new jobs in metropolitan areas are in the suburbs. Government must persuade employers that under the explosive new circumstances "supervisors cannot conduct business as usual."[13]

After Dr. Martin Luther King Jr.'s death, Shultz organized a conference in Chicago on race and unemployment. Between 1961 and 1967, the number of unemployed sixteen- to nineteen-year-old white workers fell, he pointed out at the opening session. Yet unemployed nonwhites of the same age grew by 29 percent during those years. Attributing the disparity to segmented labor markets and businesses moving out of cities to suburbs and southern states, he called for programs like the GI bill to equip unemployed and underemployed black and brown workers for the labor market. He also condemned the racialized union policies. "Nothing is more sacrosanct [for unions] than seniority," he observed. Yet African Americans have been historically denied jobs in many places. Government agencies and other employers are finally beginning to hire more blacks in new kinds of work. "Should they begin at the bottom of the ladder?" he asked.

"When it comes to layoffs, will they be among the first to go, or will some special provisions insulate them from the normal rules of the game?" As dean of the Business School at the University of Chicago, he persuaded major corporations to provide summer jobs for black students in the MBA program and thus begin to integrate corporate management.[14]

Shultz received a fellowship at Stanford University's Center for the Study of the Behavioral and Social Sciences for the academic year 1968–69. The family moved there in September, expecting to spend the year at that beautiful campus. In December, however, President-elect Nixon called Shultz and asked him to be secretary of labor in his administration. He accepted on the spot and moved to Washington. Helena and the children followed in the summer.

Shultz envisioned three objectives as secretary of labor. The first was to compel companies and unions to call a strike or announce a lockout when they were unable to compromise on contract terms despite mediation, rather than asking the Labor Department or the president to intervene. His second aim was to persuade employers and government agencies to hire more African Americans, especially teenagers, and also more Mexican Americans and underprivileged whites. The third was to help the administration slow inflation in wage and prices. He succeeded in the first area, was moderately successful in the second, but failed utterly in the third.

The Kennedy and Johnson administrations, like Truman's before them, had repeatedly pressured corporate and union presidents to compromise whenever strikes seemed to threaten the economy. Secretary of Labor Arthur Goldberg was so quick to intervene in disputes that the department staff joked about giving him a fire chief's helmet and a brass pole. Lyndon Johnson was even more insistent. Shultz considered such a strategy foolhardy. If a union and a company are unable to settle on contract terms despite mediation, they should fight it out until one party or the other concedes or until they reach a compromise, he was convinced. "The real experts on what's good for a union and its members and what's good for management and its group are the people in the union and the management. It's up to them to work out the answers to their problems," he told the press shortly after he was designated as labor secretary. He adhered to that stance once he assumed office. "It's easy to exaggerate these things," Shultz declared when a strike by longshoremen closed the major ports on the Atlantic and Gulf Coasts, brushing aside complaints by New York trading companies and Sen. Jacob Javits of New York, a Republican. Shultz similarly refused to intervene in November 1969 when 147,000 workers represented by the United Electrical, Radio & Machine Workers of America, the International Union of Electrical Workers of America, and eleven other unions struck for higher wages and cost-of-living protection at General Electric.[15]

Shultz's second major objective as labor secretary was to force unions and employers to admit and hire many more African Americans, especially teenagers, and also more Mexican Americans—-beginning with the construction industry and then extending from there. Except for poorly paid jobs as laborers, only white men were hired on jobs on construction sites—mainly Irish and Italian immigrant men and their sons and grandsons. "When I was a plumber, it never [occurred] to us to have niggers [sic] in the union," AFL-CIO president George Meany unembarrassedly remarked in a meeting with Nixon aides. In 1968 a Boston Globe reporter compiled data from the state and federal agencies on apprenticeships in construction in Massachusetts. Of the 3,134 apprentices in programs in the state in spring 1968, only 58 were African Americans. Seven blacks were being trained as plumbers, for example, but 293 whites. Twenty black men were being trained as carpenters, 341 whites. Ten black bricklayers, 249 whites. One black steamfitter, 264 whites. Not even one black man was being trained as an iron worker, roofer, sheet-metal worker, plasterer, tile or floor layer, or sprinkler fitter—and not a single woman was apprenticed in any of the trades. It was the same in Philadelphia, Chicago, and other major cities. One union leader in Detroit declared that "at the present pace of integration it would be somewhere around 2168 before Negroes achieve their full equality."[16] "We found a quota for black workers in the construction industry," Shultz remarked at the time. "It was zero."[17]

The previous labor secretary, Willard Wirtz, had tried to institute a plan that would have imposed quotas for admitting and training African Americans in the building-trade unions in Philadelphia. The comptroller general of the General Accounting Office, the congressional agency that supervises federal spending, shot down that plan, noting that Section 703 (j) of Title VII of the 1964 Civil Rights Act explicitly prohibited quotas in hiring. Sen. Everett Dirksen of Illinois, the Senate Republican minority leader, had insisted on including that ban on quotas as a condition for his support of the law.[18]

Rather than conceding, Shultz and Assistant Secretary of Labor Arthur Fletcher, a Republican African American, persuaded Nixon and Attorney General John Mitchell to back a revised version of the Philadelphia Plan. The modified version would provide "target goals" of admitting more minorities in the building trades, rather than precise numbers, with goals increasing every year but varying between cities according to their particular labor markets. This might enable the administration to get around Section 703 (j) of Title VII. For example, 30 percent of the population of Philadelphia in the late 1960s was black, yet only 1 percent of the sheet-metal workers were black. Because of retirement and attrition, about 10 percent of the sheet-metal workers were replaced with new hires every year. So if a contractor wanted to win a federal contract, the local of the sheet-metal workers with a federal contract would have to admit a "minority goal," which would rise annually. The contractor would be required to file an affirmative action program within 120 working days after signing the government contract, and the building-trade unions would have to open their membership to racial minorities. A contractor's application would be approved if he made "a good faith effort" of 4–8 percent minorities by the end of 1970. The range would rise to 19–23 percent by 1973. Employing minorities at that rate would put the contractor "in compliance." If he failed, a federal agent would investigate, and the contractor might not be eligible for future contracts. The target goals in other cities would depend on the minority share of the local population. "We must set goals, targets and timetables," Fletcher told reporters in July 1969, shortly after the Apollo 11 spacecraft landed on the moon. "The way we put a man on the Moon in less than ten years was with goals, targets and timetables."[19]

Historians and political scientists differ in their explanation of why Richard Nixon was so supportive of Fletcher and Shultz's affirmative action for blacks and other minorities while simultaneously pursuing his electoral strategy to attract white segregationist Democrats. Some saw it as a classic case of cunning behavior by "Tricky Dick," since affirmative action pitted two pillars of the Democratic Party—the National Association for the Advancement of Colored People (NAACP) and other civil-rights organizations and the AFL-CIO and the building-trade unions—against each other. Others point to a consistent record of support by Nixon for civil rights. As the chair of the President's Committee on Government Contracts in the Eisenhower administration, he learned about the extent of racial prejudice in workplaces. He had backed the 1964 Civil Rights Act, sent his daughters to an integrated public school, and donated to the Southern Christian Leadership Conference. Still others underline Nixon's concern to protect the power of his office and the executive branch vis-à-vis Congress's comptroller general.[20]

Each of these interpretations has merit, yet we also must acknowledge the backgrounds and character of Assistant Secretary of Labor Arthur Fletcher and Secretary of Labor Shultz. Renowned in the black community as "the father of affirmative action," Fletcher was the son of a career military man, son-in-law of an entrepreneur, and a veteran. A college football star, he studied under the GI Bill at Washburn University in Topeka, Kansas. Soon after graduation, he was asked to help a liberal Republican running for governor gain support from black voters. When the candidate won, Fletcher was given a job overseeing the building of highways in Kansas. There he learned how lucrative contracts were handed out and became convinced that government contracts could create jobs for minorities. During those same years, Fletcher helped raise funds to finance the lawsuit against the Topeka Board of Education that led to the Supreme Court case *Brown v. the Board of Education.* He left Kansas after some white businessmen objected to his attempts to steer contracts to minorities. Fletcher and his wife moved to Sacramento, California, where rocks were thrown at their house. The family moved to Berkeley and then to Washington State. Fletcher organized the East Pasco Self-Help Cooperative to train black youth for skilled jobs and ran for lieutenant governor in 1968. His work in that campaign caught the eye of Richard Nixon, who appointed him assistant secretary of labor for employment standards. In that capacity, Fletcher proposed a revised version of the Philadelphia Plan.[21]

Shultz firmly backed Fletcher and persuaded Nixon and Attorney General John Mitchell to support the Philadelphia Plan when it was attacked by southern Democrats, Republican minority leader Senator Dirksen, the Associated Contractors of America, and AFL-CIO president George Meany. As Hugh Davis Graham has argued, Shultz appealed to the president's "bourgeois solicitude for jobs, to the Quaker virtue of honest work, and to the prospect of creating black conservatives by giving them a stake in the middle class."[22]

A week before Christmas 1969, Senate opponents of the Philadelphia Plan inserted a rider banning target goals in hiring in an appropriation bill offering relief for hurricane victims. Shultz shot back immediately, declaring that the "country's long established commitment to affirmative action for equal job opportunity has been gravely jeopardized by the United State Senate." He termed the rider "part of an effort by some unions . . . to block affirmative steps to open skilled and high-paying jobs to blacks and other minorities." Nixon was no less direct. "Nothing is more unfair than that the same Americans who pay taxes should by any pattern of discriminatory practice be deprived of an equal opportunity to work on federal construction contracts." The Philadelphia Plan, he added, "does not set quotas, it points to goals." A coalition of moderate Republicans and liberal Democrats defeated the rider in the House. Then the Senate reversed itself, allowing the appropriation bill to pass without the rider.[23]

In February 1970 Shultz signed Order 4, which required every business in the United States with federal contracts worth $50,000 and fifty or more employees to accept the revised Philadelphia Plan. This meant that all midsized and large employers in the United States had to submit hiring goals and timetables based on "the percentages of the minority workforce" in their city with the aim of correcting any "underutilization" of minorities "at all levels" of employment. Order 4 involved a quarter-million employers throughout the nation and roughly 20 million workers, or one-third of the U.S. labor force.[24]

The Constructors Association of Eastern Pennsylvania sued Secretary Shultz to halt the order, charging that it flouted Title VII's ban on preferential hiring and the association's contracts with unions and that it represented an unconstitutional exercise of authority by the executive branch. On March 14, 1970, Charles Weiner, judge of the U.S. District for the Eastern District of Pennsylvania, ruled that the Philadelphia Plan did not violate the 1964 Civil Rights Act. "It is beyond question," the judge declared, "that present employment practices have fostered and perpetuated a system that has effectively maintained a segregated class. That concept, if I may use the strong language it deserves, is repugnant, unworthy, and contrary to present national policy." He added the Philadelphia Plan would provide "an unpolluted breath of fresh air to ventilate this unpalatable situation." In April 1971 the U.S. Court of Appeals in the Third Circuit voted unanimously to confirm the constitutionality of the revised Philadelphia Plan. In March 8, 1971, in Griggs v. Duke Power Co., the U.S. Supreme Court ruled in favor of the class action suit filed by the thirteen black workers at the electrical utility's power station in Dan River station, North Carolina. Hired as laborers, the workers wanted to be promoted to coal miners but the company had denied them the promotion for failing to pass an aptitude test and lack of a high school degree, a requirement imposed after the passage of the Civil Rights Act. The Court voted unanimously in favor of the black plaintiffs. The ruling marked the beginning of two decades of decisions by the Supreme Court in favor of affirmative action in hiring and promotion. Finally, in December 1971 Secretary of Labor James Hodgson, Shultz's successor, issued an order extending the ban against discrimination and applying affirmative action programs to women workers.[25]

The federal court rulings hardly resolved all racial and gender issues in workplaces. They were issued in an era when employment opportunities for blue-collar workers were decreasing, not expanding. Moreover, Richard Nixon reversed his attitude toward affirmative action in 1970, after one hundred thousand New Yorkers, led by Peter J. Brennan, the president of the New York City Building Trades Council, marched against antiwar demonstrators. After Nixon was reelected in November 1972, he nominated Brennan as secretary of labor. He assumed office in February 1973. In the interim Nixon moved Arthur Fletcher out of the Labor Department.

Nonetheless, the push by government agencies for affirmative action in industry continued. In January 1972 Congress passed and Nixon signed a new version of the Equal Employment Opportunity Act, which included hiring goals and timetables for employers to secure government contracts, an enlarged staff of attorneys for the Equal Employment Opportunity Commission (EEOC), and new powers to initiate lawsuits. In the ensuing years, the EEOC won consent decrees, timetables, and back pay for minority and women workers from AT&T, the major steel manufacturers, major trucking firms, other corporations, and many universities and colleges. None of this would have been possible without the actions of Shultz, Fletcher, and, very briefly, Richard Nixon.[26]

* * *

George Shultz failed in his third objective as secretary of labor: slowing wage inflation, as we saw in chapter 8. (See figure 15.) Shultz blamed corporate executives
for the rapid wage increases of the late 1960s and the 1970s. No one can expect
union leaders to not push for wage and benefit increases for their members when
consumer prices are rising, he argued. "That's got to come from management,"
he insisted. The normally taciturn cabinet secretary blew up at a private meeting
with presidents and board chairmen of multibillion-dollar corporations when
asked what the administration planned to do about the rising wages. "You're just
a bunch of crepehangers," he exploded.[27]

FIGURE 15. George Shultz promising that the Nixon administration would not impose wage controls, May 1970. Hoover Institute
Library.

By that point, however, Shultz had already begun to handle an even tougher problem facing Nixon in early 1970: desegregation of southern public schools. Even though fifteen years had passed since the U.S. Supreme Court ruled in the two cases of Brown v. Board of Education that "separate educational facilities are inherently unequal" and that school districts should begin to desegregate "with all deliberate speed," the vast majority of southern elementary and high school schools remained legally segregated when Nixon was inaugurated in January 1969. No southern governor had been willing to tackle the job, nor did Presidents Eisenhower, Kennedy, or Johnson. "If presidents felt they should speak up, or act to enforce court rulings, they risked offending conservatives, segregationists, and the [white] South. If they wanted to sit tight, they invited the wrath of liberals," an Associated Press reporter observed. Lyndon Johnson waited until March 1968, the month in which he announced his decision not to run again, to set a deadline for desegregation of southern schools. He picked September 1969 as the deadline, a date after his leaving office and returning home to Texas.[28]

Richard Nixon tried to follow the same line when he was elected president in November 1968. After defeating Senator Hubert Humphrey and Governor George Wallace in a razor-close contest that year, he adopted his "southern strategy" to lure white voters alienated by Johnson's support of civil rights into the Republican Party and attract those who had voted for Wallace. Consequently, he appointed two aides of Senator Strom Thurmond to his staff and tried twice unsuccessfully to put a conservative white southern judge on the U.S. Supreme Court. He stripped the liberal Department of Health, Education, and Welfare of authority over desegregation of southern public schools. He moved the power to the Justice Department, reasoning that enraged whites would blame judges, not his administration, for desegregating their children's schools. Finally, to win the backing of Senator John Stennis of Mississippi in a close vote on a military appropriation bill, Justice Department lawyers filed briefs in support of thirty-three Mississippi counties trying to postpone integration of public schools. This was the first time in recent years that the department had sided against the NAACP in a desegregation case.

The last move was a step too far. On October 29, 1969, in a unanimous decision in the case of Alexander v. Holmes County the U.S. Supreme Court ordered an immediate end to racial segregation in Mississippi counties and, by extension, all other southern counties that still maintained separate racial school systems by law. The decision followed the case of Green v. New Kent County of May 27, 1968, when the U.S. Supreme Court ruled unanimously that "the burden on a school board today is to come forward with a plan that promises realistically to work, and promises realistically to work now." The court's decisions put Nixon in a quandary. Although he considered defying the court order ("Let's see how they enforce it," he told aides), White House press secretary Ron Ziegler told reporters that "the Administration will carry out the mandate of the Court and will enforce the law." Attorney General John Mitchell made a similar statement. Nonetheless, as historian Dean Kotlowski observed, "Nixon and his aides had no inkling how to enforce it."[29]

After consulting with resolute defenders of racial segregation such as his aide Pat Buchanan and Senator Richard Russell of Georgia, the president decided to follow the advice of his more moderate advisers—Shultz, Daniel Moynihan, and Leonard Garment, a law partner whom Nixon chose as his adviser on civil rights and human rights. Although Buchanan urged Nixon to "tear the scab off the race issue in this country," Garment had been contacting southern attorneys, businesspeople, educators, clergy, and politicians attempting to meet the court's edicts without disrupting their communities. The Citizens' Committee of the Greenville School Board particularly caught his eye. It was a biracial committee that was arousing support for the school board's desegregation plan in their mid-sized South Carolina textile city under the slogan "Education Is the Important Thing." The committee's members were not all liberal, but they respected the law and valued public education. Surmounting resistance from a white committee opposed to busing and desegregation, they managed to peaceably desegregate the city's schools that semester. Their success attracted attention from major newspapers and television stations. Garment invited the committee's leaders to come to the White House to explain their project.[30]

In early February 1970, Nixon appointed the Cabinet Committee on Education to promote desegregation in Alabama, Arkansas, Georgia, Louisiana, Mississippi, South Carolina, and North Carolina, where separate racial school systems were mandated by law. Many northern corporations were moving factories to those states, where unions were weak and labor costs comparatively low. But public education in the region compared poorly with education in the rest of the nation. Many managers were loath to send their children to the schools. "In every State the public schools are literally the guarantees of that State's life and growth and health. Any community which permits the public school system to deteriorate condemns itself to economic and social stagnation," Nixon declared when he announced the Committee on Education. He provided three principles to guide the committee's members. The first was that desegregation plans should involve minimum disruption of children's education. The second was that neighborhood schools "should be the rule . . . to the extent possible." The third was that desegregation of the schools "should be dealt with uniformly throughout the land." In other words, in both the North and the South.[31]

As a nod to Wallace supporters, Nixon appointed Vice President Spiro Agnew to chair the committee. Agnew refused to participate, however, and resigned the position in August. Consequently, Shultz, the vice chair, assumed the responsibility, with an office in the White House. Other members of the committee were Daniel Patrick Moynihan, Attorney General John Mitchell, and Secretary of Health, Education, and Welfare Elliot Richardson. Leonard Garment was appointed chief of staff. "The courts have spoken; many schools throughout the country need help," Nixon declared when he announced the committee. "The nation urgently needs the civil statesmanship and level-headedness of thousands of private citizens and public officials who must work together in their towns and cities to carry out the law and at the same time to preserve educational opportunity. The Administration will work with them."[32]

In May 1970 Nixon requested $1.5 billion in emergency aid to help school districts dismantle their biracial systems, and the Cabinet Committee on Education established biracial State Advisory Committees to watch over the process. Shultz, Garment, and the staff started in Mississippi. Shultz and the committee and staff handpicked the committee members, among them Dr. Gilbert Mason, chair of the NAACP in Biloxi and a close friend of the late Medgar Evers. He recalled, "I, Gilbert R. Mason, great-grandson of a slave, welcomed into my den at my home back-of-town Biloxi, presidential assistant Robert Mardian, Postmaster General Red Blount of Alabama, Nixon advisor from Mississippi Gulf Coast, and Attorney General John Mitchell. There in my home we talked about school desegregation and the background to our local school desegregation suit. The next time I knew, in June 1970, I received an invitation to the White House."[33]

Shultz brought them to the Roosevelt Room, opposite the Oval Office. The discussion was polite, but participants were deeply divided, the blacks believing that desegregation would improve education, the whites chary. Shultz let them talk for a while, and then, as prearranged, Attorney General John Mitchell walked in. The attorney general had a reputation as a tough guy sympathetic to southern whites. Shultz asked him what he would do about desegregation. "I am the attorney general, and I will enforce the law," he growled. "I will enforce the law," he repeated, and then left. Shultz spoke next, telling the committee that the desegregation was going to happen, whether they liked it or not. The question is whether it would be implemented peacefully or through armed force, and how it would be the impact on their local economy. If the segregationists in their state fight, the NAACP will announce a boycott and northern corporations will stop investing and cancel conferences. He told the participants at the meeting that they had a great stake in seeing desegregation work.

Afterward he took the group to the State Department's handsome diplomatic reception rooms, pointing out the desk where Thomas Jefferson wrote the lines from the Declaration of Independence "dedicated to the proposition that all men are created equal." Lunch was served. Shultz sat with Dr. Gilbert Mason and Warren Hood, the president of the Mississippi Manufacturers Association. "I sat with the two strong men I wanted to co-chair the Mississippi advisory committee. I argued that if they would accept, the committee would immediately have great credibility with whites and blacks; their acceptance would thereby enhance the ability of the committee to attain its goal" of a desegregated school system introduced with the least disruption and greatest prospect of better education for the children. When they began talking, he left them alone. Toward the end of the lunch, Hood and Mason shook hands.

When they returned to the White House, the participants offered some suggestions about how to handle special problems. The Department of Health, Education, and Welfare had a small amount of money available for minor expenses. Shultz offered those funds. Then, as planned, he walked the group across the hall to meet the President in the Oval Office.[34] Shultz and the other committee members and staff went through the same procedure with each of the other southern state committees. They convened a meeting of the cochairs of all seven committees and their spouses with the president and the First Lady in New Orleans. When public schools opened in the South in September, the vast majority commenced peacefully with little federal presence.[35] The State Advisory Committees continued for several more years, serving as a liaison between the Cabinet Committee of Education and the local school boards, schools, and parent-teacher associations and distributing funds to distressed school districts. Important too was the fact that Nixon and his administration did not present desegregation as a question of morality, as civil-rights leaders and Lyndon Johnson had done, but simply a matter of obedience to the law. The president had garnered support from white southerners by nominating two white southern "strict constructionists" to the Supreme Court. Finally, at Nixon's insistence, the commissioner of the Internal Revenue Service revoked tax exemption for the private white academies that were started in the South as a response to desegregation.[36]

In this way Shultz and the Nixon administration managed to end de jure racial segregation in the public schools in North Carolina, South Carolina, Georgia, Alabama, Mississippi, Arkansas, and Louisiana. Their efforts hardly produced equality and peace. Violent resistance to desegregation occurred after segregation in some southern cities, among them Greenville, South Carolina. Moreover, black students were mainly bused to predominantly white schools; the reverse was rare. Similarly, black school principals were frequently appointed as assistants to white principals. And de facto segregation persisted in the South just as it did in the North, as affluent white families moved to exclusive suburbs or put their children in private schools. Nonetheless, school desegregation proceeded throughout the South in the 1970s. By 1980, 64 percent of black students in North Carolina were attending predominantly white schools, 44.3 percent in Alabama, and 23.6 percent in Mississippi. Desegregation was more substantial in the South than in the remainder of the country. In the Northeast, in contrast, racial segregation increased between 1968 and 1980.[37]

* * *

On July 1970 Nixon appointed Shultz as the first director of the Office of Management and Budget and in June 1972 selected him to succeed John Connally as secretary of the treasury. By this point, the Bretton Woods system created in 1944 to stabilize international commerce had broken down from the rising U.S. trade deficit and inflation. Traveling around the world, Shultz negotiated a new system of floating currency rates. In the process, he formed bonds with other finance ministers, including Helmut Schmidt, Valéry Giscard d'Estaing, and Takeo Fukuda who subsequently became chancellor of West Germany, president of France, and prime minister of Japan, respectively. While serving as secretary of the treasury, Shultz flew to Damascus to help Secretary of State Henry Kissinger mediate a cease-fire between Syria and Israel in the Yom Kippur War in October 1973. He mediated the dispute between the Justice Department's Civil Rights Division and the Equal Opportunity Employment Commission over the EEOC's proposed order to steel companies to reduce racial and gender discrimination in the mills. Shultz had become the Nixon administration's all-around problem solver. By late 1973 Shultz was the sole remaining member of the original Nixon cabinet and staff and, in the opinion of William Safire, "the best—morally and professionally. . . . He knows his stuff; he is incorruptible, tough-minded and sensitive. Most important, in a milieu that salivated over the trappings and luxuries of power, he remains the only man in the Nixon team who helps his wife do the dishes."[38]

Shultz resigned as treasury secretary in early May 1974, three months before Richard Nixon resigned. A day later, he accepted a post as executive vice president and member of the board of directors of the Bechtel Group, the large privately owned international construction corporation, which was based in San Francisco. Twelve months later, he was appointed Bechtel's president.[39]

Shultz might have continued for many more years directing Bechtel's operations, serving on its board and the boards of other corporations, teaching part-time at Stanford University, and conferring with President Reagan, with whom he worked as chair of the economic policy advisory board during the 1980 presidential campaign and transition—enjoyable and lucrative work. Shultz's plans changed suddenly on June 25, 1982, when Reagan asked him to return to Washington to become secretary of state. He had been on Reagan's short list for the post eighteen months earlier. The other contender had been General Alexander Haig. Conservative Republicans favored Haig, as did Nixon. Haig very much wanted the job, while Shultz was ambivalent. So Reagan chose Haig, but he proved to be dreadful—a general trying to seize control from the president. When Reagan dismissed Haig, he immediately turned to Shultz, who took a leave from Bechtel, put his assets in a blind trust, and headed back to Washington.

U.S.-Soviet relations were in a dire state when Shultz returned to Washington. The Soviet Union had had a much larger army than the United States and its NATO allies since the beginning of the Cold War. The United States had compensated with its larger navy, larger air force, and larger stock of nuclear weapons and intercontinental missiles. By the late 1970s, however, the United States lost its edge in nuclear armaments, for it reduced its military spending after withdrawing from Vietnam while the Soviet Union, benefiting from the rising value of its oil exports, increased the number and power of its intercontinental ballistic missiles (ICBMs) and deployed intermediate-range missiles, the SS-20s, which could strike Western European capitals in minutes. The balance of world power shifted further at the end of the 1970s as the Marxist-led Sandinistas overthrew the U.S.-backed dictator Anastasio Somoza in Nicaragua. The Soviet Union and Cuba intervened in Ethiopia and South Yemen on behalf of Marxist governments. Cuban troops financed by Moscow fought for control of oil-rich Angola. And the Islamic Revolution overthrew the Shah of Iran, thus threatening U.S. control of the Persian Gulf. On Christmas Eve 1979, the Soviet Union invaded Afghanistan. Finally, General Wojciech Jaruzelski imposed martial law in Poland to crush the rising social movement Solidarność (Solidarity). These were the boldest moves by the Soviet Union and its allies since the coup in Czechoslovakia in 1948.

Jimmy Carter had hoped to reduce U.S.-Soviet rivalry and both nations' armed forces when he was inaugurated president in January 1977. In his address at the University of Notre Dame in May 1977, the president expressed relief that the United States was no longer driven by an "inordinate fear of communism."[40] Consequently, he responded cautiously to the rise of the Sandinistas in Nicaragua and other developments that neoconservatives like Norman Podhoretz and Paul Nitze of the Committee on the Present Danger considered challenges to the United States. Carter reversed course after the Soviet forces invaded Afghanistan. Conceding that he had misjudged the Soviet objectives, Carter canceled U.S. grain agreements with the Soviets, withdrew from the Senate's consideration the Strategic Arms Limitation Treaty II that his administration had negotiated, proposed large increases in Defense Department spending, upgraded U.S. military ties with China, called for a boycott of the Olympic games planned in Moscow in 1980, stopped his annual meeting at the White House with Foreign Minister Andrei Gromyko, and secretly directed funds and arms to the mujahideen fighting the Soviets in Afghanistan.

President Reagan was even more assertive when he assumed office. The administration substantially increased aid to the mujahideen, sent one thousand

Marines to topple the Marxist government in Grenada, sent millions of dollars and military advisers to the Nicaraguan Contras in an attempt to overthrow the Sandinistas, and had Central Intelligence Agency (CIA) operatives drop mines in Nicaragua's harbors, an act of war, to prevent Cuban and Soviet ships from delivering armaments. At the same time, the administration requested and received billions of dollars from the Congress to rebuild U.S. armed forces and construct MX intercontinental missiles, B-1 bombers, and other new weapons. With the agreement of NATO allies, the U.S. Air Force and Army proceeded with plans to deploy the intermediate-range guided missiles Pershing II and ground-launched cruise missiles in England, the Netherlands, Belgium, West Germany, and Italy to counter the Soviet Union's SS-20 missiles. In a March 8, 1983, address to the Annual Convention of the National Association of Evangelicals, Reagan questioned the legitimacy of the Soviet government, terming it the "Evil Empire." In a televised address two weeks later, the president announced plans for the Strategic Defense Initiative designed to prevent Soviet missiles from reaching the United States.

By 1983 a prewar atmosphere prevailed in Moscow. "The U.S. President has ripped up almost all agreements earlier achieved with the Soviet Union and broken off talks on vital problems in international affairs. . . . He is prepared to risk everything for the sake of war but nothing for the sake of peace," declared Alexander Yakovlev, the Soviet ambassador to Canada. NATO forces conducted military exercises near the Warsaw Pact so realistic that Soviet embassies in West Europe watched every night for missiles heading toward Moscow and Leningrad. The CIA informed the president that the Soviet Union was preparing for nuclear war. Meanwhile, antinuclear protests convulsed Western European capitals. The Federal Emergency Management Agency developed plans to send residents of Washington, DC, and Alexandria, Virginia, to rural West Virginia if the atomic war began. Jonathan Schell's 1982 portrayal of the world after nuclear attack, *The Fate of the Earth,* sold hundreds of thousands of copies. On Sunday evening, November 20, 1983, one hundred million Americans, including Ronald and Nancy Reagan, watched the ABC televised movie "The Day After," a frightening depiction of a doctor, his wife and children, farms, and the Memorial Hospital in Lawrence, Kansas, after an exchange of nuclear missiles by the Soviet Union and the United States.[41]

George Shultz fully supported President Reagan's foreign positions, including the Strategic Defense Initiative (SDI) and Congressional funding of the Contras. "We have passed through a decade during which the Soviet Union expanded its military capacity at a steady and rapid rate while we stood still," Shultz told the Senate Foreign Relations Committee during his confirmation hearings in July 1982, adding that "President Reagan has given us the leadership to turn that position around, and just in time." Such remarks were not simply a matter of praising the commander-in-chief, although Shultz consistently defended Reagan throughout and after his presidency, much as he had remained loyal to Richard Nixon. Rather, Shultz believed that the U.S. government had to increase its military to improve its bargaining stance. "The past decade taught us once again an important lesson about United States–Soviet relations," he declared at the nomination hearing. "It is that diminished American strength and resolve are an open invitation for Soviet expansion. . . . Thus it is critical . . . that we persevere in the restoration of our strength; but it is also true that a willingness to negotiate from that strength is a fundamental element of strength itself."[42]

Shultz's belief that the United States had to increase its strength in order to negotiate set him apart from the other top foreign-policy advisers in Reagan's first term: CIA Director William Casey, Secretary of Defense Caspar Weinberger, UN Ambassador Jeanne Kirkpatrick, the director of the U.S. Arms Control and Disarmament Agency Kenneth Adelman, Professor Richard Pipes of the National Security Council staff, and their undersecretaries, assistant secretaries, and staff. Thinking of themselves as the "true Reaganites," Casey, Weinberger, Kirkpatrick, and the others considered the Soviet leaders unreconstructed Bolsheviks. They opposed further arms-control negotiations and new treaties that, in their opinion, undermined U.S. defenses. "The United States has spent more than 10 years trying to get the Soviets to limit their land-based missile force without threatening any significant unilateral action if the Soviets failed to agree. The MX, Trident, and B-1 were delayed again and again. The Soviets have understandably never felt the need to dismantle their own forces, knowing that future American deployment might never take place because of American domestic pressure," Representative Jack Kemp's adviser Robert Kagan declared in 1984.[43]

Shultz had a very different view, which is why conservatives had urged Reagan not to appoint him in the first place and continued to distrust him once he was in office. Unlike Casey, Weinberger, and other members of the National Security Council, Shultz actually had negotiated with the Soviet government: the grain agreements concluded when he was secretary of the treasury in the Nixon administration. The experience led him to conclude that Soviet leaders would hold to agreements that they considered in their interest.

"Experience . . . shows that the Soviets recognize reality and that tough, sober bargaining, when backed by American strength, can lead to mutually advantageous results," he declared in an October 1984 address at the Rand/UCLA Center for the Study of Soviet International Behavior. This perspective derived from his experience in industrial relations. "Negotiations without strength cannot bring benefits. Strength alone will never achieve a durable peace," Shultz maintained. The United States has to try to make agreements with the Soviet government, he was convinced. "The Soviet Union is powerful," he went on to argue. "It occupies a very large part of a shrinking world; and its military strength, including its vast nuclear arsenal, is a reality that we cannot ignore. And we owe it to our own people, and to the future of the planet, to strive for a more constructive pattern of relations between our countries."[44]

The assumption that rival parties could find common grounds through "tough, sober bargaining" derived from Shultz's background in industrial relations. And much of the language he used in talking about diplomacy could have been lifted from any one of the hundreds of industrial relations books and articles written in America in the latter 1940s and early 1950s, including Shultz's own writing during that era.[45]

Shultz was as hostile to communism as the other members of the National Security Council, which is why he fully backed Reagan's decision to place intermediate-range nuclear missiles in Europe and defended the SDI in public, despite private doubts about whether it would work. But with his experience in mediation and arbitration, he had a better grasp of how to win through negotiations. In his new field of foreign relations, much as in industrial relations, great powers mobilize forces (armies, navies, aircraft, and espionage in the one arena; thugs, detectives, picket lines, boycotts, strikes, lockouts, and attorneys in the other), claim to want peace, threaten war, wrangle, and ultimately settle.

Indeed, although they had drifted apart by the mid-1940s, the fields of industrial relations and international relations were originally closely intertwined. Both fields emerged in Britain and the United States in the late nineteenth century, as new, powerful unions, often led by socialists, confronted new, powerful corporations and Germany was challenging Britain on the seas and in Africa. Disturbed by increasing hostility in industry and among nations, social and political reformers advocated arbitration and mediation in both realms. Leading Progressives worked in both these areas. Theodore Roosevelt set up an arbitration board to end the coal strike in 1902 and three years later mediated the Russo-Japanese War. Jane Addams not only cofounded Hull House to aid immigrants in Chicago; she also tried to mediate the 1894 Pullman strike, joined the Civic Federation of Chicago to promote discussion between business and union leaders, founded the Women's Peace Party in 1915 to promote mediation between nations, and devoted the last twenty years of her life to trying to prevent war. As the eminent historian and diplomat E. H. Carr pointed out in his classic work *The Twenty Years' Crisis, 1919–1939: An Introduction to the Study of International Relations* (1940), "power, used, threatened or silently held in reserve" is the "essential factor" in bargaining both between unions and employers and between nations.[46]

Shultz resembled W. L. Mackenzie King, the Canadian academic who became minister of labor in 1909; developed a worker representation plan for John

D. Rockefeller after the 1913 massacre in Ludlow, Colorado; and became leader of the Liberal Party in 1919 and prime minister during the Second World War. Another counterpart, although more plebian than Shultz and Mackenzie King, was Ernest Bevin, who was born in a poor family, left school at the age of eleven, worked on the docks, led the Transport and General Workers Union, served as minister of labor and national service under Prime Minister Winston Churchill during the Second World War, and developed British strategy for the Soviet Union as foreign minister at the onset of the Cold War.

In their long flights to Moscow and Peking, Shultz often remarked to Ambassador Charles Hill, his closest aide at the State Department, about how his experience in industrial relations informed his thinking about international relations. Having had spent many hours at negotiating tables with irate union and unbending company officials, he was able to remain calm when others in the room hit the ceiling. "I have a hide like a walrus," Shultz boasted.[47] Like George Taylor, John Dunlop, and his other mentors, Shultz was able to distinguish between negotiators' stated positions and their bottom lines. Yet, unlike Clark Kerr, with whom he collaborated in a study of automation in the meat-packing industry, Shultz knew that as secretary of state he was no longer a mediator. Kerr failed at UC-Berkeley in autumn 1964 because he considered himself an intermediary.[48] Shultz knew better.

* * *

For the past thirty years, historians, political scientists, retired heads of state and diplomats, their aides, and journalists have advanced ideas to explain why the Cold War ended. Their interpretations generally fall into one of four categories:

- Former top officials of Reagan administration and other Americans who give the bulk of the credit to President Ronald Reagan. Most of these authors are conservatives who believe that the president's vision and courage, his SDI, and the buildup of U.S. air force, navy, and nuclear weapons forced the Soviet to concede defeat. Exceptions such as John Patrick Diggins and James Mann argued that Reagan ended the Cold War by *abandoning* neoconservative positions. Anatoly Dobrynin, the Soviet Union's seasoned ambassador to Washington, made the same argument in his 1995 memoir.[49]
- The second group give the bulk of the credit (or blame) to Secretary-General (later, President) Mikhail Gorbachev. This group is also divided into two groups—on the one hand, Gorbachev's advisers and European and American liberal scholars who praise the former Soviet leader's bold imagination and adroitness; and, on the other hand, other former advisers of the secretary-general and unreconstructed Marxists in Russia, Europe,

and America distressed by Gorbachev's break with the Soviet Union's past principles and policies.

- A third group finds the cause in sources other than the Soviet or U.S. leadership. Some writers attribute the Cold War's conclusion and the subsequent collapse of the Soviet Union to weaknesses in Soviet economic system. Others point to the influence of western consumer culture on young Soviet citizens, the Chernobyl nuclear plant explosion, the precipitous fall of the price of oil during the 1980s, the Soviet Army's losses in Afghanistan, or the rise of Solidarność in Poland. Still others cite the influence of other leaders, especially Pope John Paul II but also Prime Minister Thatcher, French President Mitterrand, and, in a few cases, former U.S. President Richard Nixon.

- The last group points to the defeat of the Soviet Union, the United States, or their subsidized allies in Vietnam, southern Africa, Ethiopia, the Horn of Africa, Iran, and Afghanistan as primary factors explaining the end of the Cold War. "The Cold War is still generally assumed to have been a contest between two superpowers . . . mostly centered on Europe," declared historian Odd Arne Westan. "[But t]he most important aspects of the Cold War were neither military nor strategic, nor Europe-centered, but connected to political and social developments in the Third World."[50]

Although each of these interpretations contains elements of truth, none is entirely persuasive, whether considered separately or even in combination. Mikhail Gorbachev was an audacious reformist head of state in the tradition of Alexander II and Nikita Khrushchev. Ronald Reagan stands apart from U.S. presidents during the Cold War in the way that he combined his determination to build up the U.S. armed force and fund insurgencies in Central America, Afghanistan, and Africa with a sincere desire to overcome animosity with Soviet leaders and create a nuclear-free world. Both Gorbachev and Reagan, however, faced strong challenges within their own governments and Reagan, despite his virtues, was unable to comprehend complex negotiating questions and by 1986 had begun to decline cognitively.[51] The process of arms reduction and withdrawal from Afghanistan was very difficult, and earnest efforts by the leaders of both governments to improve relations were repeatedly upset by unforeseen incidents. If Alexander Haig had remained secretary of state, the U.S.-Soviet conflict almost certainly would not have concluded by 1988.

George Shultz was essential to bringing the Cold War to a peaceful conclusion (as was Foreign Minister Eduard Shevardnadze, although he is not the focus of this chapter). Yet most historians and political scientists fail to appreciate Shultz's importance. The negligence is not surprising. While Ronald Reagan, the handsome former movie star, always attracted attention, Shultz seldom asserted himself in public or showed emotions. Indeed, he was so inscrutable that reporters called him "the Sphinx." In this respect, he resembled other industrial relations mediators like Bill Simkin and Allan Dash, who intentionally avoided attracting attention. Yet behind closed doors, Shultz's influence was immense.[52]

Shultz drew on his years of experiences at negotiating tables in industry before he became secretary of state to edge President Reagan away from Defense Secretary Weinberger, CIA Director Casey, and the other members of the National Security Council who were determined to make no concessions to the Soviet Union or to sign any new treaties. He persuaded Secretary-General Gorbachev and Foreign Minister Shevardnadze that Reagan was a fair-minded man who could be trusted, despite his reputation in the Kremlin as a warmonger, and that concessions to the United States were in their best interest. He took over for the president in the summit meetings with Gorbachev and Shevardnadze when issues became complex.[53] He directed Paul Nitze and Max Kampelman in the U.S.-Soviet arms-control negotiations in Geneva. Finally, he traveled to Moscow every eight weeks in 1987 for unpublicized meetings with Gorbachev and Shevardnadze at which he helped persuade the secretary-general to drop his insistence that the United States confine SDI tests to laboratories.

Several incidents reveal the ways that Shultz managed to overcome the conflicts within the Reagan administration and between the Soviet and U.S. governments—beginning on Lincoln's Birthday, February 12, 1983, when a blizzard halted almost all traffic in Washington, DC, preventing the Reagans from going to Camp David as they had planned. Although the president hadn't been meeting the secretary of state regularly until then, he and his wife Nancy invited Shultz and his wife Helena to the White House for dinner. After a genial dinner in the family quarters, the secretary of state and the president spoke by themselves. Shultz had just returned from a trip to Asia, including China. Reagan was fascinated by China and also asked about the Soviet Union. "He realized, I thought, that he was in a sense blocked by his own White House staff . . . and by his own past rhetoric," Shultz recalled. "Now that we were talking in this family setting, I could see that Ronald Reagan was much more willing to move forward in relations with these two Communist nations—even travel to them—than I had earlier realized."

Shultz had an appointment scheduled two days later with Soviet Ambassador Anatoly Dobrynin. He asked the president whether he would like to join the conversation. Reagan readily agreed as long as the meeting was kept secret from the National Security Council staff. Originally scheduled for fifteen minutes, the meeting between the three continued for two hours. It covered arms-reduction treaties, intermediate-range ballistic missiles, Afghanistan, Poland, and human rights—the major issues in contention. The president spoke at length about two Siberian Pentecostal families who had taken refuge in the U.S. embassy in Moscow.

He asked the Soviet government to allow the dissidents to leave for the United States. He promised to not gloat or even take credit. Shultz subsequently pressed the issue with the Soviet ambassador, seeing it as a way to make progress on larger issues. He spoke to the president about developing a plan for "systematic dialogue" with the Soviet government, including cultural exchange, consulates in Kiev and New York, a meeting with Foreign Minister Gromyko, and a plan for human rights. "We could not continue to vilify the Soviets publicly and expect them to respond by doing the things we wanted. It was time to start quiet diplomacy. The critical element was to get the president heavily engaged," Shultz recalled. The Politburo did not want to make concessions on a matter of internal policy, which they saw as an assault on their sovereignty, and were particularly resistant after Reagan's April 1983 speeches denouncing the "Evil Empire" and heralding SDI. Nonetheless, the Soviet government did release the two Siberian families and other family members in June and July 1983. At the end of July, the United States agreed to a $10 billion, five-year-long sale of U.S. farm goods to the Soviet Union. (Reagan's predecessor Jimmy Carter had canceled the wheat sales after the Soviet invasion of Afghanistan; Shultz considered "linkage" counterproductive.)[54]

Modest though they were, those acts marked the beginning of the end of the Cold War. Fortunately for Shultz, Ronald Reagan also had considerable experience in unions and negotiations before he entered government. He had served as president of the Screen Actors Guild for six years, first between 1947 and 1952, when he helped the House Un-American Activities Committee and J. Edgar Hoover of the FBI drive Communists out of that union, and then again in 1959 and 1960, when he led a five-week-long strike that forced the film companies to pay residuals to actors and actresses when movies they had performed in were shown again on television. Reagan had bargained with the president of Columbia Pictures, Harry Cohen; the president of Paramount Pictures, Frank Freeman; and the Warner brothers—all tough characters. Flying to Beijing with Shultz, Reagan would reminisce about how his meetings with the Hollywood moguls had prepared him for the Chinese and Soviet leaders. In a letter to Laurence Beilenson, the Screen Actors Guild's former attorney and an old friend, written between his first two summit meetings with Soviet leaders, Reagan wrote, "You know, those people who thought being an actor was no proper training for this job were way off base. Every day I find myself thankful for those long days at the negotiating table with Harry Cohen, Freeman, and the brothers Warner."[55]

Another event later in 1983 suggests how heated Shultz could be on occasion, despite his deceptive equanimity. Late Wednesday night, Eastern Daylight Time, August 31, 1983, a Soviet fighter pilot shot down Korean Air Lines flight 007 that had drifted three hundred miles into Soviet airspace on a flight from Anchorage to Seoul. All 269 passengers and crew were killed, including sixty-two U.S. citizens, among them a member of the U.S. House of Representatives. Secretary-General Yuri Andropov defended the pilot's action despite evidence that it was a passenger plane. The incident occurred at a critical moment, since Shultz and Foreign Minister Gromyko were scheduled to meet the next week in Madrid. Ten months earlier, the Soviets had pulled their delegates out of the arms-control meetings with the U.S. delegation in Geneva to protest the NATO deployment of the Pershing II and cruise missiles in Western Europe. The Shultz-Gromyko meeting in Madrid would be the first high-ranking consultation between the U.S. and Soviet officials since then. It was intended to lay the groundwork for a meeting with Gromyko and President Reagan in October and between Reagan and Secretary-General Andropov in spring 1984.

At the National Security Council meeting on September 2, Defense Secretary Weinberger called for canceling the meeting to dramatize that "this kind of action was intolerable" and would carry "a very high penalty." Shultz took the opposite stand, arguing that the United States must "tell him straight out our view" and that "refusing to meet with people is not the way to do it." Reagan allowed Shultz to go to Madrid but insisted that the secretary confine his remarks to the shooting down of the Korean plane. Gromyko's meeting with Shultz on September 7 turned into a shouting match. There was one moment when "both of them jumped up and it seemed would grab each other by his shoulders," Soviet Deputy Foreign Minister Gregori Korniyenko recalled. Tom Simon, chief of the State Department's Soviet desk, remembered two "red-faced and angry old men" stalking out of the room. It was "probably the sharpest exchange I have ever had with an American secretary of state, and I have had talks with 14 of them," Gromyko later recalled.[56]

Mikhail Gorbachev was chosen secretary-general of the Soviet Union by the Politburo on March 11, 1985. Reagan, Shultz, and their entourage met Gorbachev and the new Soviet foreign secretary, Eduard Shevardnadze, in Geneva in November 1985. After six years of increasing military spending and threats, both governments were willing to reduce the tension. Reagan and Gorbachev spoke about cutting strategic weapons by 50 percent and reducing intermediate-range nuclear forces in Europe. Agreement was stymied by the president's insistence on developing the SDI to defend the United States from Soviet missiles. They did agree, however, to have another summit meeting in Washington in 1986 and a third in Moscow. They concluded the summit by declaring that "a nuclear war cannot be won and must not be fought."[57]

Despite the apparent improvement, relations between the two governments stalled in 1986. The Soviets' arrest of a U.S. journalist of Russian descent, Nicholas Daniloff, on spy charges only worsened the situation. Since Gorbachev was not willing to travel to Washington without a prearranged treaty, he proposed that he meet Reagan at another site in between to discuss the issues that divided them.

Reagan promptly agreed and proposed Reykjavik, Iceland, as their meeting place on the weekend of October 11–12. There would be no formal dinners, simply plain talk among the principals. Rather than assembling in Reykjavik's best hotel, as the Icelandic government advised, they decided for security's sake to meet in the Höfði House, an old small seaside inn on a desolate hill outside the capital.

Reagan, Shultz, Gorbachev, and Shevardnadze sat at a small square table in a small room, their translators and note takers squeezed behind them, to negotiate the future of nuclear arms. Unlike the previous highly scripted U.S.-Soviet summits, the meetings were, in the words of journalist Don Oberdorfer, an "improvised affair from start to finish."[58] The Americans had expected an informal discussion to set a date and an agenda for a summit in Washington, DC. Gorbachev surprised the president and secretary of state at the first morning session by presenting a full-fledged proposal for the two superpowers to radically cut their nuclear weapon arsenals. He proposed a 50 percent cut in intercontinental ballistic missiles, a 50 percent cut in submarine-launched ballistic missiles, and a 50 percent cut in heavy bombers. Reagan, Shultz, Gorbachev, and Shevardnadze debated specifics throughout the afternoon without reaching a conclusion. Shultz termed the Reykjavik summit "the highest-stakes poker game ever played."[59] "At this precise moment, I knew Reykjavik had changed," recalled Kenneth Adelman, the director of Arms Control and Disarmament Agency, who opposed concessions to the Soviets. "No longer were the President of the United States and the General Secretary of the Soviet Union reading staff papers to each other. No longer were they blessing what their arms control teams had worked out. They would move from headquarters at base camp to the front line. They would become negotiators-in-chief."[60]

Seventy-nine-year-old adviser Paul Nitze, who had counseled every president since Truman on nuclear weapons, and Marshal Sergei Akhromeyev, chief of the General Staff of the Soviet Armed Forces, had a marathon meeting from 8 p.m. to 6:30 a.m. to narrow down differences on nuclear weapons, regional issues, and human rights. In the middle of the night, Marshal Akhromeyev woke up Gorbachev to ask about presenting their second position, which he had in his pocket: total elimination of all nuclear weapons by the year 2000. Gorbachev granted permission. When Reagan, Shultz, Gorbachev, and Shevardnadze resumed on Sunday morning, the president readily accepted the proposal. Although considered bellicose by liberals, Reagan had spoken about hoping to eliminate nuclear weapons from early in his presidency. The conservatives on the National Security Council and in the press did not take such remarks seriously, but they misjudged Reagan.

Pavel Palazchenko, Shevardnadze and Gorbachev's top translator, was surprised that Secretary Shultz did not try to intercede at that point. "I frequently wondered afterward why Shultz did not try then to restrain Reagan, who was suddenly saying something quite contrary to the U.S. strategic doctrine. . . . As an expert Shultz understood very well that what Reagan was saying was heresy, but did not interfere." Actually, it is not hard to understand why Shultz acted as he did. First, Shultz respected the judgment of President Reagan. Second, Shultz believed that, except for its nuclear weapons, the Soviet Union was weak—economically strapped, technologically retrograde, overstretched militarily, and lacking legitimacy among the youth and national minorities. Without nuclear weapons, the Kremlin could not threaten the United States or the world. Finally, although it did not become clear until after he left office, George Shultz was also an "abolitionist," in the nuclear-weapons language of that time. Like Mikhail Gorbachev and Ronald Reagan, Shultz wanted to rid the world of nuclear weapons. In his absorbing 1997 memoir, Palazchenko quotes a meeting at which George Shultz had met with Shevardnadze in New York City several years after he had retired. "When our leaders, each in his own way, began to speak of a world without nuclear weapons, the experts thought they were wrong and that this was a goal [that] could never be achieved," Shultz remarked. "But the experts did not understand that Reagan and Gorbachev were on to something: they felt what people [felt] in a profound way." Shevardnadze agreed.[61]

For a moment it seemed like the U.S. and Soviet leaders were about to agree to eliminate every kind of nuclear weapon, to the dismay to Margaret Thatcher and other NATO allies who had not been consulted. The agreement crashed late Sunday morning when Reagan refused to give up his promise to the American people that the Pentagon would test SDI in space as soon as possible, rather than confining research to laboratories for a decade, as Gorbachev insisted. The secretary-general repeatedly asked the president why testing in outer space would be necessary if both powers were demolishing their missiles. If they both were destroying their missiles, Reagan replied, why did Gorbachev object to SDI? He promised to share the new antimissile technology with Soviet scientists. Gorbachev was incredulous. "You Americans won't even share your milk-processing technology with us! Even [if] we accepted Reagan's promise, we can't depend on your successors," Gorbachev added.[62]

The argument continued like that until sunset, when Reagan, Shultz, Gorbachev, and Shevardnadze left the Höfði House disheartened. "We were that close to an agreement," the president told Donald Regan, his chief of staff. "One lousy word." That was all he needed from Gorbachev, he thought. According to Charles Hill, Shultz's close aide, Gorbachev seemed "rattled," even "losing his confidence." He was "very angry," recalled Ambassador Dobrynin. It was felt Gorbachev was going to the "guillotine," said his bodyguard.[63] Shultz seemed little better. "No one who attended the summit, or watched the secretary's televised news conference at its end, is likely to forget the sense almost of grief etched across Shultz's usually expressionless face as he told the world about the 'potential tremendous achievement' contained in 'the agreement that might have been' but was not to be. His cheeks were red and his eyes slightly glazed, the most telling signs to reporters who have long covered him that the secretary was truly upset," David Ottaway reported in the Washington Post.[64]

Although Shultz voiced hopes in the succeeding days that an agreement could be salvaged, feelings of rage and betrayal prevailed for weeks, especially in the Kremlin. Gorbachev had made extraordinary concessions to the Americans, yet, it appeared, received nothing in exchange. "Let's not chase after shit," he told his comrades after Shultz and Shevardnadze met in Vienna in late October. "We mustn't allow it to appear as if we're not getting anywhere," he told Anatoly Chernyaev, his top adviser.[65] Yet the next U.S. president might be even worse, Gorbachev decided. Twenty years younger than Brezhnev, Andropov, and Chernenko and formerly the minister for agricultural, Gorbachev was far more aware than his predecessors of the weakness of the Soviet economy. He "never thought his reform was possible without drastic reduction in nuclear arms," recalled Alexander Aleksandrovich Bessmertnykh, the deputy foreign minister who attended the Shultz-Shevardnadze meeting and all four of the Gorbachev-Reagan summits. "We are doomed to cooperate," Gorbachev remarked in 1988.[66]

Time was getting short by the winter of 1986–87. Gorbachev was beginning to be challenged in the Communist Party. The Democrats recaptured the Senate in the November 1986 Congressional elections and increased their majority in the House of Representatives. The Iran-Contra Affairs damaged Reagan's reputation and left the president befuddled. He had only two more years left in office. Nancy Reagan was anxious for her husband to succeed in foreign affairs for the sake of his legacy and her own desire for peace. Fortunately, the most truculent members of the administration were forced to resign because of their roles in the Iran-Contra scandal, lost influence, or passed away. They were succeeded by more moderate figures—Senator Howard Baker became the president's chief of staff, General Colin Powell became director of the National Security Council, and Frank Carlucci was appointed secretary of defense.

The April 1986 catastrophe at the Chernobyl nuclear power plant moved the diplomats on both sides to accommodate. "We need negotiations. Even with that 'gang' we need to negotiate. If not, what remains? Look at the Chernobyl catastrophe. Just a puff and we can all feel what nuclear war would be like," Gorbachev told the Politburo. The Chernobyl devastation "casts its shadow on everything from that moment forward: on the economy, on the moral and psychological state of society, on trust in the new leadership and the people's hopes for change," remarked his adviser Anatoly Chernyaev. According to U.S. officials, the accident at Chernobyl produced merely one-third of the radiation of the smallest nuclear bomb yet spread radiation across the Ukraine and half of Europe. "After Chernobyl, we all now realize the real danger of everything nuclear," Shultz said to Gorbachev.[67]

With Reagan unwilling to bend, Gorbachev realized he would have to break up the disarmament deal that he proposed at Reykjavik and concentrate on securing a treaty to reduce or eliminate the Pershing II missiles stationed in Western Europe—the greatest threat to Moscow. He also began to speak more fully about the restructuring reforms of perestroika, free elections for offices in the Communist Party, a free press, and human freedom as a means to undermine the Soviet bureaucrats frustrating his economic policies.

In 1987 Shultz began flying to Moscow every eighth week to meet with Secretary-General Gorbachev and Foreign Minister Shevardnadze, much as George Taylor, John Dunlop, and David Cole had with Henry Kaiser and the Steelworkers' negotiators after the 1959 steel strike. Shultz assisted Taylor in those negotiations. Now he followed Taylor's example. On April 13–15, 1987, he went to Moscow for three days of meetings with Foreign Minister Shevardnadze and Secretary-General Gorbachev. (See figure 16.)

On the first day, they discussed human rights, bilateral issues, regional problems, and arms control. That evening Shultz returned to the U.S. ambassador's residence, where he hosted a Passover Seder. He had invited sixty refuseniks— Soviet Jews denied the rights to practice their faith or move abroad. Putting a white yarmulke on his head, the Episcopalian grandson of Presbyterian missionaries walked around the huge dining table, speaking to each person, many of whom had been imprisoned by the government. "He seemed in awe of these tough, cheerful, resolute men and women bearing names familiar to him from the lists he presents at every meeting with high Soviet officials," the *New York Times* correspondent David Shipler reported.[68]

The next morning, Secretary-General Gorbachev protested U.S. interference in internal Soviet affairs. Shultz replied that he had an airplane full of reporters who would gladly give up their seats if Gorbachev allowed the refuseniks to depart. Yet this was only the beginning of their discussion that day. Shultz and Gorbachev went on to sign an accord for renewed joint U.S.-Soviet exploration in outer space. He gave a thirty-minute interview to a prominent Soviet journalist, which was broadcast on Soviet television that evening. In September Shevardnadze asked Shultz for the list of dissidents that the Americans had compiled. In October 1987 the Soviets granted exit visas to six thousand people, five thousand more than had been permitted to leave the previous year. The Soviet government stopped jamming radio broadcasts of the Voice of America and the BBC. Jim Wright, the speaker of the House of Representatives, met not only Gorbachev and Shevardnadze, but also their conservative Politburo critic Yegor Ligachyov and spoke to the Soviet people on television. Soviet and U.S. representatives began meeting

FIGURE 16. George Shultz and Mikhail Gorbachev in Moscow, circa 1987. Alamy photographs.

to discuss clashes in Nicaragua, Angola, and Cambodia. The U.S. ambassador to Moscow and the Soviet ambassador to the United States spoke at their respective military academies. Shevardnadze created an office on human rights in the Foreign Ministry, and many more Soviet citizens were allowed to leave for West Germany, the United States, and Israel.[69]

When Shevardnadze came to Washington in September 1987, he and Shultz agreed on the principles of an Intermediate-Range Nuclear Force (INF) treaty. There was a blowup in October, when Gorbachev became incensed about State Department and CIA reports questioning the honesty of his reforms. Wasn't he still sending billions to insurgents in the Third World? Wasn't he trying to make the Soviet Union a stronger adversary? The reproaches came from Robert Gates, the deputy director of the CIA, and conservative commentators critical of Reagan's policies. Shultz attributed Gorbachev's outburst to attacks he was experiencing from Boris Yeltsin in the Central Committee. He dismissed the conservative Americans. "What kind of world do they envision? A world of increasing nuclear arms? A world in which the Soviets have four times as many weapons in the INF category as we have? A world in which we would refuse to start a process of reducing nuclear arms? That took care of that particular critic," Shultz told the president.[70]

Anatoly Chernyaev, Gorbachev's foreign policy adviser, considered Shultz's meetings with Gorbachev and Shevardnadze the turning point. "Late 1987 was marked by a very important meeting between Gorbachev and U.S. Secretary of State George Shultz, on October 23. I believe this was the real turning point in the beginning of real disarmament. . . . The parameters of the future agreements on medium-range missiles in Europe were defined. . . . An unofficial but practical and consistent mechanism of negotiations was created by the two sides, by highly professional people who knew and trusted each other, not only on matters of policy but also personality. And this was the harbinger of new relations between the USSR and the United States, probably more important than public assurances. A friendly, personal understanding was forged among Gorbachev, Shevardnadze, and Shultz—a real statesman."[71]

Shultz aimed to do more than reduce nuclear and other weapons: he was trying to change Secretary-General Gorbachev's perspective on markets and the world. Shultz was an economist by trade. His wife Helena was a nurse. When they visited the Soviet Union, she visited Soviet hospitals. She would return to the embassy telling her husband about appalling conditions that she saw there. Shultz began giving informal tutorials to Gorbachev between their scheduled appointments, in which he spoke about how the Information Age was succeeding the Age of Manufacturing, how computer-directed machinery was replacing machine tools everywhere except in the Soviet Union, and how Soviet commerce was lagging behind its capitalist competitors and would fall even further if it did not open itself to a free exchange of ideas. He pulled out four-color graphs and pie charts showing global manufacturing and export trends. They showed Japan and other East Asian nations rising, while the United States and especially the Soviet Union were declining. Shultz showed Gorbachev a photograph of a shipping label that read "Made in one or more of the following countries: Korea, Hong Kong, Malaysia, Singapore, Taiwan, Mauritius, Thailand, Indonesia, Mexico, Philippines. The exact country of origin is unknown." Assistant Secretary of State Rozanne Ridgway, who accompanied Shultz on many of trips to Moscow, said that he was trying to "get into Gorbachev's mind." It seemed to have worked. The Secretary-General's depiction of ongoing international trends in his 1987 book *Perestroika* suggests Shultz's tutorials. He spoke about the "world of fundamental social shifts, of all-embracing scientific and technology change, of worsening global trends—problems concerning ecology, natural resources, etc.—and of radical change in informational technology."[72]

Several days before Gorbachev arrived for the summit in Washington in December 1987, Shultz gave an address on the Informational Age to the World Affairs

Council. None of the major newspapers covered the speech. As Don Oberdorfer later realized, however, Shultz had another audience in mind: the Soviet leaders. He had his speech translated into Russian and handed copies to the secretary-general, Raisa Gorbachev, Foreign Minister Shevardnadze, Marshal Akhromeyev, and the other ranking members of the party.[73] At the December 7–10, 1987, summit in Washington, Gorbachev and Reagan signed the Intermediate-Range Nuclear Force treaty in which they agreed that 1,500 Soviet warheads and 350 U.S. warheads would be destroyed, all verified by on-site, short-notice inspections. Shultz hosted Gorbachev at a grand luncheon at the State Department's diplomatic room on the second day of the visit. He invited key members of Congress; Ambassador Jack Matlock; all past U.S. ambassadors to the Soviet Union; prominent Americans in business, finance, the arts, and labor; and cabinet members. Shultz took pleasure in taking Mikhail and Raisa Gorbachev to the desk on which Thomas Jefferson signed sections of the Declaration of Independence, just as he had done for Dr. Gilbert Mason of the Biloxi NAACP and Warren Hood of the Mississippi Manufacturers Association. "Two world wars, an exhausting cold war, plus small wars—all destroying millions of lives. Isn't it a high enough price to pay for adventurism, arrogance, and contempt for the interests and rights of others . . .? Humanity has been forced to put up with this for too long. We can no longer allow it," Gorbachev declared in his toast to Shultz.[74]

President Reagan, Secretary Shultz, and their party flew to Moscow for a summit meeting with Secretary-General Gorbachev and Foreign Secretary Shevardnadze on May 29, 1988. Gorbachev hoped to sign a treaty reducing or eliminating intercontinental ballistic missiles that spring. The Americans did not think there was sufficient time to draft and sign the treaty and win approval from the U.S. Senate before Reagan left office. That had to wait until 1991 and 1993, when the United States signed Strategic Arms Reduction Treaties (START) with the Soviet Union and Russia. Consequently, the May 1988 summit in Moscow was mainly symbolic in nature. Those symbols were hardly insignificant, however. Reagan delivered a speech to students at Moscow State University, Gorbachev's alma mater, under a mammoth bust of Vladimir Lenin and billowing red flags. Standing on a lectern with the U.S. presidential seal, Reagan spoke about the virtues of U.S. democracy, told corny jokes as was his wont, answered questions from the students, and received a standing ovation when he concluded. Afterward, the president and Mrs. Reagan walked through Red Square. Police had cleared the area, but a few residents remained, mainly women. "I have great admiration for the women of Russia," Reagan told the group. The president was stopped by a reporter as they walked back to the Kremlin. "Do you still consider this an evil empire?" "No," he replied. "That was another time, another era." "Are you now old friends?" another asked them. "Da, da!" replied Gorbachev. "Yes," declared Reagan.

Their responses were honest. "In a curious way the fact that we did not have a START agreement finished in time to sign at the summit . . . has caused people to reflect on what may be the most important, the deeper and the more significant [thing that has happened]," Shultz told reporters in Brussels, where he had stopped to fill in the European allies after the summit. He elaborated in the same kind of language he had used a quarter-century earlier, with unions and companies. "Because underneath it all, what we are looking for is an East-West relationship, or U.S.-Soviet relationship, that is broad, that is solid, manageable, and can go through steps in a considered and solid way."[75]

The new era was broader than the détente that President Nixon and Secretary Kissinger fashioned with Secretary-General Brezhnev in the early 1970s. Since the Geneva summit in 1985, U.S. assistant secretaries of state met with the Soviet counterparts more than twenty times to discuss their policies in Latin America, southern Africa, the Middle East, and Asia. By 1988, the Soviet Union had already begun to pull troops out of Afghanistan. On December 7, 1988, Gorbachev told the United Nations General Assembly that the Soviet Union planned to remove five hundred thousand troops from Eastern Europe. And while American Jewish groups' attempts to persuade the Nixon administration to support their campaign to allow their brethren to leave the Soviet Union had failed, Reagan and Shultz's unceasingly pressure led to a large-scale emigration of Soviet Jews. Finally, between 1986 and 1988, Shultz and his staff met repeatedly with Soviet officials to discuss arms control, human rights, regional issues, and bilateral relations. Shultz and Shevardnadze themselves met twenty-six times. Gorbachev joked about Shultz receiving "frequent flyer" miles for his trips to Moscow.[76]

Shultz knew little about the intricacies of nuclear weapons and nuclear policy before he was appointed secretary of state. Nor was he a specialist on bilateral, regional, and human-rights issues. The same was true for Foreign Minister Shevardnadze, Secretary-General Gorbachev, and, needless to say, President Reagan. In part for that reason, they were willing to abandon their governments' previous positions. Shultz persuaded Reagan to trust Gorbachev and persuaded the secretary-general and the foreign minister to trust him and Reagan. It was a remarkable accomplishment, arguably the most consequential achievement of the Labor Board veterans. Ironically, Shultz succeeded in this venture as an official in an administration that undermined the labor unions and the bargaining system that he and his mentors had devoted their lives to protecting. Indeed, he considered Ronald Reagan's firing of the air-traffic controllers to be the president's most important foreign-policy decision. Soviet leaders concluded that the president's tough words would be backed up by action, if necessary.[77]

Shultz's years of working with union and company officials prepared him for the negotiations with the Soviet leaders. "Everyone reflects their own experience," he remarked at a three-day conference with Soviet Foreign Minister Alexander Bessmertnykh, Secretary-General Gorbachev's adviser Anatoly Chernyaev, Defense Secretary Frank Carlucci, Special Adviser Paul Nitze, and other U.S. and Soviet diplomats at Princeton University in 1993. "I have spent a lot of time in labor-management relations. . . . I think sometimes a good argument and a good fight over something gives people an idea of where your bottom line really is, and they test what they are able to do, and . . . and it can clear the air for something more constructive. And I think in many ways that's exactly what took place here."[78]

10

Doing the Lord's Work

*He worked literally until the last. I say it only because
it gives insight into the kind of person he was.*

—John T. Dunlop in 1959, recalling Sumner Slichter

THE LABOR BOARD CREW rose from modest backgrounds to assume positions
of considerable influence in the United States and abroad. As other chapters have
described, they were born in small and midsized towns and in the countryside
during the Progressive Era. Most of them were children of teachers, professors
and engineers, pastors and missionaries, shopkeepers, clerks and salesmen, seam-
stresses, railroad telegraphers, and farmers—the folks whom John R. Commons
in 1906 termed "this third class, which is not a class, [but] may . . . determine the
issues."[1] As youngsters, they absorbed the Social Gospel, liberal ideas, and consensus methods—some at church, others at Quaker Meetinghouses or Reform
temples, as well as from their parents. In college during the Great Depression,
they saw workers standing in breadlines and battles between strikers and scabs.
Although some of their college classmates joined the Communist Party, their
sympathies lay with the Socialist Party and they supported Franklin Roosevelt's
New Deal. Industrial relations, not politics, became their main interest. They
worked with union leaders and company managers during the Second World War
to stabilize the economy and thus help defeat the Axis powers. After the war, they
taught industrial relations, arbitrated workers' grievances for unions and companies, and gave extension classes to trade unionists. Every president of the United
States from Harry Truman to Gerald Ford turned to the Labor Board vets for help
when strikes and inflation threatened the U.S. economy. During the 1960s student
revolts, trustees of major universities appointed Labor Board vets to presidents,
chancellors, and top deanships. Several were appointed as U.S. secretaries of labor

or directors of the Federal Mediation and Conciliation Service. And their protégé George Shultz used industrial relations techniques to try, with significant success, to resolve industrial clashes, desegregate southern public schools, institute affirmative-action programs, and negotiate an end to the Cold War.

Most American men and women of their status retired when they were sixty-five or seventy years old. Afterward retirees might travel, play golf or tennis, work in their gardens, do artwork, play cards, or pursue other pastimes. The Labor Board vets could have done that too. They were well off financially.

Yet few of the leading Labor Board vets ever retired, despite suffering various illnesses and disabilities. Why should they stop? They had a mission in life. One typical example is Jean McKelvey. When she was obliged to retire from the School of Industrial and Labor Relations at Cornell University's main campus at the age of sixty-five, McKelvey directed the school's extension program in Albany, Corning, Elmira, Rochester, and Syracuse. She established a program to train women and minority men in arbitration, continued on the Federal Services Impasse Panel until she was eighty-one years old, and remained a member of the United Auto Workers Public Review Board until she died at the age of eighty-nine.[2]

Similarly, Clark Kerr, born in 1911, published *Work in America: The Decade Ahead* in 1979 and *Industrial Relations in a New Age* in 1986. A major work, *The Great Transformation in American Higher Education, 1960–1980*, appeared in 1991, when he was eighty years old. He coauthored two more books on higher education, *Troubled Times for American Higher Education: The 1990s and Beyond* and *Higher Education Cannot Escape History: Issues for the Twenty-first Century*, both published in 1994; he contributed articles to anthologies on higher education and labor relations in other venues; and he wrote a two-volume memoir about his career at the University of California and an accompanying collection of documents before he died in 2003 at the age of ninety-two.

Benjamin Aaron continued arbitrating cases and serving on the United Auto Workers Public Review Board until he died at ninety-one years old. After retiring as president of the University of Michigan, Robben Fleming became president of the Corporation for Public Broadcasting and chairman of the National Institute for Dispute Resolution. He taught part-time at the University of Michigan law school, temporarily served as president of the university again in 1988, and served on boards of colleges in North Carolina, Alabama, and elsewhere in the 1990s, wresting with problems of racial discrimination in higher education.[3]

George Shultz, the Labor Board vets' top protégé, continues working as this book is written. In the early twenty-first century, he not only informally advised President George W. Bush and his administration, he also began contributing opinion pieces to the *Wall Street Journal*, the *New York Times*, and the *Washington Post* on U.S. diplomacy, military policies, the danger of nuclear war, terrorism, federal budgetary policy, the environment, the war on drugs, communicating with Islamic countries, world population, and the world economy. In addition, Shultz wrote, coauthored, edited, or coedited numerous volumes on issues confronting the United States, including *Implications of the Reykjavik Summit on Its Twentieth Anniversary* (2007), *Putting Our House in Order: A Guide to Social Security and Health Care Reform* (2008), *Issues on My Mind: Strategies for the Future* (2013), *Blueprint for America* (2016), and *Learning from Experience* (2017). In July 2019, he coauthored an op-ed column in the *Wall Street Journal* with Pedro Aspe, the former treasury secretary of Mexico, about how the United States and Mexico could prevail upon the World Bank and the Inter-American Development Bank to fund initiatives to revitalize economies and reduce corruption in El Salvador, Guatemala, and Honduras and thus reduce emigration from that region.[4]

For more than a decade, Shultz has been warning of a nuclear holocaust if the United States and Russia do not act to prevent it. "The accelerating spread of nuclear weapons, nuclear know-how and nuclear material has brought us to a nuclear tipping point. We face a very real possibility that the deadliest weapon ever invented could fall into dangerous hands," Shultz and his coauthors—former secretary of defense William Perry, former secretary of state Henry Kissinger, and Senator Sam Nunn—wrote in the *Wall Street Journal* in January 2008. In an October 2018 column in the *New York Times*, Shultz urged the Trump administration to adhere to the Intermediate-Range Nuclear Force Treaty, which he negotiated with Secretary-General Gorbachev. If the Russian government is violating the treaty, the United States must pressure Vladimir Putin to revive inspections, he declared. The United States should also invite other countries to join the treaty, Shultz argued. "Now is not the time to build larger arsenals of nuclear weapons. Now is the time to rid the world of this threat. Leaving the treaty would be a huge step backward. We should fix it, not kill it." Unfortunately, the Trump administration ignored Shultz's plea and in August 2019 formally withdrew from the INF Treaty.[5]

John Dunlop was every bit as determined as Shultz, with mixed results. Dunlop chaired the Massachusetts Joint Labor-Management Committee for Municipal Police and Firefighters from 1977 until he died in October 2003 at the age of eighty-nine. He founded the Joint Center for Housing Studies at Harvard and MIT, which brought together academics and people in the building industry. He also helped create and direct the Harvard Center for Textile and Apparel Research, which brought people from business, government, industry, academia, and students to tour textile and apparel mills in the United States and China. When Hillary Rodham Clinton tried to reform the U.S. health-care industry in 1993–94, Dunlop consulted with the First Lady's team, insurance companies, union leaders, and industrialists. In addition, Dunlop continued to participate in the Harvard Trade

Union Program to educate promising midlevel trade unionists. On the side, Dunlop continued to mediate union-management disputes, often without pay—for example, between the board of the Hartford Symphony Orchestra and Local 400 of the American Federation of Musicians. He also continued to write, producing one more book of his own—*The Management of Labor Unions: Decision Making with Historical Constraints* (1990)—and coauthoring two others—*Mediation and Arbitration of Employment Disputes* (1997) and *A Stitch in Time: Lessons from the Apparel and Textile Industries* (1999)—and numerous essays. And he continued to teach at Harvard to the end of his life, offering a seminar to freshmen on the American workplace in spring 2003.[6]

"John Dunlop has never wanted to acknowledge it, but he is doing the Lord's work," one economist remarked.[7] Several of his initiatives later in life were innovative and quite successful. One was his work with the Harvard University Clerical and Technical Workers (HUCTW). Although most labor unions lost members in the latter 1970s and 1980s, that was not true for clerical workers at major universities. Unions were able to organize thousands of clerical workers and win contracts at the University of California, Yale University, Columbia University, Cornell University, Wesleyan University, Wayne State University, and other colleges and universities. Clerical and technical workers tried to win union recognition at Harvard University as well but lost twice in close elections.

The organizers tried again in the late 1980s. The majority were working-class women from Boston, Lynn, and other nearby old mill towns in eastern Massachusetts. Often these were their first jobs. The administration portrayed clerical and technical employment at Harvard as an opportunity for which those women ought to be grateful. They could work with distinguished professors, researchers, and doctors, meet medical students, perhaps even find a mate. Although the university negotiated with the building trade unions and the unions representing the campus police and food-service workers, they consistently opposed unionization of the clerical and technical staff. When the union won the third election supervised by the National Labor Relations Board (NLRB) in a close vote, the administration was not pleased.

The president of Harvard at the time was Derek Bok, a professor of labor law and dean of the law school. In his book *Labor and the American Community* (1970), which he coauthored with Dunlop, Bok defended labor unions and their contribution to American society. Yet in 1988 he originally argued that unions were not appropriate for clerical and technical workers at his university. He pondered for five months whether to appeal the NLRB's ruling. Finally, he invited a dozen people to his home on a Sunday afternoon to help him decide—top deans, other administrators, university lawyers, Anne Taylor from Human Resources (which opposed the union), and Dunlop. Taylor urged Bok to appeal the ruling and Dunlop advised the contrary. Bok also consulted Archibald Cox, the retired

Harvard professor of law and special prosecutor in the Watergate affair, who had coauthored with Dunlop important articles critiquing the Taft-Hartley Act. Cox also recommended accepting the NLRB's ruling.

Bok accepted Dunlop and Cox's advice and appointed Dunlop as the administration's negotiator with the union. The union officials whom Dunlop had dealt with over the course of his career were nearly all male. The Harvard Clerical and Technical Workers union was different. All but one of its leaders were women, and they aimed to promote a consciously feminine model of unionism while giving the members a voice in decision making much as the alumni, faculty, students, and other members of the university community had. Kristine Rondeau and the other leaders of the HUCTW rejected the bureaucratic form of organizing that the United Auto Workers had tried previously on the campus without success. Rather than hiring a company to poll the workers' opinions, they approached prospective members one by one, meeting them in their apartments, and discussing their personal needs as well as issues at work. And they did not denounce the university. At one rally, U.S. Representative Barney Frank declared, "It's not anti-Harvard to be pro-union." The organizers seized on the slogan, putting it on all their stickers, banners, buttons, and T-shirts. The line even became a song, performed by the Harvard Pipettes, the union's a cappella singers. "Harvard could buy us out easy," remarked Rondeau. "But this isn't about money. It's about control."

Dunlop jumped at the opportunity to work with Rondeau and her sister union members. It was partially a matter of personalities. Rondeau was born and raised in a Massachusetts mill town—daughter of a trade unionist, married to a union organizer, modest but determined. Dunlop preferred the company of trade unionists to that of the faculty, and he also could be charming, especially when it served his purposes. Dunlop had been at Harvard for a half-century. He taught in three of its schools, was the former dean of Arts and Sciences, and at that time was acting dean of the Kennedy School of Government. Dunlop considered Harvard University a disaster in its governance. He respected skilled workers and had seen how unions could improve the management of companies. He hoped that the HUCTW could do that for the university.

The feminine (Rondeau and the other organizers used that term rather than "feminist") character of the HUCTW was ideal for that purpose, and he bonded with Kris Rondeau much as he had bonded with George Meany and oldfangled male trade unionists, odd though the comparison may seem. Rondeau and Dunlop had breakfast, lunch, and dinner together every day during the negotiations, and she came to greatly appreciate the relationship, even though he dubbed her "Toots." "John was the least cynical person I ever knew," Rondeau remarked after he died. "He was the one [person in the] management who believed what we believed, that the negotiations were a rare chance to achieve resolution of Harvard's labor issues."

When Bok gave Dunlop the authority to negotiate with the union, Dunlop proposed that the union officials enter a sixty-day transition period before they formally negotiated a contract with the administration. Rondeau and the other leaders agreed, and for two months eight or nine trade unionists and an equal number of administrators met regularly—not to make demands, but to explore their past relations and how they could be improved. Rondeau brought in many clerical and technical workers who told stories about what employment was like at Harvard—both the enjoyable and distressing aspects. Dunlop suggested that the union and the administration use a mediator to facilitate their discussions. He recommended Jim Healy, a retired professor of industrial relations at the Harvard Business School, who was a former member of the Boston Regional War Labor Board and had decades of experience in mediation and arbitration. Rondeau agreed.

At the end of the sixty-day transition, Dunlop, Rondeau, and their colleagues and coworkers negotiated a unique ruleless contract. There was no specified grievance procedure, no insistence by the administration on "management's rights," no written rules on seniority, job classification, or the like. One hundred employees were elected as representatives of the union in their particular section of the huge, multifaceted university. They were the equivalent of union shop stewards, except, as the late labor journalist John Hoerr wrote, "these reps do not spend time 'policing' the workplace to find contract violations, for there are no rules to violate." Problems at a university usually involve interpersonal clashes among employees and between supervisors and workers. The HUCTW encouraged workers who had complaints to first try to work it out with their supervisors, with the union representatives offering support. If that failed, the problem would go to one of thirty local problem-solving teams, consisting of one management representative and one union representative. And if these two were unable to agree, the issue was given to the mediator—originally, Jim Healy.

The HUCTW and the university administration also agreed to set up joint councils in all schools and administrative units in the university. The councils met biweekly to handle quality-of-life issues, such as work schedules, physical comfort, office space allocation, health and safety guidelines, and reorganization of jobs. The administrators used the councils as sounding boards before instituting changes in policies. The changes were not "earthshaking," John Hoerr remarked, "but they represent real progress for a work force that never had a voice in anything." Finally, although the HUCTW had not stressed money as their principal complaint, the union won increases of 25 percent in salaries for the average clerical and technical workers in their first three years.[8]

Equally innovative and successful was Dunlop's work with the Farm Labor Organizing Committee (FLOC), the Campbell Soup Company, and midwestern tomato and cucumber farmers. The union was led by Baldemar Velásquez, a son of Texas farmworkers who annually traveled to the Midwest to pick crops late in the summer and in the fall. Inspired by the Southern civil-rights movement and Cesar Chavez, Velásquez gathered a group of volunteers to organize Latino farmworkers in northwestern Ohio and southeastern Michigan in the late 1960s. Devoting themselves entirely to the cause for years without any recompense, the Farm Labor Organizing Committee ultimately called strikes in the tomato and cucumber fields at harvest time in 1978 and 1979. They managed to get some contracts but gained little for the laborers until they connected with Ray Rogers, a New York labor activist who had directed the campaign that forced major banks to pressure the manufacturing firm J. P. Stevens to make concessions to its textile workers. Rogers agreed to mount a comparable campaign for FLOC against the Campbell Soup Company, a major procurer of Ohio tomatoes, and Vlasic Company, a subsidiary of Campbell's that bought cucumbers from Michigan farmers for its pickles.

Those companies were originally quite reluctant to deal with the union, asserting, correctly, that they did not employ any farmworkers. Pressure increased, however, as Rogers organized protests against corporate investors who sat on banks linked to Campbell's and churches supported a boycott of Campbell's, whose red-and-white tomato soup cans were ideal targets. Dunlop interceded at that point. He mediated between Velásquez, whom he greatly admired, and Campbell Soup Company officials. Within a year, the Farm Workers Organizing Committee won a unique three-way agreement between tomato farmers, the union, and the Campbell Soup Company. A five-member commission consisting of labor priest Monsignor George Higgins, former president of the United Auto Workers (UAW) Doug Fraser, an agribusiness leader from Ohio, a professor of agricultural economics at Purdue University, and Dunlop as chair monitored the agreement. Within a year, the union won a comparable contract with the Vlasic Company and the H. J. Heinz Company. They moved on to try organizing migrant tobacco-leaf workers at R. J. Reynolds fields in North Carolina. In the interim, FLOC affiliated with the AFL-CIO. The contrast between the Farm Labor Organizing Committee and the United Farm Workers led by Cesar Chavez couldn't have been sharper. While FLOC was winning contrasts and acquiring members, the UFW lost its contracts in California and Texas and degenerated into a cult for Chavez representing few workers.[9]

* * *

Despite these and other accomplishments, the biggest project that Dunlop tackled in the last decade of his life proved an utter failure: the Commission on the Future of Worker-Management Relations, which he chaired.

The 1990s are remembered today as a boom time, with jobs available for almost all, wages rising, and the Dow-Jones average surging. The depiction is accurate for the latter 1990s, but not the early 1993 when Bill Clinton was inaugurated as president. Real wages for men in the blue-collar sector were in a trough, having fallen steadily since the mid-1970s, and, although wages for women workers had risen, they remained considerably lower on average than for men doing comparable work. Unemployment rates were high in the early 1990s and employers began to hire workers contingently, with few or no benefits. More industrial corporations moved their operations from the Midwest to southern states or from the upper South to Mexico or Asia. Other major corporations, including Bethlehem Steel, Eastern Airlines, and TWA, went bankrupt. Unions suffered repeated defeats in the industrial sector during the 1980s, as aggressive corporate managers broke strikes and forced unions to accept lower compensation for new employees. Meanwhile German and Japanese manufacturers were making inroads into electrical equipment, computers, and other industries previously dominated by U.S. firms. As the economy changed, income levels in the United States were increasingly bifurcated, and the working-class families were becoming increasingly anxious.

The 1991–92 recession may appear slight in comparison with others, but the slump was bad enough to lead the majority of American voters to abandon President George H. W. Bush when he sought reelection in 1992, despite the U.S. victory in the war against Saddam Hussein in 1991, and to cast their ballots for Bill Clinton, the untested Democratic governor of Arkansas, or for the eccentric Texas billionaire Ross Perot. (It was in those years that Donald Trump first grabbed attention outside New York City by denouncing Japanese auto manufacturers.) Labor Secretary Robert Reich termed the 1991–92 slump "a watershed." He noted, "Most people who lost their jobs weren't rehired by their former employers. In fact, job insecurity is now endemic."

Soon after assuming office, President Clinton asked Secretary of Labor Robert Reich and Secretary of Commerce Ron Brown to set up the Commission on the Future of Worker-Management Relations and appointed Dunlop to chair it. Reich and Brown asked the commission to investigate the problems confronting workers and corporations in the United States and increase productivity through worker-management cooperation and employee participation.

Dunlop enlisted ten highly accomplished people to serve with him on the commission: Douglas Fraser (former president of the UAW), Paul Allaire (CEO of the Xerox Corporation, which bargained with unions), Kathryn C. Turner (CEO of Standard Technology, a health information consulting firm, which did not recognize unions), former secretaries of labor Ray Marshall and W. J. Usery, former secretary of commerce Juanita Kreps, Professor Tom Kochan of MIT,

Professor William B. Gould IV of Stanford University Law School, Professor Richard Freeman of Harvard University, and Professor Paula Voos of the University of Wisconsin.[10]

For the next twenty-one months, the Dunlop Commission, as it was promptly dubbed, conducted 21 hearings, heard from 411 witnesses, and logged in almost 5,000 pages of testimony.[11] These were serious discussions. Typical was one session held at the Department of Labor headquarters in Washington, DC, on cooperative methods introduced in a variety of industries in recent years to reduce costs and increase productivity. In the morning, the executive vice president of the Ford Motor Company spoke about the revival of that corporation in the 1980s. He attributed the improvement to cooperation between the UAW and management. He then introduced workers, union representatives, and management staff from the Sharonville, Ohio, transmission plant who had come together when confronted with the possibility of the plant closing. They had formed sixty-seven work teams to increase productivity. The management had removed several levels of supervision and increased the pay for workers who acquired more skills and took courses on team building. After a question-and-answer period, union and management representatives from Oregon spoke. The group claimed that their joint teams had reduced workers' compensation expenses for the state by $2 million over the previous three years, reduced the number of worker complaints, and enabled the state's Occupational Safety and Health Administration (OSHA) committee to concentrate on the most dangerous workplaces. Representatives of a nonunion metal fabricating shop in Ohio spoke next. They related how they surmounted a financial crisis through an employee-ownership program and problem solving, with concentration on training in health and safety.

In the afternoon, the president of a small nonunion Kansas City insurance company spoke about improvements initiated by the employee committee at her firm, including daycare, recycling, and an employee-of-the-month program. She also spoke about problems that small businesses faced complying with excessive government regulation, especially the Family and Medical Leave Act, which had been enacted that year. A union-management panel from Minneapolis and St. Paul then discussed how hospitals, the Service Employees International Union local, and other union locals in the two cities had succeeded in moving from an antagonistic to a cooperative relationship through job redesigning without layoffs. They had been assisted by the Federal Mediation and Conciliation Service. The final panel consisted of an executive and a quality action team from Federal Express's offices in Memphis, Tennessee, which had managed to reduce costs by $700,000 in a year through brainstorming. Doug Fraser interjected that, while he did not want to belittle the Memphis working party's endeavors, the commission had received statements from Federal Express workers elsewhere expressing dissatisfaction with the management, and 65 percent of the employees in one district had signed UAW authorization cards.[12]

The commission members heard presentations on many other topics, including Alternative Dispute Resolution systems, discrimination against women in the workplace, the increasing number of contingent jobs, particularly for racial minorities, new forms of company unionism, undue judicial deference to arbitration, reform of labor law to expedite union recognition and contracts, and codetermination systems in Germany. The speakers included labor historian David Brody, critical legal scholar Kathryn Stone, and other noted authorities. The commission published a lengthy fact-finding report in May 1994 and a more condensed final report in January 1995.

The commission's numerous recommendations boiled down to five categories. One urged Congress to revise labor law in ways that would expedite the organization of unions while nonetheless facilitating employee participation in nonunion workplaces. A second encouraged mediation, alternative methods of dispute resolution, and experiments in private dispute resolution to expedite conflict resolution. The third was to allow OSHA, the Equal Employment Opportunity Commission, and the Labor Department's Wage and Hours Division to encourage employees to participate in developing specific safety and health programs for their own workplaces, rather than relying on broad regulations, which were harder for employers to implement and which impinged on productivity. The fourth was to create a national forum on the workplace in which leaders of business, labor, women, and civil-rights groups could continue discussion of public policy on workplace issues. The fifth, and most important in Dunlop's opinion, advised the "establishment of a National Labor-Management Committee to discuss issues of special concern to the future of collective bargaining and worker-management relations." Parallel committees could be formed in communities, states, and industries "to encourage grass-roots experimentation and learning."[13]

All for naught. The principal business organizations did not endorse the Dunlop Commission's recommendations. Neither did AFL-CIO leaders. Although business leaders restrained themselves when the Dunlop Commission issued its fact-finding report in June 1994, the Republican triumph in the November 1994 Congressional elections squashed any chance that the commission's proposals would be adopted. Twenty of twenty-three recommendations of the commission were "totally or wholly" unacceptable, a U.S. Chamber of Commerce labor and public policy expert remarked when the final report was issued in early January 1995. "Legislatively, it is dead," declared a Chicago attorney who had served on the NLRB during George H. W. Bush's administration. Although more subdued, the top union leaders were almost as dismissive. "The Dunlop Commission got the problems facing American workers right . . . but failed to follow through on the logic of its own findings," UAW president Owen Bieber remarked. Douglas Fraser, a commission member and former president of the UAW, issued the sole dissenting opinion among the commission members, protesting the commission's willingness to allow nonunion employee-participation plans. Steve Early, a labor journalist who had testified before the commission, called John Dunlop's search for consensus "a fool's mission." "The report almost borders on the trivial. . . . It is probably already gathering dust in a government file," John Tysse, labor-law attorney for the Chamber of Commerce, snidely remarked.[14]

* * *

The failure of the Commission on the Future of Worker-Management Relations marked the end of the Labor Board vets' half-century-long struggle to build and sustain stable, balanced relations between unions and corporate management in the United States. Their efforts were part of a longer history of attempts by middle-class reformers to calm relations between labor and capital in America. Key earlier moments include Jane Addams's attempt to mediate between George Pullman and the American Railway Union in Chicago in 1894, the work of the National Civic Federation in the early twentieth century, and the activities of the National War Labor Board of 1918. However, none of these or other similar efforts had had more than a modest impact.

This was not true for the work of the Labor Board vets. For almost forty years, they were able to guide union and company representatives toward compromise on wages, hours, various benefits, and work rules on the job in manufacturing, shipping, airlines, mining, and other blue-collar lines of work. As a result, many American workers were far better paid, received unprecedented pension and medical insurance, and had more protection at their jobs than their counterparts experienced in earlier days, or than such workers receive today. Although their work was particularly beneficial for white male union members, conditions improved significantly for male workers of color and women who belonged to unions as well. When schoolteachers, sanitation workers, nurses, other government employees, and professional athletes began to join unions in the 1960s and early 1970s, the Labor Board vets developed comparable systems in those sectors.

Which is not to suggest that relationships between labor and capital were placid. That was hardly the case. Automation; new technologies; the 1959 and 1969–70 strike waves; increasing imports of steel, automobiles, and electronic goods; right-to-work campaigns; and the emergence of populistic conservatism repeatedly upset union-management relations.

Despite these challenges, the Labor Board vets managed to keep relations between the unions and top management relatively stable for decades. The success of the "New Deal Order," as many historians term that period, was not ensured by the triumph of the United States in the Second World War, laws passed by Congress, or acts of any president. Without the extraordinary abilities and grit of mediators and arbitrators like George Taylor, Sylvester Garrett, David Cole, Jean McKelvey, Pete Jensen, Ben Aaron, John Dunlop, and other War Labor Board vets, union-management relations might have broken down much sooner than they ultimately did.

But no intermediaries—regardless of their skill—could have prevented the decline of the old blue-collar unions and the curbs imposed on public-employee and service-sector unions. The compromises forged by the Labor Board vets depended on slow but steady increases in wages and producer prices and substantial return on capital. Those agreements could not survive the stagflation crisis of the 1970s. As labor costs for manufacturers mounted and productivity and profits fell, corporations mobilized against unions. At the same time, more aggressive conservatives took charge of the Republican Party, Democrats became less sympathetic to unions, and in 1980 Ronald Reagan was elected president. Federal agencies deregulated industries, imports increased, and new technologies undermined unionized businesses. Only the professional sports unions could thrive under these conditions, protected by television revenues.

When interviewed a quarter-century ago, John Dunlop called the Labor Board crew "a peculiar generation."[15] That was not completely true. The group had predecessors—mediators and arbitrators who worked with unions and employers in the railroad and garment industries in the early twentieth century. But Dunlop was accurate in another way: they did not have successors. Except for George Shultz (who moved out of industrial relations after 1970), no one followed in their footsteps. The world overwhelmed the reformers.

ACKNOWLEDGMENTS

I BECAME INTERESTED IN THE LABOR BOARD BOYS shortly after my first book was published in early 1983. Unfortunately, eighteen months later, I experienced a neurological infection that nearly took my life. Afterward, I began to suffer seizures, almost daily at first, more or less weekly for a decade. I became completely free of seizures only about eight years ago. The whole experience was quite unpleasant, and hard for my family. My greatest debt is to my wife, Cynthia Wells, our daughter Lily, and our son Sam, for their understanding, patience, and support. Their love enabled me to carry on. I am also deeply grateful to the late Dr. Susan Spencer, a brilliant, dedicated neurologist without whom I almost certainly would not be free of seizures.

I am similarly grateful to friends, relatives, and professionals who helped my family and me in too many different ways to describe here. They include David Pudlin, the late Marty Montgomery, Peter Gottlieb, Sandra Blum, the late Jeffrey Butler, David Banks, Martha Banks, Yuksel Serindag, Etti and Oded Tammuz, Peggy Best, Bill Stowe, Ann Wightman, Pat Maines, the late Dr. Roger Goettsche, and especially my late parents, Cynthia's late parents, and our extended families. I am also deeply grateful to my colleagues in the History Department and other colleagues in the Public Affairs Center for their steady support, and to Colin Campbell and Nat Greene, who were the president and vice president of the university when I became ill.

There was an unintended benefit of this otherwise dreadful experience. Namely, it forced me to slow down. I gave top priority to recovery and teaching. Nevertheless, I never stopped working on the project. Lenin's adage "Better fewer but better" became my lodestar on publication. The result is a much more ambitious, complex, and nuanced book than the one that I would have written if I had been on the normal academic track.

* * *

Many people helped me on this project in different ways, so many over such a long time that I may have forgotten someone. Please forgive me if that is so. I must begin with all the men and women who granted me interviews. They included not only the former members of the National War Labor Board staff who are subject of this book but also the late Ben Fischer, the late Daniel Bell, the late Mario Savio, the late Justice Arthur Goldberg, Elaine Bernard, George Strauss, Ambassador Charles Hill, and Secretary of State George Shultz. Without these many interviews, I would not have been able to understand this remarkable group. I also benefited by interviewing early members of the faculty at Cornell University's School of Industrial and Labor Relations not discussed in the book.

I visited almost twenty archives and libraries—too many for me to thank each helpful staff person here. But I do want to express special appreciation to Richard Strassberg, Steven Calco, Patrizia Sione, and Melissa Holland at the Cornell University's Kheel Center; Robert McKersie, the former dean of Cornell University's School of Industrial and Labor Relations; Harrison Wick, the special collections archivist at Indiana University of Pennsylvania; and Kate Wolfe, Lisa Pinette, Nancy Putnam, Diane Klare, Erhard Konerding, Alan Nathanson, and the other current and former excellent librarians at Wesleyan University's Olin Library, who provided a great deal of help over many years. I am very grateful to Don McPherson, formerly of Indiana University of Pennsylvania, who gave me transcripts of the interviews that he and Sylvester Garrett conducted with key figures in the steel industry.

It would not have been possible for me to conduct the research and write this book without the funding I received from the Wesleyan History Department's Meigs Fund, the National Endowment for the Humanities, the New York State School of Industrial and Labor Relations, Harvard University's Charles Warren Center, and Wesleyan University's Office of Academic Affairs.

Many scholars and authors helped me in different ways. David Brody, Tom Kochan, and Bruce Laurie read the first, rough draft of the manuscript. David's advice, "Write as if it was a biography of one person," proved the key for the book. Joe McCartin, Jack Metzger, George Strauss, Leon Fink, David Engerman, the late John Hoerr, Julie Greene, Ruth Milkman, and the late Mark McColloch provided comments on drafts of individual chapters of the revised version. The late David Montgomery, the late Steve Sapolsky, the late Don Meyer, Ilene De

Vault, Nick Salvatore, Sven Beckert, Liz Cohen, Pierre Gervais, Gil Skillman, Gail Radford, Cele Bucki, Erica Chenoweth, Bret Eynon, Jack Trumpbour, Laura Kalman, Victoria Smolkin, Jerry Friedman, the late Wis Comfort, Anne Greene, Amy Bloom, and Annie Dillard each offered valuable help. Brian Fay, Don Moon, Charles Lemert, and Judith Brown were also very supportive of my research.

I have been fortunate enough to be invited to give papers on this subject and receive helpful rejoinders at the Centre d'études nord-américaines, École des hautes études en sciences sociales, in Paris, the European Social Science History Conference in the Hague, the Newberry Seminar in Labor History in Chicago, the Washington, DC, Working-Class History Seminar, the University of Pennsylvania Economic History Forum, the faculty seminar at MIT's Institute for Work and Employment Relations, the interuniversity labor history seminar at Columbia University, the Harvard Trade Union Program, the Charles Warren Center, the Cornell ILR School, the University of Buffalo's History Department and Law School, the corporatism interuniversity faculty seminar at the University of Massachusetts at Amherst, the Economics Department at University of Massachusetts Amherst, the Organization of American Historians meeting, the Labor and Working-Class History Association meeting, a joint meeting of the American Historical Association and the Industrial Relations Research Association, and lectures sponsored by Wesleyan University's Center for the Humanities and Public Affairs Center.

The University of Illinois Press asked two of the best labor historians in the country, Nelson Lichtenstein and Eric Arnesen, to evaluate the manuscript. They both offered many shrewd tips. The book is better as a result. Needless to say, neither Nelson, Eric, nor others who read drafts are responsible for my interpretations or errors.

James Engelhardt, the acquisitions editor for the University of Illinois Press's labor and working-class history series, has been a steady source of advice. Michael Roux, Tad Ringo, Roberta Sparenberg, Alison Syring, Geof Garvey, and other UIP staff have also been very helpful. I am also grateful to the late Jeannette Hopkins and Suzanne Tamminen of Wesleyan University Press for their suggestions regarding publication.

Marc Eisner of Academic Affairs at Wesleyan arranged for funding to pay for the photographs in the book. Without Marc and Susanne Javorski, the art librarian at Olin Library, there wouldn't be such fine photographs to complement the text. I also received help in locating photographs from Gina Tingas at Getty Images, Tricia Gesner of AP Images, Judith Aaron Turner, Sarah Patton at the Hoover Institute Library, Diana Bachman of the University of Michigan's Bentley Historical Library, Edward Copenhagen of Harvard University Library, Celia Caust-Ellenbogen of Swarthmore College's Friends Historical Library, and Kelsey Noel at the National Archives.

257

I want to thank the students who took my seminars related to this book, several of whom also did research afterward. We are fortunate to have such fine students at Wesleyan University.

Above all, I want to thank Cindy—my sweetheart and editor suprême.

NOTES

Preface

1. Address by Governor Dewey at convocation, November 12, 1945, Founding Documents Collection, box 1, Kheel Center, 4.

2. Interview of Ben Fischer by the author, June 11, 1996 (in possession of the author). Fischer was associate research director for the United Steelworkers of America and assistant to Murray from 1944 to 1952.

Chapter 1. In the Wake of Pearl Harbor

1. William C. Murphy Jr., "Roosevelt Sends Personal Note to Emperor in 'Final' Effort to Avert War with Japan," *Philadelphia Inquirer*, Dec. 7, 1941, 1, 8; "Two Japanese Convoys Head for Thailand," *Philadelphia Inquirer*, Dec. 7, 1941, 1, 8.

2. Quoted in William Bartsch, "The Other Pearl Harbor," *Historically Speaking* 5, no. 2 (Nov. 2003): 33.

3. G. Allan Dash Jr., interview by Clare McDermott, Feb. 13, 1978, National Academy of Arbitrators Oral History Project (1982), 12.

4. Ibid., 13.

5. The most influential work in that vein are Nelson Lichtenstein's *Labor's War at Home: The CIO in World War II* (New York: Cambridge University Press, 1982) and Ruth Milkman's *Gender at Work: The Dynamics of Job Segregation by Sex during World War II* (Urbana: University of Illinois Press, 1987).

6. For further discussion, see R. J. Overy, *Why the Allies Won* (New York: W. W. Norton, 1995).

7. Hanson Baldwin, "Ominous Lull on War Front," *New York Times*, Dec. 17, 1941, section 1, 5.

8. Overy, *Why the Allies Won*, 190–92.

9. Maury Klein, *A Call to Arms: Mobilizing America for World War II* (New York: Bloomsbury, 2013).

10. U.S. Dept. of Labor, Bureau of Labor Statistics, *Handbook of Labor Statistics 1975—Reference Edition* (Washington, DC: GPO, 1975), Bulletin 1865, 389–90.

11. *Stars and Stripes* quoted in James Lacey, *The Washington War: FDR's Inner Circle and the Politics of Power That Won World War II* (New York: Bantam, 2019), 365; American Institute of Public Opinion reported in *New York Times*, Mar. 30, 1941; congressional representatives quoted in Aaron Levenstein, *Labor: Today and Tomorrow* (New York: A. A. Knopf, 1945), 27–28, 45–46; Joel Seidman, "Six Significant Strikes in 1941," *Survey Graphic* 30, no 11 (Nov. 1941): 578.

12. "Official Text of President's Plea for Labor Peace," *New York Times*, Dec. 18, 1941; "President Spurs Employers and Labor to Early Accord," *New York Times*, Dec. 18, 1941, 1, 14; James MacGregor Burns, "Maintenance of Membership: A Study in Administrative Statesmanship," *Journal of Politics*, 10, no. 1 (Feb. 1948): 107.

13. The public members devoted all their time to the board.

14. National War Labor Board, *Termination Report of the National War Labor Board: Industrial Disputes and Wage Stabilization in Wartime, January 12,1942–December 31, 1945* (Washington, DC: National War Labor Board [1948]), 2: 49–50.

15. "John Chamberlain, "Will Davis of the War Labor Board," *Fortune* 7 (Mar. 1942), 70–71, 166–67; *Dictionary of American Biography, Supplement Seven, 1961–1965* (1981), s.v. "William Hammatt Davis"; "William Hammatt Davis; Chairman of War Labor Board," *New York Times*, Aug. 15, 1964; Andrew Anthony Workman, *Creating the Center: Liberal Intellectuals, the National War Labor Board, and the Stabilization of American Industrial Relations, 1941–1945* (PhD diss., University of North Carolina, 1993), 15–18; interview of Benjamin Aaron by the author, Jan. 4, 1998.

16. Chamberlain, "Will Davis"; *Dictionary of American Biography, Supplement Seven, 1961–1965*, s.v. "William Hammatt Davis"; "William Hammatt Davis," *New York Times*; Workman, *Creating the Center*, 115–18; interview of Benjamin Aaron by the author, Jan. 4, 1998.

17. George W. Taylor, "Toward a National Labor Policy," *Atlantic Monthly* 162 (Sept. 1938), 343. Taylor's Quaker background is discussed in chapter 2.

18. Transcript of Executive Sessions, NWLB (World War II), Jan. 16, 1942, Record Group 2–2, box 8, pp. 1–2, National Archives and Records Administration, College Park, MD (hereafter, NARA).

19. Ibid., 42.

20. Ibid., 34, 38.

21. Ibid., 36, 43.

22. Jerry Flint, "David Cole, 75, Lawyer, Dead; A Noted Arbitrator and Mediator," *New York Times*, Jan. 26, 1978; for Seward and Gill, see Record Group 202, Record of the Division of Public Information, box 667, NARA, and National War Labor Board, *Termination Report*, 2: 4–6, 8, 18, 39, 43–44; for Garrison, *Who's Who in America* (1958), s.v. "William Lloyd Gar-

rison." In Feb. 1944 Garrison became a public member of the national board, replacing Wayne Morse. In Mar. 1945, when Taylor replaced Davis as chairman of the NWLB, Garrison was named vice chairman; in Sept. 1945, when Taylor left the board to organize the Presidential Labor-Management Conference, Garrison became the NWLB's last chairman.

23. Ibid.; William Weinberg, "Accommodation and Mediation," in *Industrial Peacemaker: George W. Taylor's Contribution to Collective Bargaining*, ed. Edward Shils (Philadelphia: University of Pennsylvania Press, 1979), 81, 86; transcript of interview with Ralph Seward by Richard Mittenthal, Apr. 14, 1966, in National Academy of Arbitrators, *The Early Days of Labor Arbitration*, 2nd ed. (Ann Arbor: University of Michigan, Office of the Secretary-Treasurer, National Academy of Arbitrators, Graduate School of Business Administration, 1984), 12; Benjamin Aaron, interview by the author, Jan. 4, 1998, 18 (personal possession of the author).

24. John R. Commons, *Labor and Administration* (New York: Macmillan, 1913), 72.

25. See chapter 4 for a fuller discussion of the Labor Board boys' vision of the world.

26. Rev. Dunlop and his wife lived in Cebu for almost fifty years. He became pastor of the Bradford United Church of Christ, the first Evangelical Church in Cebu, the second-largest city in the Philippines. He learned the Cebuano language and translated the Bible into Cebuano.

27. John T. Dunlop, "The Movement of Real and Money Wage Rates," *Economic Journal* 48, no. 191 (Sept. 1938): 434ff; John Maynard Keynes, "Relative Movements of Real Wages and Output," *Economic Journal* 49, no. 193 (Mar. 1939): 34–51.

28. John T. Dunlop, interview by the author, Feb. 27, 1992, 8–11; Steven Greenhouse, "John Dunlop, 89, Dies; Labor Expert Served 11 Presidents," *New York Times*, Oct. 4, 2003, A14; Ken Gewertz, "John Dunlop, Esteemed Scholar, Dies at 89," *Harvard University Gazette* 99, no. 4 (Oct. 9, 2003): 13; John T. Dunlop, "The Movement of Real and Money Wage Rates," *Economics Journal* 48 (Sept. 1938): 413–38; Dunlop, "Trends in the 'Rigidity of English Wage Rates," *Review of Economic Studies* 6 (June 1939): 189–99; Dunlop, "Real and Money Wages: A Reply," *Quarterly Journal of Economics* 55 (Aug. 1941): 683–91; Dunlop, "Wage Policies and Trade Unions," *AER—Supplement* 32 (Mar. 1943): 290–301; Dunlop and Arthur D. Hill, *The Wage Adjustment Board* (Cambridge, MA: Harvard University Press, 1950), 34–42.

29. Interview of Benjamin Aaron by the author, Jan. 4, 1998; "Benjamin Aaron, 91, UCLA Professor Mediated Labor Disputes," *Los Angeles Times*, Aug. 31, 2007, http://articles.latimes.com/2007/aug/31/local/me-aaron31; email from Judith Aaron Turner to the author, May 26, 2019.

30. Ruth Dewing Ewing, interview by the author, Sept. 2008; "Ruth D. Ewing," *Keene Transcript*, http://www.sentinelsource.com/news/obituaries/ruth-d-ewing/article_0696c613-d7ff-5e55-91ac-bc1dae465b53.html; "Ruth Ewing (1915–2014)," *Monadnock Ledger-Transcript*, http://www.legacy.com/obituaries/ledgertranscript/obituary.aspx?pid=169881050.

31. Quotations are from Jean Trepp McKelvey, interview by the author, Rochester, New York, Oct. 5, 1990, pp. 4, 6, 16–19, 23, 27, 29, 35, 38, 43, Kheel Center for Labor-Management Documentation and Archives, Ives Hall, Cornell University, Ithaca, NY [hereafter, Kheel Center]. See also curriculum vitae of Jean Carol Trepp McKelvey, Kheel Center; Jean T. McKelvey, *AFL Attitudes toward Production, 1900–1932* (Ithaca, NY: Cornell University, 1952); Elaine Gruenfeld Goldberg, ed., "The ILR School at Fifty: Voices of the Faculty, Alumni and Friends"

(privately printed, Ithaca, NY: Cornell University, School of Industrial and Labor Relations, 1996), 24; Blake F. McKelvey in memoriam, accessed Jan. 29, 2014, http://www.correction history.org/sheriffs/rochester/html/blakebio.html.

32. Clark Kerr, interview by the author, Aug. 7, 1992 (personal possession of the author); transcript of reminiscences of Clark Kerr (1998), 54–57, Oral History Research Office Collection, Rare Book and Manuscript Library, University Archives, Columbia University, New York [hereafter, Kerr reminiscences].

33. Kerr interview, Aug. 7, 1992; Kerr reminiscences, 54–57.

34. Kerr interview, Aug. 7, 1992; Kerr reminiscences 54–57.

35. Paul S. Taylor and Clark Kerr, "Whither Self-Help?" *Survey Graphic* 23, no. 7 (July 1934): 328.

36. Kerr interview, Aug. 7, 1992, 8–16; Clark Kerr, interview by George Strauss, Aug. 5, 1985, 2, 4 (personal possession of the author); Paul S. Taylor and Clark Kerr, "Uprising on the Farms," *Survey Graphic* 24 (Jan. 1935): 22; Paul Taylor, *On the Ground in the Thirties* (Salt Lake City, UT: G. M. Smith, 1983), vii, 17–158.

37. Taylor and Kerr, "Uprising on the Farms," 44.

Chapter 2. George Taylor and the War Labor Board, 1942–45

1. Douglas Lockwood, *Australia's Pearl Harbor: Darwin, 1942* (Ringwood, Australia: Penguin Australia, 1984); "The War Summarized," *New York Times*, Feb. 19, 1942; "Rain of Bombs Mark Drive on M'Arthur and Refugees," *New York Times*, Feb. 19, 1942, 1; "Bombers Chase U-Boats off Aruba; Total Tanker Toll in Area Is Four," *New York Times*, Feb. 19, 1942, 1; "'Nazis Speed Up War Production," *New York Times*, Feb. 19, 1942, 1; "Tanker Wrecked off U.S. East Coast," *New York Times*, Feb. 19, 1942, 1; the bombing of Darwin, National Archives of Australia, accessed June 11, 2013, http://www.naa.gov.au/collection/fact-sheets/fs195.aspx.

2. Quoted in Nelson Lichtenstein, *Labor's War at Home: The CIO in World War II* (New York: Cambridge University Press, 1982), 51.

3. "On the Labor Home Front," *Wall Street Journal*, Feb. 20, 1942, 4.

4. William M. Leiserson, "Diagnosis of War Labor Policy," repr. in *Labor Relations Reference Manual* (Washington, DC: Bureau of National Affairs, 1943), 9: 927–31; "Leiserson Expects Storms for NWLB," *New York Times*, Feb. 19, 1942, 12.

5. Robert Houghwout Jackson, *That Man: An Insider's Portrait of Franklin D. Roosevelt* (New York: Oxford University Press, 2003), ch. 5.

6. Lichtenstein, *Labor's War*; Katherine van Wezel Stone, "The Post-war Paradigm in American Labor Law," *Yale Law Journal* 90, no. 7 (June 1981), 1509–80; Martin Glaberman, *Wartime Strikes: The Struggle against the No-Strike Pledge in the UAW in World War II* (Detroit, MI: Bewick, 1980); Staughton Lynd, "Government without Rights: The Labor Law Vision of Archibald Cox," *Industrial Relations Law Journal* 4 (1980–81): 483ff; Lynd, "Ideology and Labor Law: Values and Assumptions in American Labor Law by James B. Atleson," *Stanford Law Review* 36, no. 5 (May 1984): 1273–98; James B. Atleson, *Labor and the Wartime State: Labor Relations and Law during World War II* (Urbana: University of Illinois Press, 1998).

7. I accepted that interpretation myself at the time but changed as I did more research.

The principal dissenter in the 1980s was Howell John Harris, whose essay "The Snare of Liberalism? Politicians, Bureaucrats, and the Shaping of Federal Labour Relations Policy in the United States, ca. 1915–1947," appeared in *Shop Floor Bargaining and the State*, ed. Steven Tolliday and Jonathan Zeitlin, 148–91 (New York: Cambridge University Press, 1985). I presented a fuller critique in "'Industrial Peace through Arbitration': George Taylor and the Genius of the War Labor Board," *Labor: Studies in the Working-Class History of the Americas* 11, no. 4 (Dec. 2014): 39–62.

8. Claudia Goldin and Robert A. Margo, "The Great Compression: The Wage Structure in the United States at Mid-century," *Quarterly Journal of Economics* 107, no. 1 (Feb. 1992): 1–34,

9. Lichtenstein, *Labor's War*, xii.

10. David Montgomery, "The Shuttle and the Cross: Weavers and Artisans in the Kensington Riots of 1844," *Journal of Social History* 5, no. 4 (Summer 1972): 411–46; Philip Scranton and Walter Licht, *Work Sights* (Philadelphia: Temple University Press, 1986), 62–65; Elliott J. Gorn, *Mother Jones: The Most Dangerous Woman in America* (New York: Hill and Wang, 2001), ch. 5; Edward Levinson, *I Break Strikes! The Technique of Pearl L. Bergoff* (New York: R. M. McBride, 1935), ch. 6; "The Philadelphia Strike Off: Some Rioting by Sympathizers with Street Car Employees—Two Women Injured," *New York Times*, Dec. 21, 1895; "Strike Leaders Facing Defeat: Philadelphia Labor Chiefs Fail to Paralyze the City's Industries," *New York Times*, Mar. 8, 1910, 2; Gladys L. Palmer, *Union Tactics and Economic Change: A Case Study of Three Philadelphia Textile Unions* (Philadelphia: University of Pennsylvania Press, 1932), appendix B, table 4; Philip B. Scranton, *The Philadelphia System of Textile Manufacture: 1884–1984* (Philadelphia: Philadelphia College of Textiles and Science, 1984), 14; *Kensington: A City within a City, A Historical and Industrial Review* (Philadelphia: Keighton, 1891).

11. Edward B. Shils, *Industrial Peacemaker: George Taylor's Contribution to Collective Bargaining* (Philadelphia: University of Pennsylvania Press, 1979), 2.

12. An 1891 directory of religious institutions in Kensington lists eighty Christian churches of all denominations, two Jewish synagogues, a Mormon church, and a spiritualist church, but not a single Quaker institution (*Kensington*, 567–79).

13. George W. Taylor, *Significant Post-war Changes in the Full-Fashioned Hosiery Industry* (Philadelphia: University of Pennsylvania Press, 1929); Taylor, *The Full-Fashioned Hosiery Worker* (Philadelphia: University of Pennsylvania Press, 1931).

14. Palmer, *Union Tactics*, 215ff.; *Dictionary of American Biography*, supp. 9, *1971–1975*, ed. Kenneth Jackson et al. (New York: Charles Scribner's Sons, 1994), s.v. "George William Taylor"; Shils, *Industrial Peacemaker*, 1–2, 89; Shils, "George W. Taylor; Industrial Peacemaker," *Monthly Labor Review*, Dec. 1995, 29–30; Joseph H. Willets, "George William Taylor (1901–1972)" Philadelphia: *American Philosophical Society*, 1973), 166–69; George W. Taylor, "Hosiery," in *How Collective Bargaining Works: A Survey of Experience in Leading American Industries*, ed. Harry A. Millis, 450–507 (New York: Twentieth Century Fund, 1942).

15. G. Allan Dash Jr., interview by Clare B. McDermott, in *The Early Days of Labor Arbitration As Recalled by G. Allan Dash, Jr., Sylvester Garrett, John Day Larkin, Harry H. Platt, Ralph T. Seward, William E. Simkin*, 2nd ed. (Washington, DC: National Academy of Arbitrators, 1984), 1. For further discussion, see Philip S. Benjamin, *The Philadelphia Quakers in the*

Industrial Age, 1865–1920 (Philadelphia: Temple University Press, 1976), 89–90ff; Howell John Harris, *Bloodless Victories: The Rise and Fall of the Open Shop in the Philadelphia Metal Trades, 1890–1940* (New York: Cambridge University Press, 2000), ch. 8; Emory R. Johnson, *The Wharton School, 1881–1931* (Philadelphia: Wharton School, 1931); Steven A. Sass, *The Pragmatic Imagination* (Philadelphia: University of Pennsylvania Press, 1982), ch. 7.

16. George W. Taylor, "Effectuating the Labor Contract through Arbitration," *The Profession of Labor Arbitration: Selected Papers from the First Seven Annual Meetings of the National Academy of Arbitrators, 1948–1954,* ed. Jean T. McKelvey (Washington, DC: Bureau of National Affairs, 1957), 22.

17. Gladys W. Gruenberg, *Labor Peacemaker: The Life and Work of Father Leo C. Brown, S.J.* (St. Louis, MO: Institute of Jesuit Sources, 1981), 41ff.; William E. Simkin, interview by Edgar Jones, in *Early Days of Labor Arbitration*, 26–27.

18. For a good discussion of the Hosiery Workers' socialism, see Sharon McConnell-Sidorick, *Silk Stockings and Socialism: Philadelphia's Radical Hosiery Workers from the Jazz Age to the New Deal* (Chapel Hill: University of North Carolina Press, 2017).

19. Dash interview, 24.

20. *Rules of Discipline of the Yearly Meeting of Friends for Pennsylvania, New Jersey, Delaware, and the Eastern Parts of Maryland* (Philadelphia: Society of Friends, Philadelphia Yearly Meeting, 1903), 11–15ff.

21. Simkin interview, 4 (emphasis in original); Walter J. Gershenfeld, "Early Years: Grievance Arbitration," Shils, *Industrial Peacemaker*, 31–34.

22. George W. Taylor, "Industrial Peace through Arbitration," draft of an article for the *American Arbitration Journal*, Oct. 1938, 3–4, in "Speeches and Articles by Dr. George W. Taylor," vol. 1, 1938–1950, Lippincott Library, University of Pennsylvania [hereafter, Taylor, "Speeches and Articles"]; John R. Commons, *Industrial Goodwill* (New York: McGraw-Hill, 1919).

23. George W. Taylor, "Toward a National Labor Policy," *Atlantic Monthly*, Sept. 1938, 336.

24. Dash interview, 40, 43.

25. Ibid., 9, 42.

26. "Umpire for G. M.," *Business Week*, no. 594 (Jan. 18, 1941), 52; Shils, *Industrial Peacemaker*, 123–30.

27. Lewis M. Gill remarks at "An Oral History of the National War Labor Board and Critical Issues in the Development of Modern Grievance Arbitration." *Case Western Reserve Law Review* 39, no. 2 (1988): 549.

28. A railroad union officer quoted in Fred Shapiro, "Mediator," *New Yorker*, Aug. 1, 1970, 40.

29. "Carnegie-Illinois Confers with C. I. O.; Others Raise Pay," *New York Times*, Mar. 2, 1937, 1, 12.

30. Ahmed White, *The Last Great Strike: Little Steel, the CIO, and the Struggle for Labor Rights in New Deal America* (Berkeley: University of California Press, 2016), ch. 11.

31. Quoted in Robert H. Zieger, *The C.I.O., 1935–1955* (Chapel Hill: University of North Carolina Press, 1995), 146.

32. "3 Steel Companies Fight Compromise on a Closed Shop," *New York Times*, Feb. 19, 1942.

33. Ibid., 12.

34. "The Role of Organized Labor in Winning the War," from Taylor, "Speeches and Articles," unpaginated.

35. Ibid.

36. Ibid.

37. National War Labor Board, *Termination Report of the National War Labor Board: Industrial Disputes and Wage Stabilization in Wartime, January 12,1942–December 31, 1945* (Washington, DC: National War Labor Board [1948]), 1: 83–84.

38. Quoted in ibid., 1: 84 (emphasis added).

39. International Harvester Company Case No. 2004-MB, repr. in National War Labor Board, *Termination Report*, 2: 287 (emphasis added).

40. In re Ryan Aeronautical Co. and UAW Local 506, San Diego, Calif., Case No. 46, June 1942, *Labor Relations Reference Manual,*" National Labor Relations Board, vol. 9 (Washington, DC: Bureau of National Affairs, July 1943): 1124.

41. "Thinking Out Loud or the Present Thoughts of One Employer," mimeographed, Feb. 18, 1942, quoted in Milton Derber, "The Principles of Dispute Settlement," *Problems and Policies of Dispute Settlement and Wage Stabilization during World War II*, Bulletin No. 1009 (n.d. [1951]), 81.

42. "The Role of Organized Labor in Winning the War," from Taylor, "Speeches and Articles," unpaginated.

43. NWLB Minutes, Mar. 18, 1942, 285–86, quoted in James MacGregor Burns, "Maintenance of Membership," *Journal of Politics* 10, no. 1 (Feb. 1948): 110–11.

44. Joel Seidman, *American Labor from Defense to Reconversion* (Chicago: University of Chicago Press, 1953), 97–98.

45. The board also ordered the companies to insert a minimum wage of at least 78 cents per hour for all its employees (except apprentices), including those on piecework. The three directive orders are reprinted in National War Labor Board, *Termination Report*, 2: 288–322.

46. Ibid., 1: 782.

47. Quoted in Allan R. Richards, *War Labor Boards in the Field* (Chapel Hill: University of North Carolina Press, 1953), 39.

48. National War Labor Board, *Termination Report*, 1: 782–84, 789.

49. Richards, *War Labor Boards*, 29–30, 39, 46, 75.

50. "Instructions to Regional War Labor Boards: Importance of Grievance Machinery," repr. in *Wage Labor Reports*, vol. 9 (1944), xxiv–xxv.

51. William H. Davis, *The Reminiscences of William Hammatt Davis,* Oral History Research Office, Part 1, No. 44, Columbia University Rare Book & Manuscript Library, University Archives, Columbia University, New York.

52. Richards, *War Labor Boards*, 246–47.

53. Benjamin Aaron, interview by the author, Jan. 4, 1998, 4–5 (personal possession of the author).

54. John Dunlop, interview by the author, Feb. 27, 1992, 8–11 (personal possession of the author).

55. George Hildebrand, interview by the author, Sept. 23, 1991.

56. National War Labor Board, *Termination Report*, 2: 36.

57. Garrett was married to Mary (Molly) Yard, who grew up in Shanghai, daughter of missionaries and a graduate of Swarthmore College. She helped found and became president of the American Student Union, a socialist student organization that mobilized against war and General Franco in the mid- and late 1930s. She consequently became deeply involved in the liberal wing of the Democratic Party in California and Pittsburgh and served as national president of the National Organization for Women from 1987 to 1991 ("Molly Yard, Advocate for Liberal Causes, Dies at 93," *New York Times*, Sept. 22, 2005).

58. Sylvester Garrett, interview by author, Jan. 11, 1996, 43–45 (personal possession of the author).

59. National War Labor Board, *Termination Report*, 1: 635.

60. Memorandum from Gill to Garrison, July 24, 1943, National Archives and Records Administration, Record Group 202 [hereafter, NARA], entry 67, box 458, folder "Lewis M. Gill."

61. Proceedings of RWLB, Philadelphia, Mar. 9, 1943, pp. 3–5, 10, entry 194, box 7, NARA.

62. Records of the Historical Section, Summary of Reports of Regional Chairmen, Feb. 21, 1944, 59, entry 77, box 487, NARA.

63. Proceedings of RWLB, Philadelphia, Mar. 16, 1943, p. 112, entry 194, box 8, NARA.

64. William M. Leiserson, "Diagnosis of War Labor Policy," repr. in *Labor Relations Reference Manual*, 9: 927–31.

65. Proceedings of RWLB, Philadelphia, Mar. 16, 1943, 8.

66. Ibid.

67. Ibid.

68. Ibid.

69. Ibid.

70. Ibid., 3–5, 8, 49–50, 61, 64, 70–71, 81, 86, 90, 96–97, NARA, entry 194, box 8.

71. Quoted in "Trouble in Philadelphia," *Time*, vol. 44, no. 7, Aug. 14, 1944, 24.

72. Records of the Historical Section, Summary of Reports of Regional Chairmen, pp. 43–44, entry 77, doc. 487, NARA.

73. Quoted in James Wolfinger, *Philadelphia Divided: Race and Politics in the City of Brotherly Love* (Chapel Hill: University of North Carolina Press, 2007), 152.

74. Wolfinger, *Philadelphia Divided*, ch. 6; Allan M. Winkler, "The Philadelphia Transit Strike of 1944," *Journal of American History* 59, no. 1 (June 1972): 82ff; "WLB Tells Union to Get Men Back on Job at Once," *Philadelphia Evening Bulletin*, Aug. 1, 1944; Theodore Spaulding, "Philadelphia's Hate Strike," *The Crisis*, Sept. 1944, 281–83, 301; "Philadelphia Hit by Transit Strike," *New York Times*, Aug. 2, 1944.

Chapter 3. On Top of the World, 1946–56

1. Advisory Committee on Labor, Supreme Commander for the Allied Powers, *Final Report: Labor Policies and Programs in Japan* (Tokyo: Advisory Committee on Labor, July 29, 1946); Helen Mears, *Mirror for America, Japan* (Boston: Houghton, Mifflin, 1948), 8, 38; John Curtis Perry, *Beneath the Eagle's Wings: Americans in Occupied Japan* (New York: Dodd, Mead, 1980), 150–52; Andrew Gordon, *The Evolution of Labor Relations in Japan* (Cambridge, MA: Harvard University Press, 1985), 329–39.

2. Benjamin Aaron, *A Life in Labor Law: The Memoirs of Benjamin Aaron* (Los Angeles: University of California—Los Angeles, Institute for Research on Labor and Employment, 2007), 66–67, 86, 121ff; Benjamin Aaron, interview by Gerry Fellman, June 1, 1989, p. 2, National Academy of Arbitrators, History Committee Interview, http://www.naarb.org/interviews/BenjaminAaron.PDF; Benjamin Aaron, interview by Jennifer Glenn, 1999, pp. 193–95, Center for Oral History Research, UCLA Library, University of California–Los Angeles; National War Labor Board, *Termination Report of the National War Labor Board: Industrial Disputes and Wage Stabilization in Wartime, January 12,1942–December 31, 1945* (Washington, DC: National War Labor Board [1948]), 2: 33.

3. The leading examples of the two approaches are Nelson Lichtenstein, *Labor's War at Home: The CIO in World War II* (New York: Cambridge University Press, 1982); and Kim Phillips-Fein, *Invisible Hands: The Businessmen's Crusade against the New Deal* (New York: Norton, 2010).

4. Sanford Jacoby, "Reckoning with Company Unions: The Case of Thompson Products, 1934–1964," *Industrial and Labor Relations Review* 43, no. 1 (Oct. 1989): 19–40; Ronald Schatz, *The Electrical Workers: A History of Labor at General Electric and Westinghouse, 1923–60* (Urbana: University of Illinois Press, 1983), chs. 7, 9.

5. I will refer to my subjects in this and subsequent chapters as "the Labor Board vets" since the NWLB closed in December 1945 and they were no longer young.

6. "Agrarian Unrest Stirs Philippines," *New York Times*, Nov. 12, 1945; Mallory Browne, "British See Threat to Empires in Asia: Rising against Dutch in Java Linked to Widespread Nationalist Moves," *New York Times*, Oct. 21, 1945, E5.

7. Louis Stark, "Basic Talks Begin," *New York Times*, Nov. 6, 1945.

8. "Labor Delegates Pass by Pickets," *New York Times*, Nov. 6, 1945.

9. Division of Labor Standards [DLS], U.S. Department of Labor, *The President's National Labor-Management Conference, November 5–30, 1945*, 6 vols. (Washington, DC: GPO, 1946), 5: 2.

10. DLS, *President's National Labor-Management Conference*, 2: 8–9 (emphasis added).

11. "Labor: Trouble at the Table," *Time*, Nov. 19, 1945, 21.

12. DLS, *President's National Labor-Management Conference*, 2: 7–9 (emphasis added).

13. Ibid., 3: 139–43.

14. See, inter alia, David Witwer, *Corruption and Reform in the Teamsters Union* (Urbana: University of Illinois Press, 2003); Allen Friedman and Ted Schwarz, *Power and Greed: Inside the Teamsters Empire of Corruption* (New York: Franklin Watts, 1989).

15. George W. Taylor, "Business Outlook," *Washington Post*, Oct. 20, 1946, M8.

16. George W. Taylor, "Effectuating the Labor Contract through Arbitration," in *The Problem of Labor Arbitration: Selected Papers from the First Seven Annual Meetings of the National Academy of Arbitrators, 1948–1954*, ed. Jean T. McKelvey (Washington, DC: BNA, 1957), 26.

17. Harry Shulman, "Reason, Contract, and Law in Labor Relations," *Harvard Law Review* 68, no. 6 (1955): 1004.

18. Ralph Seward, interview by Sylvester Garrett and Donald McPherson, Feb. 23, 1987, pp. 30, 56, Sylvester Garrett Collection, Manuscript Group 49, Addenda Inventory 2, series III, box 5, no. 7, Special Collections and University Archives, Indiana University of Pennsylvania, Indiana, PA [hereafter, Garrett Collection].

19. Monroe Lake, interview, Mar. 12, 1954, Special Collections, Columbia University Library; Kenneth F. Bannon, interview by Jack W. Skeels, Feb. 28, 1963, p. 10, box 121, folder 12, Bannon Collection, Oral History, Walter P. Reuther Library, Wayne State University, Detroit, MI; "Contract Is Hurt, Say Ford Officials," *New York Times*, Mar. 18, 1943, p. 11; "Ford Rouge Plant Strike On, Off Again," *Detroit Free Press*, Apr. 13, 1943; Aaron, *Life in Labor Law*, 46; "Harry Shulman, Ford Umpire," *Fortune* 33 (Mar. 1946), 172; Lawrence Galton, "Harry Is for the Headaches," *Nation's Business*, Aug. 1947, 49ff; Eugene V. Rostow, "Dean Harry Shulman," *Yale Law Journal* 64, no. 6 (May 1955): 802–4; Robert W. Campbell, interview by George Heliker, Feb. 25, 1954, pp. 8–9, acc. #940, box 5, folder "Labor-Heliker Interviews," Frank Hill Papers, Benson Ford Research Center, Henry Ford Museum, Dearborn, MI [hereafter, Hill Papers].

20. Aaron, *Life in Labor Law*, 46; "Harry Shulman, Ford Umpire," *Fortune* 33 (Mar. 1946), 172; Lawrence Galton, "Harry Is for the Headaches," *Nation's Business*, Aug. 1947, 49ff; Eugene V. Rostow, "Dean Harry Shulman," *Yale Law Journal* 64, no. 6 (May 1955): 802–4; Campbell interview, Hill Papers.

21. All of the opinions, many of the memoranda, and a good selection of the decisions are available in the Harry Shulman Papers, Special Collections and Archives, Sterling Library, Yale University, New Haven, CT.

22. Shulman, "Reason, Contract, and Law," 1020–21. Also see David Brody, "Workplace Contractualism in Comparative Perspective," in *Industrial Democracy in America: The Ambiguous Promise*, ed. Nelson Lichtenstein and Howell John Harris, 176–205 (Cambridge: Cambridge University Press, 1993).

23. Robert W. Campbell to George Heliker, undated [Mar. 1954], pp. 1–3, Hill Papers; John A. Byrne, *The Whiz Kids: The Founding Fathers of American Business and the Legacy They Left Us* (New York: Doubleday, 1993).

24. Bureau of Labor Statistics, U.S. Department of Labor, *Employment and Earnings, United States, 1909–75*, Bulletin 1312–10 (Washington, DC: GPO, 1976), 25.

25. For an overview, see William B. Gould, *Black Workers in White Unions: Job Discrimination in the United States* (Ithaca, NY: Cornell University Press, 1977), esp. ch. 10.

26. "Ground-Breaking Ceremony Starts Statler Hotel Job," *Los Angeles Times*, July 6, 1950; "Strife between Unions Delays Statler Work," *Los Angeles Times*, Aug. 29, 1951; 'Pay Rise Hearings Set," *New York Times*, Aug. 25, 1951.

27. John T. Dunlop, "The Arbitration of Jurisdictional Disputes in the Building Industry," in *Arbitration Today: Proceedings of the Eighth Annual Meeting, National Academy of Arbitrators, January 27 and 28, 1955*, ed. Jean T. McKelvey (Washington, DC: Bureau of National Affairs, 1955), 162.

28. Daniel Bell, interview by author, June 6, 1994, 59 (personal possession of the author).

29. Sylvester Garrett and L. Tripp Reed, *Management Problems in Multi-employer Bargaining* (Philadelphia: University of Pennsylvania Press, 1949).

30. Until the mid-1950s, the company and union employed a three-member arbitration committee, after which Garrett became the sole intermediary.

31. For a discussion of the factors that led the corporation to change its policy regarding collective bargaining, see Irving Bernstein, *Turbulent Years: A History of the American Worker, 1933–1941* (Boston: Houghton Mifflin, 1969), 457–73.

32. Jack Stieber, *The Steel Industry Wage Structure* (Cambridge, MA: Harvard University Press, 1959), 286ff; Wilbur Lohrentz, interview by Sylvester Garrett, 21, unpublished, Garrett Collection; Gabriel Alexander, interview by Donald McPherson and Sylvester Garrett, Aug. 2, 1987, unpublished, Garrett Collection.

33. J. Warren Shaver, interview by Francis Quinn, Sept. 15, 1980, pp. 21–22, box 41, folder 18, Oral History Committee of the National Academy of Arbitrators, Ithaca, NY.

34. Seward, interview by Garrett and McPherson, Garrett Collection. Punctuation changed.

35. See chapter 2 for Garrett's role in the creation of the Joint Wage Rate Inequity Negotiating Commission.

36. Stieber, *Steel Industry Wage Structure*, 42–47; Frank De Vyver, "Collective Bargaining in Steel," *Labor in Postwar America*, ed. Colston Warne et al. (Brooklyn, NY: Remsen, 1949), 389–90.

37. Robert Tilove, "The Wage Rate Rationalization Program in United States Steel," *Monthly Labor Review* 64, no. 6 (June 1947): 970; Stieber, *Steel Industry Wage Structure*, 176; Sylvester Garrett, interview by the author, Jan. 11, 1994, 14–15. See Tilove, "Wage Rate Rationalization Program," and Stieber, *Steel Industry Wage Structure*, for detailed descriptions of the plan.

38. Seward, interview by Garrett and McPherson, p. 10, Garrett Collection; Ralph Seward, interview by Sylvester Garrett, p. 25, Garrett Collection.

39. Seward interview, Feb. 23, 1954, by Garrett and McPherson, p. 11, Garrett Collection; Board of Conciliation and Arbitration, Case No. A-372 (Feb. 1, 1952), pp. 21–22, Garrett Collection.

40. Quoted in Stieber, *Steel Industry Wage Structure*, 97.

41. Seward interview by Garrett and McPherson, pp. 23, Garrett Collection.

42. Quoted in Arbitration Award, United States Steel Company, National Tube Division, Loraine Works and United Steelworkers of America, Local 1104, Case No. N-146 (Jan. 31, 1953), pp. 18, 20, Garrett Collection.

43. Board of Conciliation and Arbitration, Case No. A-372, p. 23.

44. Jack Metzger, *Striking Steel: Solidarity Remembered* (Philadelphia: Temple University Press, 2000), 34, 36.

45. "Agreement between National Tube Company and United Steelworkers of America–CIO, Production and Maintenance Employees," Apr. 22, 1947, Pennsylvania State University, Pittsburgh, Pennsylvania, 6–8, 33–41. National Tube Company was a subsidiary of U.S. Steel.

46. Jack Stieber, "Labor's Walkout from the Korean War Stabilization Board," *Labor History* 21, no. 2 (1980), 239–60; Robert Zieger, *The CIO, 1935–1955* (Chapel Hill: University of North Carolina Press, 1995), 10l; Aaron, *Life in Labor Law*, ch. 3.

47. Garrett interview, Jan. 11, 1994, 15, 22.

48. Board of Conciliation and Arbitration, Case No. A-372, pp. 49, 53, 58–59.

49. William Simkin, interview by Sylvester Garrett and Donald McPherson, Jan. 22–23, 1987, p. 6, Addenda 2 Inventory, box 2 (I), interviews, folder 8, Garrett Collection.

50. Ibid., 32–33.

51. Ben Fisher, interview by Sylvester Garrett, pp. 14—15, Addenda 3 Inventory, series IV, box 7, folder 4, Garrett Collection.

52. Board of Conciliation and Arbitration, *Quarterly Report to Parties*, Feb. 2, 1952, through Apr. 30, 1952, and Board of Arbitration, *Quarterly Report to Parties*, Jan. 1, 1957, through Mar. 31, 1957, box 1, folder 12, Garrett Collection. The board's name changed between 1952 and 1957.

53. Daniel Bell, "Steel's Strangest Strike," *Fortune*, Sept. 1956, 125, 246.

54. Clark Kerr, "Governmental Wage Restraints: Their Limits and Uses in a Mobilized Economy," in *Proceedings of the Fourth Annual Meeting of the Industrial Relations Research Association, December 28–29, 1951*, ed. L. Reed Tripp (Champaign-Urbana: IRRA, 1952), 25.

55. Clark Kerr, interview by the author, Aug. 7, 1992 (personal possession of the author).

56. Sumner H. Slichter, "How Bad Is Inflation?" *Harper's Magazine*, Aug. 1952, 53 (emphasis added). Also see "Creeping Inflation—Curse or Cure? A 'Debate in Print' between Sumner H. Slichter and Heinz Luedicker," repr. from *Journal of Commerce* (New York, 1957), 12–16, 23–28; Sumner Slichter, "Argument for 'Creeping Inflation,'" *New York Times Magazine*, May 8, 1959, 23; Ronald Schatz, "Sumner Slichter (1892–1959), Economist," *Encyclopedia of U.S. Labor and Working-Class History*, ed. Eric Arnesen (New York: Routledge, 2007), 3: 1277–78.

Chapter 4. Down-to-Earth Utopians

1. Roger Rosenblatt, *Coming Apart: A Memoir of the Harvard Wars of 1969* (Boston: Little, Brown, 1997), 114; Rosenblatt, *The Boy Detective: A New York Childhood* (Boston: Little, Brown, 2013).

2. John T. Dunlop, interview by the author, Feb. 27, 1992 (personal possession of the author), 8–11; "In Memoriam: Lloyd Reynolds," *Yale Bulletin and Calendar* 33, no. 27 (Apr. 22, 2005); Princeton University, "Richard A. Lester Dies at 89; Influential Economist and Dean of the Faculty at Princeton University," press release, Dec. 31, 1997, https://pr.princeton.edu/news/97/q4/1231-lester.html; Guide to the E. Wight Bakke Papers, Kheel Center for Labor-Management Documentation and Archives, Ives Hall, Cornell University, Ithaca, NY [hereafter, Kheel Center], accessed July 29, 2013, http://rmc.library.cornell.edu/EAD/htmldocs/KCL05522.html; Bruce Weber, "Robben W. Fleming, University President in Turbulent Times, Dies at 93," *New York Times*, Jan. 21, 2010, http://www.nytimes.com/2010/01/22/education/22fleming.html?_r=0; "James J. Healy, Harvard Business School Professor and Prominent Labor Arbitrator, Dead at 88," *Harvard Gazette*, July 21, 2005, https://news.harvard.edu/gazette/story/2005/07/james-j-healy-harvard-business-school-professor-and-prominent-labor-arbitrator-dead-at-88/.

3. Clark Kerr, *Labor Markets and Wage Determination: The Balkanization of Labor Markets and Other Essays* (Berkeley: University of California Press, 1977), 3, 11.

4. John T. Dunlop and James J. Healey, *Collective Bargaining: Principles and Case Studies*, 2nd ed. (Homewood, IL: R. D. Irwin, 1955); E. Wight Bakke and Clark Kerr, *Unions, Management, and the Public* (New York: Harcourt, Brace, 1948); Bruce Kaufman, ed., *How Labor Markets Work: Reflections on Theory and Practice by John Dunlop, Clark Kerr, Richard Lester and Lloyd Reynolds* (Lexington, MA: Lexington, 1988), ii. Also see the syllabi and case studies in Dunlop's papers (uncatalogued) at the Harvard University Archives, Cambridge, MA.

5. Clark Kerr, *Marshall, Marx and Modern Times: The Multi-dimensional Society* (Cambridge: Cambridge University Press, 1969), 17; H. H. Gerth and C. Wright Mills, eds., *From Max Weber: Essays in Society* (New York: Oxford University Press, 1946), 128, 155; Serge Guildbaut, *How New York Stole the Idea of Modern Art* (Chicago: University of Chicago Press, 1983); Richard H. Pells, *The Liberal Mind in a Conservative Age: American Intellectuals in the 1940s and 1950s* (New York: Harper and Row, 1985), ch. 3; Nils Gilman, *Mandarins of the Future: Modernization Theory in Cold War America* (Baltimore, MD: Johns Hopkins University Press, 2003), chs. 1–5; Nils Gilman, "Modernization Theory, the Highest Stage of American Intellectual History," in *Stages of Growth: Modernization, Development, and the Global Cold War*, ed. David C. Engerman et al., 47–80 (Amherst: University of Massachusetts Press, 2003).

6. See, for example, Clark Kerr, "Industrial Conflict and Its Mediation," *American Journal of Sociology* 60, no. 3 (Nov. 1954): 233.

7. Karl Mannheim, *Ideology and Utopia: An Introduction to the Sociology of Knowledge*, trans. Louis Wirth and Edward Shils (London: Routledge and Kegan Paul, 1960; originally in German, 1929), ch. 4, esp. 219–22, 224–25.

8. Bruce E. Kaufman, "Reflections on Six Decades in Industrial Relations: An Interview with John Dunlop," *Industrial and Labor Relations Review* 55, no. 2 (2002): 325.

9. Milton Derber, interview by Phil Menzel, Apr. 16, 1987, 10–14, Milton Derber Papers (1951–80), box 14 (no listed folder), Labor and Industrial Relations, Institute of Faculty Archive, University of Illinois at Urbana-Champaign.

10. Clark Kerr, interview by the author, Aug. 7, 1992 (personal possession of the author), 15, 21–22; "Catherine 'Kay' Kerr, 1911–2010," *Berkeley Daily Planet*, Dec. 22, 2010, http://www.berkeleydailyplanet.com/issue/2010-12-22/article/37047?headline=Catherine-Kay-Kerr-1911-2010—From-the-University-of-California-Press-Office.

11. Kaufman, "Reflections," 327.

12. John R. Hicks, *Theory of Wages* (London: Macmillan, 1935); Paul J. McNulty, *The Origins and Development of Labor Economics: A Chapter in the History of Social Thought* (Cambridge, MA: MIT Press, 1980), 178–80.

13. Kerr, *Labor Markets*, 5, 40 (emphasis added).

14. Richard A. Lester, "Wage Diversity and Its Theoretical Implications," *Review of Economic Statistics* 28, no. 3 (Aug. 1946): 152, 157–58.

15. Clark Kerr, "Industrial Conflict and Its Mediation," *American Journal of Sociology* 60, no. 3 (1954): 230.

16. Ibid., 233.

17. For overviews, see Committee on Labor Market Research, *Memorandum on University Research Programs in the Field of Labor* (Washington, DC: Social Science Research Council, 1946); Caroline F. Ware, "Trends in University Programs for Labor Education, 1946–1948," *Industrial and Labor Relations Review* 3, no. 1 (Oct. 1949): 54–69; Brother Justin, "The Study of Industrial and Labor Relations in Catholic Colleges," *Industrial and Labor Relations Review* 3, no. 1 (Oct. 1949): 70–75; and Robert Clewett, "Industrial Relations Research Centers in American Universities," MA thesis, UC-Berkeley, 1949.

18. Edwin E. Witte, "The University and Labor Education," *Industrial and Labor Relations Review* 1, no. 1 (Oct. 1947): 7.

19. Address by Governor Dewey at convocation, Nov. 12, 1945, p. 4, Founding Documents Collection, box 1 (unsorted), Kheel Center.

20. John McConnell, interview by the author, July 12, 1990, 24; Jean McKelvey, interview by the author, Oct. 5, 1990, 42, 68–72.

21. In the 1930s the progressive program was called the Western Summer School. *Biennial Message of Earl Warren, Gov. of California, Delivered to Senate and House of Representatives in Joint Session, Jan. 8, 1945, 6*; Tobias Higbie, *Labor Mind: A History of Working-Class Intellectual Life* (Urbana: University of Illinois Press, 2019), 78–82.

22. Quoted in Milton Derber, "A Brief History of the Institute of Labor and Industrial Relations," p. 1, series 22, box 1, folder 801, Labor and Industrial Relations Archives, University of Illinois at Urbana-Champaign (1987).

23. Mark Starr to James Healy, Aug. 31, 1951, UAV 845.50005, box 6, Harvard University Archives.

24. Derber and Menzel, "Brief History"; Mark Starr, "Cap and Gown Meets Overall," *Guidance, Practical Arts, and Vocational Education*, Jan. 1945.

25. Derber and Menzel, *Brief History*, 34–35.

26. Jean T. McKelvey, "Teaching Industrial and Labor Relations," *Labor and Nation*, Nov.–Dec. 1948, 33–34, 42.

27. *I&LR News* 3, no. 3 (Apr. 1947), p. 1, Kheel Center; McKelvey interview, p. 103, Oct. 5, 1990, Kheel Center.

28. Edmund Ezra Day, "Education in Industrial and Labor Relations," *Industrial and Labor Relations Review* 3, no. 2 (Jan. 1950): 225–26.

29. Edwin Witte, "Where We Are in Industrial Relations," in *Proceedings of the First Annual Meeting, Industrial Relations Research Association* (Champaign, IL: Industrial Relations Research Association, 1949), 17–18.

30. John Dunlop, "The Settlement of Emergency Disputes," in *Proceedings of the Fifth Annual Meeting, Industrial Relations Research Association* (Madison: IRRA, 1953), 118.

31. Clark Kerr, "Governmental Wage Restraints: Their Limits and Uses in a Mobilized Economy," *American Economic Review* 42, no. 2 (May 1952): 369–70.

32. Clark Kerr, "Industrial Relations and the Liberal Pluralist," in *Proceedings of the Seventh Annual Meeting, Industrial Relations Research Association* (Madison: IRRA, 1955), 7.

33. Sumer H. Slichter, "The Growth of Moderation," *Atlantic Monthly*, Oct. 1956, repr. in *Potentials of the American Economy: Selected Essays of Sumer H. Slichter*, ed. John T. Dunlop (Cambridge, MA: Harvard University Press, 1961), 15–21.

34. Jefferson Cowie, *Capital Moves: RCA's Seventy-Year Quest for Cheap Labor* (Ithaca, NY: Cornell University Press, 1999), chs. 1–2; Ronald Schatz, *The Electrical Workers: A History of Labor at General Electric and Westinghouse, 1923–60* (Urbana: University of Illinois Press, 1983), ch. 9.

35. Bernstein served on the staff of the Regional War Labor Board in San Francisco during the war and joined the Institute of Industrial Relations at UCLA afterward ("Irving Bernstein; Leading Labor Historian, UCLA Professor, Was 84," *Los Angeles Times*, Oct. 6, 2001).

36. Kerr, "Industrial Relations," 2 (emphasis added).

37. Lloyd M. Fisher, "The Price of Union Responsibility," *New York Times,* Aug. 31, 1947. For the refusal of workers to vote for Wallace despite urgings of leftist union officials, see Charles H. Titus and Charles R. Nixon, "The 1948 Election in California," *Western Political Quarterly* 2, no. 1 (Mar. 1949): 97–102; Donald Tormey, interviews by the author, Sept. 15, 1976, and Jan. 20, 1981 (personal possession of the author).

38. Quoted in James L. Cochrane, *Industrialism and Industrial Man in Retrospect* (New York: Ford Foundation, 1979), 62; University of California Academic Senate, "Lloyd H. Fisher, Political Science: Berkeley," *University of California: In Memoriam,* 1957, Online Archives of California, http://oac.,dlib.org/view?docId=hbow10035d&chunk.id=div00018 &brand=oac4&doc.view=entire_text.

39. Institute of International Industrial and Labor Relations, *Labor, Management, and Economic Growth: Proceedings of a Conference on Human Resources and Labor Relations in Underdeveloped Countries,* Nov. 12–14, 1953, ed. Robert L. Aronson and John P. Windmuller (Ithaca, NY: Cornell University, 1954), iii–v.

40. Clark Kerr and Abraham Siegel, "Industrialization and the Structuring of the Labor Force: A Typological Framework," in *Labor, Management, and Economic Growth,* ed. Aronson and Windmuller, 137–47. An expanded version of the paper was published a year later: Clark Kerr and Abraham Siegel, "The Structuring of the Labor Force in Industrial Society: New Directions and New Questions," *Industrial and Labor Relations Review* 8, no. 2 (Jan. 1955): 151–68. In 1954 Siegel was appointed as an instructor at the Department of Economics at MIT. He later became a professor and dean of the Sloan School of Management there.

41. Clark Kerr, Frederick H. Harbison, John T. Dunlop, and Charles A. Myers, "The Labor Problem in Economic Development: A Framework for a Reappraisal?" *International Labour Review* 71, no. 3 (Mar. 1955): 235.

42. Harbison moved from Chicago to Princeton in 1955.

43. Quoted in Cochrane, *Industrialism and Industrial Man,* 114.

44. Carton 12, folder 51, Clark Kerr Personal and Professional Papers, Bancroft Library, UC-Berkeley, summarized in Ethan Schrum, "Administering American Modernity: The Instrumental University in the Postwar United States," PhD thesis, University of Pennsylvania, 2009, 79–80.

45. Clark Kerr, John T. Dunlop, Frederick Harbison, and Charles A. Myers, *Industrialism and Industrial Man: The Problems of Labor and Management in Economic Growth* (Cambridge, MA: Harvard University Press, 1960); Kerr et al., "Industrialism and Industrial Man," *International Labour Review* 82, no. 3 (Sept. 1960): 236–50; Clark Kerr, John T. Dunlop, Frederick Harbison, and Charles A. Myers, "Industrialism and World Society," *Harvard Business Review* 39, no. 1 (Jan.–Feb. 1961): 113–29.

46. John T. Dunlop and Vasilii P. Diatchenko, eds., *Labor Productivity* (New York: Mc-Graw-Hill, 1964).

47. John T. Dunlop, Walter Galenson, and Clark Kerr, "General Impressions of Eastern Europe," box 2, folder "CFS-current," Sept. 1964, in Clark Kerr Collection on Industrialism and Industrial Man, Institute of Industrial Relations, UC–Berkeley.

48. John T. Dunlop and Nikolay P. Fedorenko, eds., *Planning and Markets: Modern Trends in Various Economic Systems* (New York: McGraw-Hill, 1969).

49. Kerr et al., *Industrialism and Industrial Man*, 7, 229, 233; Kerr, "Industrial Relations and the Liberal Pluralist," Seventh Annual Meeting, IRRA (1955), p. 2 (emphasis added); Herbert Marcuse, *One-Dimensional Man* (Boston: Beacon, 1964).

50. Kerr et al., *Industrialism and Industrial Man*, 134.

51. Ibid., ch. 3; Kerr et al., "Industrialism and World Society," repr. in Clark Kerr, *Labor and Management in Industrial Society* (Garden City, NY: Anchor, 1964), 347–48.

52. Clark Kerr, John T. Dunlop, Frederick Harbison, and Charles A. Myers, "Industrialism and Industrial Man," *International Labour Review* 82, no. 3 (Sept. 1960): 240; Clark Kerr, John T. Dunlop, Frederick Harbison, and Charles A. Myers, *Industrialism and Industrial Man*, 55–59.

53. Kerr et al., "Industrialism and Industrial Man," 240.

54. Kerr et al., "Industrialism and Industrial Man," 240–41; Kerr et al., *Industrialism and Industrial Man*, ch. 3.

55. Kerr et al., "Industrialism and Industrial Man," 240–41.

56. Kerr et al., *Industrialism and Industrial Man*, 272–77; "Ronald Reagan Address to the British Parliament, June 8, 1982," in *The History Place: Great Speeches Collection*, accessed July 29, 2013, http://www.historyplace.com/speeches/reagan-parliament.htm.

57. Kerr et al., *Industrialism and Industrial Man*, 288–93.

58. Clark Kerr, John T. Dunlop, Frederick Harbison, and Charles A. Myers, "Postscript to *Industrialism and Industrial Man*," *International Labour Review* 103, no. 6 (June 1971): 535–36.

59. Kerr et al., *Industrialism and Industrial Man*, 295.

60. Ibid., 282.

61. Kerr et al., *Industrialism and Industrial Man*, 238.

Chapter 5. War and Peace in Steel, 1959–72

1. Board of Arbitration, Cases USC-846, 848, 850, 869, Oct. 1, 1959, Arbitration Award, U.S. Steel Corporation Fairless Works and United Steelworkers of America, Local Union No. 4889, addenda, pp. 1, 1–2, 22–23, series IV, box 28, Sylvester Garrett Collection, Manuscript Group 49, Special Collections and University Archives, Indiana University of Pennsylvania, Indiana, PA [hereafter, Garrett Collection]. (At the request of the parties, Garrett did not issue the ruling until Oct. 1, 1959.)

2. On union leaders' and workers' relative calm and leeriness of strikes in the mid- to late 1950s, see, among others, Becky M. Nicolaides, *My Blue Heaven: Life and Politics in the Working-Class Suburbs of Los Angeles, 1920–1965* (Chicago: University of Chicago Press, 2002), chs. 5–7; Ronald Schatz, *The Electrical Workers: A History of Labor at General Electric and Westinghouse, 1923–60* (Urbana: University of Illinois Press, 1983), 149–60; Schatz, "Connecticut's Working Class in the 1950's: A Catholic Perspective," *Labor History* 25, no. 1 (Winter 1984): 83–101.

3. Bureau of Labor Statistics, U.S. Department of Labor, *Handbook of Labor Statistics, 1975— Reference Edition*, Bulletin No. 1865, 225, 226, 313; Bureau of Labor Statistics, *Employment and Earnings Statistics for the United States, 1909–66*, Bulletin No. 1312–4 (Oct. 1966), 16, 134–35, 310–11, 614.

4. George H. Hildebrand, "The New Economic Environment of the United States and Its Meaning," *Industrial and Labor Relations Review* 16, no. 4 (Apr. 1963): 523, 530, 533; Thomas E. Klier, "From Tail Fins to Hybrids: How Detroit Lost Its Dominance of the U.S. Auto Market," *Economic Perspectives* (Chicago: Federal Reserve Bank of Chicago, 2009), 5.

5. Silberman, "Steel—It's a Brand-New Industry," *Fortune* 62, no. 6 (Dec. 1960), 249, 256; Charles Stieber, "Steel," *Collective Bargaining: Contemporary American Experience*, ed. Gerald Somers, 155–56 (Madison: University of Wisconsin Industrial Relations Research Association, 1980); Richard Kalwa, "Collective Bargaining in Basic Steel, 1946–1983," PhD diss., Cornell University, 1985, 13ff; Jules Backman, *Steel Prices, the Steel Industry, and the National Economy* (Scarsdale, NY: Republic Steel Corporation, 1965).

6. James Reston, "Democrats Gain 13 Senate Seats," *New York Times*, Nov. 6, 1958; "Democrats' Edge Tripled in House," *New York Times*, Nov. 6, 1958; "Labor Is Dazzled by Ohio Victory," *New York Times*, Nov. 6, 1958; "Labor Batted .700 in Elections," *New York Times*, Nov. 6, 1958; Arthur Krock, "Queer Gaps in the National Pattern," *New York Times*, Nov. 6, 1958; "A.D.A. Hails Results," *New York Times*, Nov. 6, 1958; "Democratic Gubernatorial Gains Give the Party 34 State Houses," *New York Times*, Nov. 6, 1958; "Foes of Work Law Went Democratic," *New York Times*, Nov. 9, 1958; Albert Clark, "What Mandate? Democrats' Win Traces More to G.O.P.'s Collapse Than to Demand for Anything New," *Wall Street Journal*, Nov. 6, 1958; Lawrence Richards, *Union-Free America: Workers and Antiunion Culture* (Urbana: University of Illinois Press, 2008), ch. 3; Thomas W. Evans, *The Education of Ronald Reagan* (New York: Columbia University Press, 2006), 84; *Encyclopedia of American History*, 7th ed., ed. Richard B. Morris and Jeffrey Morris (New York: Collins Reference, 1996), 1185.

7. "Blough Asks Newspapers to Lead Inflation Fight," *Washington Post*, Nov. 10, 1956, A16; "U.S. Steel Chief Defends Prices," *Washington Post*, Aug. 9, 1957, A2; "Big Business Can Be Bigger, Blough Holds," *Chicago Daily Tribune*, Mar. 14, 1957; Roger M. Blough, "Price and the Public Interest," address delivered to the Economic Club of Detroit, Sept. 15, 1958, repr. in *Representative American Speeches: 1958–1959*, ed. A. Craig Baird (New York: H. W. Wilson, 1959), 65–78. On Boulware, see Schatz, *Electrical Workers*, ch. 7; Kimberly Phillips-Fein, "American Counterrevolutionary: Lemuel Boulware and General Electric, 1950–1960," *American Capitalism: Social Thought and Political Economy in the Twentieth Century*, ed. Nelson Lichtenstein (Philadelphia: University of Pennsylvania Press, 2006), ch. 11.

8. Bureau of Labor Statistics, *Handbook of Labor Statistics 1975*, 391; David L. Cole, "Where We Are and Where We Are Going in Collective Bargaining," in *Current Trends in Collective Bargaining*, ed. Arthur Max Ross (Berkeley, CA: Institute of Industrial Relations, 1960), 4; W. H. Smith, "Current Trends in Collective Bargaining," in *Current Trends in Collective Bargaining*, 15. For overviews, see "More Industries Join Steel, Struggle to Kill Restrictive Union Rules," *Wall Street Journal*," Aug. 18, 1959; Ann James Herlihy, "A Review of Work Stoppages during 1958," *Monthly Labor Review*, June 1959, 638; Loretta Nolan, "A Review of Work Stoppages during 1959," *Monthly Labor Review*, June 1959, 611; Loretto R. Nolan and Julian Malnak, "A Review of Work Stoppages during 1960," *Monthly Labor Review*, June 1961, 614; A. H. Raskin, "Deep Shadow over Our Factories," *New York Times Sunday Magazine*, Nov. 29, 1959, 20, 127–29; Daniel Bell, "The Subversion of Collective Bargaining," *Commentary*, no. 29 (1960), 185–97; Mike Davis, *Prisoners of the American Dream: Politics and Economy*

in the History of the U.S. Working Class (London: Verso, 1986), 121–24. For a good overview of the managerial revolt of the late 1950s, see David Stebenne, *Arthur J. Goldberg: New Deal Liberal* (Oxford: Oxford University Press, 1996), chs. 6–7.

9. A. H. Raskin, "2 Attitudes in Steel," *New York Times*, Oct. 16, 1959.

10. R. Conrad Cooper, "Management Planning," address to Pittsburgh Chapter, Society for Advancement of Management, Mar. 20, 1958, pp. 2, 3, 13, in Special Collections and University Archives, Indiana University of Pennsylvania, Indiana, PA (emphasis in original).

11. Quoted in "R. Conrad Cooper former U.S. Steel Corp. Executive Vice President," *New York Times*, Oct. 2, 1982, http://www.upi.com/Archives/1982/10/02/R-Conrad-Cooper-former -US-Steel-Corp-executive-vice/4763402379200/?spt=su.

12. Judith Stein, *Running Steel, Running America: Race, Economic Policy, and the Decline of Liberalism* (Chapel Hill: University of North Carolina Press, 1998), 22.

13. George J. McManus, *The Inside Story of Steel Wages and Prices, 1959–1967* (Berkeley: University of California Press), 1967, 16–17.

14. At the request of the parties, Garrett did not issue the ruling until Oct. 1, 1959 (Board of Arbitration Award, Garrett Collection; Sylvester Garrett, interview by Francis Quinn, Mar. 13, 1980, pp. 25–26, Oral History Committee, National Academy of Arbitrators, 1986–20079, Kheel Center for Labor-Management Documentation and Archives, Cornell University, Ithaca, NY [hereafter, Kheel Center]).

15. "Agreement between National Tube Company and the United Steelworkers of America-CIO, Production and Maintenance Employees, Apr. 22, 1947, Pittsburgh, Pennsylvania," Pennsylvania State University, 6–8, 33–41. National Tube Company was a subsidiary of U.S. Steel.

16. Quoted in James Rose, "The Struggle over Management Rights at U.S. Steel, 1946–1960," *Business History Review* 72, no. 3 (1998): 453.

17. "Agreement between National Tube Company and United Steelworkers," 6–8, 33–41.

18. "Oral History Conference among Martha Conley, Ralph Seward, Sylvester Garrett," Dec. 6, 1984, pp. 27–28, Sylvester Garrett Collection.

19. Saul Wallen, "The Silent Contract vs. Explicit Provisions," *Collective Bargaining and the Arbitrator's Role: Proceedings of the Fifteenth Annual Meeting of the National Academy of Arbitrators*, ed. Mark L. Kahn, 117–37 (Washington, DC: Bureau of National Affairs, 1962).

20. William Simkin, interview by Sylvester Garrett and Donald McPherson, Jan. 22–23, 1987, p. 8, addenda 2, box II(I) interviews, folder 8, Garrett Collection.

21. Pike and Fischer, Inc., *Steelworkers Handbook on Arbitration Decisions* (Washington, DC: Pike and Fischer, 1960), 29ff; Jack Stieber, "Work Rules and Practices in Mass Production Industries," *Proceedings of the Fourteenth Annual Meeting, Industrial Relations Research Association*, ed. G. Somers (Madison: IRRA, 1962), 402; Rose, "Struggle over Management Rights," 459, 467ff.

22. "R. Conrad Cooper Dies at 79; Ex-Steel Industry Negotiator," *New York Times*, Oct. 2, 1982; R. Heath Larry, interview by Sylvester Garrett and Donald McPherson, Jan. 8, 1988, p. 19, addenda 2, box III interviews, folder 5, Garrett Collection; Sylvester Garrett, interview by the author, Jan. 11, 1994, 24 (personal possession of the author); *Who's Who in Commerce and Industry* (1944); "Oral History Conference," 20.

23. Cooper and Stephens are quoted in Rose, "Struggle over Management Rights," 460.

24. Bell, "Subversion," 190–91; "Labor: Stand on Principle," *Time*, Oct. 12, 1959.

25. A. H. Raskin, "A Question of Principle," *New York Times*, Nov. 3, 1959; Raskin, "Deep Shadows over Our Factories," *New York Times Sunday Magazine*, Nov. 29, 1959, 20. The 1952 steel strike, the nearest equivalent to 1959 stoppages, was fundamentally an effort by management to force the Truman administration to allow the companies to raise their prices.

26. Jack Metzger, *Striking Steel: Solidarity Remembered* (Philadelphia: Temple University Press, 2000), 73.

27. A. H. Raskin, "Hope for Steel Pact in 80 Days Dim," *New York Times*, Nov. 15, 1959, E7; Raskin, "Steel Peace Move by Nixon Rejected; Industry Adamant," *New York Times*, Jan. 1, 1960; Joseph A. Loftus, "All-Night Session: Work Practices Issue Shelved—Cost Put at 41c an Hour," *New York Times*, Jan. 5, 1960; "Nixon Counters Steel Pact Foes," *New York Times*, Jan. 24, 1960; "Steel Union Signs with Firms, Hails Mitchell's Role," *Wall Street Journal*, Jan. 6, 1960, 3: "Gains Scored by Industry, Steel Union," *Hartford Courant*, Jan. 7, 1960, 8A. The union did make a concession in one area. They gave up the cost-of-living adjustment to the members' wages, a benefit they had won in 1956.

28. Arthur Krock, "The State of the Union and George Meany," *New York Times*, Jan. 8, 1960; Evelyn Ora Harper, letter to the editors, *Los Angeles Times*, Feb. 8, 1960, B4.

29. George W. Taylor quoted Dunlop in his address "Collective Bargaining: New Approaches to the Problem of Achieving Agreements," 122, at the conference Critical Issues Affecting Labor-Management Relations, Seventh Annual Meeting, Industrial Relations Conference, Mar. 29–30, 1961, section on Labor Relations Law, State Bar of Michigan, Labor and Industrial Relations Records, Bentley Historical Library, Institute of Labor and Industrial Relations, University of Michigan–Wayne State University, Ann Arbor, MI.

30. "Taft-Hartley: 'Not Adequate to Handle Big Strikes,'" *U.S. News and World Report*, Oct. 19, 1959, 70–71. Clark Kerr and his fellow panelists made the same suggestions in President's Commission on National Goals, *Goals for Americans: Programs for Action in the Sixties* (Englewood Cliffs, NJ: Prentice-Hall, 1960), 161.

31. "Text of Report Submitted to the President by the Steel Board," *New York Times*, Oct. 20, 1959.

32. "Death of an Idea," *Pittsburgh Press*, Oct. 5, 1965.

33. Raskin, "2 Attitudes"; Raskin, "Steel: The Mood of Both Sides," *New York Times*, Oct. 18, 1959, E5; Raskin, "Kaiser to Sign with Steel Union, Ending Industry's United Front, Major Producers Standing Firm," *New York Times*, Oct. 26, 1959; Milton Esterow, "Kaiser's Site and Mines Helps Make Company an Independent," *New York Times*, Oct. 26, 1959; "Kaiser-Union Joint Statement and Company Discussion of the New Steel Contract," *New York Times*, Oct. 27, 1959; "Kaiser Steel to Sign Separate Contract with Union, Breaking Industry Ranks," *Wall Street Journal*, Oct. 26, 1959; National Broadcasting Company, *Meet the Press*, Guest Edgar F. Kaiser, vol. 3, no. 37 (Sunday, Nov. 1, 1959), 3–4.

34. "Kaiser Signs Pact," *Los Angeles Times*, Oct. 27, 1959; "Kaiser Steel Advisers on Progress Announced," *Los Angeles Times*, Dec. 9, 1959, B7; "Work Practices Named at Kaiser Plant," *Los Angeles Times*, Dec. 22, 1959; "Union and Kaiser Map Study," *Wall Street Journal*, Dec. 22, 1959; A. H. Raskin, "Panel to Meet Today to Seek Long-Term Steel Peace Plan," *New*

York Times, Mar. 9, 1960; A. H. Raskin, "Progress Noted by Kaiser Panel," *New York Times,* Mar. 10, 1960; "Recommendations of Kaiser-USA Long-Range Committee," *Monthly Labor Review,* Feb. 1961, 137; "The Kaiser-Steelworkers Agreement," *Monthly Labor Review,* Dec. 1959, 1345–46; Stebenne, *Goldberg,* 210, 254, 279–84; *Meet the Press,* 5.

35. "Why Committee Failed," *Iron Age,* Dec. 8, 1960, 8; Simkin interview, 34.

36. Abel quoted in *Creative Collective Bargaining: Meeting Today's Challenges to Labor-Management Relations,* ed. James Healey and James Henderson (Englewood Cliffs, NJ: Prentice-Hall, 1965), 205; "Steel and Union to Meet on Jobs," *New York Times,* Jan. 4, 1961; Stebenne, *Goldberg,* 286; for the increase in steel imports and decline in domestic steel manufacturers' profits, see Kalwa, "Collective Bargaining," tables 1.1 and 1.3; R. Heath Larry, "Steel's Human Relations Committee," *Steelways,* Sept. 1963, 18.

37. Healey and Henderson, *Creative Collective Bargaining,* 203, 207–8; Joseph Loftus, "All-Night Session," *New York Times,* Jan. 5, 1960.

38. "Work Rules Talks Stay Deadlocked," *Iron Age,* Dec. 8, 1960, 81.

39. Marvin Miller, *A Whole Different Ball Game: The Inside Story of the Baseball Revolution* (Chicago: Ivan Dee, 2004), 19–20; Robert F. Burk, *Marvin Miller: Baseball Revolutionary* (Urbana: University of Illinois Press, 2015), 48–51, 80–90.

40. "United Steelworkers–Steel Industry Human Relations Committee," p. 2, folder 20, Marvin Miller Collection, United Steelworkers of America Collection Papers, Historical Records and Labor Archives, Pattee Library, Pennsylvania State University, Philadelphia [hereafter, Miller Collection]; "M'Donald Hails His Union's Gains," *New York Times,* Dec. 27, 1962; 'USW Wants Experience with Kaiser Pact before Seeking It at Other Steel Firms," *Wall Street Journal,* Dec. 27, 1962.

41. "Work Rules Talks Stay Deadlocked," *Iron Age,* Dec. 8, 1960, 81; "United Steelworkers–Steel Industry Human Relations Committee," undated [1963?], folder 20, Miller Collection; Larry, "Steel's Human Relations Committee," 18; 'USW Wants Experience"; David Feller, "The Steel Experience: Myth and Reality," *Proceedings of the Twenty-First Annual Meeting Industrial Relations Research Association, December 29–30, 1968,* ed. G. Somers (Madison: IRRA, 1969), 157.

42. Confidential: United States Steel Corporation and United Steelworkers of America, "Review of Grievance and Arbitration Procedure," May 4, 1966, viii, box 5, folder "Joint Review of Grievance Procedure," Miller Collection.

43. Edward J. Lally, "Industry, USW Set Talks for Revising Complaint Procedure," *American Metal Market,* Mar. 31, 1961, 20.

44. R. Conrad Cooper, "Let's Look at the Doughnut," Oct. 10, 1961, address, repr. in *Representative American Speeches, 1961–1962,* ed. Lester Thonssen (New York: H. W. Wilson, 1962), 158.

45. Memo from Marvin Miller to Ben Fischer re Agenda for Human Relations Research Study Committee on Grievance and Arbitration Problems, undated [1961?], folder 20, Miller Collection; Ben Fischer, "Arbitration: The Steel Industry Experiment," *Monthly Labor Review,* Nov. 1972, 7–8, 8–10; Miller quoted in McManus, *Inside Story,* 41–42; Feller, "Steel Experience," 156–57; A. H. Raskin, "Nonstop Talks Instead of Nonstop Strikes," *New York Times Sunday Magazine,* July 7, 1963, 7, 12, 30.

46. "Dr. George W. Taylor to the Men and Women of Kaiser Steel, Dec. 16, 1962," box 19, folder 5, USWA Research Department, Kaiser Steel Corp., Long-Range Committee, Historical Collections and Archives, Pattee Library, Pennsylvania State University, Philadelphia; "Kaiser Plan to Share Costs Wins Approval," *Los Angeles Times*, Mar. 14, 1966; John Pomfret, "Kaiser Nears Pact with Steel Union to Share Savings," *New York Times*, Dec. 14, 1962; Harry Bernstein, "Kaiser Committee Approves Savings Sharing Plan," *Los Angeles Times*, Dec. 18, 1962; Gladwin Hills, "Bonus Plan Working at Kaiser," *New York Times*, Mar. 26, 1964; A. H. Raskin, "Approach to Automation: The Kaiser Plan," *New York Times Sunday Magazine*, Nov. 3, 1963, 11; Miller to Fischer memo re Agenda.

47. Dr. George W. Taylor to the Men and Women of Kaiser Steel, United Steelworkers Research Department, Kaiser Steel Corp., Long-Range Committee, box 29, folder 20, Pennsylvania State University; Edgar Kaiser quoted in "The *Facts* of the Kaiser Steel Agreement," United Steelworkers Research Department, Kaiser Steel Corp., Long-Range Committee, box 29, folder 20, Pennsylvania State University; "Kaiser Steel Company–United Steelworkers of America Plan for Economic Progress by Employee, Company and the Public" (official text), Dec. 17, 1962, United Steelworkers Research Department, Kaiser Steel Corp., Long-Range Committee, box 29, folder 20, Pennsylvania State University; "Kaiser Steel Reported to Yield $20 in Two Savings in Two Years," *American Metal Market,* Apr. 7, 1965, #709, box 17, folder 7; "Long Range Sharing Plan for Kaiser Steel Corp. Employees," *Monthly Labor Review*, Feb. 1963, 154–61; Raskin, "Automation Has Made Strikes Senseless," *New York Times Sunday Magazine*, Oct. 31, 1965, 185.

48. "A Proposal for Establishing Administrative Machinery for the Exploration and Settlement of Problems and Disputes between the Steel Industry and United Steelworkers of America," United Steelworkers Research Department, Kaiser Steel Corp., Long-Range Committee, box 9, folder 7, Historical Collections and Labor Archives, Pennsylvania State University.

49. Ibid.

50. Ibid.

51. Ibid.

52. Ibid.

53. Stebenne, *Goldberg*, ch. 8.

54. Ibid., 274–78ff; Jack Stieber, "The President's Committee on Labor-Management Policy," *Industrial Relations* 5, no. 2 (1966): 1–19.

55. Ben Fischer, interview by Sylvester Garrett, pp. 14–15, box 7, Garrett Collection.

56. John Pomfrets, "President's Role in Steel Accord Called Decisive," *New York Times*, Sept. 5, 1965; David Jones, "Johnson Reports Accord on New Steel Contract after Suggesting Terms," *New York Times*, Sept. 4, 1965; David Jones, "Union Ratifies New Steel Pact Covering 3 Years," *New York Times*, Sept. 6, 1965,; I. W. Abel, "Basic Steel's Experimental Negotiating Agreement," *Monthly Labor Review*, Sept. 1973, 41; Miller, *Whole Different Ball Game*, 25–29; McManus, *Inside Story*, 175–82.

57. Board of Arbitration Case USC 719; "Union Seeks Bonuses for All Steelworkers, Arbitrators Are Told," *Wall Street Journal*, June 17, 1969; "Incentive System for Steelworkers Ordered Changed," *Wall Street Journal*, Aug. 6, 1969; "Arbitrator Sets Date for U.S. Steel to

Make Proposal on Incentives," *Wall Street Journal*, June 10, 1970; "National Steel Corp. and Allegheny Ludlum Agreed on Incentive Pay," *Wall Street Journal*, July 13, 1970; "U.S. Steel and USW Return to Arbitration on Incentive Pay Issue," *Wall Street Journal*, Aug. 3, 1970; "U.S. Steel and Union Set Aug. 26 Arbitration on Incentive Pay Issue," *Wall Street Journal*, Aug. 5, 1970; "Incentive-Pay Coverage Is Extended at U.S. Steel," *Wall Street Journal*, Nov. 19, 1970; "Ganging Up on the Public," *Wall Street Journal*, June 26, 1970.

58. William T. Hogan, *The 1970s: Critical Years for Steel* (Lanham, MD: Lexington, 1972), 7, 45, 49.

59. Robert Crandall, *The U.S. Steel Industry in Recurrent Crisis* (Washington, DC: Brookings Institution Press, 1981), table 2–7; Philip Shabecoff, "Labor Meets Managers on Steel Output," *Wall Street Journal*, Dec. 15, 1972, 69; Hogan, *The 1970s*, 5; Report of Officers, United Steelworkers of America 16th Constitutional Convention, Sept. 18–22, 1972, box 12, folder 12, Garrett Collection; "No-Strike Accord Reached on Steel," *New York Times*, Mar. 30, 1973.

60. Molony quoted in speech by Conrad Cooper, "General Statement," June 5, 1968," box 1, R. Conrad Cooper Papers, 1927–1980, AIS.1991.01, Archives Services Center, University of Pittsburgh, Pittsburgh, PA; Bernard D. Nossiter, "Steel Pay Pact Is Reached," *Washington Post*, Mar. 29, 1962; Michael K. Drapkin, "Steelworkers Ratify Anti-strike Accord; Buying Hopes It Signals End of Stockpiling," *Wall Street Journal*, Mar. 30, 1973; John Hoerr, "The Steel Experiment," *Atlantic Monthly*, Dec. 1973, 25; Experimental Negotiating Agreement, collection #5588, box 22, Kheel Center.

61. Drapkin, "Steelworkers Ratify Anti-strike Accord."

62. Ibid.; Garrett interview, 21; "ABA Talk on ENA," p. 3, Garrett Collection, box 2, folder 4.

Chapter 6. When the Meek Began to Roar:
Public Employee Unionism in the 1960s

1. Meany quoted in Charles R. Morris, *The Cost of Good Intentions: New York City and the Liberal Experiment, 1960–1975* (New York: W. W. Norton, 1980), 87. Joseph Slater's *Public Workers: Government Employee Unions, the Law, and the State, 1900–1962* (Ithaca, NY: ILR, 2004), offers an excellent overview of that era.

2. Quoted in Damon Stetson, "Transit Mediation Method Made More Flexible," *New York Times*, Nov. 16, 1967, 42.

3. George Taylor, "Collective Bargaining in the Public Sector," *The Next Twenty-Five Years of Industrial Relations*, ed. Gerald Somers (Madison, WI: IRRA, 1973), 27.

4. David L. Cole's notes during a meeting of the Governor's Committee on Public Employee Relations, undated, collection 5588, box 16, folder 1, Kheel Center for Labor-Management Documentation and Archives, Catherwood Library, Cornell University, Ithaca, NY [hereafter, Kheel Center] (emphasis added).

5. "Labor Secretary May Aid Schools," *New York Times*, Jan. 6, 1961; Leonard Buder, "City Schools Pick 5 Labor Advisers," *New York Times*, Feb. 16, 1961; Walter H. Waggoner, "Clara Tea4d, Ex-Head of Briarcliff," *New York Times*, Mar. 4, 1980, D19; Robert McG. Thomas Jr., "Walter Gellhorn, Law Scholar and Professor, Dies at 89, *New York Times*, Dec. 11, 1995, D10;

"Collins Back on RWLB," *New York Times*, Sept. 16, 1945; "Concerns Penalized for Wage Increases," *New York Times*, Nov. 11, 1944.

6. Quoted in Stephen Cole, *The Unionization of Teachers* (New York: Praeger, 1969), 76.

7. Benjamin Fine, "Teacher Strikes Growing in Nation," *New York Times*, Feb. 14, 1947.

8. "Legislature Sets Records in Action: Teacher Pay Rise, Anti-strike, Budget Bills Prominent among Its Measures," *New York Times*, Mar. 19, 1947; "A Legislative Milestone," *New York Times*, Mar. 15, 1947; Slater, *Public Workers*, 94; Anne M. Ross, "Public Employees and the Right to Strike," *Monthly Labor Review* 92, no. 3 (Mar. 1969): 14–15.

9. Leonard Buder, "Night School Teachers Threaten to Quit Unless City Raises Pay," *New York Times*, Jan. 3, 1959; "Night Teachers Act to Resign on February 2," *New York Times*, Jan. 11, 1959; Gene Currivan, "High School Unit Rejects Pay Offer," *New York Times*, Jan. 14, 1959; Leonard Buden, "Teacher Dispute to Be Aired Today," *New York Times*, Feb. 7, 1959; David Selden, *The Teacher Rebellion* (Washington, DC: Howard University Press, 1985), 30.

10. Buder, "Night School Teachers," 3; Gene Currivan, "Theobald Resists Teachers' Threat," *New York Times*, Jan. 4, 1959; "Night Teachers Act"; Currivan, "High School Unit"; Selden, *Teacher Rebellion*, 30.

11. Leonard Buder, "Teachers Resign at High Schools," *New York Times*, Feb. 3, 1959; Buder, "15 Night Schools in City Are Shut," *New York Times*, Feb. 4, 1959; Buder, "5 Centers Set Up in Night Schools," *New York Times*, Feb. 5, 1959; "Night Teachers Protest Hiring," *New York Times*, Feb. 6, 1959; "Teachers Parley Today," *New York Times*, Feb. 9, 1959; Buder, "2nd Mediation Fails in Teachers' Fight over Night Salary," *New York Times*, Feb. 10, 1959; Buder, "Theobald Decries Teachers' Tactics," *New York Times*, Feb. 11, 1959.

12. "City Teacher Unit Sanctions Strike," *New York Times*, Mar. 26, 1960; Myron Lieberman and Michael H. Moscow, *Collective Negotiations for Teachers* (Skokie, IL: Rand McNally, 1966), 36.

13. Robert Terte, "New Union Votes for Teacher Strike," *New York Times*, Apr. 28, 1960; "N.Y. Teachers Strike Will Start Today," *New York Times*, Nov. 7, 1960; Selden, *Teacher Rebellion*, 40–46.

14. Leonard Buder, "Scope Is Disputed—15,000 Join Walkout, Union Head Says," *New York Times*, Nov. 8, 1960; "Teacher Absence by Area," *New York Times*, Nov. 8, 1960; "The Teachers' Outlaw Strike," *New York Times*, Nov. 8, 1960; Robert Terte, "Students Treat Strike as Lark," *New York Times*, Nov. 8, 1960.

15. "Organizations That Wish to Be Considered As Possible Bargaining Agents," box 3, unsorted, George W. Taylor Papers, Manuscript Collections, Biddle Law Library, University of Pennsylvania, Philadelphia [hereafter, Taylor Papers].

16. "Public Hearing: Commission of Inquiry of the Board of Education," Mar. 3, 1961, pp. 22, 72, box 3, unsorted, Taylor Papers.

17. George W. Taylor et al. to Charles H. Silver, president, Board of Education of the City of New York, May 17, 1961, box 3, unsorted, Taylor Papers; Appendix A, "What Is 'Collective Bargaining'?," box 3, unsorted, Taylor Papers; Advisory Ballot for the Commission of Inquiry of the Board of Education," box 3, unsorted, Taylor Papers; "Unions' Methods Puzzle Teachers," *New York Times*, Mar. 29, 1961; Selden, *Teacher Rebellion*, 68.

18. George W. Taylor to Jesse Freidin, June 14, 1961, box 3, Taylor Papers; George W. Taylor

to Charles H. Silver, June 22, 1961, box 3, unsorted, Taylor Papers; "Bargaining Issue Facing Teachers," *New York Times*, June 1, 1961; "School Board's Labor Advisers Resign in Dispute over Report," *New York Times*, June 15, 1961; "Labor Aide Quits School Board Job—He Sided with Commission on Bargaining Poll," *New York Times*, June 22, 1961.

19. Steven Greenhouse, "Theodore W. Kheel, a Go-To Labor Peacemaker in New York, Dies at 96," *New York Times*, Nov. 15, 2010, A27.

20. "Talks Stepped Up in Drive to Avery Teachers' Strike," *New York Times,* Sept. 1, 1963; "Teachers' Strike Barred by Court; Union Is Defiant," *New York Times*, Sept. 6, 1963.

21. Leonard Buder, "School Strike Is Averted; Teachers Accept Offer of $580 Two-Year Raise," *New York Times*, Sept. 9, 1963.

22. Fred Shapiro, "Mediator," *New Yorker,* Aug. 1, 1970.

23. Quoted in A. H. Raskin, "What Makes Teddy Run," *New York Times Sunday Magazine*, Dec. 5, 1965, 52.

24. Leonard Buder, "Mayor Appoints 3 to Try to Head Off Strike by Teachers," *New York Times*, Aug. 24, 1965; "Teachers' Union Gives Deadline," *New York Times*, Aug. 25, 1965.

25. Leonard Buder, "Donovan Refuses to Offer Pay Rise," *New York Times*, Aug. 26, 1965.

26. Leonard Buder, "School Talks Make Some Progress," *New York Times*, Sept. 5, 1965; Joseph Michalak, "Mayor Steps into Teacher Talks," *New York Herald Tribune*, Sept. 8, 1965.

27. Draft of letter to Robert Wagner, Sept. 10, 1965, box 3, unsorted, Taylor Papers; Leonard Buder, "One Issue Is Left in Teacher Talks: Only 'Money Matters' Remain in Negotiations," *New York Times*, Sept. 10, 1965; Buder, "New School Pact Averts a Strike; Terms Approved," *New York Times*, Sept. 11, 1965; Buder, "Teachers' Strike Avert but Questions Are Raised," *New York Times*, Sept. 12, 1965, E11; "New Pay Increases," *New York Times*, Sept. 11, 1965.

28. "Lloyd K. Garrison, Lawyer, Dies; Leader in Social Causes Was 92," *New York Times*, Oct. 3, 1991, D20; "School Board Statement," *New York Times*, Sept. 11, 1965; Leonard Buder, "New School Pact Averts a Pact; Terms Approved," *New York Times*, Sept. 11, 1965.

29. Homer Bigart, "New Talks Today: Quill Scores Mayor—Says Walkout Could Last a Month," *New York Times*, Jan. 2, 1966. As it turns out, it was Quill himself, not the judge, who died suddenly after the strike.

30. "Protecting the Cities," *New York Times,* Jan. 16, 1966, E12; "Transit Walkout Termed Obsolete, Reuther Urges New System to End Public Strikes," *New York Times*, Jan. 18, 1966; "Javits Bill Seeks New Strike Curbs," *New York Times*, Jan. 21, 1966; "New Mediation Law Is Urged for State," *New York Times*, Jan. 23, 1966; A. H. Raskin, "Search for That Elusive No-Strike Law," *New York Times*, Jan. 31, 1966.

31. Emanuel Perlmutter, "Rockefeller Seeks New Way to Curb Municipal Strikes," *New York Times,* Jan. 16, 1966; Lloyd Reynolds, "A Tribute to E. Wight Bakke," in *The Next Twenty-Five Years of Industrial Relations*, ed. Gerald Somers (Madison, IRRA, 1973), 205–7.

32. "Panel on Public Strike to Hold Hearing Here," *New York Times*, Feb. 27, 1966.

33. Notes by David L. Cole, undated, p. 1, box 16, folder 1, David L. Cole Papers, Kheel Center [hereafter, Cole Papers].

34. Ibid. (exclamation in the original).

35. Ibid. (emphasis in the original). Cole forgot that John L. Lewis repeatedly sanctioned coal miners' strikes that threatened the welfare of the public during and after World War II.

36. Ibid.

37. Ibid.

38. Ibid. (emphasis added).

39. Ibid. (emphasis in the original).

40. Ibid.

41. David L. Cole's notes on Governor's Committee on Public Employee Relations meeting, Jan. 29, 1966, collection 5588, box 14, folder 13, Kheel Center.

42. Governor's Committee on Public Employee Relations, *Final Report*, Mar. 31, 1966, iv, 2ff, box 3, unsorted, Taylor Papers.

43. Ibid., 9–14, 18–19.

44. Ibid., 9–14, 18–19, 21–34, 25, 27–28, 41–44.

45. Ibid., 51–57; Robert Helsby, "Impact of the Taylor Law on Public Schools (1968–1970)," *Journal of Collective Negotiations* 1, no. 1 (Feb. 1972): 13; Sydney Schanberg, "State Panel Calls for Replacement of Condon-Wadlin," *New York Times*, Apr. 8, 1966, 1–58.

46. Governor's Committee, *Final Report*, 53, 57.

47. Ibid., 60–65, 68.

48. Ibid., 65–67.

49. Ibid., 27, 71–80.

50. Will Lissner, "Union Aides Decry State Labor Plan," *New York Times*, Apr. 10, 1966; Frank S. Adam, "Preparing a Basic New Law for New York," *New York Times*, Apr. 18, 1966; Richard L. Madden, "Travia Rejects Experts' Plan to Replace Condon-Wadlin Act," *New York Times*, Apr. 13, 1966; Madden, "State Bill Scored on Public Strikes," *New York Times*, May 7, 1966.

51. Richard L. Madden, "Compromise on City's Tax Plan Held Vital for Albany Approval," *New York Times*, Apr. 16, 1966; Madden, "State Bill Scored"; A. H. Raskin, "Wanted: A Substitute for Condon-Wadlin," *New York Times*, Apr. 17, 1966; Ronald Donovan, *Administering the Taylor Law: Public Employee Relations in New York* (Ithaca, NY: ILR, 1990), 45ff.

52. Donovan, *Administering the Taylor Law*, 49–53; Sydney Schanberg, "Accord Reached on No-Strike Law: Governor and Legislative Leaders Compromise," *New York Times*, Apr. 2, 1967; Peter Millones, "Architect of Taylor Law Says Right to Strike Is Overemphasized," *New York Times*, Oct. 16, 1968.

53. Peter Millones, "Governor Signs New State Law to Curb Public Employee Strikes," *New York Times*, Apr. 22, 1967; Millones, "Public Employee Unions Say Condon Law Substitute Will Increase Walkouts," *New York Times*, Apr. 4, 1967.

54. David Jones, "Militancy Sweeps Schools in U.S. as Teachers Turn to Strikes, Sanctions and Mass Resignation," *New York Times*, June 11, 1967.

55. Damon Stetson, "500,000 in the City Go without Heat in Housing Strike," *New York Times*, Jan. 28, 1967; "Sewer Workers Walk Out Here," *New York Times*, May 12, 1967; "End of Walkout at Garages Seen," *New York Times*, Feb. 4, 1968.

56. Leonard Buder, "There Will Be No Teachers, No Schools," *New York Times*, Sept. 10, 1967; Fred Hechinger, "Fallout from the Strike," *New York Times*, Sept. 24, 1967; Richard Kahlenberg, *Tough Liberal: Albert Shanker and the Battles over Schools, Unions, Race, and Democracy* (New York: Columbia University Press, 2007), 77–81.

57. "Sanitation Dispute Issues," *New York Times*, Feb. 6, 1968; Mark Tolchin, "150 Firemen on Patrol to Control Burning Trash," *New York Times*, Feb. 10, 1968; Martin Arnold, "Union Leaders Say Mayor's Call for the Guard Solidified Labor," *New York Times*, Feb. 17, 1968.

58. Memo from George W. Taylor to Sol Corbin, May 9, 1968, box 13, folder 4, Cole Papers; memo from Richard Winfield to Governor's Committee, Apr. 11, 1968, box 14, folder 4, Cole Papers.

59. David L. Cole's notes, p. 3, box 14, folder 3, Cole Papers (emphasis in the original).

60. Damon Stetson, "Firemen Remove No-Strike Clause," *New York Times*, Aug. 21, 1968; Stetson, "Goldberg Renews Mediation Effort: Sanitation Union Warns of Possible Strike Next Week," *New York Times*, Oct. 10, 1968; Stetson, "Goldberg Presses to Avert a City Garbage Strike," *New York Times*, Oct. 12, 1968; Stetson, "2 Leaders of Hospital Strike Enter Jail as Hundreds Protest," *New York Times*, Dec. 14, 1968; A. H. Raskin, "The Trouble with the Taylor Law," *New York Times*, Nov. 3, 1968.

61. Current Developments Section, Bureau of National Affairs, *Daily Labor Report*, No. 204, Oct. 17, 1968, "Conference on Public Employee Relations Hears New York Lab Debated and Debated," AA1, box 16, folder 3, Cole Papers; Raskin, "Trouble with the Taylor Law." The quotation is from "Goldberg Cautions in Labor Disputes," *New York Times*, Oct. 15, 1968.

62. Damon Stetson, "Taylor Law Held Failure by Kheel," *New York Times*, Oct. 13, 1968.

63. "'Impasse Procedure—the Finality Question': Remarks of Dr. George W. Taylor at Governor's Committee on Public Employee Relations" (official text), box 16, folder 3, collection 5588, Cole Papers; Bureau of National Affairs, *Daily Labor Report*, Oct. 17, 1968, EE1—5, Kheel Center; Millones, "Architect of Taylor Law," 32.

64. Governor's Committee on Public Employee Relations, *Report of Jan. 23, 1969*, 3ff, Kheel Center.

65. "Poll Find Majority Would Ban Strikes by Teacher Unions," *New York Times*, Mar. 20, 1968.

66. Quoted in A. H. Raskin, "Taylor Law: Another Effort to Prevent Public Strikes," *New York Times*, Mar. 9, 1969, E6; Peter Millones, "The Antilabor Mood Reflected: Stiffer Provisions in Taylor Law Show Public Reaction," *New York Times*, Mar. 15, 1969.

67. A. H. Raskin, "Taylor Law: Another Effort to Prevent Public Strikes," *New York Times*, Mar. 9, 1969, E6; Bill Kovach, "State G.O.P. Pressing Strike-Law Vote," *New York Times*, Mar. 5, 1969.

68. Damon Stetson, "Revised Taylor Law Is Called 'Unduly Harsh' by Dr. Taylor," *New York Times*, June 8, 1969.

69. On the last point, see chapter 8 in this volume.

70. Current Developments Section, Bureau of National Affairs, *Daily Labor Report*, No. 204, Oct. 17, 1968; "Conference on Public Employee Relations Hears New York Lab Debated and Debated," AA-7, box 16, folder 3, Cole Papers; Stetson, "Revised Taylor Law"; David Cole, interview by Martha Ross, p. 75, Federal Mediation and Conciliation Service Papers, Nov. 11, 1974, George Washington University Library.

Chapter 7. "How Can We Avoid a Columbia?"
The Student Revolt, 1964–71

1. "Master Planner," *Time*, Oct. 17, 1960, 69.

2. On Kerr's efforts to persuade the regents to change university policies on free speech in the late 1950s and early 1960s, see Ray Colvig, *Turning Points and Ironies: Issues and Events— Berkeley, 1959–67* (Berkeley: University of California Press, 2004).

3. Lawrence Davies, "Clark Kerr Takes Key Role in Urging Peace Talks," *New York Times*, Feb. 11, 1968.

4. Grace Hechinger, "Clark Kerr, Leading Public Educator and Former Head of California's Universities, Dies at 92," *New York Times*, Dec. 2, 2003, A28.

5. For summaries, see *Priorities for Action: Final Report of the Carnegie Commission on Higher Education* (New York: McGraw-Hill Education, 1973); *Sponsored Research of the Carnegie Commission on Higher Education* (New York: McGraw-Hill Education, 1975); *A Digest of Reports of the Carnegie Commission on Higher Education* (New York, McGraw-Hill, 1974); and Carnegie Council on Policy Studies in Higher Education, *Three Thousand Futures: The Next Twenty Years for Higher Education* (San Francisco: Jossey-Bass, 1980).

6. Paul Goodman, "Thoughts on Berkeley," *New York Review of Books*, Jan. 14, 1965, repr. in *The Berkeley Student Revolt: Facts and Interpretations*, ed. Seymour Martin Lipset and Sheldon Wolin (Garden City, NY: Anchor, 1965), 316.

7. Kerr quoted in A. H. Raskin, "The Berkeley Affair: Mr. Kerr vs. Mr. Savio & Co.," *New York Times Magazine*, Feb. 14, 1965.

8. Clark Kerr, *The Uses of the University*, 3rd ed. (Berkeley: University of California Press, 1982), vii, 1; William W. Scranton, *The Report of the President's Commission on Campus Unrest* (Washington, DC: President's Commission, n.d. [1970]).

9. Clark Kerr, interview by the author, Aug. 7, 1992 (personal possession of the author), 7–8.

10. Jacques Barzun, *The American University: How It Runs, Where It Is Going* (New York: Harper and Row, 1968), 67, 70.

11. Robert Nisbet, *Teachers and Scholars: A Memoir of Berkeley in Depression and War* (New Brunswick, NJ: Transaction, 1992), 199, 201ff.

12. William Clyde DeVane, *Higher Education in the Twentieth-Century America* (Cambridge, MA: Harvard University Press, 1965), 127, 131; Kerr, *Uses of the University*, ch. 2; Grace Hechinger, "Clark Kerr, Leading Public Educator and Former Head of California's Universities, Dies at 92," *New York Times*, Dec. 2, 2003, A28.

13. "Master Planner," *Time*, Oct. 17, 1960, 59; Kerr, *Uses of the University*, 7–8.

14. Smelser quoted in Page Smith, *Killing the Spirit: Higher Education in America* (New York: Viking, 1990), 156; Clark Kerr, *TG&B* (Berkeley: University of California Press, 2001), 2: xx; "Master Planner," *Time*, Oct. 17, 1960, 60.

15. Kerr, *Uses of the University*, 103–4.

16. Max Heirich and Sam Kaplan, "Yesterday's Discord," in Lipset and Wolin, *The Berkeley Student Revolt*, 10–35; Robert Cohen, *When the Old Left Was Young: Student Radicals and America's First Mass Student Movement, 1929–1941* (New York: Oxford University Press,

1993), chs. 2, 3, 5; Kerr, *TG&B*, 2: 124–25. The line about Berkeley's ultraleft reputation is from Nisbet, *Teachers and Scholars*, 55.

17. Kerr, *TG&B*, 2: 126–27; Jo Freeman, "A Short History of the University of California Speaker Ban" (2000), http://www.jofreeman.com/sixtiesprotest/speakerban.htm; Freeman, "From Freedom Now! to Free Speech: The FSM's Roots in the Bay Area Civil Rights Movement," in *The Free Speech Movement: Reflections on Berkeley in the 1960s*, ed. Robert Cohen and Reginald E. Zelnick, 73–82 (Berkeley: University of California Press, 2002).

18. Kerr, *TG&B*, 2: 180; Clark Kerr, "Fall of 1964 at Berkeley: Confrontation Yields to Reconciliation," in Cohen and Zelnick, *Free Speech Movement*, 362–64; "The Seventh Alexander Meiklejohn Award," *Bulletin of the AAUP* 50, no. 2 (June 1964): 185–87.

19. Kerr, *TG&B*, 2: 129, 154; dissenters quoted in Heirich and Kaplan, "Yesterday's Discord," 26; Robert Cohen, "The Many Meanings of the FSMs," in Cohen and Zelnick, *Free Speech Movement*, 13–15.

20. "Don Mulford—Longtime Assemblyman," *SF Gate*, Mar. 28, 2000, https://www.sfgate.com/news/article/Don-Mulford-Longtime-Assemblyman-2792988.php; "U.C. Rights Stand Hit by Legislators," *Oakland Tribune*, Apr. 28, 1964; memo of Sheriffs to Kerr, May 19, 1964, box 70, file no. 165–95–12 ("Civil Rights Demonstrations"), collection CU-149, Bancroft Library, University of California, Berkeley. These protests are described in Jo Freeman, *At Berkeley in the '60s: The Education of an Activist, 1961–1965* (Bloomington: Indiana University Press, 2004), chs. 17–23; W. J. Rorabaugh, *Berkeley at War: The 1960s* (New York: Oxford University Press, 1989), ch. 2.

21. Waldo Martin, "Holding One Another: Mario Savio and the Freedom Struggle in Mississippi and Berkeley," in Cohen and Zelnick, *Free Speech Movement*, 83–102; Bradford Cleveland, "A Letter to Undergraduates," *SLATE Supplement Report* 1, no. 4 (Sept. 1964), repr. in Lipset and Wolin, *The Berkeley Student Revolt*, 72 (emphasis in the original).

22. Sheriffs to R. A. Hudgens, Mar. 20, 1964, box 70, file no. 165–95–12 ("Civil Rights Demonstrations"), collection CU-149, Bancroft Library, University of California, Berkeley; Robert Cohen, *Freedom's Orator: Mario Savio and the Radical Legacy of the 1960s* (New York: Oxford University Press, 2009), 79–81; Max Heirich, *The Beginning: Berkeley 1964* (New York: Columbia University Press, 1971), ch. 2.

23. Kerr, *TG&B*, 2: 180.

24. Ibid., 1: 20.

25. Clark Kerr, "The University: Civil Rights and Civil Responsibilities," in *Documentary Supplements to TG&B* (Berkeley, CA: Berkeley Public Policy Press, 2003), 65, 76; Cohen, *Freedom's Orator* (New York: Oxford University Press, 2009), 79–82ff.

26. Kerr, *TG&B*, 2: 180.

27. Katherine A. Towle, statement to presidents or chairmen and advisers of all student committees regarding enforcement of provisions of the policy on "Use of University Facilities," Sept. 14, 1964, in Kerr, *Documentary Supplements to TG&B*, 79–81.

28. Matthew Dallek, *The Right Moment* (New York: Oxford University Press, 2004), 86–88ff; Kerr, *TG&B*, 2: 212–13.

29. Freeman, *At Berkeley*, 219; Lange quoted in Linda Gordon, *Dorothea Lange: A Life beyond Limits* (New York: W. W. Norton, 2009), 416; Cohen, *Freedom's Orator*, 214; Kerr, *TG&B*, 2: 215.

30. Robert H. Cole, "Dec. 1964," in Cohen and Zelnick, *Free Speech Movement*, 422.

31. Mario Savio, "We Want a University," published in *Humanities, an Arena of Critique and Commitment*, no. 2 (Dec. 1964), repr. in Lipset and Wolin, *Berkeley Student Revolt*, 216–19.

32. Ibid.

33. Mario Savio, "The Uncertain Future of the Multiversity," *Harper's Magazine*, Oct. 1966, 88–89; Savio, "We Want a University," repr. in Lipset and Wolin, *Berkeley Student Revolt*, 208.

34. Robert H. Cole, "Dec. 1964," in Cohen and Zelnick, *Free Speech Movement* (2002), 425.

35. Lisa McGirr, *Suburban Warriors: The Origins of the New American Right* (Princeton, NJ: Princeton University Press, 2001), chs. 1–3; Dallek, *Right Moment*, esp. ch. 9.

36. Heirich, *Beginning*, 229–50; Sheldon Wolin and John Schaar, *The Berkeley Rebellion and Beyond* (New York: Vintage, 1970), 49.

37. "Kerr Fired by Regents at Berkeley: University Head Was Criticized by Governor Reagan," *Washington Post*, Jan. 21, 1967, A1.

38. Quoted in Fred M. Hechinger, "Reagan vs. Kerr—Contest at Berkeley," *New York Times*, Jan. 15, 1967, E13.

39. Tom Bates, *Rads: The 1970 Bombing of the Army Math Research Center at the University of Wisconsin and Its Aftermath* (New York: HarperCollins, 1992).

40. James Angell to Roswell Ham, box 71, folder 31, Collection CU-149, Bancroft Library, University of California, Berkeley; "Another Campus Crisis: Finding a President," *Newsweek*, Aug. 31, 1970; "New Presidents Named at Duke, Penn State, Nebraska, Tennessee: 270 Other Colleges Looking," *Chronicle of Higher Education*, Jan. 5, 1970.

41. Remark by Clark Kerr in conversation with the author in his UC-Berkeley office, Aug. 7, 1992.

42. Robben W. Fleming, interview, tapes 1–4, Oral History Project, University of Wisconsin, Madison; Fleming, *Tempests into Rainbows: Managing Turbulence* (Ann Arbor: University of Michigan Press, 1996), 87; Ralph E. Hansen, Director of Department of Protection and Security, to George Alderson, Clerk of Courts, Dane County Courthouse, Apr. 30, 1968, Robben Fleming Collection, Bentley Historical Library, University of Wisconsin–Madison [hereafter, Fleming Collection]; "UW Student Demonstration against Dow Chemical Co," *Connections* 1, no. 4 (Apr. 16–30, 1968); "The Romance of Robben Head," *Connections* 1, no. 4 (Apr. 16–30, 1968).

43. Memo from "jhh" to senior staff, Sept. 5, 1969, box 111, folder "Vietnam War Teach-in, Sept. 1969"; memo, Robben W. Fleming to executive officers, Sept. 5, 1969; Robben W. Fleming to Regents memo, "Speech at Viet Nam Forum," Sept. 9, 1969; "Action Teach-in on the Viet Nam War"; "Vietnam—Time's Up!" (emphasis in original), all in Fleming Collection.

44. "Reflections on Viet Nam: An Address by RWF to the 'Action Teach-In,' Ann Arbor, Mich. Sept. 19, 1969," Fleming Collection.

45. "Fleming Grabs Tiger by Tail," *Detroit News*, Sept. 23, 1969; Robben W. Fleming memo to Michael Radcock, Sept. 22, 1969, Fleming Collection.

46. Columbia Strike Coordinating Committee, 1968, SDS, "Create Two, Three, Many Columbias, That Is the Watchword!," https://studentantiwar.blogs.brynmawr.edu/stories -from-the-frontlines/frountline-in-usa/create-two-three-many-columbias-that-is-the- watchword/.

47. Robben W. Fleming to Linowitz, Oct. 9, 1969, box 99, folder "ACE—Special Committee (1)," Presidential Files Collection, Bentley Historical Library, University of Michigan–Ann Arbor [hereafter, Presidential Files].

48. "Colleges Urged to Develop Better Links to Students," *New York Times*, Apr. 2, 1970.

49. "How Can We Avoid a Columbia?," Sept. 13, 1969, box 7, folder "Students," Fleming Collection.

50. Albert Reiss Jr. to Robben Fleming, July 2, 1968, folder "Student Unrest," Fleming Collection.

51. "How Can We Avoid a Columbia?" (emphasis added), box 7, folder "Students," Sept. 13, 1969, Fleming Collection; Wilbur K. Pierpont to Peter W. Forsythe, memorandum—confidential, Fleming Collection; A. B. Ueker to J. P. Brinkerhoff, memorandum, June 4, 1969, Fleming Collection; "Building Service Security," June 5, 1969, Fleming Collection; memo [no date or author listed], Fleming Collection.

52. John O'Connor, "Fleming Assaults FBI 'Dirty Tricks,'" *Ann Arbor News*, Nov. 25, 1977, box 17, folder "Interviews: TV; Newspaper; Magazine" (1), Fleming Collection. For the FBI's effort to undermine Kerr at Berkeley, see Seth Rosenfeld, *Subversives: The FBI's War on Student Radicals and Reagan's Rise to Power* (New York: Farrar, Straus and Giroux, 2012).

53. Robben W. Fleming to Senate Assembly, Mar. 31, 1971, and "The UM University Judiciary System" proposed draft, Mar. 31, 1971, box 202, unlabeled folder, College of Literature, Science & the Arts Collection, Bentley Historical Library, University of Michigan–Ann Arbor; Hester Pulling, "Discipline: Fall Issue at 'U'?," *Michigan Daily*, June 24, 1970, box 7, unsorted, College of Literature, Science and the Arts Collection, Bentley Historical Library, University of Michigan–Ann Arbor.

54. David D. Dill, Case Studies in University Governance, National Association of State Universities and Land-Grant Colleges, final draft (1970), pp. vii, 253, 257, box 102, folder "NASULGC," Presidents' Office Collection, Bentley Historical Library, University of Michigan–Ann Arbor; "Some Proposals for the Governance of the College of Literature, Science, and the Arts," box 2, folder "Testimony (Robben W. Fleming), Aug. 12, 1974," p. 3, Fleming Collection; John McConnell, interview by the author, July 12, 1990, 66, Kheel Center for Labor-Management Documentation and Archives, Cornell University, Ithaca, NY.

55. Scranton, *The Report of the President's Commission*.

56. Malcolm G. Scully, "Teaching Assistants' Strike at Wisconsin Raises Issue of Faculty Control over Educational Policy," *Chronicle of Higher Education*, Mar. 30, 1970, 1.

57. Robert Sherrill, "Spiro Agnew: Is This Our Spirit of '76?" *The Nation*, Oct. 30, 1972, 395; "Strike Ends at U. of Michigan; Pact Calls for 10% Blacks in '73," *New York Times*, Apr. 3, 1970; Fleming, *Tempests into Rainbows*, 207, 214, 217–18; "Statement of the Board of Regents, University of Michigan," box 111, folder "Policy, 1969–70," Presidential Files; "Students Reject Apology by Aide," Mar. 31, 1970, https://www.nytimes.com/1970/03/31/archives/students-reject-apology-by-aide-strikers-at-michigan-want-president.html.

58. Robben Fleming, "Faculty Strike Policy," undated handwritten note [June 1970?], box 103, folders "Strike and Boycott Policy" and "Faculty Pay Policy during Strikes," Sept. 4, 1970, Presidential Files.

59. "399 Students Seize Building at Harvard and Eject 9 Deans," *New York Times*, Apr. 10,

1969; "400 Police Quell Harvard Uprising—41 Students Reported Hurt," *New York Times*, Apr. 11, 1969; Richard Lee Howell, "Harvard University and the Indochina War: From the Takeover of University Hall in the Spring of 1969 through the Aftermath of the Invasion of Cambodia and the Kent State Killings in the Spring of 1970," PhD thesis, Michigan State University, 1987, 64–66. Several students, among them the U.S. secretary of the Air Force's children and historian Arthur Schlesinger's children, escaped arrest by jumping out of windows.

60. Huntington quoted in Seymour Martin Lipset and David Riesman, *Education and Politics at Harvard: Two Essays Prepared for the Carnegie Commission on Higher Education* (New York: McGraw-Hill, 1975), 225.

61. Roger Rosenblatt, *Coming Apart: A Memoir of the Harvard Wars of 1969* (Boston: Little, Brown, 1997), 112–13, 194–97.

62. Harvard University New Office, press releases, Sept. 12, 1969, and June 16, 1971, Dunlop biographical clippings file (uncatalogued), Harvard University Archives, Pusey Library, Harvard University, Cambridge, MA; Phyllis Keller and Morton Keller, *Making Harvard Modern* (New York: Oxford University Press, 2001), 362.

63. Lawrence E. Eichel et al., *The Harvard Strike* (Boston: Houghton Mifflin, 1970), 340–43; Committee on Governance, "Organization and Structure on Governing Boards and the President's Office," Mar. 1971, quoted in Keller, *Making Harvard Modern*, 362–63.

64. "One Perspective from 5 University Hall," revised draft, Aug. 27, 1986, p. 4, Asc. 11522, box 17, folder "350th Celebration," John T. Dunlop Papers, Harvard University Archives, Pusey Library, Harvard University, Cambridge, MA.

65. Dan Swanson, "Good-bye, John," *Harvard Crimson*, Feb. 20, 1973 (emphasis in original).

66. Clark Kerr, "Industrial Relations and University Relations," *Proceedings of the Twenty-First Annual Winter Meeting, Industrial Relations Research Association, December 28–29, 1968*, ed. Gerald Somers (Madison, WI: IRRA, 1969), 18, 19.

Chapter 8. A Whole Different Ball Game, 1968–81

1. Quoted in Richard Goldstein, "Robin Roberts Dies at 83; Led Phillies Whiz Kids to Pennant," *New York Times*, May 7, 2010, B15.

2. Robin Roberts with C. Paul Rogers III, *Throwing Hard Easy* (Chicago: Triumph, 2003), 217–19.

3. "Interview with Marvin Miller" by Fay Vincent, Mar. 26, 2004, tapes 2 and 5, Oral History Collection, Society for American Baseball Research, Walter Cronkite School of Journalism and Mass Communication, Arizona State University, Phoenix.

4. Robert F. Burk, *Marvin Miller: Baseball Revolutionary* (Urbana: University of Illinois Press, 2015), 56–65.

5. See chapter 5 for a discussion of the Kaiser Steel Long-Range Planning Committee.

6. James B. Dworkin, *Owners versus Players: Baseball and Collective Bargaining* (Boston: Auburn House, 1981), 27–28; Luther Evans, "Majors Clear Way for New Coordinator," *Miami Herald*, Mar. 5, 1966, repr. in *Late Innings: A Documentary History of Baseball, 1945–1972*, ed. Dean Sullivan (Lincoln: University of Nebraska Press, 2002), 203–4.

7. Marvin Miller, *A Whole Different Ball Game: The Inside Story of the Baseball Revolution* (Chicago: I. R. Dee, 2004), 23ff.

8. John Helyar, *Lords of the Realm*, 33; Carmen Lee, "Obituary: J. Bruce Johnston/Tenacious Negotiator for Steel Companies," *Pittsburgh Post-Gazette*, July 7, 2001: http://old.post-gazette.com/obituaries/20010707johnston0707p2.asp.

9. Helyar, *Lords*, 33.

10. Ed Edmonds and Frank Houdek, *Baseball Meets the Law* (Jefferson, NC: McFarland, 2017), 114–17.

11. Ibid., 118–23. *Flood v. Kuhn*, 407 U.S. 258, 281 (1972).

12. Edmonds and Houdek, *Baseball*, 119–20, 122; Robert McFadden, "John Gaherin, 85, Negotiator for Newspapers and Baseball," *New York Times*, Jan. 31, 2000, A23.

13. Quoted in Robert Korstad and Nelson Lichtenstein, "Opportunities Found and Lost: Labor, Radicals and the Early Civil Rights Movement," *Journal of American History* 75, no. 3 (1988): 811.

14. Lewis Gill, interview by Jim McDonald, Aug. 29, 1990, National Academy of Arbitrators, History Committee Interview, https://naarb.org/interviews/LewisGill.PDF; Burk, *Marvin Miller*, 153; Jerry Flint, "David L. Cole, 75, Lawyer, Dead; Noted Mediator and Arbitrator," *New York Times*, Jan. 26, 1978.

15. Burk, *Marvin Miller*, 148; Damon Stetson, "Peter Seitz, 78, the Arbitrator in Baseball Free-Agent Case," *New York Times*, Oct. 19, 1983, D25.

16. Statement from the Major League Baseball Players Association, Dec. 16, 1974, #5733, box 1, folder 22, Peter Seitz Papers [hereafter, Seitz Papers], Kheel Center for Labor-Management Documentation and Archives, Catherwood Library, Cornell University, Ithaca, NY [hereafter, Kheel Center].

17. Statement by Chairman of Arbitration Panel, #5733, box 2, folder 2, Seitz Papers; Decision No. 29, Grievance Nos. 75–27 and 75–28, in the Matter of the Arbitration between the Twelve Clubs . . . and Major League Baseball Players Association, Dec. 23, 1975, box 2, folder 2, Seitz Papers; Joseph Durso, "Arbitrator Frees 2 Baseball Stars," *New York Times*, Dec. 24, 1975; Red Smith, "Wanted: New Ghostwriters," *New York Times*, Dec. 28, 1975, 139.

18. Joseph Durso, "Arbitrator Frees 2 Baseball Stars," *New York Times*, Dec. 24, 1975.

19. Murray Chass, "A Pink-Slip Thanks for a Major Decision," *New York Times*, Aug. 22, 2013, B16; Roberts quoted in Richard Goldstein, "Marvin Miller, Union Leader Who Changed Baseball, Dies at 95," *New York Times*, Nov. 27, 2012.

20. If inflation is included, the GDP increased more than 1,100 percent during those years (Susan B. Carter et al., eds., *The Historical Statistics of the United States, Millennial Edition* [New York: Cambridge University Press, 2006]), table Ca74–90, Gross Domestic Product, by Major Component, 1929–2002; Carter et al., *Historical Statistics*, table 149–158, Implicit Price Deflation for Gross Domestic Product and Major Components: 1929–2002; Carter et al., *Historical Statistics*, table Cg281–291, Indexes of National Productivity, by Sector and Type of Goods: 1947–2000).

21. Robert J. Samuelson, *The Great Inflation and Its Aftermath* (New York: Random House, 2008), 28–29, 261–62.

22. Carter et al., *Handbook of Labor Statistics 1975—Reference Edition* (Washington, DC:

U.S. Department of Labor, Bureau of Labor Statistics, 1975), table Ce69–90, Gross Savings and Investments, by Sectors and Types: 1929–2002; Roger Lowenstein, *While America Aged* (New York: Penguin, 2008), 9.

23. Bureau of Labor Statistics, U.S. Department of Labor, *Historical Labor Statistics*, 389. By 2016, unions had fallen to merely 10.7 percent of the labor force—lower than at any time since 1930; Bureau of Labor Statistics, U.S. Department of Labor, "Union Membership Rate 10.7 Percent in 2016," *Economics Daily*, Feb. 9, 2017, https://www.bls.gov/opub/ted/2017/union-membership-rate-10-point-7-percent-in-2016.htm.

24. Carter et al., *Handbook of Labor Statistics*, table 97, Average Union Rates for Selected Trades, by City, 1947–73, 236; Carter et al., *Handbook of Labor Statistics*, table 123, The Consumer Price Index and Major Groups, 1935–1974, 314.

25. Carter et al., *Handbook of Labor Statistics*, table 96, Indexes of Average Straight-Time Hourly Earnings of Men in Selected Production Occupation in Nonelectrical Machinery Manufacturing, Selected Metropolitan Areas, 1945–73, 235.

26. Bureau of Labor Statistics, U.S. Department of Labor, *Employment and Earnings, United States, 1909–1975*, Bulletin 1312–10 (Washington, DC: U.S. Department of Labor, 1976), 303; Lowenstein, *While America Aged*, 35–36.

27. Quoted in A. H. Raskin, "What Makes Teddy Kheel Run," *New York Times Sunday Magazine*, Dec. 5, 1965, 161.

28. Carter et al., *Handbook of Labor Statistics*, table Cb18–22, Real Gross Domestic Product—Trends and Fluctuations: 1952–2001; Carter et al., *Handbook of Labor Statistics*, table Cc1–2, Consumer Price Indexes for All Items—1774–2003; Carter et al., *Handbook of Labor Statistics*, table Cb24–27, Unemployment Rates: 1940–2003; Alan S. Blinder, *Economic Policy and the Great Stagflation* (New York: Academic Press, 1979), 64; Leonard Silk, "Productivity and Inflation," *New York Times*, Jan. 12, 1979, D2; Steven Rattner, "Productivity Rate Causes Worry: Expert Warn Nation about Slower Growth," *New York Times*, May 8, 1979, D1–2; David Warsh, "US Slips Again in Productivity," *Boston Globe*, July 31, 1979; Alfred L. Malabre Jr., "Factory Labor Costs Soar in U.S. but Hardly Budge in Japan," *Wall Street Journal*, Oct. 15, 1980; Bureau of Labor Statistics, U.S. Department of Labor, Economic News Release, Table 1, Work Stoppages Involving 1,000 or More Workers, 1947–2016, last modified Feb. 9, 2018, https://www.bls.gov/news.release/wkstp.t01.htm.

29. Carter et al., *Handbook of Labor Statistics*, table 159, Work Stoppages in the United States, 188–1973, 391. For the militancy of the early 1970s, see *Rebel Rank and File: Labor Militancy and Revolt from Below in the Long 1970s*, ed. Aaron Brenner et al. (London: Verso, 2010).

30. Joseph Kraft may have been the first columnist to use the phrase in the United States. See "The Battle: Stagflation," *Washington Post*, Feb. 25, 1971, A21.

31. Carter et al., *Handbook of Labor Statistics*, table Ba478–486, Labor Force, Employment, Unemployment: 1938–2000. High inflation and high unemployment persisted into the mid-1980s. Unemployment was even worse for African American workers—usually twice that of white workers.

32. "Can Capitalism Survive?" *Time* 106, no. 2, July 14, 1975.

33. The 1950–53 war in Korea ended in a ceasefire.

34. Philip Shabecoff, "Building Leaders Move to Control Pay-Price Spiral," *New York Times*, Jan. 22, 1971; Thomas O'Hanlon, "The Unchecked Power of the Building Trades," *Fortune* 78, no. 6 (Dec. 1968), 102–3; David Lipsky and Henry Farber, "The Composition of Strike Activity in the Construction Industry," *Industrial and Labor Relations Review* 29, no. 3 (Apr. 1976): 388; Bureau of Labor Statistics, U.S. Department of Labor, *Employment and Earnings, United States, 1909–75*, Bulletin 1312–10 (Washington, DC: Government Printing Office, 1976), 3, 26; Bureau of Labor Statistics, *Handbook of Labor Statistics*, 105–7, 409. For new construction as a proportion of gross national product, see Richard Clough, *Construction Contracting*, 4th ed. (New York: Wiley, 1981), 23.

35. Bryon E. Calame, "An Iron Hand: How a Business Agent Runs His Union Local with No Interference," *Wall Street Journal*, Apr. 26, 1972, p. 1.

36. Shultz quoted in "Nixon Establishes Building Bargaining Panel," *Wall Street Journal*, Sept. 23, 1969. Also see Merriman Smith, "Nixon Sets Agency for Job Rows," *Chicago Daily Defender*, Sept. 23, 1969; Robert Young, "Board to Seek Building Peace," *Chicago Tribune*, Sept. 23, 1969; "Building Industry Ills under Study," *Chicago Tribune*, Nov. 16, 1969, D1.

37. John T. Dunlop, "Wage and Price Controls As Seen by a Controller," *Proceedings of the 1975 Annual Meeting of the Industrial Relations Research Association*, ed. James L. Stern and Barbara D. Dennis (Madison, WI: Industrial Relations Research Association, 1976), 462–63. Also see Dunlop and Arthur D. Hill, *The Wage Adjustment Board: Wartime Stabilization in the Building and Construction Industry* (Cambridge, MA: Harvard University Press, 1950), 75.

38. Testimony on William E. Dunn, Hearings before the Committee on Banking, Housing and Urban Affairs, United State Senate, 92nd cong., 1st sess., on S. 2712, Nov. 1–5, 1971 (Washington, DC: Government Printing Office, 1971), 277; "Wage Settlements in Construction Pared by Federal Panel," *Wall Street Journal*, Jan. 5, 1972, 18; Byron E. Calame, "Nixon Panel Bars Painters' Pay Rises in First Rejection," *Wall Street Journal*, June 7, 1971, 2; Elliot Carlson, "Panel Nears Pay Stabilizing Breakthrough," *Wall Street Journal*, July 9, 1971, 3; "President Takes First Firm Step to Stop Building Cost Escalation," *Wall Street Journal*, Feb. 24, 1971, 3; Dunlop, "Wage and Price Controls," 457–63.

39. Howard G. Foster, "Industrial Relations in Construction, 1970–1977," *Industrial Relations* 17, no. 1 (Feb. 1978): 3.

40. James P. Gannon, "Contract Seen Hurting Steel Firms, Economy and Eventually Unions," *Wall Street Journal*, Aug. 3, 1971; "Steelmakers Boost Most Quotes 8% in Record Across-the-Board Sweep," *Wall Street Journal*, Aug. 3, 1971; "Steel Layoffs, Price Increases Keep Spreading," *Wall Street Journal*, Aug. 4, 1971; "Steel Output Last Week Fell 51.8% to Low since '59, Dropping Operating Rate to 25%," *Wall Street Journal*, Aug. 10, 1971.

41. "Two Big Can Firms Grant 52-Week Layoff Pay to Steelworkers Union," *Wall Street Journal*, Aug. 15, 1955.

42. Gannon, "Contracts Seen Hurting Steel Firms," 1, 29; "Steelmakers Boost Most Quotes," 3; "Steel Layoffs, Price Increases," 3; "Steel Output," 3; Ben Fischer, interview by the author, June 11, 1996 (personal possession of the author); Ben Fischer, interview by Sylvester Garrett, p. 80, Sylvester Garrett Collection, Special Collections and University Archives, Indiana University of Pennsylvania, Indiana, PA [hereafter, Garrett Collection]; "Steel Industry Conference Approves New Bargaining Plan," *Steel Labor* 38 (Apr. 1973), 3; "The Experimental Negotiation Agreement," box 22, folder 12, David L. Cole Papers, Kheel Center [hereafter, Cole Papers].

43. Philip Shabecoff, "Growth of Arbitration Appears to Point to Era of Labor Peace," *New York Times*, Apr. 22, 1973; David L. Cole's notes, box 21, folder 10, Cole Papers; Bernard Cushman, "Current Experiments in Collective Bargaining," *Proceedings of the Twenty-Sixth Annual Meeting of the Industrial Relations Research Association*, Dec. 28–29, 1973, ed. G. Somers (Madison, WI: IRRA, 1974), 129–36; United States Steel Corporation and United Steelworkers of America, "Review of Grievance and Arbitration Procedure," table B, box 5, Garrett Collection; John P. Moody, "USW Weighs Grievance Setup," *Pittsburgh Post-Gazette*, Nov. 11, 1970; "After Two Years, New Grievance System Pleases Mills, Union, and Is Extended," *Wall Street Journal*, Aug. 8, 1973; National Commission for Industrial Peace, *Report and Recommendations* (Washington, DC: U.S. President Executive Office, 1974).

44. "Client Seminar, Dec. 11–13, 1974: Summary of Proceedings," Asc. 14984, box 8, folder "Economic Policy," John T. Dunlop Papers, Harvard University Archives, Pusey Library, Harvard University, Cambridge, MA.

45. For further discussion, see Philippe C. Schmitter, "Still the Century of Corporatism?" in *Trends toward Corporatist Intermediation*, ed. P. Schmitter (London: Sage, 1982); Schmitter, "Neo-Corporatism and the State," in *The Political Economy of Corporatism*, ed. Wyn Grant (New York: St. Martin's Press, 1983); Claus Offe, "The Attribution of Public Status to Interest Groups: Observation on the West German Case," in *Organizing Interest Groups in Western Europe: Pluralism, Corporatism, and the Transformation of Politics*, ed. Suzanne Berger (Cambridge: Cambridge University Press, 1981); Ronald W. Schatz, "From Commons to Dunlop: Rethinking the Field and Theory of Industrial Relations," in *Industrial Democracy in America*, ed. Nelson Lichtenstein and Howell John Harris, 87–112 (New York: Cambridge University Press, 1993).

46. For brief description, see Dunlop and Hill, *Wage Adjustment Board*, ch. 7. He continued to do the same work under private auspices from 1948 to 1957 as chair of the National Joint Board for Settlement of Jurisdictional Disputes, a committee of building contractors' associations and the building trade unions.

47. John T. Dunlop, "Comments on 'Collective Bargaining, Wages, and the Price Level,'" in *Proceedings of the First Annual Meeting, Industrial Relations Research Association, December 29–30, 1948*, ed. Milton Derber (1949), 53–54.

48. John T. Dunlop, "Consensus and National Labor Policy," in *Proceedings of the Thirteenth Annual Meeting, Industrial Relations Research Association*, Dec. 28–29, 1960, ed. Gerald G. Somers, 2–15 (Madison, WI: IRRA, 1961).

49. Wirtz and Dunlop quoted in A. H. Raskin, "Why Labor Doesn't Follow Its Leaders," *New York Times*, Jan. 8, 1967; "New Basic Steel Pact to Have Major Impact on 1974 Bargaining Pattern," *Daily Labor Report*, Oct. 16, 1973, 6–7 CC; "A Framework for Labor-Management-Government Discussions in the Construction Industry in 1975," box 177, folder "Dunlop (1)," William Seidman Collection [hereafter, Seidman Collection], Gerald R. Ford Presidential Library and Museum, Ann Arbor, MI [hereafter, Ford Library]; Cole's notes on Mar. 5, 1974, session of the National Commission for Industrial Peace, Cole Papers; *United States Code, Congressional and Administrative News*, 86th Congress, first session, 1959, vol. 1, PL 86–257; National Commission for Industrial Peace, *Report and Recommendations*, 9, 11.

50. Philip Shabecoff, "A.F.L.-C.I.O. Plan Seeks to Strengthen Organizing," *New York Times*, Sept. 9, 1973; Hearings before the Committee on Labor and Public Welfare, U.S. Senate, 94th

cong., 1st sess., on John T. Dunlop, of Massachusetts, to be Secretary of Labor, Feb. 25, 1975 (1975), 34.

51. James Strong and Philip Warden, "Nixon, Labor Leaders Move toward a New Era of Accord," *Chicago Tribune*, Feb. 20, 1973; TRB, "Nixon's Efforts to Win Labor Over to His Coalition," *Los Angeles Times*, Feb. 20, 1973, C7; "Co-opting Labor," *New York Times*, Jan. 5, 1973; "Who Is Co-opting Whom?," *New York Times*, Feb. 21, 1973; Philip Shabecoff, "Meany Role Cited in Ending Freeze," *New York Times*, Jan. 13, 1973, 1; Rowland Evans and Robert Novak, "Meany and Nixon: A New Phase to Their Friendship," *Washington Post*, Jan. 15, 1973, A21.

52. On in-fighting among Republicans after the 1972 election, see A. James Reichley, *Conservatives in an Age of Change: The Nixon and Ford Administrations* (Washington, DC: Brookings Institution, 1981), 242–49; George Shultz, interview by A. James Reichley, Jan. 4, 1978, Ford Library, 8.

53. Arnold R. Weber, "The Game Plan after Controls: A Lot of Old-Time Religion," *New York Times*, Apr. 28, 1974; Michael C. Jensen, "Severe Economic Problems Are Being Left by Nixon," *New York Times*, Aug. 9, 1974; Roger B. Porter, *The U.S.-U.S.S.R. Grain Agreement* (New York: Cambridge University Press, 1984), 26–27; Carter et al., *Handbook of Labor Statistics*, table Cb5–8, Business Cycle Turning Dates and Duration—Monthly: 1854–200; Carter et al., *Handbook of Labor Statistics*, table Cj797–807, Common Stock Prices: 1802–1999.

54. James P. Gannon, "Shultz to Leave Treasury Post in May; Simon, Dunlop Mentioned as Successors," *Wall Street Journal*, Mar. 15, 1974; Timothy D. Schellhardt, "Ford Realigns Economic Policy Team, Will Detail Battle Plan Early Next Week," *Wall Street Journal*, Sept. 30, 1974; James L. Rowe, "Ford Appoints Management, Labor Panel," *Washington Post*, Sept. 29, 1974, A15; "Two New Economic Panels," *New York Times*, Sept. 29, 1974.

55. Roger B. Porter, *Presidential Decision Making: The Economic Policy Board* (New York: Cambridge University Press, 1980), 54; James Cannon, *Gerald R. Ford: An Honorable Life* (Ann Arbor: University of Michigan Press, 2013), 311.

56. "The President's Remarks at the Swearing In of John T. Dunlop, with Mr. Dunlop's Response, March 18, 1978," *Presidential Documents: Gerald R. Ford, 1975*, vol. 11, no. 12, Ford Library, 281–82; "The Tiger," *Newsweek*, Feb. 17, 1975, 72; "John T. Dunlop: An Economic Activist Moves Closer to Power," *Business Week*, Apr. 7, 1975, 63–68.

57. Ben Rathbun, "Dunlop . . . His Addition Is Hard Work," *Boston Globe*, Jan. 19, 1976; Edward Cowen, "Power Struggle Reporter on Simon Treasury Role," *New York Times*, Apr. 3, 1974.

58. James L. Rowe Jr., "Ford Appoints Management and Labor Panel," *Washington Post*, Sept. 29, 1974, A15; Gerald R. Ford, "Executive Order 11809—Establishing the President's Labor-Management Committee," 39 FR 35565; Oct. 2, 1974; John T. Dunlop, "Highlights of a Brief Tenure, 1975–76," in *The Ford Presidency*, ed. Kenneth Thompson (Lanham, MD: University Press of America, 1988), 297.

59. Dunlop, "Comments," 53–54.

60. John Robert Greene, *The Presidency of Gerald R. Ford* (Lawrence: University Press of Kansas, 1995), 71–75; Porter, *Presidential Decision Making*, 101–4, 110, 114d; Eileen Shanahan, "Dunlop Favors Continuing Tax Cutbacks Indefinitely," *New York Times*, Oct. 1, 1975;

"Dunlop to Press for Further Tax Cuts," *Boston Globe*, Sept. 1, 1975; "Simon to Delay Action on Tax Cuts," *Boston Globe*, Sept. 8, 1975; Richard T. Cooper and Paul E. Steiger, "Tax and Cost Cuts: How Ford Decided," *Los Angeles Times*, Nov. 23, 1975, A1; Jerald derHorst, "Tax Plan Puts Ford a Step Ahead," *Chicago Tribune*, Oct. 10, 1975.

61. A. H. Raskin, "Labor: Public Aggression, Private Cooperation," *New York Times*, Aug. 31, 1975, section 3: 1, 5; "Ford Plans Spur for U.S. Utilities," *New York Times*, June 14, 1975; James P. Gannon, "Ford to Propose Aid to Electric Utilities," *Wall Street Journal*, June 3, 1975; Dennis Farney, "Ford Plan to Spur Power-Plant Building via Tax Breaks Faces Doubtful Future," *New York Times*, June 16, 1975; Carroll Kilpatrick, "Ford Seeks Tax Breaks to Spur Energy Plants," *Los Angeles Times*, June 14, 1975; "Ford Supports Tax Breaks to Spur Utilities: Up to $1 Billion in Credits," *New York Times*, June 13, 1975; Bill Neikirk, "Dunlop Dons Various Hats in Labor Post: Keeps a Low Profile," *Chicago Tribune*, Oct. 5, 1975.

62. "Housing's Sluggish Recovery Prompts Key Ford Aides to Draft New Initiatives," *Wall Street Journal*, Sept. 25, 1975; "Presidential Panel Has Few New Ideas to Revive Housing," *Wall Street Journal*, Nov. 7, 1975; "White House Interest in Housing Aid Indicated," *Washington Post*, Sept. 27, 1975; Kenneth R. Harney, "U.S. Housing: Hills Get Way with Subsidies," *Washington Post*, Nov. 1, 1975, C1; John Betz, "Ford to Review Housing Plight," *Los Angeles Times*, Oct. 12, 1975, H8.

63. "Teamsters' Central States Pension Fund Is Being Investigated Anew, Dunlop Says," *Wall Street Journal*, Oct. 17, 1975.

64. Robert G. Kaiser, "Old Grain Policy Unworkable, U.S. Officials Found," *Washington Post*, Sept. 11, 1975, A25; David Rosenbaum, "Unions Halt Fight over Soviet Grain," *New York Times*, Sept. 10, 1975; Porter, *U.S.-U.S.S.R. Grain Agreement*, 54–67; Dennis Hevesi, "Theodore Gleason, 92, Who Led Longshoremen's Union, Is Dead," *New York Times*, Dec. 27, 1992.

65. Dunlop's memorandum was reprinted in John T. Dunlop, "The Limits of Legal Compulsion," *Labor Law Journal* 27, no. 2 (Feb. 1976): 67–74. Also see David Burnham, "Dunlop Asks Policy Shift on Regulatory Agencies," *New York Times*, Nov. 9, 1975; John T. Dunlop, "Some Recollections of a Brief Tenure," *Monthly Labor Review*, Feb. 1988, 46–47.

66. *Electrical Workers v. Labor Board*, 341 U.S. 694 (1951).

67. The Construction Users' Anti-inflation Roundtable was renamed the Business Roundtable in 1975. See Marc Linder, *Wars of Attrition: Vietnam, the Business Roundtable, and the Decline of the Construction Unions*, 2nd rev. ed. (Iowa City, IA: Fănpìhuà Press, 1999); Benjamin C. Waterhouse, *Lobbying America: The Politics of Business from Nixon to NAFTA* (Princeton, NJ: Princeton University Press, 2014), chs. 3–6; Herbert R. Northrup and Howard G. Foster, *Open Shop Construction* (Philadelphia: University of Pennsylvania, Wharton School, Industrial Research Unit, 1975); Herbert R. Northrup and David O. Northrup, *Open Shop Construction Revisited* (Philadelphia: University of Pennsylvania, Wharton School, Industrial Research Unit, 1984).

68. "Statement of John T. Dunlop, Secretary of Labor, June 10, 1975," Hearings before the Subcommittee on Labor-Management Relations of the Committee on Education and Public Welfare, House of Representatives, 94th cong., 1st sess., on H.R. 5900, 7; Leonard Silk, "Labor's Turn at Bat: Unions Seek to Catch Up with Prices, Which Outran Wages during Controls," *New York Times*, June 19, 1974; James P. Gannon, "Power Play in Washington," *Wall Street Journal*,

July 15, 1975; James L. Rowe Jr., "Some Get Big Gains in Wages," *Washington Post*, May 4, 1975; "Construction Wage Increase," *Washington Post*, June 28, 1978, D22.

69. Text of H.R. 5900, Hearings before the Subcommittee on Labor-Management Relations of the Committee on Education and Public Welfare, House of Representatives, 94th cong., 1st sess., on H.R. 5900, 4.

70. Walter Mossberg, "Overhaul of Construction Bargaining Is Aim of Bill Labor Agency Is Drafting," *Wall Street Journal*, July 25, 1975; "Dunlop Suggests More Safeguards in Job-Site Picketing," *Wall Street Journal*, June 6, 1975, 3; Lee Dembart, "Common Situs Picket Rights for the Building Unions," *New York Times*, Nov. 6, 1975.

71. "Statement of John T. Dunlop, Secretary of Labor, June 10, 1975," Hearings before the Subcommittee on Labor of the Committee on Labor and Public Welfare, U.S. Senate, 94th cong., 1st sess., on S. 1479, 16; Edward Cowan, "U.S. Role in Wage Dispute Is a Clue to Dunlop Aims," *New York Times*, Feb. 10, 1975.

72. For overviews of those developments, see Judith Stein, *Pivotal Decade* (New Haven, CT: Yale University Press, 2010); Barry Bluestone and Bennett Harrison, *The Deindustrialization of America* (New York: Basic, 1982); Charles Craypo, "The Decline in Union Bargaining Power," in *U.S. Labor Relations, 1945–1989: Accommodation and Conflict*, ed. Bruce Nissen, 3–44 (New York: Garland, 1990); Nelson Lichtenstein, "Market Triumphalism and the Wishful Liberals," in *Cold War Triumphalism*, ed. Ellen Schrecker, 103–25 (New York: New Press, 2004).

73. Reprinted in John Hoerr, *And the Wolf Finally Came* (Pittsburgh, PA: University of Pittsburgh Press, 1988), 521.

74. The best studies of the Business Roundtable are Waterhouse, *Lobbying America*, esp. chs. 3–7, and Linder, *Wars of Attrition*. Also see Kim Phillips-Fein, *Invisible Hands: The Making of the Conservative Movement from the New Deal to Reagan* (New York: W. W. Norton, 2009).

75. Barry Chiswick to Alan Greenspan, memorandum re: common situs from Nov. 21, 1975, box 178, folder "Dunlop (2)," Seidman Collection; Max Friedersdorf to the president, memorandum re: common situs from Dec. 10, 1975, Seidman Collection; Friedersdorf to the president, memorandum re: Senator John McClellan, Dec. 18, 1975, Seidman Collection; L. William Seidman notes re: Meeting with Economic Policy Board Executive Committee, Dec. 17, 1975, Seidman Collection; Jim Cannon to the president, memorandum re: common situs picketing, undated [mid-Dec. 1975], Seidman Collection; Dennis Farney, "Picketing Bill Vetoed by Ford in Dunlop Defeat," *Wall Street Journal*, Dec. 23, 1975; A. H. Raskin, "Hard Hats and Their Focal Role," *New York Times*, Jan. 4, 1976, F1, F9.

76. Stein's *Pivotal Decade* provides the best discussion of this development.

77. Quoted in "Moderation's Chance to Survive," *Business Week*, Apr. 19, 1982, 36.

Chapter 9. George Shultz at the Negotiating Table

1. For a selection of his articles, see George P. Shultz, *Thinking about the Future* (Stanford, CA: Hoover Institute Press, 2019). He is continuing to work. See, for example, his article, coauthored with James A. Baker and Ted Halstead, "The Strategic Case for U.S. Climatic

Leadership: How America Can Win with a Pro-market Solution," *Foreign Affairs*, vol. 9, no. 2 (May–June 2020), 28–38.

2. Michael Bowman, "Kissinger, Shultz Warn of Rising Nuclear Perils," *VOA News*, Jan. 25, 2018, https://www.voanews.com/a/kissinger-shultz-warn-of-rising-nuclear-perils/4224920.html.

3. George P. Shultz, *Turmoil and Triumph* (New York: Charles Scriber's Sons,1993), 24; Henry Stamm IV, *People of the Wind River: The Eastern Shoshones, 1825–1900* (Norman: Oklahoma University Press, 1999), ch. 10, epilogue; *Minutes of the General Assembly of the Presbyterian Church of the U.S.A. with an Appendix* (Philadelphia, 1900), 796. In a 2015 interview, Shultz said that his maternal grandparents were Episcopal missionaries, not Presbyterians, as he wrote in *Turmoil and Triumph*. See also "Problems and Principles: George P. Shultz and the Uses of Economic Thinking," conducted by Paul Burnett in 2015, Oral History Center of the Bancroft Library, University of California, Berkeley, 2.

4. Shultz, *Turmoil and Triumph*, 24–25; John Braeman, "Charles A. Beard: The Formative Years in Indiana," *Indiana Magazine of History* 78, no. 2: 93–127; Charles Beard and Birl Shultz, *Documents on the State-wide Initiative, Referendum, and Recall* (New York: Macmillan, 1912). Birl Shultz, *The History of the Appropriations in the Legislative Session of 1916, New York State*, PhD diss., Columbia University, 1916); Birl Shultz, *The Securities Market and How It Works* (New York: Harper and Row, 1942); Birl Shultz, *Stock Exchange Procedure* (New York: New York Stock Exchange Institute, 1936).

5. Shultz, *Turmoil and Triumph*, 25; George P. Shultz '38, accessed Mar. 25, 2018, https://www.loomischaffee.org/about-us/news-calendar/news-post/~post/george-p-shultz-38-speaks-at-convocation-oct-27-20171027.

6. George P. Shultz, "The Agricultural Program of the Tennessee Valley Authority," BA thesis, Princeton University, 1942, 10, 20, 65–66; Shultz, *Turmoil and Triumph*, 25–26.

7. Shultz, *Turmoil and Triumph*, 27; "Problems and Principles," 10. Helena O'Brien Shultz died in 1995. Two years later, Shultz married Charlotte Mailliard Swig.

8. Robert B. McKersie, "End of an Era: Industrial Relations Section Turns Fifitysomething," *MIT Management*, winter term, 1995, 4–8.

9. Charles A. Myers and George P. Shultz, *Nashua Gummed and Coated Paper Company and Seven AFL Unions* (Washington, DC: National Planning Association, 1950); George P. Shultz and Robert P. Crisara, *The LaPointe Machine Tool Company and the United Steelworkers of America* (Washington, DC: National Planning Association, 1952).

10. Charles Myers and George P. Shultz, *The Dynamics of a Labor Market* (New York: Prentice-Hall, 1951); George P. Shultz, *Pressures on Wage Decisions* (New York: Wiley, 1951); John Coleman and George P. Shultz, *Labor Problems* (New York: McGraw-Hill, 1953, 1959); George P. Shultz and George Baldwin, *Automation: A New Dimension to Old Problems* (New York: Public Affairs Press, 1955); George P. Shultz and Thomas Whisler, *Management Organization and the Computer* (Glencoe, IL: Free Press, 1960); Thomas Whisler and George P. Shultz, "Automation and the Management Process," *Annals of the American Academy of Political and Social Science* 340 (Mar. 1962): 81–89; Albert Rees and George P. Shultz, *Workers in an Urban Labor Market* (Chicago: University of Chicago Press, 1970); George P. Shultz, *Strikes: The Private Stake and the Public Interest*, Selected Papers no. 8 (Chicago: University of

Chicago, Graduate School of Business, 1963); George P. Shultz and Arnold Weber, *Strategies for the Displaced Worker: Confronting Economic Change* (New York: Harper and Row, 1966); George P. Shultz and Robert Z. Aliber, *Guidelines, Information Controls, and the Market Place* (Chicago: University of Chicago Press, 1966).

11. Letter by George Shultz to the author, Apr. 9, 2019 (personal possession of the author).

12. George P. Shultz, interview by Stephen Kott, Marc Selverstone, and James Young, Dec. 18, 2002 (Charlottesville: University of Virginia, Miller Center of Public Affairs), 1, https://millercenter.org/the-presidency/presidential-oral-histories/george-p-shultz-oral-history-secretary-state.

13. George P. Shultz, "Priorities in Policy and Research for Industrial Relations," *Proceedings of the Twenty-first Annual Winter Meeting, Industrial Relations Research Association*, ed. Gerald G. Somers (Madison, WI: IRRA, 1969), 2–4.

14. George P. Shultz, "Race and Unemployment: Some Issues and Ideas," Selected Papers, no. 30 (n.d. [Apr. 1968]), 2, 5, 10, 12; George P. Shultz, "Issues for Manpower Action Programs," *Issues on Labor Policy*, ed. Stanley M. Jacks (Cambridge, MA: MIT Press, 1971), 35; "Jobless Talk on WTTW-TV," *Chicago Daily Defender*, Apr. 10, 1968; Judith Stein, "Affirmative Action and the Conservative Agenda: President Richard M. Nixon's Philadelphia Plan," *Labor in the Modern South*, ed. Glenn T. Eskew (Athens: University of Georgia Press, 2001), 188–89.

15. William Greider, "Shultz: On Labor Disputes," *Washington Post*, Dec. 14, 1968, A4; Edwin Dale, "Nixon Aide Backs Loose Labor Rein," *New York Times*, Dec. 14, 1968; Edward A. Morrow, "Philadelphia Unit Bars I.L.A. Aid," *New York Times*, Jan. 27, 1965; George Hornes, "Dock Strike's Cost Nears $2 Billion," *New York Times*, Feb. 2, 1969, S23; A. H. Raskin, "G.E. Strike: Administration's Role So Far Is Hands Off," *New York Times*, Nov. 2, 1969.

16. Ian Forman, "The Economics of White Racism: The Labor Picture," *Boston Globe*, June 16, 1968, E6ff; Terry Anderson, *The Pursuit of Fairness* (New York: Oxford University Press, 2004), 115–16; Meany was quoted in Dean Kotlowski, *Nixon's Civil Rights* (Cambridge, MA: Harvard University Press, 2001), 99.

17. Quoted in Anderson, *Pursuit*, 118.

18. Ibid., 115–16.

19. Ibid., 115–17.

20. For thoughtful discussions of this issue, see Kotlowski, *Nixon's Civil Rights*, ch. 4; Kotlowski, "Richard Nixon and the Origins of Affirmative Action," *Historian* 60, no. 3 (Spring 1998): 523–41; J. Larry Hood, "The Nixon Administration and the Revised Philadelphia Plan for Affirmative Action in Expanding Presidential Power and Divided Government," *Presidential Studies Quarterly* 23, no. 1 (Winter 1993): 145–67; and John Skrentny, *The Ironies of Affirmative Action* (Chicago: University of Chicago Press, 1996), ch. 7.

21. Fletcher quoted in Anderson, *Pursuit*, 116–17; "Arthur Fletcher, G.O.P. Adviser, Dies at 80," *New York Times*, July 14, 2005; "1968 Lt. Gubernatorial General Election Results—Washington," USElectionAtlas.org, last revised Nov. 11, 2007, https://uselectionatlas.org/RESULTS/state.php?fips=53&year=1968&f=0&off=6&elect=0; David Hamilton Golland, "Arthur Allen Fletcher, 'the Father of Affirmative Action,'" BlackPast.org, Oct. 30, 2011, http://www.blackpast.org/perspectives/arthur-allen-fletcher-father-affirmative-action.

22. Hugh Davis Graham, *The Civil Rights Era* (New York: Oxford University Press, 1990), 325.

23. Arthur Fletcher, *The Silent Sell-out* (New York: Third Press, 1974), 65–69; Anderson, *Pursuit*, 123–25.

24. Anderson, *Pursuit*, 124–25; Melvin Small, *The Presidency of Richard Nixon* (Lawrence: University Press of Kansas, 1998), 175–76; "Labor Agency Issues Minority Hiring Rules," *Wall Street Journal*, Feb. 4, 1970; "Shultz Warns 18 Cities to End Bias in Building Jobs," *New York Times*, Feb. 10, 1970.

25. Donald Janson, "U.S. Judge Upholds Controversial Philadelphia Plan to Increase Hiring of Minorities in Building Industry," *New York Times*, Mar. 15, 1970 30; ; Donald Janson, "Minority Hiring Upheld by Court," *New York Times*, Apr. 24, 1971; "U.S. Job Bias Ban to Include Women," *Washington Post*, Dec. 3, 1971, A2; Anderson, *Pursuit*, 127–29.

26. For further information, see David Golland, *A Terrible Thing to Waste: Arthur Fletcher and the Conundrum of the Black Republican* (Lawrence: University Press of Kansas, 2019), ch. 4; and Anderson, *Pursuit*, 141–44.

27. Robert M. Smith, "Reflective Administrator," *New York Times*, June 11, 1970; A. H. Raskin, "Said Nixon to George Shultz: 'I Track Well with You,'" *New York Times Sunday Magazine*, Aug. 20, 1970.

28. Douglas B. Cornell, "White House Pattern in Desegregation: Reticence Became the Rule after Court Decisions Put Presidents on the Spot," *Los Angeles Times*, Dec. 3, 1969, A2; Dean Kotlowski, "With All Deliberate Delay: Kennedy, Johnson, and School Desegregation," *Journal of Policy History* 17, no. 2 (2005): 155; Kotlowski, "Nixon's Southern Strategy Revisited," *Journal of Policy* 10, no. 2 (1998): 215.

29. Louis Kohlmeier, "High Court Bars Integration Delay Sought by Nixon," *Wall Street Journal*, Oct. 30, 1969; Robert Donovan, "Court Drops 'Deliberate Speed,' Orders Desegregation 'at Once,'" *New York Times*, Oct. 30, 1969; Fred Graham, "President Vows to Enforce Edict on Desegregation," *New York Times*, Oct. 31, 1969; Kotlowski, "Nixon's Southern Strategy," 218–19 (emphasis in the original).

30. Leonard Garment, *Crazy Rhythm: My Journey from Brooklyn, Jazz and Wall Street to Nixon's White House, Watergate, and Beyond* (Cambridge, MA: Da Capo, 2001), 207, 214ff. Garment's account notwithstanding, sharp opposition to integration and busing arose in Greenville in fall 1970. For a balanced account, see S. Russell Merritt, "The Success of Greenville County, South Carolina, in Avoiding Public School Resegregation, 1970–1990," *Equity and Excellence in Education* 28, no. 3 (1995): 50–56.

31. Quoted in Gareth Davies, "Richard Nixon and the Desegregation of Southern Schools," *Journal of Policy History* 19, no. 4 (2007): 383; Carroll Kilpatrick, "Nixon Asks Obedience on Schools," *Washington Post*, Feb. 17, 1970, 1, 7.

32. "Nixon Forms Panel on Desegregation," *New York Times*, Feb. 17, 1970; Jonathan Spivak, "Plan to Integrate Nation's Schools Sent to Congress," *Wall Street Journal*, May 22, 1970; David Lawrence, "Southern Counsel Sought by Nixon," *Hartford Courant*, July 6, 1970; Rowland Evans and Robert Novak, "Agnew Withdraws from Segregation Committee," *Hartford Courant*, Aug. 20, 1970.

33. Gilbert R. Mason, *Beaches, Blood, and Ballots: A Black Doctor's Civil Rights Struggle* (Jackson: University Press of Mississippi, 2000), 186–87.

34. Shultz, *Turmoil and Triumph*, 1045–49; Shultz, "How a Republican Desegregated the South's Schools," *New York Times*, Jan. . 8, 2003, A23.

35. James Wooten, "South Peaceful as Many Schools Are Integrated," *New York Times*, Sept. 1, 1970; Wooten, "Confusion but Still Progress in South's Schools," *New York Times*, Sept. 20, 1970; John Herbers, "Confusions on Extent of Integration," *New York Times*, Sept. 24, 1970; "Southern Schools Make Desegregation Strides," *Hartford Courant*, Sept. 2, 1970; "Few Incidents in Dixie As Schools Desegregate," *New Journal and Guide*, Sept. 5, 1970, B1; "Desegregated Schools," *New Journal and Guide*, Sept. 5, 1970, B10; "Integration in Schools Working," *Chicago Daily Defender*, Sept. 17, 1970.

36. Davies, "Richard Nixon," 388–89; Kotlowski, *Nixon's Civil Rights*, 19–20; Harry Dent, *The Prodigal South Returns to Power* (New York: Wiley, 1978), 187–88.

37. Gary Orfield, *Public School Desegregation in the United States, 1968–1980* (Washington, DC: Joint Center for Political Studies, 1983), 3, 6; Merritt, "Success of Greenville County," 51.

38. William Safire, "Who's What around the White House," *New York Times*, Nov. 11, 1973.

39. "George Shultz Takes Job as Executive at Bechtel," *Wall Street Journal*, May 10, 2009; R. W. Apple Jr., "Shultz Leaving Treasury; Simon May Be Successor," *New York Times*, Mar. 15, 1974; "Shultz Is Moved Up at Bechtel," *New York Times*, May 29, 1975.

40. James Wooten, "Carter Calls Failure on the Mideast Now Could Be Disastrous," *New York Times*, May 23, 1977, p. 1.

41. Alexander Yakovlev, *On the Edge of an Abyss* (Moscow: Progress, 1985), 340; Pavel Palazchenko, *My Years with Gorbachev and Shevardnadze* (University Park: Pennsylvania State University Press, 1997); Taylor Downing, *1983: Reagan, Andropov, and a World on the Brink* (New York: Da Capo, 2018); Jonathan Schell, *The Fate of the Earth* (New York: Knopf, 1982).

42. George P. Shultz, nomination hearings before the Committee on Foreign Relations, U.S. Senate, 97th cong., 2nd sess., July 13 and 14, 1982 (1982), 9

43. Robert Kagan, "Why Arms Control Failed: It Didn't Stop the Alarming Buildup of Soviet Missiles," *Policy Review* no. 27 (Winter 1984): 33.

44. George P. Shultz, *Managing the U.S.-Soviet Relationship over the Long Term*, Current Policy No. 624 (Washington, DC: U.S. Department of State, 1984), 2–3.

45. Myers and Shultz, *Nashua Gummed*; Shultz and Crisara, *LaPointe Machine Tool*.

46. E. H. Carr, *The Twenty Years' Crisis, 1919–1939* (London: MAC, 1940), 277.

47. Shultz, *Turmoil and Triumph*, 512.

48. George Shultz, interview by the author, Aug. 8, 2000, 7–8 (personal possession of the author).

49. John Patrick Diggins, *Ronald Reagan: Fate, Freedom, and the Making of History* (New York: W. W. Norton, 2007); James Mann, *The Rebellion of Ronald Reagan* (New York: W. W. Norton, 2007); Anatoly Dobrynin, *In Confidence: Moscow's Ambassador to America's Six Cold War Presidents (1962–1986)* (New York: Times Books, 1995), 611.

50. Odd Arne Westad, *The Global Cold War: Third World Interventions and the Making of Our Times* (Cambridge: Cambridge University Press, 2005), 396.

51. On Reagan's declining abilities, see Don Oberdorfer, *From the Cold War to a New Era: The United States and the Soviet Union, 1983–1991*, updated ed. (Baltimore, MD: Johns Hopkins University Press, 1998), 262–63; Anatoly Chernyaev, *My Six Years with Gorbachev*

(University Park: Pennsylvania State University Press, 2000)53; Mikhail Gorbachev, *Memoirs* (New York: Doubleday, 1995), 409, 416–17; Palazchenko, *My Years with Gorbachev*, 55.

52. A handful of authors recognize Shultz's impact. Principally Oberdorfer, *From the Cold War*; James Graham Wilson, *The Triumph of Improvisation: Gorbachev's Adaptability, Reagan's Engagement, and the End of the Cold War* (Ithaca, NY: Cornell University Press, 2014); and Robert Service, *The End of the Cold War, 1985–1991* (New York: PublicAffairs, 2015). Yet even those authors seem not to realize how Shultz's experience in industrial relations influenced his behavior in diplomacy. The exceptions are Carolyn McGiffert Ekedahl and Melvin A. Goodman, *The Wars of Eduard Shevardnadze* (University Park, PA: Pennsylvania State University Press, 1997).

53. On Shultz's handling everything in summit meetings beyond generalities, see Gorbachev, *Memoirs*, 410ff; Chernyaev, *My Six Years*, 54–55; William C. Wohlforth, ed., *Witnesses to the End of the Cold War* (Baltimore, MD: Johns Hopkins University Press, 1996), 43; Louis Sell, *From Washington to Moscow: US-Soviet Relations and the Collapse of the USSR* (Durham, NC: Duke University Press, 2016), 130–31.

54. Dobrynin, *In Confidence*, 517–20; Shultz, *Turmoil and Triumph*, 163–71, 267, 277–78; Oberdorfer, *From the Cold War*, 18–21. See George P. Shultz, "Light-Switch Diplomacy," *Business Week*, May 28, 1979, 24, 26, for Shultz's opposition to linkage.

55. Wayne Federman, "What Reagan Did for Hollywood," *Atlantic*, Nov. 14, 2011; Charles Hill, interview by the author, Aug. 6, 1998; Reagan quoted in Diggins, *Ronald Reagan*, 385; see also Oberdorfer, *From the Cold War*, 188–89.

56. Quotations are from Oberdorfer, *From the Cold War*, 49–62, and Sell, *From Washington to Moscow*, 139.

57. Quoted in Oberdorfer, *From the Cold War*, 153.

58. Ibid., 189.

59. Quoted in David Ottaway, "The Rise of George Shultz: Summit Confers New Responsibility for Arms Strategy," *Washington Post*, Oct. 17, 1986, A1, A28.

60. Kenneth Adelman, *The Great Universal Embrace* (New York: Simon and Schuster, 1989), 63.

61. Palazchenko, *My Years with Gorbachev*, 57.

62. Michael Beschloss, *Presidential Courage* (New York: Simon and Schuster, 2007), 306.

63. William Taubman, *Gorbachev: His Life and Times* (New York: W. W. Norton, 2017), 301–2.

64. David Ottaway, "The Rise of George Shultz: Summit Confers New Responsibility for Arms Strategy," *Washington Post*, Oct. 17, 1986, A1; David Hoffman, "Iceland Talks: One Word Chills Hope," *Washington Post*, Oct. 19, 1986, A1, A42. On NATO allies' displeasure, see, for example, Jeanne Kirkpatrick, "Grumbling about Reykjavik," *Washington Post*, Oct. 15, 1986, A15.

65. Quoted in Taubman, *Gorbachev*, 305.

66. *Witnesses*, xiii, 164–65; Jack Matlock, Jr., *Autopsy on An Empire* (New York: Random House, 1995), 98; Gorbachev quoted in William Safire, "Doomed to Cooperate?" *New York Times*, June 2, 1988, A27.

67. Gorbachev quoted in Andrei Grachev, *Gorbachev's Gamble* (Cambridge, UK: Polity,

2008), 81; Chernyaev, *My Six Years*, 64–65; Shultz quoted by Bessmertnykh, *Witnesses to the End of the Cold War*, 33.

68. David Shipler, "Shultz Visits Embassy Seder for Noted Soviet Dissidents," *New York Times*, Apr. 14, 1987.

69. Sarah Snyder, *Human Rights Activism and the End of the Cold War* (New York: Cambridge University Press, 2011), 194; Henry Kamms, "U.S. and Soviet Sign a Pact over Exploration in Space," *New York Times*, Apr. 16, 1987; Bill Keller, "Shultz Open on Soviet TV," *New York Times*, Apr. 16, 1987, A14; David K. Shipler, "A Busy Week of Diplomacy," *New York Times*, Apr. 19, 1987, E1; Taubman, *Gorbachev*, 397–98.

70. Document 66241, Nov. 1987, box 92158, Soviet Union—1987–88 Memos, etc., Nelson Ledsky Files, Archives, Ronald Reagan Presidential Library, Simi Valley, CA; Taubman, *Gorbachev*, 398–400.

71. Chernyaev, *My Six Years*, 142.

72. Quoted in Cyril Black et al., eds., *Rebirth: A History of Europe since World War II* (Boulder, CO: Westview, 1992), 234.

73. Oberdorfer, *From the Cold War*, 223–24; Taubman, *Gorbachev*, 281–82, 395–96, 401. Also see Shultz, *Turmoil and Triumph*, 590–91.

74. Shultz, *Turmoil and Triumph*, 1011–13; Taubman, *Gorbachev*, 405–6.

75. Robert McCartney, "NATO Welcomes Summit's 'Success,'" *Washington Post*, June 3, 1988.

76. Don Oberdorfer, "4th Summit Reflects a New Era: Interaction Different in Style, Substance," *Washington Post*, May 29, 1988, 26.

77. Peggy Noonan, *When Character Was King: A Story of Ronald Reagan* (New York: Viking, 2001), 226.

78. Wohlforth, *Witnesses to the End of the Cold War*, 74–75.

Chapter 10. Doing the Lord's Work

1. John R. Commons, "Class Conflict: Is It Growing in America, and Is It Inevitable," presented at the American Sociological Society, December 1906, repr. in Commons, *Labor and Administration* (New York: Macmillan, 1913), 82.

2. Wolfgang Saxon, "Jean McKelvey, 89, Professor and Labor Arbitration Expert," *New York Times*, Jan. 14, 1998, 2017.

3. Benjamin Aaron, *A Life in Labor Law: The Memoirs of Benjamin Aaron* (Los Angeles: University of California–Los Angeles, Institute for Research on Labor and Employment, 2007), chs. 14, 15, 17, 18; Robben W. Fleming, *Tempests into Rainbows: Managing Turbulence* (Ann Arbor: University of Michigan Press, 1996), ch. 17; "U-M Remembers Former President Robben Wright Fleming," January 22, 2010, https://news.umich.edu/u-m-remembers-former-president-robben-wright-fleming/.

4. Many of those columns are reprinted in George P. Shultz, *Thinking about the Future* (Stanford, CA: Hoover Institute Press, 2019). Also see George P. Shultz, *Communicating with the World of Islam* (Stanford, CA: Hoover Institution Press, 2008), and George P. Shultz and Pedro Aspe, "Making Central America Great Again," *Wall Street Journal*, July 11, 2019, A15.

5. George P. Shultz, William J. Perry, Henry A. Kissinger, and Sam Nunn, "Toward a Nuclear-Free World," *Wall Street Journal*, January 15, 2008, A13; George P. Shultz, "We Must Preserve This Nuclear Treaty," *New York Times*, October 25, 2018; Hearing to Receive Testimony on Global Challenges and U.S. National Security Strategy, Committee on Armed Services, U.S. Senate, 115th cong., 2nd sess., January 25, 2018, 1, 15–16, https://www.armed-services.senate.gov/imo/media/doc/18–06_01–25–18.pdf; James Cameron, "The U.S. Officially Withdrew from the INF Treaty," *Washington Post*, August 3, 2019. See "Wise Man: An Interview with George Shultz," *Octavian Report*, vol. 3, no. 1 (Summer 2019), https://octavianreport.com/article/george-shultz-americas-greatest-challenges/, for the secretary of state's reflections of other issues, including climate change and public education.

6. Ken Gewertz, "John Dunlop, Esteemed Scholar, Dies at 89," *Harvard University Gazette*, October 9, 2003; Kathleen Teltsch, "Foundation Seeks to Restore U.S. Competitive Edge," *New York Times*, July 22, 1990; Fred Andrews, "It's Not the Product That's Different, It's the Process," *New York Times*, December 15, 1999, C14; Robert Pear, "Health Initiative Tilting toward Price Regulation," *New York Times*, February 16, 1993, A14; Steve Curwood, "John Dunlop: Problem-Solver: Officially 'Retired' from Harvard, He Continues to Work on Labor Issues," *Boston Globe*, August 25, 1985, A13, A15; John T. Dunlop, *The Management of Labor Unions: Decision Making with Historical Constraints* (Lexington, MA: Lexington, 1990); John T. Dunlop and Arnold M. Zack, *Mediation and Arbitration of Employment Disputes* (San Francisco: Jossey-Bass, 1997); Frederick H. Abernathy, John T. Dunlop, Janice H. Hammond, and David Weil, *Lean Retailing and the Transformation of Manufacturing—Lessons from the Apparel and Textile Industries* (New York: Oxford University Press, 1999); Abernathy et al., "Globalization in the Apparel and Textile Industries: What Is New and What Is Not," in *Locating Global Advantage: Industry Dynamics in the International Economy*, ed. Martin Kenney and Richard Florida, 23–51 (Stanford, CA: Stanford University Press, 2004).

7. George Perry of Brookings Institute quoted in "An Economic Activist Moves Closer to Power," *Business Week*, April 7, 1975, 68.

8. John Hoerr, "Solidaritas at Harvard: Organizing in a Different Voice," *American Prospect*, no. 14 (summer 1993), 67, 82; Hoerr, *We Can't Eat Prestige: The Women Who Organized Harvard* (Pittsburgh, PA: University of Pittsburgh Press, 1997); Ken Gewertz, "John Dunlop Honored for His Accomplishments," *Harvard University Gazette*, January 8, 2004.

9. "Tomato Fields in Ohio Struck by Farm Group in Dispute over Pay," *Wall Street Journal*, August 30, 1978; "Effects Are Disputes as Migrant Continue Ohio Tomato Walkout," *New York Times*, October 22, 1979, A11; William Serrin, "Migrant Workers Organize a Boycott of Campbell," *New York Times*, July 2, 1984, A10; "Farm Group Boycotting Campbell Puts Focus on Financial Concerns," *New York Times*, November 27, 1984, A15; Keith Schneider, "Campbell Soup Accord Ends a Decade of Strife," *New York Times*, February 24, 1986, B7; "Heinz Reaches Accord with Migrant Workers," *New York Times*, April 12, 1987; "Four New Members Will Oversee FLOC," *Philadelphia Tribune*, A8; "For Migrant Workers, a Sweet Victory at Campbell," *Business Week*, July 8, 1985, 50; W. K. Barger and Ernesto M. Reza, *The Farm Labor Movement in the Midwest: Social Change and Adaption among Migrant Farmworkers* (Austin: University of Texas Press, 1994); Matt García, *From the Jaws of Victory: The*

Triumph and Tragedy of Cesar Chavez and the Farm Worker Movement (Berkeley: University of California Press, 2012).

10. Robert Reich, *Locked in the Cabinet* (New York: Knopf, 1997), 177; "Brown and Reich Announce Worker-Management Commission," U.S. Department of Labor press release, March 24, 1993; Commission on the Future of Worker-Management Relations, mission statement; list of Commission Members; Commission Fact Sheet, retrieved May 11, 2020, from Connell University, School of Industrial and Labor Relations site, https://rmc.library .cornell.edu/EAD/htmldocs/KCL06220.html.

11. John Logan, "'All Deals Are Off': The Dunlop Commission and Employer Opposition to Labor Law Reform," in *The Right and Labor in America: Politics, Ideology, and Imagination*, ed. Nelson Lichtenstein and Elizabeth Tandy Shermer (Philadelphia: University of Pennsylvania Press, 2012), 279; Stephen Franklin, "'Distrust and Animosity' on Job," *Chicago Tribune*, June 3, 1994, C1.

12. John T. Dunlop, "Minutes of the July 28, 1993, Meeting of the Commission on the Future of Worker-Management Relations" (Ithaca, NY: Cornell University, School of Industrial Relations, 1993), http://digitalcommons.ilr.cornell.edu/key_workplace/423.

13. Dunlop Commission on the Future of Worker-Management Relations, *Final Report* (Washington, DC: U.S. Department of Labor and U.S. Department of Commerce, 1994), https://digitalcommons.ilr.cornell.edu/cgi/viewcontent.cgi?article=1004&context=key_ workplace.

14. Robert Rose, "Labor Loses with Defeat of Pro-Union Lawmakers," *Wall Street Journal*, November 10, 1994, A8: Stephen Franklin, "Blueprint for Labor Peace Feeds Fire of Contention," *Chicago Tribune*, January 10, 1995, C1, C10; "Dead on Arrival," *Industry Week*, February 6, 1995, 56; Steve Early, "Worker Abuse Is Documented; Now Action," *Los Angeles Times*, June 14, 1994, 15; Douglas A. Fraser, "Dissenting Opinion of Douglas A. Fraser," retrieved July 24, 2018, http://digitalcommons.ilr.cornell.edu/key_workplace/424.

15. John T. Dunlop, interview by the author, February 27, 1992, 49 (personal possession of the author).

INDEX

RONALD W. SCHATZ is a professor of history at
Wesleyan University. He is the author of
*The Electrical Workers: A History of Labor at
General Electric and Westinghouse, 1923–60.*

THE WORKING CLASS IN AMERICAN HISTORY

The University of Illinois Press
is a founding member of the
Association of University Presses.

———————————————

Composed in 10.75/13 Arno Pro
with DIN display
by Jim Proefrock
at the University of Illinois Press
Manufactured by Sheridan Books, Inc.

University of Illinois Press
1325 South Oak Street
Champaign, IL 61820-6903
www.press.uillinois.edu